THE POLITICS OF THE JUDI

J. A. G. GRIFFITH was born in 1918 and educated at Taunton School and the London School of Economics and Political Science (LSE). He has been on the staff of the LSE since 1948, becoming Professor of English Law in 1959 and of Public Law from 1970 until his retirement in 1984. From 1956 to 1981 he edited *Public Law*. His books include *Principles of Administrative Law* (with H. Street), *Central Departments and Local Authorities, Government and Law* (with T. C. Hartley), *Parliamentary Scrutiny of Government Bills, Public Rights and Private Interests* and *Parliament* (with Michael Ryle).

From the reviews of *The Politics of the Judiciary:*

'In his soberly, ordered, authoritative exposition and in his telling selection of examples, he has rendered sterling service to all — academic, practitioner and sober citizen alike.'
ANDREW CURRIE, *TES*

'[A] brilliant little book, which is all the more powerful for being closely and soberly argued and is no mere polemic.'
ANTHONY GREY, *Freethinker*

'Highly readable, and as much to be recommended to the general reader as to those having a special interest in the subject.' J. A. ANDREWS, *British Book News*

'The first thinker to rip the mask off the sacred name of justice and reveal the political passions pulsing underneath was Thrasymachus. Justice, he asserted, was nothing but the interest of the stronger. In spite of the logical difficulties exposed by Socrates, Thrasymachus has not lacked for successors ... *The Politics of the Judiciary* is a lively contribution to this tradition.' KENNETH MINOGUE, *TLS*

J. A. G. GRIFFITH

The Politics
of the Judiciary

Fifth Edition

FontanaPress
An Imprint of HarperCollins*Publishers*

Fontana Press
An imprint of HarperCollins*Publishers*
77–85 Fulham Palace Road,
Hammersmith, London W6 8JB

This fifth edition published by Fontana Press, 1997
1 3 5 7 9 8 6 4 2

First published in Great Britain by
Fontana in 1977 in the series
'Political Issues of Modern Britain',
edited by B. Crick and P. Seyd.

ISBN 0 00 6863817

Set in Postscript Times by
Rowland Phototypesetting Ltd
Bury St Edmunds, Suffolk

Printed and bound in Great Britain by
Caledonian International Book Manufacturing Ltd, Glasgow

To BEN
who helped

To BARBARA
who sustained

Juger l'administration, c'est aussi administrer
J.-E.-M. PORTALIS, 1745–1807

The vanity of appearing as model employers of labour had not then, apparently, taken possession of the council, nor had the council become such ardent feminists as to bring about, at the expense of the ratepayers whose money they administered, sex equality in the labour market . . . The council would, in my view, fail in their duty if, in administering funds which did not belong to their members alone, they put aside all these aims to the ascertainment of what was just and reasonable remuneration to give for the services rendered to them, and allowed themselves to be guided in preference by some eccentric principles of socialistic philanthropy, or by a feminist ambition to secure the equality of the sexes in the matter of wages in the world of labour.

LORD ATKINSON in *Roberts v. Hopwood* [1925] AC 578

The Government recognizes that the judges are the great enemies of every government, because they're always supporting people who allege that they're being downtrodden by government.

LORD DONALDSON MR in an interview on Channel 4 on 10 February 1989 (as reported in the *Guardian*).

Contents

Preface to the Fifth Edition   xi

Prologue   xiii

Part One: The Judiciary

1 Courts and judges   5
  Introduction   5
  Appointment   8
  Social and political position   18
  A simplified note on the structure of
    the courts   22

2 Extrajudicial activities   25
  Commissions, inquiries, reports and
    the like   25
  Industrial relations   30
  Northern Ireland   33
  The Nolan Committee   36
  The Scott Inquiry   37
  Legislative process   38
  Participation in public debate   42
  The consultative function   45
  Judges and the public service   46
  Lord Mackay's proposals   53
  Conclusion   56

Part Two: Cases

3 Industrial relations   63
  The early cases   63
  Picketing   68
  The right to strike   70
  Inducing breach of contract   71
  Industrial Relations Act 1971   72
  The Law Lords restrain Denning   79
  The Conservative attack   84
  The uses of the labour injunction   90
  The later cases   98

4 The control of discretionary powers   103
  The earlier cases   103
  *The changes in attitude and the growth
    of interventionism*   104
  Judicial review   112
  The giving of reasons   116
  Ministerial policy   119
  The Fares Fair litigation   126
  Local policy   133
  Local government finance   134
  Homelessness   137
  Education   145
  Social services   148
  Social security   149

5 Personal rights   152
  Individual freedom   152
  Police powers   158
    The earlier cases   158

The Police and Criminal Evidence
     Act 1984   162
Prisoners   171
Race Relations   175
     The earlier cases   175
     The CRE cases   178
Immigration   182
Deportation, asylum, extradition and
     exclusion   190
Miscarriages of justice   204

6 Contempt, confidentiality and censorship 214
The meaning of contempt   214
Prejudicial statements   215
Confidentiality   220
The Spycatcher cases   223
Disclosure of documents   232
Arms to Iraq   239
Restrictions on freedom of expression   244
The protection of sources   251
Official Secrets   256

7 The moral maze   260
Moral behaviour   260
Demonstrations and protests   266
Matters of life and death   273

Part Three: Policy

8 Judicial creativity   281

9 The political role   290

The traditional view   290
The myth of neutrality   292
The public interest and its application   295

The interests of the State   297
Law and order   301
Social and political issues   310
Means and ends   326
More power to the judges?   331
Conclusion   334

Books referred to in the text   345

General Index   347

Index of Cases   363

Preface to the Fifth Edition

Twenty years on and I apologize for the old-age spread though I have deleted much material. The book was never intended to be a statement of judicial politics at the date of publication but a chronicle of its development. Some wheels have come three-quarter circle and *Roberts v. Hopwood* is not so distant today as it was when Lord Greene MR upheld *Wednesbury* corporation in 1948.

Nowadays judges are refreshingly freer in their written and spoken thoughts about social as well as legal problems. Lord Taylor C J told the Home Affairs Committee that judges recognized their 'accountability'. Sir Richard Scott not only produced the most comprehensive and highly critical account of how Whitehall goes about our business but vigorously defended his views in public after he had reported. All this was encouraging.

Industrial relations came to occupy much less of the courts' time, but the homeless, immigrants and asylum seekers occupied more. A seminar was held in the upper chamber on the law relating to public interest immunity certificates. Freedom of expression took some nasty blows, as did demonstrators, homosexuals in the armed forces, and sado-masochists. Local authorities have been asked to take their disputes elsewhere. Some ministerial policies have been invalidated and immediately restored by Parliament. Progress has been made in requiring bureaucrats to provide reasons for their conduct, and Lord Rees-Mogg was awarded a personal *locus standi*. Sir John Laws has given a new meaning to celestial jurisprudence, and the senior judiciary transferred some of their dislike for the Lord Chancellor to the Home Secretary. Territorial disputes have broken out over sentencing. The constitution changes and remains the same.

My special thanks go to Russell Campbell, Cyril Glasser, Maurice Sunkin and Eddie Yaansah. My colleagues at LSE continually had their more important studies interrupted: Carol

Harlow, Joe Jacob, Richard Rawlings, Robert Reiner, Bill Wedderburn and Michael Zander. Other helpful academics included Reuben Hasson, Andrew Le Sueur, Stephen Livingstone and Martin Loughlin. Further information and advice came from David Bookbinder, Ann Dummett, Paul Foot, Stephen Grosz, Joshua Rozenberg and John Wadham. Very few of these saw any draft of what I had written. None saw a final version. Factual errors, logical fallacies, non sequiturs, mistaken opinions, and stylistic lapses are mine and mine alone. And I acknowledge with thanks the services provided by the staff of the British Library of Political and Economic Science.

My technical incompetence is almost total. I cannot type. I don't understand computers or word processors. I am barely able to pick up a phone and get the right number. With Fats Waller, I can just about write myself a letter. Colleen Etheridge does all these things with charm and great ability; once more I am deeply in her debt. At Fontana Press, Toby Mundy provided encouragement and understanding as good editors should.

JOHN GRIFFITH
MARLOW
November 1996

Prologue

In the preface to the last edition, in October 1990, I noted that there had been many changes during the previous six years. Now, after a similar period, it is necessary once again to assess the nature of the relationship between ministers and judges.

At the centre of the relationship between the judiciary and the executive government stands the Lord Chancellor. He is the president of the Supreme Court, and a cabinet minister in charge of the department that bears his name. The Lord Chancellor appoints all judges of the High Court, as well as hundreds of members of tribunals; he is consulted by the Prime Minister – and his advice is highly persuasive – on all judicial appointments and promotions to the Court of Appeal and the House of Lords, and on the appointments of the Lord Chief Justice and the Master of the Rolls. Directly and indirectly, the Lord Chancellor determines many of the terms and conditions under which judges are employed. The administration of justice is largely funded and controlled, like other public services, by the government.

For much of the present century the Lord Chancellor's Department saw itself – and was seen by others – as a 'broker or hinge, mediating between the profession and government, carefully safeguarding the interests of both'.[1] Sir Claud Schuster, who was Permanent Secretary of the department from 1915 to 1944, preferred to describe the Lord Chancellor's role as that of a 'link or buffer' between the judiciary and the executive.[2] The judges looked to the Lord Chancellor and his department to represent them in the highest political circles while recognizing that his ministerial responsibilities might conflict with their interests.

During the 1960s, senior judges roused themselves from the

1 . Cyril Glasser, 'The Legal Profession in the 1990s – Images of Change', in *10 Legal Studies*, volume 1 (1990).
2 . Robert Stevens, *The Independence of the Judiciary* (1993), p. 3.

relative torpor of the postwar years and, under the leadership of Lord Reid, re-established the courts as a power in the world of politics. The divided and more turbulent 1970s saw the courts involved, whether they liked it or not (some, notably Lord Denning, clearly liked it) in labour disputes from which it was difficult to emerge with much credit. In 1976, the Law Commission report on administrative law remedies was followed by the reformed judicial review, enthused over by public law judges who then, in the early 1980s, discouraged its use when it proved too popular with immigrants and the homeless.

'When Mrs Thatcher became Prime Minister in 1979,' says Robert Stevens, 'the judiciary was treated much as any other Quango'[3] and this heralded a change in the relationship between the judges and the new Lord Chancellor, Lord Hailsham, who was a highly political holder of the office. Although a champion of the independence of the judiciary, he gave little public support to the expressions of alarm voiced by some senior judges at the growth of managerialism in the administration of justice. The department was ceasing to be special within the structure of central government and beginning to operate 'like any other government department'[4] and to be subject to the same financial constraints. The consequences of other changes, having earlier origins, became apparent: since the mid-century the Bar had grown several fold, helped by the development of legal aid which enabled more people to engage in civil litigation; the courts came under greater pressure and delays in the process lengthened. For many judges in the 1980s their social and professional lives were changing; they came under much greater scrutiny in the press, on radio and television, and not all found adjustment easy.

Another source of contention was judicial salaries. Over the years since the middle of this century judges sought to establish that those in the High Court should be paid more than the most senior civil servants. Comparisons are difficult as not all permanent secretaries receive the same salary; but today it would seem that High Court judges are paid about the same as the average payment to permanent secretaries: about

3 . *Op. cit.*, p. 172.
4 . *Op. cit.*, p. 165.

£105,000 a year. Nevertheless, they have a feeling of grievance: immediately before appointment they may well have
been earning £250,000 a year.

Their dissatisfaction was accentuated when in 1991, for the
first time in twenty years, the recommendations of the Top
Salaries Review Board were rejected by the government and
judges held to a modest increase. Moreover, until 1990, judges
had to serve fifteen years before they could draw their full
pension; now they must serve twenty years. Shortly after his
appointment as Lord Chief Justice in 1996, Lord Bingham
spoke of the gap between the salaries of judges and the high
incomes of leading QCs, and warned that unless judges were
paid sufficient to attract the ablest candidates the ranks of the
judiciary would be filled by the second best.

An important part of government policy in the 1980s was
to weaken or remove any countervailing sources of power or
influence. Along with the attack on the trade unions (for which
there were historic political reasons) came confrontation with
intermediate institutions including the civil service, local authorities, the BBC, the universities and other professional bodies.
Some of these were much weaker than others. Local government officers and civil servants had few weapons to fight with;
university teachers could not rely on public support; the medical profession were handicapped by their obligation to put
first the interests of patients, though they could draw on the
popularity of the national health service.

During the 1980s, the public reputation of the senior judiciary was seriously damaged. In a series of political decisions,
the judges seemed to lose their sense of political balance: the
curtailment of local authority powers in *Bromley v. GLC*; the
banning of trade union membership at GCHQ; the farce of
the *Spycatcher* affair; above all, the ineptitude in handling
miscarriages of justice. In 1987 Mrs Thatcher appointed Lord
Mackay as Lord Chancellor.

It is against this background that the fierce response to Lord
Mackay's proposals in 1989 for reform of the legal profession
must be understood. As we will see (pp. 53–6), the most
senior judges, past and present, condemned the proposals in
extravagant terms. When barristers are elevated to sit as senior
judges in the High Court they remain closely associated with

their Inns of Court and the Bar, so the judges' protests were on behalf of the profession as a whole to safeguard the administration of justice. The Law Society, representing solicitors, who stood to benefit from those proposals that extended rights of audience before the courts, remained relatively silent.

Lord Lawson, then Chancellor of the Exchequer, tells us that Lord Mackay warned the Cabinet that his proposals would be bitterly opposed by the judiciary. 'There are', he wrote, 'few pressure groups as redoubtable as the [British Medical Association]; but even they were easy meat compared with the lawyers.'[5] And so it turned out; the proposals were weakened before being passed into legislation, and, on rights of audience, the most senior members of the judiciary were given an effective veto. The strength of the judiciary is that, like the police (who proved similarly resilient), judges are indispensable, being an essential part of the machinery of government. So far, in this conflict, the advantage lies with them. Lord Mackay remains highly unpopular among large sections of the profession. He is seen as the agent of changes they deeply resent.

All these developments have led to a distancing of the judiciary from the other organs of the State. But the recent conflicts with the executive, apparent since 1990, have a separate and additional cause. The change in the relationship has been brought about principally because some ministers, particularly the Secretaries of State for the Home Department and Social Security, have adopted harsh policies and have been willing to act in ways which they must have known were on the margins of legality. In other words they have taken a view of where the public interest lies which does not accord with the judicial view. Judges have therefore been forced by ministerial action much closer to the political heat of the kitchen than they would wish.

Outside the courts, it might have been expected from past history that the Lord Chancellor would have intervened at an early stage to seek to avoid the serious breach between the most senior judges and the Home Secretary on sentencing policy. But, so far as we know, this did not happen, and the general lack of sympathy between the judges and the Lord

5 . Nigel Lawson, *The View from No. 11* (1992), p. 619.

Chancellor may have made such an intervention difficult, even impossible. Judges have largely ceased to influence policy-making. It remains to be seen whether the relationship will change under the new Lord Chancellor.

Several explanations have been given for the recent robustness of the courts in their attitude to ministers (this is discussed on p. 326). But these judicial decisions must not be exaggerated; they have been directed to only a few areas of governmental activity, mostly where ministers have been secretive or devious or dishonest. We must be glad that the courts forced these cases into the open. But in many other circumstances the courts have been supportive of government, particularly in the hard cases on homelessness, immigration and extradition. Many senior judges also demonstrated their support when they chose publicly to back the opinion of the Attorney-General against Sir Richard Scott in the dispute over the duties of ministers to sign public interest immunity certificates in the arms-for-Iraq affair. And this greatly helped the government in its vigorous efforts to avoid responsibility.

The increased robustness of the judiciary in its attitude to the executive, together with the more extravagant challenges to the sovereignty of Parliament, may be seen as an attempt to regain lost ground and to establish or re-establish the judiciary as an important and influential constitutional force. It is not surprising that so many senior judges have expressed their support for the campaign to incorporate the European Convention on Human Rights into UK domestic law. If this succeeds – and the present indications are that Labour in government will introduce legislation to this end – the powers of the judiciary will be greatly enhanced. This is discussed on pp. 333–4.

Throughout modern history, the relationship between the executive, Parliament and the courts has determined the shape of the constitution. Judicial review of administrative action is no novelty. Its development during this century, and especially over the last thirty-five years, has brought great benefits and has been a restraint on overweening princes. But, as Lord Devlin and others have warned, there are dangers in going too far and claiming too much. Where the line is to be drawn will always be controversial.

Part One

The Judiciary

There is one matter which I ought to mention. All the judges, without exception, are members of the Athenaeum, and I presume you will wish to be a member. If so, may I have the pleasure of proposing you? There is a meeting of the Committee early next week.

Lord Cozens-Hardy, MR to Lord Buckmaster — as he became — on the latter's appointment to the Lord Chancellorship, in a letter dated 26 May 1915, quoted by R. F. V. Heuston, *The Lives of the Lord Chancellors 1885–1940*, p. 269.

The most politically influential of the judges, however, has been the Master of the Rolls, Lord Denning ... With his own modest roots he dismisses the attacks on a class-based judiciary: 'The youngsters believe that we come from a narrow background — it's all nonsense — they get it from that man Griffith.'

Anthony Sampson, *The Changing Anatomy of Britain* (1981), p. 159.

I would think about 10 or 15 per cent [of judges are Labour Party voters]. I would think it's a diminishing number because I think that a large number of judges who would have voted for Mr Clement Attlee would look askance at voting for some of his successors, with all respect to them.

Lord Templeman, in an interview on Radio 4 with Hugo Young on 13 April 1988.

Since nearly all High Court judges are appointed when they are between about 45 and 57 it is likely that they will have shed such political enthusiasms as they may have had when young and have formed firm views about how the country should be run.

Sir Frederick Lawton (former Lord Justice), *Solicitors Journal*, 2 November 1990.

Mr Mullin: *It does seem remarkable to someone who is not a lawyer that only one woman has ever got in the top thirty or so judges, and she turned out to be the daughter of a High Court judge and the sister of the Lord Chancellor. Do you think any woman who has not got those qualifications could have made it?*
Lord Taylor of Gosforth: *Absolutely.*
Mr Mullin: *Why has not one then?*
Lord Taylor: *That particular judge actually came from being a Registrar in the Family Division. That was the route by which she got on to the Bench, and . . . she turned out to be extremely good and was appointed higher on merit. Good heavens, let us not take that away from her. One of the reasons why we are very much against increasing the number of women on the Bench simply in order to be able to say, 'Look we have more women on the Bench' is that we do not want to practise reverse discrimination, because it is unfair to the women who get there on merit. Your saying that the one woman who has made it to the top was because her brother was the Lord Chancellor is very offensive.*
Mr Mullin: *I do not say that at all. I am perfectly prepared for the possibility that she has one of the finest legal minds in the country. I just note she is the only one ever.*
Lord Taylor: *I promise there will be more and*

they will not all be the sisters of the Lord Chancellor!

Evidence given to Home Affairs Committee of the House of Commons on 14 June 1995 (H. C. 52-II of 1995–96 Qq 278–80).

It is a great temptation to cast the judiciary as an elite which will bypass the traffic-laden ways of the democratic process. But it would only apparently be a bypass. In truth it would be a road that would never rejoin the highway but would lead inevitably, however long and winding the path, to the authoritarian state.

Lord Devlin, *The Judge* (1970), p. 17.

1. Courts and judges

Introduction

This book is concerned with the relationship between the judiciary and politics. In the courts political questions may come before the judges because the matter is already in public controversy, like race or industrial relations; or because it is claimed that a public authority has exceeded its powers; or because the matter concerns the activities of the police; or because the matter impinges on the individual rights of citizens, affecting their freedom or their property.

The laws relating to civil and criminal wrongs are made either by Parliament in the form of Acts of Parliament (also called statutes) or by the judges themselves (called the common law). The common law is made as judges decide cases and state the principles on which they are basing their decisions, this accumulation of principles building into a body of law. Some parts of this common law have long fallen into disuse as having no contemporary relevance. Other parts have evolved to meet social changes. Statute law, however, predominates over common law wherever there is conflict, and much statute law is made to change and to replace parts of the common law.

Statute law itself cannot be a perfect instrument. A statute or one section of a statute may be made to deal with some particular subject – perhaps with immigration, or drugs, or housing or education – but a situation arises where doubt is cast on the meaning of the words of the statute. Does the situation fall within these words or not? For example, do the words 'national origins' include 'nationality' (see pp. 175–6)? The judges then must decide how to interpret the statute and by so doing they define its meaning. Not only therefore do the judges 'make law' through the development of the common law. They also do so by this process of statutory interpretation.

Judges are employed to decide disputes. Sometimes these disputes are between private individuals when neighbours disagree or one person is injured by another in an accident. Sometimes these disputes may be between large private organizations when companies argue about the terms of a commercial contract. But public bodies − government departments, local authorities, and others − are also legal persons and also become involved in disputes which lead to judicial activity. Most importantly, the courts may entertain applications for judicial review of administrative action.

Such disputes are dealt with by the civil law and in the civil courts. The judgment given will say where the rights and wrongs lie and the court may award damages to one party or even order a party to take certain positive steps or to refrain from certain action.

In criminal law, the dispute is with the State. Over the years laws have been made and amended declaring certain kinds of action to be criminal and punishable with imprisonment or fines. This has been done because it is believed that the State has an interest in seeking to prevent those actions and to punish those who so act. So we have crimes called murder, manslaughter, rape, conspiracy, theft, fraud, assault, and hundreds of others, some of them quite trivial. They are dealt with in the criminal courts.

If the judicial function were wholly automatic, not only would the making of decisions in the courts be of little interest but it would not be necessary to recruit highly trained and intellectually able men and women to serve as judges and to pay them handsome salaries.

It is the creative function of judges that makes their job important and makes worthwhile some assessment of the way they behave, especially in political cases. It must be remembered that in most cases for most of the time the function of the judge (with the help of the jury if there is one) is to ascertain the facts. But when questions of law do arise, their determination may be of the greatest importance because of the effect it will have on subsequent cases.

A note on the structure of the courts[1] appears below (pp. 22–3), where it will be seen that the most senior judges are Lords of Appeal in Ordinary (or Law Lords) who are members of the House of Lords and sit, in their judicial function, in the Appellate Committee of that House. Each is referred to as Lord So-and-so. The next senior are Lords Justices of Appeal who sit in the Court of Appeal (presided over by the Master of the Rolls and the Lord Chief Justice). Each is referred to as Lord or Lady Justice So-and-so. Next come judges of the High Court each of whom is referred to as Mr or Mrs Justice So-and-so. There are also Deputy High Court judges who sit part time. The High Court, the Crown Court and the Court of Appeal are together called the Supreme Court. Next in seniority come the Circuit judges (often referred to as County Court judges when they are sitting in that court) each of whom is referred to as Judge So-and-so. Recorders and Assistant Recorders are senior barristers or solicitors who sit as judges a few weeks each year. There are also District and Deputy District judges; stipendiary magistrates who act full time; and Justices of the Peace (JPs) who act part time and are unpaid.

The purpose of this book is to look at the ways in which judges of the High Court, the Court of Appeal, and the House of Lords have in recent years dealt with political cases which have come before them. By political I mean those cases which arise out of controversial legislation or controversial action initiated by public authorities, or which touch important moral or social issues.

When people like the members of the judiciary, broadly homogeneous in character, are faced with such situations, they act in broadly similar ways. It will be part of my argument to suggest that behind these actions lies a unifying attitude of mind, a political position, which is primarily concerned to protect and conserve certain values and institutions. This does not mean that the judiciary invariably supports what governments do or even what Conservative governments do. Individually, judges may support the Conservative or Labour or the Liberal parties. Collectively, in their function and by their

1 . Unless otherwise indicated, this book concerns the system in England and Wales only.

nature, they are neither Tories nor Socialists nor Liberals. They are protectors and conservators of what has been, of the relationships and interests on which, *in their view*, our society is founded. They do not regard their role as radical or even reformist, only (on occasion) corrective.

Appointment

The most remarkable fact about the appointment of judges is that it is wholly in the hands of politicians. High Court and Circuit judges, Recorders, stipendiary and lay magistrates are appointed by the Lord Chancellor who is a member of the government.[2] Appointments to the Court of Appeal, to the Appellate Committee of the House of Lords,[3] and to the offices of Lord Chief Justice, the Master of the Rolls, the Vice Chancellor of the Chancery Division, and President of the Family Division are made by the Prime Minister after consultation with the Lord Chancellor. The Lord Chancellor's Department has been headed, since the 1880s, by a permanent secretary. The department is the centre for the collection of information about the activity, the legal practice, and the reputation of members of the bar, including those more senior – almost always Queen's Counsel (the conferment of which status is in the gift of the Lord Chancellor) – from whom senior judicial appointments will be made. Inevitably the officials in the department exercise some influence but its extent varies and is difficult to assess. In 1990, all but one of the Law Lords and all the Lords Justices of Appeal had been appointed by Mrs Thatcher.

> In respect of appointments to the High Court and above, senior officials of the Lord Chancellor's Department regularly meet Supreme Court Judges and Law Lords who are asked to give their views on the work and suitability for appointment of practitioners and serving

2 . In *R. v. The Lord Chancellor ex parte Witham*, the Divisional Court on 7 March 1997 held that the L.C. had acted beyond his powers in fixing compulsory fees for issuing writs.

3 . Referred to hereafter as the Law Lords.

judges. The Lord Chancellor also consults the four Heads of Divisions, together with the Senior Presiding Judge, when considering candidates for appointment to specific posts on the High Court Bench. He also consults senior members of the judiciary before recommending persons for appointment to the Court of Appeal or the House of Lords.[4]

The Heads of Divisions are the Lord Chief Justice, the Master of the Rolls, the President of the Family Division, and the Vice Chancellor.

Appointments to the High Court bench are made by invitation. Suitably qualified candidates may indicate that they are interested in appointment, but this is not necessary; candidates will normally have sat as deputy High Court judges and often as Recorders. Save for those few who are appointed on promotion from the Circuit Bench (who may include solicitors), appointments are made from members of the Bar who have practised for twenty to thirty years. Junior Counsel to the Treasury, who appear for the government, may be appointed directly to the High Court bench. Lords Justices of Appeal are now invariably appointed on promotion from the High Court, Lords of Appeal in Ordinary generally from the Court of Appeal (in England and Wales, and Northern Ireland) or the Court of Session (in Scotland).

How far the Prime Minister uses his or her power of appointment or, to put this another way, merely accepts the Lord Chancellor's advice, varies with different Prime Ministers and differing circumstances. It seems to be unusual for the Prime Minister or the Lord Chancellor to consult other ministers (except that the Lord Chancellor may discuss the matter with the Attorney-General and the Solicitor-General) unless any such minister happens to be also a distinguished member of the bar, as was Sir Stafford Cripps in Mr Attlee's administration from 1945. But it would be a mistake to assume that Prime Ministers are mouth-pieces of their Lord Chancellors

---

4. *Judicial Appointments*, published by the Lord Chancellor's Department (1995); for a detailed account, see Memorandum of Lord Chancellor's Department to Select Committee on Home Affairs inquiry into Judicial Appointments Procedures (H. C. 52-II of 1995–96, Appendix 1).

when making influential appointments such as Lord Chief Justice and Master of the Rolls. In July 1995, the Lord Chancellor (Lord Mackay) limited himself to saying that he had 'supported absolutely' the nominations of the Prime Minister.[5] It was reported that the appointments of Lord Justice Bingham as LCJ and Lord Woolf as MR in 1996 were strongly resisted by some on the right wing of the Conservative party.

Lord Simon of Glaisdale has written, 'in 1951 Sir Winston [Churchill] particularly wanted [Sir Walter Monckton] in the unenviable post of Minister of Labour, and (presumably by way of compensation) undertook in writing that he should be appointed Lord Chief Justice on the next vacancy'.[6]

Such an undertaking was of very little value. Lord Goddard was then in only his sixth year as Lord Chief Justice, never looked like someone about to retire, and indeed continued in office for three years after Sir Winston gave way as Prime Minister in 1955. But the story shows that Sir Winston had no doubt the office was in his gift.

In January 1997, the Lord Chief Justice was paid £132,147; Lords of Appeal in Ordinary and the Master of the Rolls, £122,203; Lords Justices of Appeal, £117,164; judges of the High Court, £104,415.

Judges of the High Court and above, with the exception of the Lord Chancellor, may be removed from office only on an address presented by both Houses of Parliament. No English judge has been removed under this provision which derives from the Act of Settlement 1701. Circuit judges and Recorders, however, may be removed from office by the Lord Chancellor on the ground of incapacity or misbehaviour.[7] Since 1993 judges must retire at seventy years of age (previously seventy-five) with possible annual extension by invitation to seventy-five. This reduction caused some resentment, especially as the period of service for a full pension was raised from 15 to 20 years. In 1977 a full-time salaried judge in Scotland was removed from his office for misbehaviour: he was deemed to have engaged in public political activity. Sheriff Peter

---

5 . See Note 4, paras 448, 459.
6 . 81 *Law Quarterly Review*, 295 (1965).
7 . Recorders are appointed for three-year terms which are renewable.

Thomson published a pamphlet advocating the holding of a plebiscite on Scottish home rule. In accordance with the Sheriff Courts (Scotland) Act 1971, the Secretary of State for Scotland asked two senior Scottish judges (the Lord President of the Court of Session and the Lord Justice Clerk) to investigate and they reported their finding of misbehaviour which, as for Circuit judges and Recorders in England and Wales, was a ground for dismissal. The Secretary of State, having taken into account that Sheriff Thomson had been previously warned, at the time of a similar offence in 1974, made an Order for his dismissal. The Order was laid before Parliament and there debated on 6 December 1977. The case caused much discussion, especially as it could scarcely be said that his activity was directly connected with his duties as a judge.[8] Thomson asked for permission to make a statement at the bar of the House of Commons but this was denied.[9]

In December 1983, the Lord Chancellor dismissed for misbehaviour an Old Bailey Circuit judge who had been fined £2000 on two charges of smuggling whisky and cigarettes.

In addition to his powers of dismissal of Circuit judges and others, the Lord Chancellor may rebuke or reprimand any judge in person or in writing, in public or in private. And he has great influence in persuading a judge at any level that he should retire on the grounds of ill-health or with any other excuse. The Lord Chancellor tried to remove some of the ambiguities and uncertainties by releasing a letter in July 1994 addressed to the judiciary in which he indicated what were the limits of acceptable behaviour. In particular he said that a conviction of driving under the influence of drink or drugs was so grave as to amount prima facie to misbehaviour; so might offences involving racism and sexual harassment.

Cases are reported in the press from time to time of such rebukes and reprimands as the result of a variety of incidents such as drink-driving, a fracas with a cab driver, an 'over-familiar greeting' of a court officer, and kerb crawling. Very

8. See 940 HC Deb. col. 1288–1332; also 939 HC Deb. col. 922–5.
9. A summary of the statement was contained in a letter from Mr Thomson to *The Times* on 16 December 1977. See also *Stewart v. Secretary of State for Scotland* [1996] SLT 1203.

rarely is a judge of the High Court (or above) involved.

The danger of criticizing the appointment of particular judges was shown when in June 1980 a Belfast jury awarded £50,000 damages to a Northern Ireland county court judge for a libel contained in an article in the *Economist* suggesting that his appointment had been based, as *The Times* put it in a leading article, not so much on his ability but on the fact that he was a Roman Catholic. The *Economist* appealed and the matter was settled on undisclosed terms, the damages being 'adjusted' and the editor expressing himself as extremely satisfied.

Sometimes counsel for one of the parties in a case will make objection to a particular judge hearing the case. And the judge may then decide not to sit. In 1978 Lord Denning MR acceded to such a request when told that the Church of Scientology of California felt that in his court there was an unconscious influence operating adversely to the church.[10] In 1996, it was reported that a High Court judge had stepped down after defence counsel had argued that his role as a prominent freemason might lead to 'possible bias'.[11] In January 1978, the Lord Chancellor announced that Judge Neil McKinnon had said that he wished not to preside in future over cases involving racial questions; and that this wish would be given effect to. Judge McKinnon had been widely criticized for comments made during his hearing of a case of inciting racial hatred.

Occasionally the Lord Chancellor will publicly reprimand a judge, as happened in 1978 when Mr Justice Melford-Stevenson was rebuked for describing an Act of Parliament as a 'buggers' charter'. In January 1982, Lord Hailsham repudiated the comment of a judge that a rape victim who hitch-hiked a lift was guilty of contributory negligence and that the rapist's penalty should accordingly be reduced. In January 1984, Lord Hailsham reprimanded a Recorder who attacked as an affront to British justice a decision by Woolworths to prosecute a widow aged seventy-seven for shop-lifting.

More seriously, Judge Argyle was severely reprimanded by Lord Havers 'for a number of unfortunate remarks made by

10. See *The Times*, 21 February 1978.
11. The *Guardian*, 19 September 1996.

him in the course of a speech at Trent Polytechnic, Nottingham, on Friday, March 13, 1987'.[12] It was reported that he had said the Government 'had fallen flat on its face in dealing with the situation', adding that law and order did not exist in this country at the moment; that there could be up to five million illegal immigrants in Britain; and that judges should be able to impose the death sentence on anyone convicted of an offence carrying more than a fifteen-year sentence.

In November 1988, Circuit Judge Cassel was reported as having said, when putting a husband on probation for indecent assaults on his twelve-year-old daughter, during his wife's pregnancy, that the wife's lack of sexual appetite led to considerable problems 'for a healthy young husband'. The Lord Chancellor, Lord Mackay, said it was regrettable that the judge should have expressed himself in this way. It appeared that the judge had tendered his resignation on the grounds of ill health in a letter sent to the Lord Chancellor the day before his controversial comments.

In February 1989, the Lord Chancellor was reported as having sought an explanation of remarks made at a dinner by Sir James Miskin, Recorder of London. Sir James was reported as having called for a return of capital punishment, launched an attack on the parole system, favoured the abolition of the right to silence for accused persons, referred to a black person as a 'nig-nog', and made a remark about 'murderous Sikhs' involved in a case he was hearing at the time. The Court of Appeal subsequently upheld convictions in the case, saying that although the remarks 'raised the appearance of bias', and were 'doubly deplorable' as involving a respected ethnic minority, they could not have affected the outcome of the trial.

To what extent, if at all, do the Lord Chancellor or the Prime Minister take into account the political allegiance of those whom they consider for appointment to judicial office? The wider question is the extent to which an active political life, and particularly membership of the House of Commons, is regarded by the Lord Chancellor as a positive qualification for appointment to a judgeship. Practice has differed over the years.

12. 488 HL Deb. col. 1376 (21 July 1987).

Lord Halsbury was Lord Chancellor for far longer than any other during the last hundred years. He had three periods in that office which he held, in all, for over seventeen years between 1885 and 1905. His judicial appointments were much criticized on the ground in effect that 'Halsbury appointed to the High Court, and to a lesser extent to the county court, men of little or no legal learning whose previous career in public life had been largely in the service of the Conservative Party or else were relations of his own.'[13] Professor Heuston has examined such criticisms. Of the judges appointed by Halsbury to the High Court, eight were MPs at the date of their appointment and of these six were Conservatives. Five others had been unsuccessful parliamentary candidates, three of them being Conservatives. One other had been a Conservative MP nearly twenty years before. So fourteen out of the thirty appointments were, in those senses, of politicians – and ten were Conservatives. Heuston concludes that of Halsbury's thirty appointments to the High Court, four or five were men of real distinction, eighteen or nineteen were men of competent professional attainments, leaving no more than seven 'whose appointments seem dubious'. Four of these seven were Conservative MPs at the date of the appointment, one had been a Conservative MP, and another had twice been an unsuccessful Conservative candidate. We may say, therefore (this is my conclusion not Heuston's), that of the ten Conservative politicians whom Halsbury appointed, six were bad appointments. Every Lord Chancellor, especially if he holds office as long as did Halsbury, will make some mistakes (and Heuston suggests that as many as three of the six were 'unlucky' appointments), but Halsbury's experience may suggest that the proportion of bad appointments is likely to be statistically higher amongst appointments made from the Lord Chancellor's political associates.

Certainly at that time it was accepted that a political career was likely to be an advantage for a barrister aspiring to a judgeship, though it was important that his seat should be safe, as no government would wish to run the possibility of

13. R. F. V. Heuston, *The Lives of the Lord Chancellors, 1885–1940,* (1964), p. 36.

diminishing its strength in the House. Heuston tells us how Lord Halsbury when he was a Parliamentary candidate was congratulated by Sir Edward Clarke on his election defeat by nine votes in 1874. Clarke explained that if Halsbury had won by such a majority he could not have expected elevation to a judgeship. But, as it was, he could expect to be made Solicitor-General and found a safe seat. This is indeed what happened although he held the office for over a year until the seat was found for him in 1877. (During the interval he was in fact offered a judgeship, which he declined, but it was made clear that the government could not long countenance a Solicitor-General without a seat in the House of Commons.)

In August 1895, arising out of argument about the fees payable to the law officers, Lord Salisbury, as Prime Minister, promised Sir Edward Clarke that he would be appointed Attorney-General if a vacancy occurred within two years. In 1897, a new Master of the Rolls had to be appointed. If the Attorney-General (Sir Richard Webster) took the post, Clarke would have to be appointed Attorney-General. Lord Salisbury, who had a poor opinion of Clarke's abilities (as had Halsbury), wrote in much perplexity to the Lord Chancellor but saying that the Rolls should be offered to Clarke 'on party grounds' because he would do less harm as a judge than as Attorney-General. Salisbury continued:

There remains the third course, to throw Clarke over altogether and tell him that the highest point of his career has been reached. I confess that the more I consider this alternative, the more I dislike it. It is at variance with the unwritten law of our party system; and there is no clearer statute in that unwritten law than the rule that party claims should always weigh very heavily in the disposal of the highest appointments ... It would be a breach of the tacit convention on which politicians and lawyers have worked the British Constitution together for the last 200 years. Perhaps it is not an ideal system – some day no doubt the MR will be appointed by competitive examination in Law Reports, but it is our system for the present; and we should give our party arrangements a wrench if we throw it aside.

Lord Salisbury did offer the Rolls to Clarke, who declined it on the ground that it would put an end to his political career, though he added that he would accept being made a Law Lord. But that offer did not come.[14]

The change in the attitude to the appointment of barrister-politicians as judges is said to date from Lord Haldane's Chancellorship (1912–15) when legal and professional qualifications became the criteria, though at first the change was not extended to the most senior appointments. Lord Haldane himself expressed his 'strong conviction that, at all events for a judge who is to sit in the Supreme Tribunals of the Empire, a House of Commons training is a real advantage. One learns there the nuances of the Constitution, and phases of individual and social political life which are invaluable in checking the danger of abstractedness in mental outlook.'[15]

But a little later Lord Sankey, who was Lord Chancellor from 1929 to 1935, when resignations occurred, replaced five Law Lords who had had political backgrounds by others whose reputations rested on their professionalism as lawyers.[16]

In recent years Lord Chancellors have differed in their opinions about the value of judges having had experience as politicians.[17] During the 1950s, being an MP came once again to be regarded as a qualification for appointment to a judgeship. In 1964, Lord Gardiner, who shortly afterwards became Lord Chancellor himself, said that since 1951 'one of two' Lord Chancellors (there had been only three) 'felt that the standard of members of the bar going into the House of Commons has fallen noticeably since the war, and if you want the right men in the House of Commons then you must reward the man who votes the right way with a judgeship'.[18] Lord Gardiner thought that political views ought not to affect judicial appointments at all and pursued this policy during his period as Lord Chancellor (1964–70). Today, being a known supporter of a political party seems to be neither a qualification nor a disqualification for

14. On all this see Heuston, *op. cit.*, pp. 52–4, 323–4.

15. Quoted in Heuston, *op. cit.*, p. 39.

16. Abel-Smith and Stevens, *Lawyers and the Courts* (1967).

17. In 1948, Prime Minister Attlee appointed a front bench Opposition spokesman, J. S. C. Reid, directly to be a Law Lord.

18. *Economist*, 28 March 1964, p. 210.

appointment. Frequent public involvement in political activity may give rise to doubts in the minds of some Lord Chancellors about suitability for the judicial role.

It must be remembered that Lord Chancellors in making their appointments to the High Court have a relatively small group to select from. Effectively, the group consists of experienced barristers between the ages of forty-five and sixty and the number of genuine possibilities – the short list – may be as small as half a dozen. Personal characteristics must be taken into account. A man or woman whose social or personal habits are unconventional or uncertain is not likely to be risked. Officially no regard is paid to ethnic origin, gender, marital status, sexual orientation, religion or (if otherwise fit) disability. Political opinions should fall within the ordinary range represented in the House of Commons.

Politically one of the most important judicial appointments is that of Master of the Rolls. As president of the Court of Appeal his view on the proper relationship between the executive government and the individual, including powerful private organizations, is crucial. When Sir John Donaldson was appointed to succeed Lord Denning in July 1982, this was seen as a strongly political appointment and one which the Prime Minister favoured. Sir John had been a Conservative councillor and had presided over the National Industrial Relations Court for the two and a half years of its existence during the Heath administration. On its demise he reverted to his position as a judge of the High Court and was not promoted during the years of the Labour government 1974–9. From the beginning of 1984 when it seemed probable that Lord Hailsham would soon resign as Lord Chancellor, Sir John was widely discussed as his probable successor in the Thatcher Cabinet. This highlighted his political characteristics and qualifications and may have led to his decision not to preside over the Court of Appeal when it considered the appeal by the government against the decision of Glidewell J rejecting the decision to ban trade union membership at GCHQ.[19]

When the characteristics of judges are considered, the outstanding common factor is that all have spent twenty-five or

19. See p. 156.

more years prior to their first appointment as practising members of the Bar. Increasingly over recent years, their professional careers have absorbed their time and their aspirations. The atmosphere and culture of the Inns of Court have been the greatest influence on their attitudes.

Social and political position

Over the last 40 years there have been many surveys of the social background of the judiciary. Most have concentrated on the educational institutions attended. Fees at the top public schools are affordable only by wealthy parents and so are an indicator of social class. Admission to the universities of Oxford and Cambridge was similarly restricted during the 1940s and 1950s when today's judges were at that stage of their educational careers.

An ambitious survey by Jenny Brock analysing social class from 1820 to 1968 appeared in the report of a *Justice* subcommittee in 1972 (see table on following page).[20]

Another survey, published in 1975, covers the period 1876–1972 and, with a few omissions, analyses the 317 judges who sat in the High Court, the Court of Appeal and the House of Lords during that period. The author does not, however, break down these ninety-six years into shorter periods, so trends within the whole are not apparent. He considers school background and finds that 33 per cent attended one of the so-called Clarendon Schools (Charterhouse, Eton, Harrow, Merchant Taylors, Rugby, St Paul's, Shrewsbury, Westminster, Winchester), while 70 per cent attended Oxford or Cambridge Universities.[21]

In 1956 the *Economist*[22] published a short survey. This covered 69 judges of the Supreme Court, House of Lords and Judicial Committee of the Privy Council and showed that 76

20. Class assignment is according to father's occupation or rank. The judges in this table are those of the High Court, the Court of Appeal and the House of Lords, or their equivalents.

21. C. Neal Tate, 'Paths to the Bench in Britain', 28 *Western Political Quarterly* 108.

22. 12 December 1956, pp. 946–7.

Period of Appointment	1820–1875	1876–1920	1921–1950	1951–1968	1820–1968	Number
Social class	%	%	%	%	%	
I Traditional landed upper class	17.9	16.4	15.4	10.5	15.3	59
II Professional, commercial and administrative upper class	8.5	14.6	14.3	14.0	12.7	49
III Upper middle class	40.6	50.5	47.3	52.3	47.4	183
IV Lower middle class	11.3	9.7	8.8	8.1	9.6	37
V Working class	2.8	1.0	1.1	1.2	1.3	6
Not known	18.9	7.8	13.2	14.0	13.5	52
	100	100	100	100	100	
Number	106	103	91	86	386	386

per cent had attended 'major public schools' (not further defined) and the same percentage had been to Oxford or Cambridge. In May 1970 *New Society*[23] looked at 359 judges including those offices surveyed by the *Economist* but also, amongst others, county court judgeships and metropolitan magistrates. It found that 81 per cent had attended public schools and 76 per cent had attended Oxford or Cambridge. In 1975 Hugo Young analysed the educational background of 31 appointees to the High Court during the previous five years. He found that 68 per cent went to public schools and 74 per cent to Oxford or Cambridge.[24]

The *New Society* survey compared County Court judges in three recent years. In 1947, in 1957 and in 1967, seven County

23. 14 May 1970 (by Kevin Goldstein-Jackson).
24. *Sunday Times*, 5 October 1975.

Court judges were appointed. Of these 21 judges, all but 1 in 1947, 2 in 1957 and 1 in 1967 had attended public schools; all but 3 in 1947, 2 in 1957 and 3 in 1967 had attended Oxford or Cambridge. In 1978, of 74 High Court judges listed, over 75 per cent had attended public schools and, of these, 41 per cent had attended one of the Clarendon Schools.[25] Of the 17 High Court judges appointed between 1 January 1980 and 1 May 1982, 76 per cent attended public schools and 88 per cent Oxford or Cambridge.[26]

In 1987 Labour Research surveyed the educational background of the senior judiciary and repeated this in 1994.[27]

| | Public school | | Oxbridge | |
	1987 %	1994 %	1987 %	1994 %
House of Lords	90	91	80	82
Court of Appeal	83	77	86	87
High Court	62	80	78	80
All	70	80	80	87

Highly significant for future trends is the big increase in the percentage of High Court judges attending public schools shown in these figures. In June 1996, the six most recent appointees to the High Court bench were educated at Bryanston, Charterhouse, Blackfriars, Repton, Mill Hill and Rugby schools; four graduated from Cambridge and one from Oxford universities.

The decline in the number of 'political' judges is also shown. The *Economist*'s survey of 1956 recorded that 23 per cent of their 69 judges had been MPs or parliamentary candidates. Since 1977, no judge sitting in the High Court, or the Court of Appeal or the House of Lords (as a Law Lord) had formerly been a member of the House of Commons.

According to the Labour Research report of 1994, only two present members of the senior judiciary (High Court and

25. 950 HC Deb. col. 107–10, 16 May 1978.
26. LAG *Bulletin*, August 1982 (Phil Cohen).
27. *Labour Research*, January 1987, p. 9; October 1994, p. 10.

above) had ever stood as a candidate for the House of Commons (both in 1959) and only one other had been elected to a local authority. Twenty-six others (all Circuit judges) had stood for Parliament (two successfully) or had been elected to local authorities. This is a remarkable decline from the earlier years of this century when the advancement of barrister MPs to the bench was common.[28]

In January 1994 the average age, the number of women, and those from the ethnic minorities were:

	Average age	Women	Ethnic minorities	Total number
Law Lords	66.5	0	0	10
Heads of Division	63.0	0	0	4
Lords Justices	63.0	1	0	29
High Court judges	57.6	6	0	95
				138

Of 514 Circuit judges in post on 1 December 1994, 29 were women, and 4 were of ethnic minority origin. In 1996 there were 7 female judges on the High Court bench.

In summary, 80 per cent of the senior judiciary are products of public schools and of Oxford or Cambridge, with an average age of about sixty; 5.1 per cent are women; 100 per cent are white. Some explanation of the gross disproportions in gender and colour can no doubt be found in the structure of the legal profession, in the financial and other difficulties facing those wishing to qualify as barristers, and then needing to support themselves in the early years of practice. Another part of the explanation is sexual and racial discrimination within the profession.

The process of appointment to the judiciary and of promotion rests broadly, as we have seen, on consultation by the Lord Chancellor and his department. But the decisions are all

28. See p. 14; and Joseph M. Jacob, 'From privileged Crown to interested public', in [1993] *Public Law* 121, and *The Republican Crown*, especially chapter 6.

his or the Prime Minister's after consultation with him. In 1995 the Lord Chancellor said that he encouraged greater numbers of women and ethnic minority practitioners to apply to become judges but that he had no plans to reconstitute the professional judiciary to reflect the composition of society as a whole. Little comfort is to be obtained from the official view of the Lord Chancellor's Department who told the Home Affairs Committee in 1995,

> This is not to say that the Lord Chancellor does not appreciate the value of the judiciary more closely reflecting the make-up of society as a whole. Other things being equal, that should tend over time to result from ensuring the fullest possible equality of opportunity for persons in all sections of society who wish to enter the legal profession and who aspire to sit judicially. This implies equality of opportunity at all levels of the educational system and the legal profession as well as in the appointments system itself.[29]

These are weasel words indeed from which all meaning has been extracted. The gross imbalance in the representation of women and those from the ethnic minority is to await the day when they are treated equally by society as a whole. Judges are appointed and promoted by the most senior judge, advised by other senior judges. The system is self-perpetuating and it would be remarkable if the products were not homogeneous.

A simplified note on the structure of the courts

In 1996 there were 12 Law Lords; 35 Lords Justices; 96 High Court judges; 457 part-time deputy High Court judges (of whom 255 were Circuit judges); 517 Circuit judges; 1245 part-time Recorders and assistant Recorders; 92 stipendiary magistrates; some 30,000 JPs.

Usually 5 Law Lords sit together to form a court; as do 2 or 3 Lords Justices; High Court judges sit alone (with a jury in Crown Court). For certain cases 2 or 3 High Court judges

29. HC 52-II, p. 130.

CIVIL JURISDICTION

House of Lords (Appellate Committee)
(Lords of Appeal in Ordinary, also called Law Lords)

↑

Court of Appeal
(Master of the Rolls and Lords Justices of Appeal)

↑

County Courts	*Divisional Court of Queen's Bench*	The Divisions of the High Court:
(Circuit Judges)	(Lord Chief Justice and Judges of Queen's Bench)	*Queen's Bench, Chancery, Family* (High Court Judges)

CRIMINAL JURISDICTION

House of Lords (Appellate Committee)
(Lords of Appeal in Ordinary, also called Law Lords)

↑   ↑

Divisional Court of Queen's Bench
(Lord Chief Justice and Judges of Queen's Bench)

Court of Appeal
(Lord Chief Justice, Lords Justices of Appeal and High Court Judges)

↑

Crown Court
(Queen's Bench and Circuit Judges, Recorders, JPs)

↑   ↑

Magistrates' Courts
(JPs, stipendiaries)

sit together to form a Divisional Court. Circuit judges sit singly, as do Recorders (sometimes joined by 2 to 4 JPs).

All the above are barristers, *except* 1 High Court judge, 72 Circuit judges, and 150 Recorders and assistant Recorders, all of whom are solicitors. Sixty-two per cent of stipendiary magistrates are solicitors, the rest being barristers. JPs are lay men and women. High Court judges may be asked to sit in the Court of Appeal, and Circuit judges to sit in the High Court, from time to time.

2. Extrajudicial activities

Commissions, inquiries, reports and the like

Judges are frequently called upon by the government of the day to preside over commissions, committees and administrative tribunals of different kinds. Some of these are concerned with matters deep in political controversy.

Royal Commissions are appointed by the Crown to enquire into selected matters of concern.[1] Committees are appointed by ministers for the same purpose. As the Crown acts on the advice of ministers in this matter, and as they deal with comparable matters, the distinction between the two is not substantial. Royal Commissions have more prestige but nothing of real consequence flows from this, and the matters which these bodies investigate vary greatly in importance.

Dr T. J. Cartwright has recorded that 640 such bodies were appointed between 1945 and 1969 and he examined 358. These included 24 Royal Commissions; and 334 'major' departmental committees which he defined as those dealing with matters of direct concern to the government of Britain and whose reports were published as command papers.

The mean size of the twenty-four Royal Commissions was thirteen members, but when comparable committees are added the mean size falls to eight members. Of the twenty-four Royal Commissions, judges chaired seven. Only academics equalled them in number of Royal Commission chairs and no one group[2]

1 . See T. J. Cartwright, *Royal Commissions & Departmental Committees in Britain* (1975); see also G. Rhodes, *Committees of Inquiry* (1975).

2 . See Cartwright, *op. cit.*, p. 72. His other groups are civil service; retired central government; other government (active or retired); legal profession; business, finance, industry; medical profession; trade unions; other; no information.

of persons held half as many chairs of departmental committees. Altogether, judges chaired 118 out of Dr Cartwright's 358 bodies.

Judges chaired commissions or committees concerned with, among other things, Justices of the Peace (1946–8), medical partnerships (1948), police conditions of service (1948–9), the industrial health services (1949–50), State immunities (1949–51), taxation of profits and income (1951–5), marriage and divorce (1951), dock workers (1955–6), the interception of communications (1957), prison conditions (1957–8), the working of the monetary system (1957–9), legal education for African students (1960), security in the public service (1961), the security service and Mr Profumo (1963), children and young persons in Scotland (1961–4), jury service (1963–5), the port transport industry (1964–5), pay for dock workers (1966), tribunals of enquiry (1966), 'D' notices (1967), the age of majority (1965–7), trade unions and employers' associations (1965–8), Scottish inshore fisheries (1967–70), the constitution (1969–73), one-parent families (1969–74), the adoption of children (1969–72), contempt of court (1974), defamation (1975), and the Brixton disorders (1981). Many of these were highly political, some also highly controversial. Since 1969, important departmental committees chaired by judges have included those on the interrogation of terrorists (1971–2), crowd safety (1971–2), legal procedures to deal with terrorists (1972), the working of the Abortion Act (1971–4), the Red Lion Square disorders (1974–5), standards of conduct in public life (1974–6), and police pay (1977–8).

All those related to affairs within the United Kingdom. In addition, judges have frequently been employed on overseas matters. One of the most famous of these in post-war years was the Nyasaland Commission of Enquiry of 1959 led by Mr Justice Devlin who reported in terms of which the government of the day did not wholly approve. In 1972, Lord Pearce chaired a Commission on Rhodesian Opinion appointed to ascertain directly from all sections of the population of Rhodesia whether or not certain proposals for the government of that country were acceptable. The number of such judicial appointments for overseas territories is considerable.

In December 1973, Mr John Morris MP asked how many

judges had carried out non-judicial duties in the form of inquiries, commissions and reports, or similar tasks, during the previous twenty years. He was told that, including Law Lords and Lords Justices but excluding standing bodies such as the Law Commission, the total was 79 judges. The Labour Government of 1964–70 appointed more, on average, than did the Conservative Governments during this period from 1953 to 1973.[3] On 12 July 1984, Mr Morris tried the same question again for the period since 1973. This time the Attorney-General replied that the figures for the period before 1982 were 'not fully available or reasonably accessible', which can mean only that no one in his office was prepared to make the count. However he did say that in the years ending June 1983 and June 1984 the total number of High Court judges so involved was 28.[4] As no details were given, this figure is almost meaningless, but if the categories counted were similar to those for the period of 1953–73 those two later years show almost a doubling, on average.

More recently, in 1985–6, Mr Justice Popplewell reported on crowd safety and control at sports grounds, following the Bradford fire; in 1988, Lord Justice Butler-Sloss on suspected child abuse cases in Cleveland; in 1988 Mr Justice Barry Sheen on the sinking of the *Herald of Free Enterprise*; in 1988, Lord Cullen on the *Piper Alpha* oil rig explosion; in 1989, Lord Justice Taylor on the Hillsborough stadium disaster. In 1990, Lord Justice Woolf was appointed to inquire into the circumstances surrounding the riot at Strangeways prison and associated matters.

From time to time, the judicial process itself comes under scrutiny and the outstanding defects of expense, delay and difficult access are re-examined. In June 1995 Lord Woolf, a Lord of Appeal in Ordinary, published an interim report on the civil justice system in England and Wales. This was followed in 1996 by proposals for major reforms to promote greater access to the courts. Specifically a judge is chairman of the Law Commission, which is the permanent body concerned with law reform. Judges are therefore constantly involved in the process

3 . For full details see 865 HC Deb. col. 478–82 (7 December 1973).
4 . 63 HC Deb. col. 630 (12 July 1984).

of making recommendations for improvement in the law and this includes not only technical legal subjects but those on the boundaries of law and politics, like conspiracy. The Scottish Law Commission, also chaired by a judge, became deeply involved in the debate on devolution, submitting memoranda particularly dealing with the distribution of powers between the United Kingdom Parliament and the proposed Scottish Assembly.[5] These memoranda, although generally avoiding comment that might be regarded as politically partisan on the question of the desirability or otherwise of devolution, contain passages which were bluntly, even scathingly, critical of the statements of the means by which the government hoped to achieve their objectives.

One of the Scottish Law Commission's proposals was that if the area of devolution was sufficiently extensive, responsibility for the courts should also be transferred to the Scottish Assembly. A few months earlier Lord Wheatley spoke on behalf of all the High Court judges in Scotland. He accepted that a judge, as a member of a Royal Commission or a departmental Committee of Enquiry, might have to explain publicly the recommendations arrived at. However, he continued:

> When the subject enters the political arena and becomes politically controversial, we assume an elective silence on the political issues and confine ourselves, if we intervene at all, to constitutional or legal questions or views on practical matters affecting the law and its administration where our views may naturally be expected and sought.[6]

He went on to say that the unanimous view of the High Court judges in Scotland was that the Scottish courts should remain the responsibility of the United Kingdom and not become the responsibility of the Scottish Assembly.

It is difficult to see how this disagreement between the Scottish Law Commission and the Scottish High Court judge could be thought of as other than political.

Judges are used to head permanent bodies concerned with

5 . See Scottish Law Commission: memorandum no. 32 incorporating also an earlier memorandum.

6 . 367 HL Deb. col. 837 (27 January 1976).

national security. In April 1980, Lord Diplock was appointed to review the interception of communications (mostly phone-tapping) undertaken by the police, Customs and Excise, and the security services.[7] Mr Robin Cook, MP objected to Lord Diplock's suitability on the ground that he had been chairman of the Security Commission since 1971, and had not formerly indicated any understanding of the concern for civil liberties and privacy which had given rise to public and press anxiety about the procedures of the security services. Cook also referred to Diplock's 'evident distaste for trade unions' and said it was well known that 'taps' were frequently placed on trade unionists involved in trade disputes. The Home Secretary rejected the criticism.[8] Subsequently, the Speaker ruled in the House of Commons that it was offensive, even in relation to these extrajudicial activities, to refer to Lord Diplock as 'a Tory judge.'[9] Under the Interception of Communications Act 1985, the appointment was made statutory and Lord Nolan was the Commissioner in 1996. Complaints may be taken to a tribunal presided over by Mr Justice Macpherson of Cluny.

Under the Security Service Act 1989, Lord Justice Stuart-Smith was appointed Security Service Commissioner with a general supervisory role over the security services. Lord Justice Simon Brown was appointed as the president of the complaints Tribunal under the Act.

High Court judges are the deputy chairmen of the Parliamentary Boundary Commissions.

An important permanent body is the Judicial Studies Board. Its function is to provide training for judges, especially for those acting as assistant Recorders or deputy Registrars, and for lay magistrates; but also for other judges through refresher seminars, attended by civil servants as well. Originally limited to training in the criminal jurisdiction (with an emphasis on sentencing), the Board is now concerned also with the civil and family courts and tribunals. There is a Main Board, chaired by a Lord Justice of Appeal; the committees on the different jurisdictions are also chaired by judges.[10]

7 . 982 HC Deb. col. 205–20.
8 . 996 HC Deb. col. 824–6 (18 December 1980).
9 . 987 HC Deb. col. 651 (3 July 1980) and *The Times*, 11 July 1980.
10. See Report for 1983–87 (HMSO 1988).

Judges also preside over enquiries set up under the Tribunals of Enquiry (Evidence) Act 1921. These are nowadays reserved for investigations into matters which may involve the reputation of ministers or public officials. Between 1945 and 1970 there were five: in 1948—9 into questions of possible bribery of ministers, chaired by Mr Justice Lynskey; in 1957—8 into leakage of bank rate, chaired by Lord Justice Parker; in 1959 into allegations of police assault on a boy, chaired by Lord Sorn; in 1962—3 into a case of spying in which a minister's moral behaviour might have been involved, chaired by Lord Radcliffe; and in 1966—7 into the responsibility for the Aberfan disaster, chaired by Lord Justice Edmund Davies. Since 1970, this procedure has been used twice in Northern Ireland, as we shall see.[11] In 1972 a Tribunal of Enquiry presided over by Mr Justice James enquired into the collapse of the Vehicle and General Insurance Company and reported in terms which were critical in particular of one civil servant.[12] In 1978 a Tribunal was appointed, under the chairmanship of Mr Justice Croom-Johnson, to investigate the activities of the Crown Agents.

Two outstanding examples of the use of the judiciary in politics have concerned industrial relations, and Northern Ireland.

Industrial relations

Under statutory powers[13] the minister may set up courts of enquiry into trade disputes. Many of these have been presided over by judges, normally with two experienced non-lawyers. They are far from being solely fact-finding. The terms of reference frequently require the court to have regard to the public interest or the national interest or the national economy or considerations like 'the need for an efficient and competitive'

11. See pp. 33—6; and generally Cmnd 3121.
12. HC 133 of 1971—2.
13. Formerly the Industrial Courts Act of 1919; see now Trade Union and Labour Relations (Consolidation) Act 1992, sections 215—16.

industry.[14] In one enquiry[15] into the electricity supply industry, Lord Wilberforce asked the Treasury to submit a memorandum on the significance of the dispute to the interests of the national economy and the Treasury responded with a document that argued for a progressive and substantial reduction in the levels of settlements.[16] This request from the court caused some difficulties as it was argued that the government was seeking to impose its views and even a favoured solution of the dispute upon the court. Lord Wilberforce sought to rebut this, but the request clearly, in the minds of some, showed that the court was not independent or impartial.

The status and function of these courts came into question during one of the most critical of these enquiries, that presided over by Lord Wilberforce in 1972 into the dispute about miners' pay[17] which had led to a widespread stoppage of work. The extent to which the courts could become involved in the politics of such disputes had been shown a few years earlier when Lord Cameron presided over an enquiry into a dispute on London building sites.[18] The report then expressed the opinion that certain workmen should be eligible for re-employment if they sought it but not in any circumstances for election as shop stewards; and that other workmen should not be offered re-employment.

In the miners' dispute Lord Wilberforce became deeply enmeshed in job evaluation, the social and physical conditions in the pits and, above all, the need to produce a settlement under which the miners would go back to work. Lord Wilberforce discovered that there were two factors in any possible wage increase. One was the periodic factor – that wages did increase from time to time – and the other was what he called the adjustment factor which meant that a time might come in any industry when a distortion or trend had to be recognized as such for correction. 'The existence of these two quite separate factors', said the report, 'appears to have been overlooked until

14. See Cmnd 3025 – the industry was shipping.
15. See Cmnd 4594.
16. See Cmnd 4579.
17. Cmnd 4903.
18. Cmnd 3396.

the present Enquiry brought it to light.' If a large increase could not be paid for by the National Coal Board then the government should meet it.

The *Economist* referred to the device of 'calling in a High Court judge to write incredible economic nonsense',[19] but whatever view is taken of the justice or the wisdom of the report which recommended a considerable wage increase and which formed the basis of the settlement, the impression given was that the government had set up this enquiry to produce a report which would enable them to yield to the miners' claim without total loss of face.

When in 1970 the Minister was introducing in the Commons legislation which created the National Industrial Relations Court, he said that the NIRC's existence showed 'in fact as well as in symbol' that the provisions of the Bill[20] would not be arbitrarily implemented by the Secretary of State of the day but would 'depend on the rule of the law'. The court, he said (inaccurately), would be 'something new in British justice' and would consist of judges and laymen sitting together.[21]

Many kinds of dispute arising out of industrial relations could find their way to the NIRC which, because of its status as a superior court of record and the powers given it by statute, was able to order the payment of fines and, if that or any other of its orders was disregarded, could imprison for contempt. The application of that sanction led to the involvement of the ordinary courts. Here I am concerned to emphasize that the NIRC was required by the legislation under which it operated to make decisions which were likely to lead, and did in fact lead, to considerable and widespread political protest.

Whether the NIRC always acted with the greatest wisdom may be debatable. But its failure was due not primarily to the way it performed its functions but to the nature of those functions. Many people doubted whether the issues before the Restrictive Practices Court were justiciable. What the NIRC was required to do was to make binding decisions, and to see that they were enforced, in the context of disputes between

19. 26 February 1972.
20. This became the Industrial Relations Act 1971.
21. 808 HC Deb. col. 982.

trade unions, individual workmen, employers, and employers' federations. This, as many said at the time, was not a function which judges and courts could perform successfully.

Under the Employment Protection Act of 1978 an Appeal Tribunal consists of a legally qualified chairman and of others having special knowledge or experience of industrial relations, either as representatives of employers or as representatives of workers. The president is Mr Justice Mummery. So in structure, if not in other ways, it is similar to the NIRC. It can hear appeals from tribunals under or by virtue of the Equal Pay Act 1970, the Sex Discrimination Act 1975 and others, as well as the Employment Protection Act itself. It is a somewhat curious body in that much of its jurisdiction is to hear appeals on questions of law, for which the lay members might appear unfitted. Perhaps we are seeing, as an evolution (the origins of which can be traced to the nineteenth century), the emergence of a genuine hybrid tribunal, in which case to suggest that this body is a further example of the use of judges for extrajudicial activities is only one way to describe it. It could also be said to be an example of the developed use of experienced laymen to assist in the determination of disputes.

Northern Ireland

In Northern Ireland the first involvement of judges acting outside their courts was in 1969 when the Governor appointed Lord Cameron to lead a commission of enquiry into disturbances.[22] Then in 1971 Sir Edmund Compton (not a judge but the former Parliamentary Commissioner for Administration) chaired an enquiry into allegations of physical brutality by the security forces. Sir Edmund found there had been cases of physical ill-treatment such as wall-standing, hooding, noise, deprivation of sleep, and diets of bread and water. The Home Secretary rejected any suggestion that the methods authorized for interrogation contained any element of cruelty but he appointed three Privy Councillors to consider those methods. One was Lord Parker (who had just retired as Lord Chief

22. Cmd (N.I.) 532.

Justice) and another was Lord Gardiner (who had been Lord Chancellor from 1964 to 1970). Lord Parker and the third Privy Councillor (Mr J. A. Boyd-Carpenter) concluded that these methods, subject to proper safeguards, and limiting the occasions on which and the degree to which they could be applied, conformed to the authority given. Lord Gardiner said that they were secret, illegal, not morally justifiable and alien to the traditions of what he believed still to be the greatest democracy in the world. The disagreement was wide.[23]

In April 1972, two reports were published. Lord Widgery (who had succeeded Lord Parker as Lord Chief Justice) had been appointed as a one-man tribunal of enquiry to enquire into the events of 'Bloody Sunday' which led to thirteen civilian deaths in Londonderry. This tribunal was set up under the Tribunals of Enquiry (Evidence) Act 1921, the procedure of which is designed to elicit facts. The line between matters of fact and opinions deduced from facts is not always easy to draw. Lord Widgery spoke about the justifiability of decisions taken by army commanders and soldiers, about actions which, he concluded, did 'not require censure', and in using such language caused dispute and argument about the nature of his findings.[24]

In the meantime Mr Justice Scarman had since 1969 been enquiring with two others into the violence and civil disturbances of that year. This tribunal also operated under the Act of 1921 and its report was substantial. It investigated a large number of incidents and drew conclusions about fault and responsibility. It assessed the social cost in terms of deaths, personal injuries, damage to property, damage to licensed premises, intimidation and displacement of persons.[25]

At the end of 1972 a commission under the chairmanship of Lord Diplock reported on the legal procedures to deal with terrorist activities in Northern Ireland. It concluded that the main obstacle to dealing efficiently with terrorist crime in the regular courts of justice was intimidation of would-be prosecution witnesses. It recommended that trials of scheduled

23. Cmnd 4901 (March 1972).
24. HC 220 of 1971–2.
25. Cmd (N.I.) 566.

terrorist offences should be conducted without a jury; that members of the armed services should be given power to arrest and to detain for up to four hours to establish identity; that bail should not normally be granted; that the onus of proof as to the possession of firearms and explosives should in certain circumstances be shifted to the accused; and that the rules about the admissibility as evidence of confessions and signed statements should be relaxed.[26]

That commission led to the passing of the Northern Ireland (Emergency Provisions) Act 1973. In 1974 Lord Gardiner was appointed chairman of a committee to consider what provisions and powers, consistent to the maximum extent practicable in the circumstances with the preservation of civil liberties and human rights, were required to deal with terrorism and subversion in Northern Ireland, including provisions for the administration of justice; and to examine the working of the Act of 1973. The committee reported early in 1975,[27] and made a large number of recommendations, some endorsing the Diplock Commission and the Act, others being critical and proposing amendments to the law. In particular, it proposed the ending of detention without trial as soon as was politically possible, and it condemned as a serious mistake the establishment of a 'special category' for convicted prisoners claiming political motivation.

So from the beginning of 1972 there have been involved in five major enquiries relating to Northern Ireland a former Lord Chancellor (twice), a present and a former Lord Chief Justice, a Lord of Appeal, and a High Court judge. On one occasion, two of these were seen to be in open disagreement about the legitimacy and desirability of actions taken by the authorities; on another occasion, one of these was set up, in effect, to review recommendations made by another. It may be that a judge is well qualified to conduct enquiries to establish what took place on particular occasions. But it is impossible for him in his findings not to interpret events. He must draw deductions about what he thinks took place from the evidence that is presented to him. And so he will be involved in political

26. Cmnd 5185.
27. Cmnd 5847.

controversy and, in circumstances like those prevailing in Northern Ireland, inevitably accused of bias, of whitewashing, of serving certain political masters.

Most recently, two major issues of political significance have been referred to judges for their investigation and report.

The Nolan Committee

Following a finding by the Committee of Privileges of the House of Commons that the conduct of two Members who had agreed to table parliamentary Questions in return for payment 'fell short of the standards the House is entitled to expect of its Members' and general concern about 'sleaze' in public life,[28] a standing Committee on Standards in Public Life was appointed in November 1994 with Lord Nolan, a Lord of Appeal in Ordinary, as chairman. The first report of the Committee was published in May 1995;[29] it made recommendations about the practices governing the relationships between Members and outside interests, and proposed the appointment of a Parliamentary Commissioner for Standards. The House of Commons approved the proposals and even extended their application.[30]

This Committee is intended to be a continuing body examining many aspects of public and political life. Its members have been appointed for three years in the first instance. Although its terms of reference extend beyond strictly governmental and parliamentary bodies – the universities were an early subject for examination – its activities do impinge on scrutinies constitutionally conducted by committees of the two Houses of Parliament and to that extent weaken their authority, and reflect the decline in their reputation.

28. 248 HC Deb. col. 757–70 (25 October 1994).
29. Cm 2850.
30. 263 HC Deb. col. 1739 (19 July 1995); 265 HC Deb. col. 608–82 (6 November 1995).

The Scott Inquiry

In October 1985 Sir Geoffrey Howe, the Foreign Secretary, told the House of Commons that under guidelines laid down by the government the previous year, orders for defence equipment to Iran and Iraq, then at war, which 'would significantly enhance the capability of either side to prolong or exacerbate the conflict', should not be approved.[31] After a ceasefire in 1988, the guidelines were relaxed but Parliament was not informed.

In October 1990 three senior executives, including Mr Paul Henderson, of a company known as Matrix Churchill, were arrested and subsequently charged with offences under the Customs and Excise Management Act 1979 relating to illegal exports. The case for the defence was that government agencies were well aware of the activities of the company and that Mr Henderson had supplied the security services with valuable information; also that the Minister for Trade (Mr Alan Clark) had encouraged exporters to stress in their licence applications the peaceful use to which machine tools could be put even though they were intended to be used for the manufacture of parts of conventional weapons. When Mr Clark, under cross-examination, admitted this, the Crown withdrew, the trial collapsed, and the accused were acquitted.

On 16 November 1992, the Prime Minister announced the setting up of an Inquiry into 'the export of defence equipment and dual-use goods to Iraq and related prosecutions', whether responsible Ministers operated in accordance with policies of the government, and to report on decisions taken by the prosecuting authority and those signing PII certificates.[32]

To conduct the inquiry the Prime Minister appointed Lord Justice Scott (later appointed head of the Chancery Division of the High Court). This inquiry turned out to be a remarkable event. Its Report[33] was massive, being based on much written and public oral evidence. Senior Ministers (including the Prime Minister and Lady Thatcher) and senior civil servants were

31. 84 HC Deb. col. 450 (29 October 1985).
32. 214 HC Deb. col. 74 (16 November 1992).
33. HC 115 of 1995–96.

examined. The internal workings of government departments were exposed. Some of those interviewed, led by Lord Howe, former Foreign Secretary, criticized the procedure heavily. Before the report was published, attempts were made to denigrate its findings. On publication the government mounted an extensive defensive operation aimed at minimizing its adverse aspects, although the most serious allegations against ministers had not been substantiated.

For our present purposes, the inquiry was noteworthy in that a senior judge was appointed to deal with matters deep in party politics and fraught with constitutional implications. In the face of criticism, amounting at times to abuse from public persons, Sir Richard responded vigorously. Neither side kept to the rules of gentlemanly conduct which usually govern such disagreements at the highest level. There were no ministerial resignations.[34]

Legislative process

The most senior judges sit in the House of Lords[35] and may take part in its legislative and other activities. Lords of Appeal in Ordinary – Law Lords – receive life baronies on appointment unless they are already ennobled. A survey has been made[36] of the twenty-six judges who were active Law Lords during the period 1952–68, together with two Lord Chief Justices, two Masters of the Rolls and one president of what was then the Probate, Divorce and Admiralty Division. The authors of the survey say that there was very little 'in the way of political activism' on the part of the Law Lords whose contribution to debates on bills was largely that of acting as 'resident technical consultants to the legislature on legal points' and it seems that those with records of overt political affiliation did not speak more than others.

While participating Law Lords agreed with one another more frequently than they disagreed, the authors of the survey

34. See further, pp. 239–44.
35. I.e., the Upper House of Parliament.
36. L. Blom-Cooper and G. Drewry, *Final Appeal* (1972), ch. 10.

list thirteen items between 1956 and 1967 where there was a substantial measure of disagreement and of these several were not matters of technical law. They included capital punishment, artificial insemination, adultery, the minimum age for the death penalty, corporal punishment of young offenders, and disputes concerning majority verdicts, suspended sentences and parole. In one debate, five Law Lords, in an unprecedented way, spoke against a legislative proposal which provided that in assessing damages payable to a widow on the death of her husband, her remarriage or prospects of remarriage should not be taken into account. Two other Law Lords participated and all the Law Lords with two exceptions attended the debate on 6 May 1971. 'In the face of almost certain defeat in the Lobby,' say Blom-Cooper and Drewry, 'the Law Lords, as decorously as they were able, withdrew their amendment and retired once more into their judicial shells.'[37]

Where technical law ends and political controversy begins is not always easy to determine. It is clear, however, that Law Lords while for the most part restricting themselves to the obviously technical are not averse to speaking on social questions like capital punishment, the treatment of offenders and adultery. They do occasionally assume the role of 'self-appointed guardians of the nation's conscience'.[38]

A well-known example from earlier in this century of a Law Lord speaking on a political matter in the House of Lords arose when Lord Carson in 1921 strongly attacked the proposal to establish an Irish Free State. His right to do so was challenged by Lord Chancellor Birkenhead and defended by former Lord Chancellor Finlay during a debate in 1922 on Law Lords and party politics.[39]

Highly political was Lord Salmon's contribution in 1975 to the debates on the government's controversial Trade Union and Labour Relations (Amendment) Bill. He said:

We cannot shut our eyes to the fact that there are groups, very small numerically but extremely cohesive and tenacious, who have infiltrated the unions with the intention

37. Ibid., p. 215.
38. Ibid., p. 204.
39. 49 HL Deb. col. 931–73.

of seizing power if they can. Their objects and ideas are entirely different from those of the trade unions, which we all know and respect. Their avowed purpose is to wreck the Social Contract and the democratic system under which we live. Their ethos derives from foreign lands where individual liberty is dead, and where the courts and trade unions are mere tools of the Executive, to do its will.[40]

The argument is familiar – Lord Gordon-Walker said he had heard it for forty years – but, even more, it is a political argument. Lord Salmon clearly felt strongly and spoke in the name of freedom and democracy. He posed the question whether the disadvantage of a judge speaking on matters which in one form or another – such as unfair dismissal from employment or from a trade union – might well come before him when he was on the bench, was outweighed by the advantage of hearing his views or by the argument that he should not be prevented, by convention or otherwise, from speaking in Parliament on such a matter.

In 1984, when the Police and Criminal Evidence Bill was being debated in the House of Lords, Lord Scarman, who had spoken at second reading, moved two amendments during the Committee stage. The first concerned unlawfully obtained evidence and had the object of strengthening the deterrent effect of the Bill in dealing with problems of the misuse of police power. He returned to the same matter during the Report stage and his amendment was carried, against the Government, on a division. Subsequently, the Government inserted a clause of their own which went some way to meet Lord Scarman's amendment.[41] On third reading, he moved a second amendment to make racially discriminatory behaviour by the police a specific disciplinary offence. This was also carried on a division; the government accepted their defeat[42] and did not seek to reverse the decision. Both these matters were deep in political

40. 358 HL Deb. col. 27.

41. 452 HL Deb. col. 431–6 (4 January 1984); 454 col. 931–4, 946–8 (11 July 1984); 455 col. 653–74 (31 July 1984).

42. 455 HL Deb. col. 1219–27 (19 October 1984).

controversy, the second in particular being strongly resisted by the police as well as by the government.

Occasionally, a Law Lord may introduce a Bill, as did Lord Templeman in 1987–8 when he took the Land Registration Bill through the House of Lords on behalf of the Law Commission. The participation of judges in the debates on the Courts and Legal Services Bill 1989–90 is discussed below.[43]

In 1993 the Home Secretary announced that the statutory scheme for compensation for victims of violent crime would not be implemented and that he proposed to introduce a new scheme under his prerogative powers. A leading opponent and critic of this proposal was Lord Ackner, and he was supported in a debate on 2 March 1994 by Lords Simon, Brightman and Bridge.[44] All four were former Law Lords, who would not consider themselves bound by the same proprieties as those affecting Law Lords in active service. Lord Ackner pursued his campaign when the Government introduced new legislation[45] following the decision by the Law Lords in the Fire Brigades case.[46] Lord Ackner frequently intervenes in debates in the upper chamber.[47]

On 25 January 1995 when the House of Lords gave a second reading to Lord Lester's Human Rights Bill, Lord Taylor C. J. and Lords Browne-Wilkinson and Lloyd spoke in support. In the debate on third reading on 1 May 1995, they were joined by Lord Slynn. Lord Woolf also sent his support, as did Sir Thomas Bingham MR, and Lords Scarman and Simon (former Law Lords). So at least four active Law Lords and the Lord Chief Justice gave their public support. A former Master of the Rolls (Lord Donaldson) spoke on the other side.[48] The purpose of the Bill – to incorporate into UK domestic law the European Convention on Human Rights – touches on some of the most controversial of political issues.

43. See pp. 54–6.

44. 552 HL Deb. col. 1071–1124.

45. See 566 HL Deb. col. 307 (19 July 1995).

46. *R. v. Secretary of State for the Home Department ex parte Fire Brigades Union* [1995] 2 AC 513 (see pp. 122–5).

47. See 'Cet Animal Est Mechant', Lord Ackner's presidential address to the Holdsworth Club on 13 March 1992.

48. 560 HL Deb. col. 1136–74; 563 HL Deb. col. 1271–85.

Participation in public debate

In July 1955, the Director-General of the British Broadcasting Corporation (Sir Ian Jacob) wrote to the Lord Chancellor (Lord Kilmuir) about a project for broadcasting a series of lectures about great judges of the past, in which Sir Ian hoped members of the judiciary would participate. The Lord Chancellor consulted the Lord Chief Justice, the Master of the Rolls and the President of the Probate, Divorce and Admiralty Division of the High Court, who all agreed with his reply. The Lord Chancellor began with the complacent and highly debatable observation that 'we are likely . . . to get a better assessment of the qualities of some eminent judge of the past through an existing member of the judiciary than from anyone else.' He continued in words which became known as the Kilmuir rules:

> But the overriding consideration, in the opinion of myself and my colleagues, is the importance of keeping the judiciary in this country insulated from the controversies of the day. So long as a judge keeps silent his reputation for wisdom and impartiality remains unassailable: but every utterance which he makes in public, except in the course of the actual performance of his judicial duties, must necessarily bring him within the focus of criticism. It would, moreover, be inappropriate for the judiciary to be associated with any series of talks or anything which could be fairly interpreted as entertainment . . . My colleagues and I, therefore, are agreed that as a general rule it is undesirable for members of the judiciary to broadcast on the wireless or to appear on television . . . We consider that if judges are approached by the broadcasting authorities with a request to take part in a broadcast on some special occasion, the judge concerned ought to consult the Lord Chancellor, who would always be ready to express his opinion on the particular request.

Lord Kilmuir added that he had no sort of disciplinary jurisdiction over Her Majesty's judges, each of whom, if asked to broadcast, would have to decide for himself whether he considered it compatible with his office to accept.[49]

In January 1986, the then Lord Chancellor (Lord Hailsham) said that the rules had been reviewed from time to time and the judiciary of the Supreme Court and the Circuit bench consulted. He himself had consulted the judges in 1971, 1979 and 1985. On each occasion the 'overwhelming consensus' was that there should be 'no change at all'. The course adopted, said Lord Hailsham, was to channel invitations for participation in journalism, appearances on the media, and other public engagements through the Lord Chancellor's office.

Certain kinds of publications seem not to have caused difficulties. Lord Scarman was a judge in the Court of Appeal when he gave and published the Hamlyn lectures in 1974, which were controversial, as was the Dimbleby lecture given by Lord Denning in 1980. There have also been conflicts. The 'controversies of the day' certainly included the dispute over clause 43 of the Administration of Justice Bill in 1985, by which the government proposed to end the citizen's right to go to the Court of Appeal when a lower court refused to give leave to apply for judicial review of the decision of a minister or other public authority. Among the many public critics were two Lords Justices of Appeal. This, said Lord Hailsham, was 'utterly improper'. The judges were reported to have apologized. There were other reports that judges had been refused permission to appear on television in the early 1980s.

Extended to journalism, the rules were directly challenged by Circuit Judge Pickles. In March 1985, he came into conflict with the Lord Chancellor over an article he had written for the *Daily Telegraph* on government pressure on the judiciary to shorten sentences and on the inadequacies of the prison system. The Lord Chancellor told him that, prima facie, the article constituted 'judicial misbehaviour' which is a ground for dismissal. In August 1985, Judge Pickles wrote a second article for the newspaper and was interviewed by the Lord Chief Justice.

In February 1986, he wrote an article in the *Guardian* attacking the Kilmuir rules as 'much too wide' and setting out the

49. For the full text of the letter see [1986] *Public Law* 383–6.

attempts to silence him, quoting letters from the Lord Chancellor (Hailsham). He also recorded programmes about law and society for the British Broadcasting Corporation. In other public statements he was openly critical of the Lord Chancellor and his department, accusing it of being secretive and antiquated. In April 1987, Judge Pickles published an outspoken autobiography. It was reported that, in 1985 and 1986, objection was taken by the Lord Chancellor to Lord Justice Browne-Wilkinson's participation in public debates, as a result of which he did not appear.

It seems to be accepted that peers are not expected to contact the Lord Chancellor's department before they speak extrajudicially in public. Lord McCluskey, in the Reith lectures of 1986, expressed many criticisms and warnings. Lord Templeman in the same year took part in radio and television programmes. In 1987, the Lord Chief Justice (Lord Lane) publicly backed police demands for the abolition of the suspect's 'right to silence';[50] and was reported as attacking politicians for delay in passing tougher laws on sentencing policy, a question on which the judiciary was divided. Whether these three informed the Lord Chancellor that they intended to speak on these lines is not known. It seems improbable. It is sometimes said that judges are entitled to make extrajudicial statements critical of the existing law and advocating reform. Perhaps Judge Pickles's utterances were disapproved of more for their style than for their content.

In November 1987, Lord Mackay, the newly appointed Lord Chancellor, ended the practice whereby judges were expected to seek the guidance of the Lord Chancellor's Department before making public statements or taking part in radio or television programmes. They were now to be trusted to use their own discretion. It appears however that in October 1989 Lord Mackay wrote to the then Lord Chief Justice, Lord Lane, stressing that, above all, judges 'should avoid any involvement, either direct or indirect, in issues which are or might become

50. When this 'right' was abolished for proceedings in Northern Ireland in 1988, as part of anti-terrorist measures, three senior Ulster judges openly criticized the Secretary of State when he attended a social function in the province.

politically controversial'. This letter was re-circulated to all judges in June 1991 with a paper written by Lord Mackay's head of information. The paper stated that circuit and district judges should always (save in an emergency) consult one of the presiding judges before speaking to the Lord Chancellor's press office and should never speak directly to the press without consulting a presiding judge. High Court judges and judges of the Court of Appeal should likewise consult heads of divisions.[51] How far this advice has been followed is doubtful.

The consultative function

From mediaeval times, the sovereign and his or her principal ministers have consulted with the judges, those 'lions under the throne'. The advice they gave was not always to the sovereign's liking, as the famous conflicts between James I and Chief Justice Coke showed. The peers also consulted the judges on occasion; when they did so in 1614 over the long-debated matter of the right of the King to tax through 'impositions' without parliamentary approval, Coke took the view that the judges should not be required to give an opinion 'on the ground that they were expected in judicial course to speak and judge between the King's majesty and his people, and likewise between His Highness's subjects, and in no case to be disputants on any side'.[52] It is tempting to see this as the first occasion when the judges insisted on independence on this principle. We shall see that the conflicts between the different roles played by the judge in the political order persist today.

Government departments, especially the Home Office, frequently consult the judges on matters which require law reform. Departments have their own legal advisers but the view of the judges, who will be required to interpret and apply the legislation, may be thought valuable. The Judges' Council of the Supreme Court and the Council of Circuit Judges may be consulted. So may individual judges.

Thus on 7 June 1988, the House of Commons debated a

51. See article by Joshua Rozenberg in the *Guardian*, 12 April 1994.
52. S. R. Gardiner, *History of England 1603–1642* (1883), vol. 2, p. 242.

proposal that juries should be empowered to recommend the use of the death penalty. The Home Secretary asked the Lord Chief Justice for his opinion and, said the Home Secretary, 'I can tell the House that he would be strongly opposed' to the proposal, on the ground that it was for Parliament, not the judges, to decide which types of murder should be met with death.

Sometimes the relationship goes beyond consultation. Lord Justice Butler-Sloss presided over the Cleveland inquiry into child abuse. Later, in June 1989, it was reported that she was proposing to the Lord Chancellor that the Children Bill should reverse a decision which she and other members of the Court of Appeal had felt obliged to make excluding hearsay evidence. In September 1989, following a private conference, the Lord Justice was reported as launching an education programme for judges on sentencing and treatment of child sex abusers.

It was also reported in August 1989 that Circuit Judge Bracewell was to play a vital role in the administration of the Children Act, advising on the system needed to match individual cases to the court best fitted to deal with them. In this connection, she was reported to have been co-opted to the Judicial Studies Board.

In September 1989, it was reported that the Home Secretary had begun a series of private discussions with public officials including the Lord Chancellor, the Lord Chief Justice (who had hitherto been reluctant to participate in such discussions lest they were seen as prejudicing judicial independence) and the senior Lord Justice of Appeal. The discussions were seen as preliminary to the government policy paper on criminal justice.

Judges and the public service

The relationship between the judiciary and the government has been changed by developments over the last twenty years and especially over the last five years or so.

The longer term has seen a greater willingness on the part of the judiciary to challenge the exercise by ministers and civil servants of their discretionary powers. An early example is

shown in *Padfield v. Minister of Agriculture* (1968).[53] The procedure by way of judicial review was simplified in 1977 and
the number of applications rose considerably.[54] In some areas
the judiciary seems more willing to limit the exercise of discretionary powers; in others, less willing, even reluctant. In
1987 a pamphlet, prepared by the Treasury Solicitor's Department in conjunction with the Management and Personnel
Office of the Cabinet Office, was published under the title *The
Judge Over Your Shoulder*. This was directed to civil servants
as an introduction to the basic principles of judicial review. It
attributed the growth of judicial review to, amongst other
things, 'an increasing willingness on the part of the judiciary
to intervene in the day-to-day business of government, coupled
with a move towards an imaginative interpretation of statutes'.
The pamphlet explained, in simple terms, how civil servants
could protect themselves from the possibility of having their
actions and decisions overturned by the courts.

A more direct conflict between the judiciary and the government arose because of an alleged change in the attitude of the
Lord Chancellor's Department. The dispute centred on the way
the courts were administered and was a result of the application
of managerial principles propagated by the Thatcher administrations of the 1980s. Before this, the judges themselves, and
especially the Master of the Rolls, whose responsibility it was
seen to be, considered and made the necessary recommendations
to the department on staffing and other administrative arrangements of the courts. Because public expenditure was involved,
the judges did not always get all the changes they wanted. But
theirs was the initiative; and it was usually successful. Those
arrangements can seriously affect the work of the courts, being
concerned with assessing the needs of the courts and securing
resources, organizing the internal structures of the courts so that
they can best deal with the caseloads arising, laying down pre-
trial and trial procedures, managing the case-flow, measuring
and monitoring court performance, managing court records, and
planning necessary reforms to court structures and processes.[55]

53. [1968] AC 997; see p. 105.
54. See p. 112–4.
55. I. R. Scott, 'The Council of Judges in the Supreme Court of England
and Wales' in [1989] *Public Law* 379.

In November 1987, the head of the Chancery Division of the High Court, then Sir Nicolas Browne-Wilkinson, in a public lecture[56] spoke of a threat to the independence of the legal system arising 'by reason of the executive's control of finance and administration'. He was explicit: 'There appear to be those in the Lord Chancellor's Department who perceive its role as being far wider than is consistent with any concept of the independence of the judiciary.' He referred to the political reforms introduced by the Treasury in other departments and to the Financial Management Initiative. This had affected staffing levels, prejudicing the proper administration of justice. It had resulted in the allocation of funds based not on the best interests of justice but on value for money.

Behind this lay the complaint that the judiciary had been effectively excluded from policy-making. A year later, the then Lord Chancellor (Lord Hailsham) replied by claiming that the essential function of the Lord Chancellor was to defend the independence and integrity of the judiciary. He denied that the Lord Chancellor was 'the lackey or dupe of the Chief Secretary of the Treasury' and scorned the idea that judges should be permitted 'to run a sort of legal Arcadia'.[57]

In March 1996, the Lord Chief Justice, Lord Taylor, complained in a public lecture, 'In addition to this hectic catalogue of legislative activity there has been unleashed on the courts an invading army equipped with clipboards conducting management reviews, feasibility projects and pilot studies all of which add to the pervading sense of frenzy and uncertainty.'[58]

In 1993 the conflict took fire when judicial independence was seen to be involved. The Employment Appeal Tribunal Rules 1980 provide that where it appears to the Registrar that the stated grounds of appeal do not give the tribunal jurisdiction, the Registrar shall notify the appellant informing him of the reasons for his opinion and no further action is to be taken on the appeal. It was the practice of the EAT to hold preliminary hearings in many cases. The Lord Chancellor considered

---

56. 'The Independence of the Judiciary' in [1988] *Public Law* 44.
57. 8 *Civil Justice Quarterly* (1989) 308.
58. 'Continuity and Change in Criminal Law', delivered at King's College London on 6 March 1996.

this practice contributed to a mounting backlog of cases and was unauthorized. The President of the tribunal (Mr Justice Wood) considered the practice to be within the rules. On 19 March 1993 the Lord Chancellor wrote to the President disagreeing with him about the applicability of the rule and demanding his 'immediate assurance that Rule 3 is henceforth applied in full' and stating 'If you do not feel that you can give me that assurance, I must ask you to consider your position.' The President replied, 'You have demanded that I exercise my judicial function in a way which you regard as best suited to your Executive purposes, but I have to say that in all the circumstances ... I cannot regard compliance with your demand as conducive to justice.' The President retired from the Bench soon afterwards.

It was reported in the press that judges were 'outraged' by this attempt by the Lord Chancellor to pressurize (as it was seen by some) a High Court judge to change his view of the law in order to save money for the Treasury. Such an interference with the independence of the judiciary, including a suggestion that the President should resign, would have been a serious breach of the constitution. The Lord Chancellor denied any such intention and the matter was debated at some length in the House of Lords.[59]

In 1988 the Lord Chief Justice (Lord Lane) re-instituted the Judges Council of the Supreme Court. The report of the Review Body on Civil Justice[60] said the Council 'should enable the judiciary to plan for the allocation of High Court caseloads and judge power in the light of needs and resources of that court as a whole rather than of individual Divisions. It will also enable it to put a common view to the Lord Chancellor about needs for resources and about priorities for some needs.'

The Council consists of the Lord Chief Justice, the Master of the Rolls, the President of the Family Division, the Vice Chancellor as head of the Chancery Division, the senior presiding judge and two judges of the High Court, one of whom is a presiding judge. Its staff is provided by the Lord Chancellor's Department. It is too early to assess its general impact. In the

59. 553 HL Deb. col. 751–804 (27 April 1994).
60. Cm. 394 para. 322.

meantime, it is clear that many judges consider that the Lord Chancellor's Department has ceased to act as an intermediary or 'hinge' between themselves and the executive government and has become as much a part of the governmental machinery as any other department of State. Judges feel that in this process they have lost a privileged position which helped to preserve their independence. This conflict between the judges and the Lord Chancellor's Department erupted when Lord Mackay put forward his proposals for the reform of the legal profession.[61]

So also, it must not be assumed that ministers and civil servants regard judicial decisions as necessarily embodying the ultimate wisdom, especially where those decisions limit their powers. Indeed, their immediate reaction may be to seek ways which circumvent judicial pronouncements. A striking example of this occurred in 1989 when a decision of the Divisional Court interpreting immigration rules[62] was considered by the Treasury Solicitor's Department to be wrong and too advantageous to the prospective immigrant. As a result, a senior member of the Treasury Solicitor's staff sent an advisory letter to the President of the Immigration Appeal Tribunal saying that the decision undermined the rules and that the judge went 'much too far'. On the authority of the President, the letter was distributed to immigration adjudicators, with a copy of the decision and a briefing to counsel defending such applications for judicial review. The advice suggested: 'we must try, by adopting a uniformly more robust and aggressive approach, to recover some lost ground' and accused the Divisional Court 'almost invariably' of looking for errors or ambiguities so as to upset the determinations of adjudicators. As a result of the publicity given to these events,[63] it was decided that the Treasury Solicitor would no longer act as solicitor for the tribunal.

A similar attitude was shown in 1986 when the Law Lords stated that the Trustee Savings Bank and its assets belonged

61. See below, pp. 53–6.
62. *R. v. Immigration Appeal Tribunal ex parte Khatab* [1989] Imm. AR 313.
63. *Independent*, 6 June 1989.

not to depositors but to the state, shortly before the bank was floated on the Stock Exchange. This view was contrary to that of the government. It was ignored by the Treasury.

Sentencing policy is a source of disagreement between judges and the Home Office. Arguments have arisen over proposals to introduce automatic parole for short-term prisoners; also over the possibility of dividing every sentence of three years or under into three parts: imprisonment, supervised release, and remission (which Lords Justices on the criminal side of the Court of Appeal made clear they did not like). Ministers from time to time make statements seeming to indicate to judges generally what sentencing policy should be, within the range of punishments laid down by statutes for different crimes. Similarly, when life sentences are reviewed, the trial judge makes a recommendation to the parole board, but complaints have been made that too frequently junior ministers in the Home Office depart from the recommendation, usually by increasing the length of the period of imprisonment. This is seen by some judges as usurping their function.

The dispute over sentencing policy became more intense when disagreement developed in public between Lord Taylor (then Lord Chief Justice) and the Home Secretary (Mr Michael Howard). In a debate in the House of Lords in May 1996 on the Government's White Paper[64] (which was to lead to a Bill), Lord Taylor said that never in the history of our criminal law had such far-reaching proposals been put forward on the strength of such flimsy and dubious evidence; and that the figures in the White Paper were shallow and untested. Minimum sentences were to be introduced, which, said Lord Taylor, 'must involve a denial of justice'. Lord Donaldson, a former Master of the Rolls, condemned the policy of mandatory sentences and said that the White Paper gave a loud and clear message to the public that judges were not to be trusted. Lord Nolan said that the proposed minimum sentences were 'unnecessary and profoundly unjust'.[65] The debate was not con-

64. *Protecting the Public* (Cm 3190).
65. 572 HL Deb. col. 1025–76 (23 May 1996).

fined to the legislature.[66] Although the issue is one which particularly concerns the judges, depriving them in part of their historic role, it is also intensely political, particularly in the months before a general election when the political parties are competing for public support for their policies on law and order. Inevitably the judiciary is drawn into this controversy.

On 5 June 1996, Lord Irvine initiated a debate in the House of Lords on the judiciary and public controversy.[67] Speaking from the Opposition front bench, his position was somewhat more conservative than that of Lord Mackay. Lord Irvine said:

> There is a distinction between judicial participation in public controversy of a political nature and the judges' participation in public controversy concerning the effective administration of justice. The debates about legal aid, maximum and minimum sentences and the size of the prison population, all concern the administration of justice. But at the same time they are issues of deep political controversy. For myself, I think that the judges would be wise to confine themselves to controversy about the administration of justice.

Lord Woolf referred to the judiciary's role when presiding over government inquiries. Perhaps with Sir Richard Scott's inquiry into arms for Iraq in mind he called for restraint to be exercised 'not only by the judiciary in making comments as a result of such inquiries, but also on the part of those, either in the Executive or in the legislature, who are desirous of criticising the judge who is responsible for making the contribution'. The Scott Report had been published some three months before this debate. It had been preceded by personal attacks on its procedure by former ministers. After publication the criticism widened, with Sir Richard, as we have seen, defending himself and his team.

66. See, for example, Lord Taylor's lecture of March 1996 (Note 58); also the attack on the Home Secretary by Lord Woolf MR and Lord Bingham CJ on the second reading of the Crime (Sentences) Bill on 27 January 1997.
67. 572 HL Deb. col. 1254–1313.

Lord Mackay's proposals

In January 1989, the Lord Chancellor, Lord Mackay, published his proposals for reform of the legal profession in three policy papers.[68] Some of the proposals – including those which threatened the monopoly of barristers in superior courts, required all advocates to have certificates of competence, and permitted multi-disciplinary partnerships – aroused considerable opposition from within the profession. Most remarkable was the language used by some senior members of the judiciary. The Lord Chief Justice, Lord Lane, referred to the first paper on the profession as 'one of the most sinister documents ever to emanate from Government'. The Master of the Rolls, Lord Donaldson, said he had 'absolutely no disagreement' with Lord Lane over the main issues. Lord Scarman criticized the papers as being 'ill-considered', 'superficial' in their reasoning and 'flawed' in their logic. Lord Ackner spoke of the proposals as involving 'at the very least a substantial risk of the destruction of the Bar', of 'the myopic application of dogma' and much else besides. The former Lord Chancellor, Lord Hailsham, was reported as saying that the government was 'thinking with its bottom and sitting on its head'.

This dispute emphasizes the ambiguity of the judges' position. They want, at one and the same time, to be 'independent' of government and to be involved in the processes of government. But, like everyone else, once they enter into discussions on policy with ministers and civil servants they compromise their vaunted independence.

In debate,[69] the senior judges renewed their attack. Lord Lane said:

Oppression does not stand on the doorstep with a tooth-brush moustache and a swastika armband. It creeps up insidiously; it creeps up step by step; and all of a sudden

68. *The Work and Organisation of the Legal Profession* (Cm 570); *Contingency Fees* (Cm 571); *Conveyancing by Authorised Practitioners* (Cm 572). These are referred to also as the Green Papers.

69. 505 HL Deb. col. 1307–1480 (the debate lasted from 9.56 a.m. until 10.41 p.m.).

the unfortunate citizen realizes that [freedom] has gone
. . . One asks whether we are now seeing tools being
fashioned which by some future, perhaps less scrupulous,
Government may be used to weaken the independent
administration of justice and so undermine the rule of
law.

Lord Donaldson spoke of the further proposed fragmentation of
the profession as 'an unmitigated disaster'; of 'an irreversible
plunge into the unknown'; of 'an affront to the constitutional
doctrine of the separation of power'; of freedom disappearing
'by gradual erosion'. And he reserved the right to say to the
government 'Get your tanks off my lawn'. Lord Bridge spoke
of a 'deep sense of unease' felt by the great majority of the
judiciary and of 'hasty and ill-considered legislation'. Lord
Goff referred to multi-disciplinary partnerships as 'most objectionable', and Lord Griffiths called them a 'profound mistake'.
Lord Ackner inveighed against 'political considerations, political dogma and doctrine which are about to do untold harm to
the future quality of the administration of justice.' Lord Oliver
spoke of the Government taking 'a terrible and unjustifiable
risk' and of the papers containing much that was 'quite
unacceptable'.

In May 1989, the Judges' Council set out the majority views
of High Court and Court of Appeal judges. To a considerable
extent these views supported those of the Bar Council in seeking to retain the monopoly of barristers in the superior courts,
in rejecting multi-disciplinary partnerships, and in objecting to
the Lord Chancellor having power to make final decisions on
the training, conduct and rights of audience of advocates.

In July, Lord Mackay published a White Paper which abandoned the proposal of a single accreditation for advocates,
gave the judges a veto over the rules for accreditation of solicitors, and did not continue to propose multi-disciplinary partnerships. The effect may be to limit greatly the opportunity for
solicitors to act as advocates in more serious criminal cases.

On 19 December 1989, the Courts and Legal Services Bill
was given a second reading in the House of Lords.[70] The general

70. 514 HL Deb. col. 122–37, 146–248.

temperature of the debate was lower than that on 7 April. Much of the strongest criticism was voiced not by the judges in the House but by non-lawyers such as Lord Benson who had chaired the Royal Commission on Legal Services[71] which reported in 1979. Lord Ackner, however, remained unsubdued. He said:

> I am convinced that the probable long-term – and not all that long – collective effect of this Bill as it now stands will be to inflict serious damage on the quality of justice in this country . . . The ever-increasing megafirms, with their growing litigation departments, growing both in size and cost, with full rights of audience in all courts, will cause the Bar to wither away. The district attorney system will take over the criminal prosecutions, and the corrupt philosophy of the contingency fee will pervade the whole system. The strong and independent judiciary, acknowledged by the Government in the Green Paper to be one of the central supports upon which our liberties are based and upon which the rule of law depends, will be weakened by the diminishing quality of available recruits and the growing political influence in their appointments.

And he quoted Chief Justice Cardozo of the Supreme Court of the USA:

> We must always take care to safeguard the law against the assaults of opportunism, the expediency of the passing hour, the erosion of small encroachments, and the scorn and derision of those who have no patience with general principles.[72]

When the Bill was debated in committee and on report, language was again more restrained. To a remarkable extent, speeches and interventions by judicial peers were dominated by Lords Ackner and Donaldson. Lord Ackner spoke on over 80 occasions and moved 17 amendments. Lord Donaldson spoke on 54 occasions. On third reading, Lords Ackner and Donaldson spoke on 17 occasions, Lord Ackner moving two

71. Cmnd. 7648.
72. 514 HL Deb. col. 204–5 (19 December 1989).

more amendments. During all these proceedings six other judicial peers spoke on a total of 16 occasions. On third reading, Lord Ackner returned to the attack.[73]

With the particular merits and demerits of these proposals I am not here directly concerned. But the reaction of the most senior members of the judiciary – the Law Lords, the Lord Chief Justice and the Master of the Rolls – was felt by many of the general public, I believe, to conflict with the image which the judiciary have been at pains to promote. Judges, it was thought, did not enter into open controversy with politicians, certainly not in such outspoken language. Lord Benson referred to the debate of 7 April when he commented on 'the degrading spectacle of the Lord Chancellor and virtually the whole of the judiciary in open conflict'. This conflict was uncharacteristic both because judges usually avoided speaking against the government on matters of party policy and because judges usually worked behind the scenes to advance their causes or to influence legal reforms. Senior professional persons have traditionally not descended into the open political pit because they have not needed to, having more effective ways to achieve their ends. But, until recently, senior professional persons have not been directly challenged over what Bernard Shaw called their conspiracies against the laity. This conflict showed that judges, no less than physicians and surgeons, churchmen, academics, and practising lawyers, would seek, for a variety of reasons (some being more elevated than others) to defend their professional status with much vigour and little subtlety.

Conclusion

Public criticism of judges has increased over the last two decades, fuelled especially by the discovery of major miscarriages of justice often inadequately investigated by the courts. At the same time judges have themselves become more critical of ministers. One outcome has been far greater participation by judges in public debate and in extrajudicial contributions

73. 516 HL Deb. col. 1758–9 (15 March 1990).

to public debate in lectures and articles in learned and less learned periodicals. This is to be welcomed. But one of its dangers was exemplified when Lord Bingham, giving a lecture on the law of privacy, said that, if legislation was not forthcoming, cases would arise in the courts in which the need to give relief was obvious and pressing. 'When such cases do arise,' he said, 'I do not think the courts will be found wanting.' This was interpreted by some as a suggestion that the judges might themselves make a new law, if Parliament failed to do so.[74]

If it is accepted, as I argue, that a judge, when sitting in his court, is frequently required to make decisions which involve an assessment of where the public interest lies and so to make a political decision, then he cannot be said to act neutrally, although he may still be the person best suited to make that particular decision. Also he may be the best person to make certain extrajudicial decisions and his opinions on a range of public matters may be worth hearing. There is nothing inherently improper in consultations between a judge and public officials on general matters of policy concerning the administration of the judicial system. But judges should not be involved in the making of decisions for which they are unsuited.

The falseness arises when judges are presented, or present themselves, as neutral arbiters capable of providing unpolitical solutions to political problems or of expressing unpolitical opinions on political issues. It is when the claim to neutrality is seen, as it must be, as a sham that damage is done to the judicial system.

74. See Lord Irvine in 572 HL Deb. col. 1258–9; and Lord Mackay, col. 1311 (5 June 1996).

Part Two

Cases

The Court's position had not been made any easier by suggestions that it was possible for the Government to influence its decisions. The Court was surprised that those suggestions should have been made, and the Court owed it to its members and to all concerned to make it clear that no attempt had been made by anyone directly or indirectly, otherwise than in open court, to influence its decision.

Sir John Donaldson, President of the National Industrial Relations Court, in *Midland Cold Storage Ltd v. Turner and Others*, as reported in *The Times*, 28 July 1972.

It was a matter of real concern that the divisional court, exercising the power of judicial review, was increasingly . . . being used for political purposes superficially dressed up as points of law. The proper remedy was the ballot box and not the court. If a rating or precepting authority over-rated or over-precepted, the remedy was in the hands of the electorate . . . The impropriety of coming to the court when political capital was sought to be made could not be overstressed. It was perhaps even worse when public servants were or felt constrained to file affidavits which demonstrated a political purpose.

McNeill, J. in *R. v. Greater London Council ex parte Kensington and Chelsea LBC* dismissing an application for judicial review of a precept issued by the GLC, as reported in *The Times*, 7 April 1982.

The intellectual isolation of appellate judges, who resolve 'hard cases' with reference to notions of social justice and public policy which they are singularly (and collectively) ill-equipped to understand ... remains a deeply worrying feature of our judicial process.

Mr Gavin Drewry in 47 *Modern Law Review* (1984), p. 380.

Spycatcher is a very interesting case, in this respect. Some people say we're all establishment minded and other people say we're all something else minded. But in fact in Spycatcher we're not. No one can sack us, no one can take our pensions away, in Spycatcher three of us decided in favour of Mrs Thatcher and against the editor of the Sunday Times, *and those three of us didn't care a damn for the editor of the* Sunday Times. *Two of us decided in favour of the* Sunday Times *and against Mrs Thatcher, and those two didn't give a damn for Mrs Thatcher, we each of us decided it was a matter of principle, knowing that we were bound to be criticised, whatever we did, and we decided it, and there's an end of it.*

Lord Templeman, in an interview on Radio 4 with Hugo Young on 13 April 1988.

I hope that in future local authorities will bite on the bullet and not seek to persuade the courts to absolve them from compliance with the Secretary of State's guidance ... Persuasion should be offered not to the judges, who are not qualified to listen, but to the department, the minister, all members of parliament and ultimately to the electorate.

Lord Templeman in *Nottinghamshire CC v. Secretary of State for the Environment* [1986] 2 WLR 1 at 23.

The cat is now out of the bag. I am the political innocent who had not seen it all along. The cat is that there has been a satanic pact between the two main political parties to see that this ill-considered legislation is forced through without proper examination by this House, because neither is prepared to forego the hope of outbidding the other for the populist vote in the law and order debate leading up to the election. That is the truth of the matter and, to my mind, it is a deplorably cynical attitude to the administration of justice

Lord Bridge in the House of Lords on the Crime (Sentences) Bill in 579 HL Deb col. 780 (18 March 1997).

3. Industrial relations

The early cases

From the middle ages, Parliament has been concerned with the problems, central to the national economy, of productivity and the control of wages. And for hundreds of years workers who were thought to be failing in their duties were subjected to imprisonment and other penalties.

The use of the penal law against workers, especially when it involves imprisonment, or the possibility of imprisonment, is one of the most persistent sources of conflict between labour and management, and between labour and governments. Parliament legislated extensively against the combination of workers but the judges also, through their power of interpreting statutes and of making and extending the common law, were a powerful source of constraint on the emerging trade union movement in the industrial society of the nineteenth century. Two outstanding characteristics of labour law during the second half of that century were the intermittent recognition by politicians in government and Parliament that control of trade unionism by the imposition of penalties was of doubtful efficacy; and the recurrent attempts by the courts to preserve the penal method.[1]

Statutes of 1859, 1871 and 1875 were designed to relieve trade unions of criminal liability, especially for conspiracy. Specifically, the Conspiracy and Protection of Property Act 1875 provided that an agreement by two or more persons to do or procure to be done any act in contemplation or furtherance of a trade dispute should not be a criminal conspiracy unless the

1 . I am much indebted to Lord Wedderburn on whose writings and advice I have freely drawn in preparing and revising this chapter. See generally *The Worker and the Law* (3rd edn, 1986).

act itself was punishable as a crime. So to strike ceased to be a crime.

The last decade of the nineteenth century saw the development of a considerable antipathy to trade unionism among influential public opinion. This was in part due to the emergence of New Unionism which sought to organize unskilled workers. Professor Saville has written that the old unions 'were able to rely upon the skill of their members as a crucial bargaining weapon' but 'the new unionists were at all times, even in years of good trade, subject to the pressures of an over-stocked labour market'. So 'the employers, too, in the semi- and unskilled trades were more uncompromising than their fellows in industries where unionism had long been established'. The industrial offensive against the trade unions in the early years of the 1890s was 'most successful against the dockers, the seamen and the casual trades' but all the New Unions lost heavily in membership.[2]

It is against the background of this offensive that the judicial decisions[3] of 1896–1901 must be seen. Although the right to strike had been established, some of the judges were not to be so easily defeated. In addition to the crime of conspiracy, there is the civil wrong (or tort) of conspiracy, consisting of an agreement which has been acted on and which is made in order to attain either an unlawful object or a lawful object by unlawful means. It was to this that some judges turned their attention.

In *Allen v. Flood*[4] a dispute arose between the ironworkers' union and woodworkers, the former objecting to certain work being done by the latter. Ironworkers told one of their officials that they would stop working if the woodworkers were continued in employment. The official informed the employers accordingly and the employers lawfully dismissed the woodworkers, who then brought an action against the official.

2 . John Saville, 'Trade Unions and Free Labour: the Background to the Taff Vale Decision' in *Essays in Labour History* (eds Asa Briggs and John Saville, 1960) vol. 1, p. 317.

3 . Including *Lyons v. Wilkins* (see p.68).

4 . [1898] AC 1.

The case was first argued in December 1895 before seven members of the House of Lords[5] including Lord Chancellor Halsbury and a former Lord Chancellor, Herschell. 'From the very beginning,' says Professor Heuston, 'Lord Halsbury took a view strongly adverse to the position of the trade union and expressed his firm opinion that the plaintiffs . . . were entitled to damages for an interference with their right to work. It was also clear, however, that on this point he would be unable to carry with him a majority of his colleagues.' Apparently, Halsbury then 'conceived the idea that the case should be re-argued before an enlarged body of Law Lords and that, in addition, the House should adopt once more the practice of summoning the High Court judges to advise', a practice generally thought to be obsolete. Lord Herschell was angered by this idea and, says Professor Heuston, 'the High Court judges at that time, many of whom were Halsbury's own appointments, were not on the whole notable for progressive views on social or industrial matters.'[6]

Between 25 March and 2 April 1897 the case was re-argued before the original seven Law Lords and two others. Of the eight High Court judges who attended, and gave their 'opinions', six agreed with Lord Halsbury and two disagreed. But when the nine Law Lords delivered their judgments in December 1897, Lord Halsbury's views were supported by only two of his colleagues, with Lord Herschell and five others in the opposing majority. So the trade unions remained protected.

Then in 1901, in *Quinn v. Leathem*,[7] the effect of that decision was reversed. For many years, L supplied a butcher with meat. The trade union sought to persuade L not to employ non-union men. When this failed, the union instructed their members working for the butcher that, if he continued to buy L's meat, they were to cease work. So the butcher took no more meat from L, who brought an action against the union

5 . Here and elsewhere this means the House in its judicial capacity.

6 . R. F. V. Heuston, *The Lives of the Lord Chancellors 1885–1940*, pp. 119–20; and see his article on 'Judicial Prosopography' in 102 *Law Quarterly Review* 90 (1986).

7 . [1901] AC 495.

officials for conspiracy to injure him. The House of Lords decided unanimously in his favour.

From the trade unionists' viewpoint the effect of *Quinn v. Leathem* was seriously to curtail their power to operate in ways which would strengthen the working-class movement against employers. This was thought by trade unionists to be inconsistent with the leading decision of ten years before which had protected employers' associations from conspiracy on the ground that the acts had been done 'with the lawful object of protecting and extending their trade and increasing their profits' without employing unlawful means, although the consequence had been to injure their competitors.[8]

These judicial decisions caused great political upheaval and resulted in the passing of the Trade Disputes Act 1906 which followed the same pattern as the Act of 1875, protecting trade unions from actions for civil conspiracy if the acts were done in furtherance or contemplation of a trade dispute.

Another struggle centred on trade union funds. In law, property may be held either by a natural person, or by a number of such persons, or by an incorporated body such as a company. Trade unions fell into the second of these groups, but, because of their large and fluctuating membership and because of certain provisions in the Trade Union Act 1871, it was assumed that it was impracticable to bring actions against them so as to make their funds liable. In 1900 a dispute arose because it was said that the Taff Vale Railway Company had victimized a trade unionist who led a wage demand. The House of Lords held that trade unions could be sued, in effect, for losses sustained by employers as a consequence of strike action.[9] Lord Halsbury gave one of the five unanimous judgments. As Professor Heuston says, the decision left 'a legacy of suspicion and mistrust . . . to poison relations between the courts and the unions for many years'. He adds: 'One of Baldwin's favourite themes was the folly of this *Taff Vale* decision: "The Conservatives can't talk of class-war: they started it," he would remark to G. M. Young.'[10]

8 . *Mogul Steamship Co. v. McGregor Gow & Co.* [1892] AC 25.
9 . *Taff Vale Railway Co. v. Amalgamated Society of Railway Servants* [1901] AC 426.
10. Heuston, *op. cit.*, p. 76; G. M. Young, *Stanley Baldwin* (1952), p. 31.

The *Taff Vale* decision was a serious blow to trade unionism. The law had seemed 'so clearly settled to the contrary', wrote Lord Asquith, that 'public opinion was unprepared for any such decision'. Liberal opinion strongly favoured its reversal. This was effectively carried through by the strong Liberal government elected in 1906 in the Trade Disputes Act of that year.

A few years later, the judiciary again intervened, this time by invoking the doctrine of *ultra vires*. This doctrine applies mainly to public authorities exercising statutory powers and to companies registered under the Companies Acts to pursue certain objects described in their constitutions. If powers or objects are exceeded, action can be brought to restrain those authorities or companies. Trade unions had for some time been supporting candidates for the House of Commons and spending union funds for this purpose. In 1909, a member of the Amalgamated Society of Railway Servants successfully challenged this practice.[11] This of course was also a severe blow to the emerging Labour Party, and again the politicians had to try to restore what had been understood to be the position by passing the Trade Union Act 1913.[12]

For much of the interwar period and for some years after 1945, the judges seemed to withdraw from the conflict or, when asked to intervene, tended to adopt a neutral position. Indeed, such decisions as were made were markedly more generous in their recognition of the legitimacy of the purposes of trade unions. Moreover, during the 1930s, employers did not need to seek the help of the courts, the unions being in a weak condition. As we shall see, judicial intervention was not noticeably restrained at this time in other political cockpits.

But the 1960s gave rise to certain assumptions about the nature and the power of trade unions which, true or false, have coloured and affected the attitudes of the middle classes and, in consequence, the policies of the Conservative, Labour and Liberal parties. Once again, the judges have become central figures in these political issues.

11. *Amalgamated Society of Railway Servants v. Osborne* [1910] AC 87.
12. See S. and B. Webb, *The History of Trade Unionism* (1920 edn), pp. 608–11.

Picketing

Picketing is a practice which stands uneasily across the boundary, as variously interpreted, of legal and illegal action. It can become conduct likely to cause a breach of the peace, or obstruction, or even assault. The Conspiracy and Protection of Property Act 1875 restated the criminal offence of 'watching or besetting' but excluded from that activity 'attending at or near the house or place where a person resides, or works, or carries on business, or happens to be ... in order merely to obtain or communicate information'. But in *Lyons v. Wilkins*[13] the Court of Appeal had decided against the officers of a trade union who, having ordered a strike against the plaintiffs and against S (who made goods for the plaintiffs only), organized pickets to seek to persuade work-people not to work for the plaintiffs. That, said Lindley LJ, was not merely obtaining or communicating information. It was putting pressure on the plaintiffs by persuading people not to enter their employment. And that was illegal. It was further decided that such watching and besetting might be a nuisance at common law and illegal on that ground also. Once again the legislature reversed the courts and by the Trade Disputes Act 1906 made picketing lawful if in contemplation or furtherance of a trade dispute and if the purpose was peacefully obtaining or communicating information or 'peacefully persuading any person to work or abstain from working'.

The interpretation of the law remained contentious. During a trade dispute in 1960, a police officer found two pickets standing at the front entrance of a factory, four standing at the back entrance and ten or twelve outside the back entrance. The officer told the defendant three times that he considered two pickets at each entrance were sufficient but the defendant, persisting in his intention to join the pickets, 'pushed gently past' the police officer, 'was gently arrested', and was charged with obstructing the police in execution of their duty. The Divisional Court held that he was properly convicted on the ground that the police officer had reasonable grounds for antici-

13. [1896] 1 Ch. 811; [1899] 1 Ch. 255.

pating that a breach of the peace was a real possibility.[14] In *Tynan v. Balmer*[15] (1966) forty pickets in a continuous circle around a factory (which had the effect of sealing off the highway) were held not to be legalized by the Act of 1906 because their action was a nuisance at common law and an unreasonable use of the highway. In 1972, a strike picket held a placard in front of a vehicle on a highway, urging the driver not to work at a site nearby and preventing him from proceeding along the highway. The picket was charged with obstruction of the highway although the whole incident lasted for not more than nine minutes. The House of Lords upheld the prosecution.[16] Lord Reid said it would not be difficult to infer, as a matter of fact, that pickets who assemble in unreasonably large numbers do have the purpose of obstructing free passage. The following year, a police cordon prevented pickets from approaching a coach carrying workers out of a site. The defendant was involved in a scuffle with a constable and was successfully charged with obstructing him in the execution of his duty.[17] The result of these cases was greatly to limit the right to picket. They enlarged the scope within which the police could prevent picketing and they greatly narrowed the scope within which picketing could lawfully be undertaken.[18]

Moreover, the use by the courts of these common law devices of obstruction, breach of the peace and nuisance is difficult to legislate against as the essential purpose (which before the 1960s had been more or less achieved with police co-operation) is to permit 'reasonable' picketing, including the right to accost for a short period within which arguments can be advanced, without putting persons in fear or to immoderate inconvenience.

'The attendance', said counsel for the defendant in *Hunt v. Broome*, 'is for the purpose of peacefully persuading a man not to work so the attendance must be in a position where the persuasion can be carried out; otherwise its purpose is frus-

14. *Piddington v. Bates* [1960] 3 All ER 660.
15. [1967] 1 QB 91.
16. *Hunt v. Broome* [1974] AC 587.
17. *Kavanagh v. Hiscock* [1974] 2 WLR 421; see also *Hubbard v. Pitt* [1975] 3 WLR 20, pp. 269–70.
18. See also *R v. Jones* [1974] ICR 310.

trated . . . Attendance for the purpose of peaceful persuasion is what is protected by the Act . . . not mere attendance, standing with banners; the attendance is for oral communication.'[19]

As the courts presently interpret the law this purpose is often difficult and sometimes impossible to achieve. It is also true that the right to picket may be abused.

The right to strike

In 1964 the House of Lords in *Rookes v. Barnard*[20] delivered a judgment which seemed like a return to the early heady days of the century. R worked for BOAC with whom his union had an agreement that all workers should be union members. In 1955 R left the union after a disagreement with union members. Two local union members, and a district union official employed by the union, threatened BOAC that labour would be withdrawn if R were not removed within three days as required by a resolution passed at a members' meeting. Such a strike would have been a breach of contract by each member. BOAC gave R long notice and lawfully discharged him. R sued the two members and the official for conspiracy.

Under the Trade Disputes Act 1906 no action for conspiracy would lie unless the act would be unlawful if done by a person alone. So the Law Lords considered whether a threat to strike could be 'unlawful' in this sense. And they held it could be.

This decision was seen by trade unionists as a direct attack on the right to strike. The Law Lords certainly seemed to stretch themselves to arrive at their conclusion. Lord Devlin, for example, could find 'nothing to differentiate a threat of a breach of contract from a threat of physical violence'. It was a time when strikes were being blamed for most of the country's ills, and Lord Hodson said: 'The injury and suffering caused by strike action is very often widespread as well as devastating and a threat to strike would be expected to be certainly no less serious than a threat of violence.' Once again

19. Mr John Mortimer, QC.
20. [1964] AC 1129.

the politicians had to seek to reverse their Lordships' decision and passed the Trade Disputes Act 1965.

Inducing breach of contract

In 1952, certain drivers and loaders told Bowaters Ltd, the paper suppliers, that they might not be prepared to deliver paper to the plaintiffs, who were printers and publishers. Bowaters told the plaintiffs and they brought an action against officers of the unions to which the drivers and loaders belonged. The Court of Appeal held that the evidence did not establish that there had been any direct procurement by the defendants of any wrongful acts by the drivers or loaders or that the latter had committed any wrongful acts; also that there was no evidence of any actual knowledge by the defendants of any contract between Bowaters and the plaintiffs. So the plaintiffs lost their action.[21]

In 1964, the House of Lords considered a case in which a union were met by a refusal of a company to negotiate with them on terms and conditions of service although they organized the majority of the men concerned, being watermen in the Port of London. Another union organized the minority. So the first union issued instructions that none of their men would man, service or tow empty barges belonging to the company. The company owned and hired out barges but did not employ any of the union men, but union action meant that barges were not returned and so the company's business came to a standstill. The company brought an action against the union officials. The House of Lords found for the company on the ground that the union had knowingly induced breaches of the hiring contract and their members' contracts of employment. Most importantly, their Lordships decided that there was, on the facts, no trade dispute within the meaning of the Trade Disputes Act 1906 because the basis of the embargo was trade union rivalry.[22]

This attitude of the courts was strengthened by the decision

21. *Thomson & Co. v. Deakin* [1952] 1 Ch. 646.
22. *Stratford v. Lindley* [1965] AC 269.

of the Court of Appeal in *Torquay Hotel v. Cousins*.[23] Union members picketed the Torbay Hotel, cutting off fuel oil supplies, and later, when the manager of the plaintiff hotel was reported as having called for a stand against the union, picketed that hotel with the same result. The union also told an alternative oil supplier not to supply the plaintiff hotel. The Court of Appeal held that as the plaintiffs employed no union members the union's actions were not in furtherance of a trade dispute and injunctions were issued against the union. As Professor Wedderburn has observed, the result of this decision could be that where an association of employers is fighting off a trade union, it may be able to 'keep its smaller members in the front line and avoid any of its bigger members being parties to the dispute'.[24] The trade unions' 'golden formula' of action 'in furtherance of a trade dispute' looks weaker as a protection than it did.

No wonder that, in 1968, a member of the Royal Commission on Trade Unions and Employers' Associations wrote:[25]

> A thing that worried me all through the deliberations . . . was this: supposing we made all the right recommendations and supposing the Government gave effect to them in legislation, how long would it be before the judges turned everything upside down?

Industrial Relations Act 1971

But the most dramatic judicial intervention was yet to come. In 1971 was passed the Industrial Relations Act. This measure of a Conservative government was strongly opposed, in and out of Parliament, by the trade union movement and the Labour party. It established the National Industrial Relations Court (NIRC), presided over by Sir John Donaldson, formerly a judge of the High Court. The NIRC had

23. [1969] 2 Ch. 106.
24. Wedderburn, *op. cit.* (2nd edn), p. 336.
25. Quoted by Wedderburn, *op. cit.* (2nd edn), p. 8.

wide jurisdiction to consider complaints arising under the Act, to impose penalties, and to punish those who disregarded its orders.

In recent years, the amount of work available for dock-workers has drastically declined because of the growing prac-tice of loading and unloading goods in containers at depots outside the port areas. From mid-1971, the Transport and Gen-eral Workers' Union authorized the practice of selective 'black-ing' of the goods carried by certain road haulier firms to ports. When the Act of 1971 came into force in February 1972, the union became liable to complaints and penalties for this blacking. The first complaint was made on 23 March 1972 and the NIRC ordered the union, its officers, servants and agents to refrain from certain specific blacking. The union's officers advised their shop stewards to obey this order but the advice was rejected. On 29 March the NIRC found the union in wilful contempt of the order and, following subsequent complaints, imposed fines totalling £55,000.[26]

On 13 June the Court of Appeal decided that the union was not accountable for its shop stewards and set aside the fines.[27] But the next day the NIRC ordered three London dockers who had defied an order against blacking made on 12 June to be committed to prison for contempt of court. The war-rants for their arrest were to be issued on 16 June, and widespread strikes became imminent. However, as the result of a curious intervention by the Official Solicitor (an officer of the court), the Court of Appeal was able to review the decision to imprison, although the three dockers did not ask for it to be reviewed; and the decision was set aside. So the dockers did not go to prison and the strikes were avoided.[28]

For a fortnight there was a breathing space. Then on 3 July another complaint was lodged with the NIRC against seven dockers including two of the original three. On 7 July, the NIRC ordered them to refrain from their actions and, after further proceedings, on 21 July committed five of the seven

26. *Heaton's Transport (St Helens) Ltd v TGWU* [1972] 1 ICR 285.
27. Ibid. 308; [1973] AC 15.
28. *The Times*, 12 and 14 June 1972.

to prison for contempt. Unofficial dock strikes began at once and the threat of widespread stoppages of work became very real.

On 24 July the General Secretary of the Trades Union Congress went to see the Prime Minister who said, according to *The Times*, that he would not intervene. On 25 July, the Official Solicitor visited the dockers in prison, but they made clear that they did not intend to give any undertakings of obedience to the NIRC or to apologize – which is normally essential before those in contempt are released. Nevertheless the Official Solicitor on that day tried to persuade the NIRC to convene immediately so that he could apply for the committal orders to be discharged. But he was told to come back not later than the afternoon of the next day.

On 25 July the situation seemed to have reached an impasse. Sir John Donaldson, president of the NIRC, had said in June: 'By their conduct these men are saying they are above the rule of law. No court should ignore such a challenge. To do so would imperil all law and order.' On 21 July he said: 'These breaches are serious and were deliberately committed, quite literally in contempt of this court ... The issue is whether these men are to be allowed to opt out of the rule of law ... It is a very simple issue but vastly important for our whole way of life is based upon acceptance of the rule of law.' The NIRC had committed the men to prison. The men showed no intention of modifying their position. Dock strikes were occurring and a general strike was clearly impending. How could industrial action on a wide scale be avoided and the face of the NIRC be saved?

We have seen that on 13 June the Court of Appeal had decided in *Heaton*'s case that the Transport and General Workers' Union was not accountable for the action of its shop stewards. From that decision, leave was given to appeal to the House of Lords. That appeal was heard between the 10th and 19th of July. Their Lordships reserved judgment and then, with almost unprecedented speed (at least eight weeks normally elapse), Lord Wilberforce delivered their joint opinion, on the morning of 26 July – that 'next day' intimated to the Official Solicitor. And the House of Lords reversed the Court of Appeal and decided that the union was responsible for its shop stewards.[29] Immediately the NIRC convened and, avowedly because of that decision, released the dockers from prison.[30]

The difficulty is finding any necessary connection between two cases. The House of Lords' decision determined an important question of law concerning the liability of trade unions for the actions of their shop stewards. But the five dockers' case was about the 'very simple issue' of punishment for men who had defied the order of the NIRC and had expressed their intention to continue in that defiance. In releasing the dockers, the president of the NIRC said that, because of the House of Lords' decision, the situation was 'entirely changed'. The unions were accountable and the burden of their task would be 'immeasurably increased' if the dockers remained in prison. 'The cause of the rule of law will not be advanced by placing an avoidable burden upon the unions.' Nevertheless five men, who had been imprisoned because they deliberately and flagrantly disobeyed the orders of the NIRC, and so imperilled the rule of law and 'our whole way of life', were released although they had not asked to be released and had made clear that they had no intention of apologizing to the court for their behaviour or of desisting from that behaviour.

A political and economic crisis of possibly considerable dimensions was avoided by two actions. First, the speeding-up of the delivery of the House of Lords' decision; and second, the discovery by the NIRC that, because of that decision, they could release the dockers. It appeared very much as if the judicial system had bent itself to the needs of the politicians and that, in particular, the principles of the rule of law to which the NIRC earlier paid such respect had been sacrificed to the expediency of the political and economic situation.

This last example of judicial activism in political affairs differs from the others. The latter have shown a conservative judiciary interpreting legislation and developing the common law in ways which government and Parliament sought to

29. [1972] 1 ICR 308: [1973] AC 15. Subsequently, however, it appeared that this was not a proposition of general application: see *General Aviation Services v. TGWU* [1976] IRLR 224, a decision which seemed to indicate a desire by the House of Lords (Lord Salmon dissenting) to put the decision in *Heaton*'s case behind them.

30. *The Times*, 27 July 1972.

reverse. The establishment of the NIRC was a political act aimed at trying to contain trade union power within particular rules prescribed by the Industrial Relations Act 1971. The experiment failed and the NIRC was abolished in 1974. But the apparent willingness of the House of Lords to expedite the delivery of their judgment coupled with the highly eccentric use made of that judgment by the NIRC to release the five dockers was so convenient for the government of the day that it aroused the strong suspicion of judicial compliance with political expediency.

A later industrial dispute was a pretty example of the intermingling of the exercise of powers in the high places of government in the United Kingdom. In October 1973, the NIRC fined the Amalgamated Union of Engineering Workers £100,000 for contempt of court when they refused to obey the court's order to call off a strike.[31]

To obtain payment of the fine the court sequestrated against assets held in the political fund of the union. Labour MPs put down a motion in the House of Commons calling for the removal from office of the president of the NIRC for 'political prejudice and partiality'. Sir John Donaldson defended himself in a public speech saying that the court had not known that the assets had been earmarked for a political or any other purpose. At this point Lord Hailsham, then Lord Chancellor, in a public speech and as head of the judiciary, attacked those who had signed the motion and said that the public should note the identity and party of the Members concerned. Whereupon Labour Members tabled another motion condemning the Lord Chancellor and alleging 'a gross contempt of the House of Commons'.[32]

In the event neither of the motions was debated and the matter lapsed.

The conflict between the courts and trade unions showed itself in the second half of the nineteenth century and the first decade of the twentieth as an expression of class conflict. The trade unions were growing in militancy, especially during the years after 1890, and were displaying powers which dismayed

---

31. *Con-Mech (Engineers) Ltd v. AUEW* [1973] ICR 620.
32. See 865 HC Deb. col. 1089–91, 1291–7.

a large part of middle-class society. The dismay was in part because of the anticipated economic consequences of this militancy, but also because it threatened the existing social order of late Victorian England.

Many politicians, from Disraeli onwards, had realized that trade union power was an economic factor which had to be taken seriously into account and certainly was not capable of being overcome by crude shows of force. Her Majesty's judges, however, were less prescient and less capable of adjusting legal principles and traditions to the new pressures. So, under men like Halsbury, they reacted to the legislation of the later nineteenth century with all the inflexibility of those who are determined that what was good enough for their fathers' social and economic structures was good enough for them. And in the more general upheaval of political beliefs which accompanied 'the strange death of liberal England', influential judges were more often to be found towards the right of the spectrum of opinion.

The most recent developments may prove to be of the utmost importance and to have the most lasting consequences. What litigation might have been promoted by the Labour government's aborted proposals in the late 1960s[33] we shall never know. But the much more rigorous policy embodied in the Conservatives' Industrial Relations Act of 1971 was a revolution in the long story. For this act deliberately sought to use the courts and the judges to achieve political ends. The institution of the NIRC reflected the new techniques and reintroduced the old arguments. The identification of 'law' and 'policy' made almost impossible the continuance of the interplay between the judges and politicians which had provided a valuable tolerance. Had the act succeeded, the damage to the reputation of judicial institutions would have been considerable; but it was always highly probable that this attempt to use the judges for these political purposes would fail. The failure was forecast by almost all those with the greatest knowledge of the working of industrial relations in this country and, more particularly, abroad. But the circumstances of its failure, and the manoeuvrings of politicians and judges which accom-

33. See *In Place of Strife* (Cmnd 3888).

panied that failure, combined to produce a calamity which went far beyond the collapse of a doomed policy, for the failure directly resulted in a deep distrust of the judicial system. Trade unionists, as we have seen, had little cause to look to the judiciary for the protection of their statutory rights. Now the suspected subservience of the judiciary to the politicians seemed to be made manifest. There is no evidence that the judges at any time protested to Her Majesty's government in or out of Parliament against the proposals to involve them directly and indirectly in the administration of the act of 1971. Their failure to do so rests with the Lord Chancellor (Lord Hailsham), the Master of the Rolls (Lord Denning), and, to a lesser extent, the Lord Chief Justice (Lord Widgery).

The events of 1972 finally persuaded the leaders of organized labour (and the great mass of trade union members) that the judges were not to be trusted. Today the relations between the trade unions and the judiciary are worse than they were in the period immediately following the *Taff Vale* decision in 1901. Mr Heath deliberately employed the judges as instruments of his policy, enmeshed trade unionists in new legal rules, and then, in chorus with the judges, condemned them, in the name of the rule of law, for seeking to extricate themselves.

Less easy to understand is the apparent willingness of the judiciary to lend themselves to this manoeuvring. It is difficult to believe in the political naïveté of judges, but Sir John Donaldson, president of the NIRC, looking back on the short history of that court, has expressed views which are bewildering in their ingenuousness. He emphasized the need for guidelines in all aspects of industrial relations and continued:

> With such guidelines, the courts could be given their traditional role of investigating the merits of disputes and helping the party who is right . . . The public suffers from every industrial dispute. Ought they not to know who is right? Adopting this new approach they *would* know, for the court which investigated the dispute would tell them. Those who suffered injustice would then be supported by the courts.[34]

34. *Lessons from the Industrial Court* (1975) 91 LQR at 191–2.

On this evidence it seems possible that a large part of the conflict that arose in the administration of the NIRC was the result of a belief of its president that, in industrial conflicts, one side can be discovered, after proper examination by judges, to be 'right' and the other side 'wrong'. But industrial conflicts are not of this kind. They can be solved only by compromise and by the exercise of economic and political strength, not by the application of legal principles or guidelines. This may be unfortunate but it is the reason why the NIRC was bound to fail.

The Law Lords restrain Denning

In a group of cases in 1978 and 1979 the Court of Appeal sought considerably to limit the immunities of trade unionists from criminal and civil liabilities for acts done 'in contemplation or furtherance of a trade dispute'.[35] Then, in three cases decided between July 1979 and February 1980, the House of Lords reversed this development. Both the substance and the manner in which this was done throw further light on the politics of the judiciary in dealing with industrial relations.

The first of these cases was *NWL Ltd v. Woods*.[36] The International Transport Workers' Federation blacked a ship in an attempt to force its owners to pay wages in accordance with the Federation's scales. Since the crew of the ship were not directly involved, the owners argued that there was no trade dispute. Two years before, in *BBC v. Hearn* (1977),[37] trade union officials had threatened that their workers would refuse to allow the BBC to televise the cup final so that it could be seen in South Africa, because of the union's disapproval of the racial policies of the government of that country. The Court of Appeal had held that there was no trade dispute and so no protection for the trade union officials. In *NWL* the House of

---

35. *Beaverbrook v. Keys* [1978] ICR 582; *Star Sea Transport of Monrovia v. Slater 'The Camilla M'* [1978] IRLR 507; *Associated Newspapers Group Ltd v. Wade* [1979] ICR 664.

36. [1979] 1 WLR 1294.

37. [1977] 1 WLR 1004.

Lords did not question that decision. But in 1978, the Court of Appeal had decided, in '*The Camilla M*',[38] where the facts were similar to those in *NWL*, that the presence of an 'extraneous motive' for trade union action was sufficient to prevent that action being a 'trade dispute'.[39]

In *NWL* the House of Lords rejected this test. Lord Diplock said that even if the predominant motives were 'to bring down the fabric of the present economic system by raising wages to unrealistic levels', that would not make the dispute any less one connected with the terms and conditions of employment and therefore a trade dispute. Similarly Lord Scarman said that if the dispute were connected with one of the matters referred to in the statute (for example, terms and conditions of employment) then 'it is a trade dispute, and it is immaterial whether the dispute also relates to other matters or has an extraneous, e.g. political or personal, motive. The connection is all that has to be shown.' The legislative purpose of the Trade Union and Labour Relations Act 1974, said Lord Scarman, was 'to sweep away not only the structure of industrial relations created by the Industrial Relations Act 1971, which it was passed to repeal, but also the restraints of judicial review which the courts have been fashioning one way or another since the enactment of the Trade Disputes Act 1906 . . . Briefly put, the law is now back to what Parliament had intended when it enacted the Act of 1906 – but stronger and clearer than it was then.'

In *Express Newspapers v. McShane*,[40] there was a dispute over pay between the proprietors of provincial newspapers and members of the National Union of Journalists. The national executive of the union called out on strike all its members on provincial newspapers. These newspapers used news copy supplied by the Press Association and the union called on PA journalists to strike also. This strike affected national newspapers. The union instructed its members on the *Daily Express*

38. See Note 35.
39. The Court of Appeal in *NWL* discharged the injunction given in the lower court on the ground that the union had not made 'impossible demands' and so distinguished '*The Camilla M*'.
40. [1979] 2 All ER 360.

and other nationals to refuse to use copy sent out by the PA.

The plaintiffs sought an injunction against the members of the national executive of the union to restrain them from inducing or procuring their members not to use PA copy. The defendants claimed that what they were doing was in furtherance of their dispute with the provincial newspapers. The judge at first instance granted the injunction and the Court of Appeal upheld his decision, Lord Denning MR saying that there was no evidence that the blacking at the *Daily Express* had had any effect on the provincial dispute. So the Court of Appeal held that the acts were not done in furtherance of a trade dispute. 'Furtherance' was to be tested objectively by the courts as well as subjectively by reference to the defendants' intentions.

The House of Lords overruled the Court of Appeal,[41] giving its reasons on 13 December 1979. Four of their Lordships held that 'in furtherance' referred only to the subjective state of mind of the defendant and that he so acted if his purpose was to help the parties in the dispute to achieve their objectives and if he honestly and reasonably believed his actions would do so. Lord Wilberforce, while agreeing in the result, said that the test was whether the act done, pursuant to the general intention, was reasonably capable of achieving its objective. Lord Denning, said Lord Wilberforce, 'finally settled, I think, upon practical effect. This, I think, with respect goes too far.'

Six weeks later, on 26 January 1980, the Court of Appeal decided *Duport Steels v. Sirs*.[42] Steelworkers in the public sector had for some time been in dispute with their employers, the British Steel Corporation, and had come out on strike. Their union, the Iron and Steel Trades Confederation, in order to bring pressure on the government (who, the union hoped, would then put pressure on the BSC to settle the strike), decided to extend the strike to the private sector of the steel industry. Certain private steel companies sought injunctions to prevent this.

The Court of Appeal granted the injunctions on the ground that the extension had generated a second dispute, between the

41. [1980] 2 WLR 89.
42. [1980] 1 All ER 529.

ISTC and the government, which was separate from the union's dispute with the BSC, and not a trade dispute because the government was not the employer. Lord Denning MR added the further reason that the acts done were too remote to be regarded as furtherance. As a leading article in *The Times* put it: 'Undaunted by the superior timidity of the House of Lords the Court of Appeal persevered in its determination to set limits to the scope of the immunities granted to trade unions by statute.'[43]

This 'second dispute' argument was not advanced by counsel for the steelworkers but emanated from the bench. Counsel thought so little of it that he did not seek to sustain it before the House of Lords. On the legal substance of the case, the House of Lords had little to add to the principles on which they had decided *Express Newspapers v. McShane*. The 'connection' between the strike in the private sector and the strike in the public sector was obvious, as was the honest and reasonable belief of the union that that extension would further their dispute with the BSC. So their Lordships again overruled the Court of Appeal.[44]

In another group of cases the courts grappled somewhat variously with a new institution.

The Advisory, Conciliation and Arbitration Service (ACAS) was established by the Employment Protection Act 1975. It is charged with the general duty of promoting the improvement of industrial relations, and in particular of encouraging the extension of collective bargaining and the development and, where necessary, reform of collective bargaining. One of its powers is to make recommendations requiring an employer to recognize a particular trade union as a negotiating body. Its functions were not at first regarded by the courts with much enthusiasm.

It is therefore clear that as a result of the statutory machinery an individual can have a substantial measure of control over his own working life compulsorily delegated to an agent, a trade union, which he has not selected and

43. *The Times*, 28 January 1980.
44. [1980] 1 All ER 529.

may even have his own contract of service varied without his consent. These are very large powers, every bit as large as powers of compulsory acquisition of property; and, in my judgment, the court should seek to ensure that, just as in the case of compulsory purchase powers, the conditions for the exercise of the powers conferred by the 1975 Act are strictly observed.[45]

In the case from which that quotation is drawn the court set aside a questionnaire issued by ACAS on the ground that it was an unlawful exercise of discretion. Much more seriously, the House of Lords in *Grunwick Processing Laboratories Ltd v. ACAS* (1978)[46] effectively made the resolution of recognition disputes dependent on the co-operation of employers. This could be seen as an example, from the other side, of the dangers of seeking to impose legal and compulsory arbitration over industrial relations. The union request for recognition was referred to ACAS which sent questionnaires to union members at Grunwick's but not to the rest of the workers because the employers would not supply ACAS with their names and addresses. The duty of ACAS under the statute was to 'ascertain the opinion of the workers to whom the issue relates'. The failure of ACAS to ascertain the opinion of the non-union members (who numbered two-thirds of all those employed) rendered void ACAS's recommendation of recognition for the union.

The next two cases, however, show a broader understanding of what ACAS was supposed to be doing. In *United Kingdom Association of Professional Engineers v. ACAS* (1980)[47] the Association sought recognition from a company already well supplied with trade unions. ACAS refused to recommend recognition partly because to do so would arouse strong opposition from the other unions with a risk of industrial action which would be damaging to the industry. In the Court of Appeal, Lord Denning MR saw this as 'another story of David and Goliath . . . a small union pitted against a great one'. He set aside ACAS's report, saying that the threats of industrial strife

45. Browne-Wilkinson J in *G. C. Powley v. ACAS* [1977] IRLR 190.
46. [1978] AC 655.
47. [1979] 2 All ER 480 (CA); [1980] 1 All ER 612 (HL).

should have been ignored. But the House of Lords (Lord Scarman delivering the main opinion) reversed the Court of Appeal and upheld the report. Similarly, in *Engineers' and Managers' Association v. ACAS* (1980)[48] the House of Lords by a majority held that ACAS had not acted unreasonably in postponing its statutory enquiries for the time being because another union was also seeking recognition and the plaintiff Association was also suing the Trades Union Congress. Lord Scarman said: 'ACAS has to form its view as to what is best for the promotion of industrial relations and the extension of collective bargaining. The Court of Appeal erred in substituting its judgment for that of ACAS.'

ACAS has had a troubled life and its powers have been limited and subjected to greater ministerial control by the Employment Act 1980.

The Conservative attack

Legislation since 1979 has greatly affected industrial relations, often in line with the expressed views of the Court of Appeal and the House of Lords.

Section 17 of the Employment Act 1980 is designed to limit 'secondary action', that is action taken by workers in support of a trade dispute between other workers and their employers. The section defined secondary action in relation to a trade dispute as arising when a person induces another to break a contract of employment if the employer under the contract of employment is not a party to the trade dispute.

Marina Shipping Ltd v. Laughton (1982)[49] was one in a long line of cases[50] arising out of attempts by the International Transport Workers Federation (ITF) to force ship owners employing cheap labour recruited abroad to pay European standard rates of wages. In this case, ITF officials blacked a ship with the result that lock-keepers, in breach of their contract with port authorities at Hull, refused to operate gates and so

48. [1980] 1 All ER 896.
49. [1982] 2 WLR 569.
50. See, for example, *NWL v. Woods* (p. 79).

prevented the ship from sailing. Section 17(3) of the Act permits secondary action if (a) the purpose or principal purpose of the secondary action was directly to prevent or disrupt the supply during the dispute of goods or services between an employer who is a party to the dispute (here the ship owners) and the employer under the contract of employment to which the secondary action relates (here the port authorities); and (b) the secondary action was likely to achieve that purpose. This would seem to cover the action of the lock-keepers in this case. But section 17(6) provides that references to the supply of goods and services between two persons are references to the supply by one to the other in pursuance of a contract between them. The Court of Appeal held that there was no contract between the owners and the port authority and so the secondary action was illegal.

Very similar facts were considered by the House of Lords in *Merkur Island Shipping Corporation v. Laughton* (1983).[51] Here the ITF persuaded tugmen, in breach of their contract with their employers, to refuse to operate tugs to enable the ship to leave port. The House of Lords held that since the ship owners were not party to any contract with the tug owners (the arrangements had been made by the charterers of the ship) the secondary action was, again, illegal.

The effect of these decisions is to prevent the ITF from pursuing its aim of requiring owners of ships flying 'flags of convenience' to pay wages at levels compatible with collective agreements made by 'bona fide organizations of ship owners and seafarers' in accordance with the recommendations of the International Labour Organization. It has been strongly argued that the interpretation is mistaken. As the law stands, everything turns on the fortuitous circumstance of the existence or non-existence of a formal contract between two parties even though the reality of the supply of goods and services from one of the principals to another within the meaning of section 17(3) is not in question. If the *purpose* is to interrupt an apparent contract and the secondary action would be likely to achieve that purpose, then the secondary

51. [1983] 2 All ER 189. See also *Union Traffic v. TGWU* [1989] ICR 98 and *Shipping Company Uniform v. ITF* [1985] IRLR 71.

action should be legitimate even if no such contract exists in fact.[52]

In *Cheall v. Association of Professional, Executive, Clerical and Computer Staff,*[53] the House of Lords overruled a majority of the Court of Appeal. Cheall resigned from one trade union (ACTSS) and joined another (APEX). In accepting Cheall, without first enquiring of ACTSS whether it objected, APEX breached the Bridlington principles designed to prevent unions poaching members from one another. As a result the Trades Union Congress Disputes Committee required APEX to dismiss Cheall and advise him to rejoin his former union. This APEX did, in accordance with its own rules, whereupon Cheall sought a declaration that his dismissal was invalid. In the Court of Appeal,[54] Lord Denning MR decided in favour of Cheall, invoking the European Convention on Human Rights, which declared that everyone had a right to join a trade union, which proposition Lord Denning identified with the common law. He also referred to the case of the three railwaymen, dismissed for refusing to join a trade union, who had succeeded before the Court of Human Rights,[55] and he reached the conclusion that the relevant article of the Convention was 'part of the law of England or at any rate the same as the law of England'. Had this view been upheld, it would have destroyed the Bridlington principles. Slade LJ also decided in favour of Cheall but on more modest grounds. Donaldson LJ disagreed. He quoted Lord Atkin that the doctrine of public policy 'should only be invoked in clear cases in which the harm to the public is substantially incontestable, and does not depend upon the idiosyncratic inferences of a few judicial minds'.[56] Donaldson LJ continued:

> Above all I think that judges must beware of confusing political policy with public policy ... Whether judges are better or less able than others to assess the merits

52. See Wedderburn, 45 *Modern Law Review* (1982) 317, and 46 *Modern Law Review* (1983) 632. See also Employment Act 1990 section 4.

53. [1983] 2 WLR 679.

54. [1982] 3 WLR 685.

55. *Young v. United Kingdom* [1981] IRLR 408.

56. *Fender v. St John-Mildmay* [1938] AC 1.

and demerits of political policies is beside the point, because that is not their function.

... We are being invited to apply considerations of political rather than public policy. This I absolutely decline to do.

The Law Lords unanimously rejected Cheall's application on the ground that there was no principle of law which prevented the union from relying on its own rules which also bound Cheall. 'My human sympathies', said Lord Diplock, 'are with Mr Cheall, but I am not in a position to indulge them; for I am left in no doubt that upon all the points that have been so ingeniously argued, the law is against him.' But Lord Diplock suggested that different considerations might apply if the effect of Cheall's expulsion from APEX were to have put his job in jeopardy because of the existence of a closed shop or for some other reason.

In *Carrington v. Therm-A-Stor Ltd*,[57] a group of employees decided to try to introduce a trade union into the factory where they worked. By late April 1980 between sixty and sixty-five of the seventy employees had joined or applied to join. The district secretary of the union wrote to the managing director setting out the union's case for recognition. Two days later the employers' managing committee decided to dismiss twenty of the employees and instructed the chargehands to decide who should be chosen. Four of those chosen brought this action for unfair dismissal. The industrial tribunal found that the reason for the dismissals was that the managing director was strongly anti-union but that none of the four could show that the reason for his dismissal was his own union membership or activities. The Court of Appeal, with regret, rejected their claim on the ground that, although the relevant statutory provision declared a dismissal to be unfair if the reason for it was that the employee proposed to join a trade union or take part in union activities, the provision was 'not concerned with an employer's reactions to a trade union's activities, but with his reactions to an individual employee's activities in a trade union context' (Sir

57. [1983] 1 WLR 138.

John Donaldson MR). The narrowness of this interpretation is self-evident.

The British Telecommunications Act 1981 established BT as a public corporation and transferred telecommunication functions to it from the Post Office. By a government licence under the Act, Mercury Communications, a private company, was authorized to establish a communications system. An agreement between BT and Mercury provided for interconnections between the two systems. The Post Office Engineering Union waged a campaign against the licensing of competitors of BT and against proposals, in a Bill before Parliament, on privatization of BT. The union instructed its members not to make the interconnection, there was a day of action and a series of selective strikes. The union also instructed its members to 'black' BT services at Mercury's premises. There was a threat of industrial action against Mercury's shareholders. Mercury applied to the court for interlocutory injunctions to restrain the union and its members from inducing breach of contract between Mercury and BT.

We have seen that a persistent principle since 1906 had been that an act done by a person in contemplation or furtherance of trade dispute could not be actionable in tort on the ground of inducing another person to break a contract. By the Employment Act 1982 the definition of a trade dispute is narrowed. Disputes between workers and workers – demarcation disputes – are excluded; so are disputes between workers and an employer unless he is their own. Also it is no longer sufficient that the dispute should be 'connected with', in the instant case, termination of employment; now it had to relate 'wholly or mainly' to that. The Court of Appeal readily allowed new evidence to be admitted and held that since the risk to jobs did not appear to be a major factor in the dispute, it seemed unlikely that the union would be able to bring itself within the definition of a trade dispute and so the injunction should be granted.

Sir John Donaldson MR said it was important in such disputes, which gave rise to strong, indeed passionate, feelings, that 'everyone should know where the courts stand. They are on neither side. They have an independent role, akin to that of a referee . . . Parliament makes the law and is solely responsible for what the law is. The duty of the court is neither to make nor to alter nor to pass judgment on the law. Their duty is simply to apply it as they understand it.'[58] The effect of the decision was to make clear that the courts, under the new legislation, will decide in what circumstances industrial action is, in their view, 'political' and when not. And this, far more than in the past, will determine the legality or illegality of the action.

The House of Lords shows every sign of adopting a hard line against trade unions when interpreting the new legislation, as this next case demonstrates.

The Dimbleby newspapers had been printed by an associated company, Dimbleby Printers Ltd, which became engaged in a closed shop dispute with the National Graphical Association. As a result of that dispute, the NGA members were on strike and the Dimbleby newspapers were not being printed. So the Dimbleby company turned to TBF (Printers) Ltd, which was itself a company closely associated with (same shareholdings, same management) T. Bailey Forman Ltd, with whom the NUJ was engaged in a trade dispute and had been since 1979. The NUJ instructed its members employed by Dimbleby newspapers not to supply copy to Dimbleby newspapers and argued that, because of their effective identity, TBF (Printers) Ltd, as well as T. Bailey Forman Ltd, was an 'employer who is party to the dispute' between the NUJ and T. Bailey Forman Ltd, within the meaning of that phrase in section 17(3) of the Act of 1980. But the House of Lords rejected this argument.[59]

Lord Wedderburn has summarized several of these recent developments thus:

> So, workers may picket, but only at their own place of work. Sympathy or solidarity action must be made tortious *because* it is 'secondary', i.e. it transgresses the rule about staying within employment unit boundaries. Access to tribunals for unfair dismissal of strikers is narrowed to victimization in the complainant's own 'establishment'; workers taking part in it elsewhere no

58. *Mercury Communications v. Scott-Garner* [1983] 3 WLR 914.
59. *Dimbleby and Sons Ltd v. National Union of Journalists* [1984] 1 WLR 427.

longer count as his fellows. And the 'trade dispute' itself
– the central concept of the system of immunities – is
now confined to disputes with a worker's *own* employer
only and to disputes which relate wholly or mainly to
the industrial conditions of the workers in that employment unit only. As it faces the power of capital organized
in interlocking but legally separate corporate entities,
labour is now cut up into atomized units of which the
boundaries are by law coterminous with the employers'
definitions of employment units in both private and
public sectors. Trans-enterprise solidarity is no longer
acceptable to the law. Any doubtful points are increasingly swept aside by Law Lords who found that the old
immunities stuck in their 'judicial gorges'. And if need
be, there are always new common law liabilities ready
to hand not necessarily protected by immunities.[60]

The last sentence refers particularly to the development of the
notion of 'economic duress' as creating liabilities for trade
unions.[61]

The uses of the labour injunction

An injunction may be issued whenever the court 'finds it just
and convenient to do so'. This very wide discretion the judge
may exercise in different ways in different cases or in different
types of cases. Labour injunctions are sought by employers or
dissident trade unionists or others to prevent or to stop industrial action, including strikes, by trade unions or their officials
which the plaintiff claims is illegal. If the action continued,
he argues, damage would result to his business or personal
interests which would be irreparable and for which the subsequent payment of compensation would be an inadequate

60. 'Labour Law Now: a Hold and a Nudge' in 13 *Industrial Law Journal*
(1984) 73.
61. See *Universe Tankships of Monrovia Inc. v. International Transport
Workers Federation* [1982] 2 WLR 803; but note *Hadmor Productions v.
Hamilton* [1982] 2 WLR 322: see also *Associated British Ports v. TGWU*
[1989] 1 WLR 939 (below, p. 94).

remedy. The plaintiff seeks an interim or interlocutory injunction, being an order of the court requiring the defendant to desist from his action in order to maintain the status quo until its legality or illegality can be determined at a subsequent trial. Where the case is urgent, the application to the court is made *ex parte*, that is, without the other side being present. If not urgent, two clear days' notice is required but is often waived.

The question for the court used to be whether the applicant had shown prima facie evidence, or a probability, that his legal rights were being infringed. He also had to show that he would suffer more harm if the interim remedy were not granted than the defendant would suffer if it was (the 'balance of convenience'). But in 1975, the Law Lords said this test caused confusion. Lord Diplock said the court need be satisfied only that the applicant's claim was not 'frivolous or vexatious' and that there was 'a serious question to be tried.'[62]

This made the granting of an interim injunction much easier to obtain. The balance of convenience still had to be shown by the plaintiff to be in his favour but, as Wedderburn says, the threat of irreparable harm to the employer's 'property' in his business interests could not be outweighed by the defendant union. Failure to abide by the terms of an injunction leads to proceedings for contempt of court, followed by fines and by possible sequestration (seizure) of the assets of the union.[63]

For the union, an interim injunction prevents the calling of a strike or other action at a time which the union has decided is the most effective. As the full trial is not likely to take place until weeks or months later, the bargaining position of the union is greatly weakened. Very frequently the full trial never takes place because the dispute is ended one way or another. Throughout the 1980s government legislation progressively reduced the number of situations in which unions or individuals could legally take industrial action.

In *Messenger Newspapers Group v. NGA* (1984)[64] the union called a strike to support the policy of 100 per cent union

62. *American Cyanamid Ltd. v. Ethicon* [1975] AC 396.
63. See Wedderburn, 'The Injunction and the Sovereignty of Parliament', in 23 *The Law Teacher* (1989) 4.
64. [1984] IRLR 397 (the 'Eddie Shah' case).

membership which had been departed from in some subsidiary companies belonging to the Group. Picketing led to violence and one company dismissed the union workers on strike. The group company obtained injunctions to stop secondary picketing and attempts to prevent advertisers taking space in the newspapers. The union disregarded the injunctions and was fined £50,000 for contempt of court. When mass picketing continued a further £100,000 fine was levied and the union's assets were sequestrated. Further violent demonstrations by mass pickets led to £525,000 additional fines being imposed. Also the union had to pay aggravated and exemplary damages amounting to over £125,000. It was this case that first showed the considerable legal sanctions available against unions under the new legislation.

During the miners' strike in 1984, members of the South Wales area of the National Union of Mineworkers supported the strike call but, months later, a few of them returned to work under extensive protection from the police. Demonstrations and pickets collected at pit gates and shouted abuse at them as they passed through in coaches. Injunctions were sought to prevent this, but the judge had some difficulty in finding that the demonstrators were acting illegally. However he decided that the protest was 'a species of private nuisance, namely unreasonable interference with the victims' right to use the highway'.[65] This was an example of judicial creativity at its most blatant.

In another case,[66] the National Union of Mineworkers was fined £200,000 for refusal to obey an interim injunction and the judge ordered sequestration of its assets, some of which had been transferred abroad. It was claimed that trustees of the NUM (the President, the Vice-President and the Secretary) were in breach of their duties, and the High Court ordered them to recover these assets and hand them over to the sequestrators. When this was not done, the judge ordered a receiver to be appointed as an officer of the court in place of the trustees.

The powers of the courts in such cases spread very wide. A strike was called by a joint negotiating committee of several

65. *Thomas v. NUM (South Wales area)* [1985] 2 WLR 1081.
66. *Clarke v. Heathfield* [1985] ICR 203, and (No. 2) at 606.

unions, one of which (TASS) had two representatives on the committee of thirty-six members. Contrary to statutory requirements, no ballot had been held and interim injunctions were granted requiring the unions to withdraw and cancel their instructions and take all practical steps to inform their members to desist. Contempt proceedings were brought for failure to comply. TASS argued that they had nothing to withdraw, not having taken the original decision to strike. Nevertheless they were held to be in contempt but, the strike having collapsed, no penalty was imposed.[67]

The statutory liability of unions for the actions of their members has given rise to many difficulties. In *Express and Star v. National Graphical Association*,[68] the plaintiff newspapers obtained an interim injunction requiring the union to withdraw a direction to their members to take industrial action. The union circulated all its branches accordingly. But the court subsequently found two specific breaches involving officers of the union and held the union guilty of contempt. The Court of Appeal upheld this decision and ruled inapplicable to contempt proceedings statutory protection provided to unions under the Employment Act 1982.

The *Spycatcher* litigation[69] may have serious implications for trade union liability. Injunctions were issued against the *Observer* and the *Guardian* newspapers to prevent them from publishing extracts from Peter Wright's book, and the Court of Appeal, overruling the judge at first instance, held that although publication by the *Independent* newspaper and others could not be a breach of those injunctions nevertheless, since they knew of their issue, they could be guilty of contempt of court if their publication interfered with the course of justice. Presumably this principle would apply to trade unions taking action in the same dispute where their fellow members had been injuncted.

In no recent case has the Court of Appeal gone further in its attempt to control trade union activity than in the dispute

---

67. *Austin Rover Co. v. AUEW (TASS)* [1985] IRLR 162. But a penalty of £250,000 was imposed on the TGWU after the strike was settled.

68. [1986] ICR 589.

69. See pp. 223–32.

over the government's suddenly announced decision in April 1989 to abolish the National Dock Labour Scheme. In May, Associated British Ports sought interim injunctions to prevent the Transport and General Workers Union from calling a national docks strike after a favourable ballot of 9,400 dockers employed under the scheme. The Court of Appeal, overruling the High Court judge, granted the injunction on the ground that in 'the balance of convenience' the wish to strike at this time was more than counterbalanced by the financial loss to the employers and the inconvenience to the public. The Court of Appeal said the strike was not in the public interest. This was a novel formulation. The 1967 scheme provided that workers should 'work for such periods as are reasonable' and the employers argued that this made the strike illegal. The Court of Appeal said that difficult questions of law were raised, that there was a 'serious issue' to be decided and that, pending the full trial, the injunction should be granted. Not surprisingly and not for the first time, trade union leaders wondered whether it had become impossible to mount a legal strike. Over 2,000 dock workers immediately walked out despite the judgment and despite the advice given by their leaders not to do so.

The union appealed to the House of Lords and the unofficial action was abandoned. The Law Lords allowed the appeal on the ground that the clause in the scheme relied on by the employers could not have the meaning attributed to it.[70] The Bill to abolish the scheme was meanwhile being rushed through Parliament, and a fresh ballot was needed for the strike. A few days later a second action brought by the newly created Commissioner for the Rights of Trade Union Members seeking an injunction was rejected by the High Court. When the Act was passed, the strike collapsed.

During the dispute in 1984, striking miners travelling in convoy on the motorway in Nottinghamshire were stopped within a few miles of four collieries. They were told by the police that there was reason to fear a breach of the peace if they proceeded and, when they attempted to push through, they were arrested for obstructing the police.[71] In another case,

70. *Associated British Ports v. TGWU* [1989] 1 WLR 939.
71. *Moss v. McLachlan* [1985] IRLR 76. This was not a case on injunctions.

the judge suggested that mass picketing was of itself capable of amounting to intimidating conduct, echoing Lord Reid in *Hunt v. Broome* (see p. 69) and so contrary to section 7 of the Conspiracy and Protection of Property Act 1875.[72] In *Read (Transport) Ltd v. NUM (South Wales)*,[73] road hauliers with contracts to take coke from British Steel Corporation works were subjected to mass picketing, abuse and threats. They obtained an interim injunction directed against the union, which then agreed to comply. But breaches of the injunction continued and the union officials were held to be in contempt, the union being fined £50,000 with sequestration of assets to follow, if needed.

In 1984, it became common for bail conditions, following arrests during the strike, to require those charged not to visit any premises or place for the purpose of picketing or demonstrating in connection with the current trade dispute between the NUM and the National Coal Board, other than peacefully to picket or demonstrate at their usual place of employment. In *R. v. Mansfield Justices ex parte Sharkey*,[74] the court added: 'It does a bench of justices no credit if their clerk is affixing standard conditions to bail forms while applications for unconditional bail are being made.' But that was the limit of their comment, except to admit that the large numbers involved did sometimes make it difficult to avoid an appearance of 'group justice'.

The dispute between, on the one side, the News International newspapers (*Sun* and *News of the World*), the Times Group (*The Times* and the *Sunday Times*) and others, and, on the other side, the unions (SOGAT 82, the NGA and others) which centred on the new site at Wapping, followed the breakdown of negotiations and the dismissal of all those on strike. There were daily (and nightly) demonstrations involving thousands of protestors and large numbers of police. Actions were begun by the employing newspapers alleging nuisance, intimidation, harassment and interference with commercial contracts.[75]

72. *Thomas v. NUM (South Wales Area)* [1985] IRLR 136 (see p. 92).

73. [1985] IRLR 67.

74. [1985] QB 613. This was not a case on injunctions.

75. *News Group Newspapers and others v. SOGAT 82 and others* [1986] IRLR 337; and [1987] ICR 716, where the assets of a union branch were held not subject to sequestration.

Injunctions were issued and some of the unions instructed their members to stop the forbidden activities. Several unions were held to be in contempt, were fined and had their assets sequestrated.

The requirements of a ballot before strike action have been variously interpreted by the courts. The requirements in Area union rules were held not to have been fulfilled by the NUM in Derbyshire and an order followed restraining the union from using funds in this connection.[76] But British Rail failed to obtain an interim injunction against the NUR, the court holding that the union was likely in the highest degree to be able to show that their ballot was valid.[77] London Underground, however, were granted an injunction to prevent a ballot being held on the ground that the issues did not constitute trade disputes.[78] And when the Employment Act 1988 tightened the ballot requirements, the Union of Communication Workers had their ballot declared invalid.[79]

In 1988, disputes arose between British shipowners, who proposed to introduce changes to existing terms and conditions of work for their employees, and the National Union of Seamen. The union decided to ballot its members on industrial action but P & O and Sealink successfully applied for injunctions to prevent the holding of ballots.[80] The basis of these decisions was that strikes would result in unlawful 'secondary' action involving employers who were not parties to the dispute. Unofficial strike action followed and the union's own bankers were granted an injunction prohibiting the NUS from transferring any of their property abroad, on the principle that third parties must ensure that they gave no aid to any action which might occur if the union's property were sequestrated as a result of some future contempt of court. Such a sequestration was ordered on the application of Sealink. The NUS persuaded its members to end their unlawful industrial action but the

76. *Taylor v. NUM (Derbyshire)* [1984] IRLR 440; [1985] IRLR 65, 99.
77. *British Rail v. NUR* [1989] IRLR 345, 349.
78. *London Underground v. NUR* [1989] IRLR 341, 343. But see Millett J. in *Associated British Ports v. TGWU* [1989] IRLR at 301.
79. *Post Office v. Union of Communication Workers* [1990] 1 WLR 981.
80. *P & O European Ferries (Portsmouth) Ltd. v. NUS, The Independent*, 28 March 1988.

courts 'transferred' the sequestration to apply to a separate complaint by P & O that NUS workers were unlawfully picketing its premises. Fines were also imposed and crippling fines were threatened.

At the same time as the dispute over the Dock Labour Scheme was moving rapidly through the courts,[81] the British Railways Board was being denied an injunction against the National Union of Railwaymen. The board claimed that a ballot on industrial action had not been validly conducted, but the High Court judge said the evidence for this 'did not come anywhere near justifying injunctive relief'. The judge seemed unimpressed by the argument that a rail strike would cause 'enormous public inconvenience'. The Court of Appeal dismissed the appeal, Lord Donaldson MR taking the high ground that the function of the independent judiciary under the rule of law was simply to decide whether there had been compliance with the statute requiring the holding of a ballot, however unpopular the strike might be with the travelling public.[82]

The extent to which trade unions are disadvantaged by the rules developed by the judiciary is shown in a case involving the National Union of Teachers. It is well known that teachers undertake a number of tasks which appear to be additional to their contractual duties and so voluntary. The union called on teachers in certain schools to take action by refusing to supervise in lunch periods, or to attend meetings outside school hours. No ballot was held, as was legally required if the action was in breach of contract. An interim injunction was granted to the local authority employers by the judge on the ground that it was 'improbable' that there was 'no serious issue to be tried'.[83] As Wedderburn says, a further advantage accrues to the plaintiff when the test is turned into this negative form. And he continues: 'The judge may as easily say "This is all too difficult for interlocutory motion. It must go to trial, so I will *not* grant an injunction", as he may conclude, "so I *will*

---

81. See p. 94.
82. *British Railways Board v. National Union of Railwaymen* [1989] IRLR 345, 349.
83. *Solihull MB v. NUT* [1985] IRLR 211.

grant an injunction".[84] But the judge usually takes the second course in cases concerning industrial relations.

The later cases

The legislation of the Thatcher period, the rise in unemployment, and the general uncertainty about future job prospects greatly diminished the status and influence of trade unions. The courts ceased to be a prominent arena for political conflict. There were, however, several significant decisions.[85]

On 13 October 1992 the British Coal Corporation announced its intention to close thirty-one of the fifty deep mine collieries and stated that the usual procedure for reviewing colliery closures would not be followed. On the same day the Secretary of State for Trade and Industry told Parliament he had accepted the decision. A remarkable outburst of public indignation was provoked and a few days later the minister said that only ten of the closures would be proceeded with for the time being. The next day it became clear that the review procedure which involved reference to an independent body would not be applied to the closure of the ten pits. Mineworkers at those pits obtained judicial review, the Divisional Court holding that there was a duty placed on the corporation to consult and a legitimate expectation that the procedure would be followed. Not to apply this to the ten pits was irrational.[86]

A second decision upholding the rights of trade unionists under existing legislation concerned threatened industrial action on London Underground. The employers sought an injunction to prevent the action because the union had called for support from newly-recruited members who had not been balloted. The Court of Appeal held that this did not mean the union had not 'the support of a ballot' as required by statute.[87]

84. *The Worker and the Law* (3rd edn), p. 700.

85. See Lord Wedderburn, 'Laski's Law Behind The Law', in R. Rawlings (ed.) *Law, Society and Economy* (1997); K. D. Ewing, Democratic Socialism and Labour Law, in 24 *Industrial Law Journal* (1995) 103, and 'The Law and Social Rights' in *Soundings* (Spring 1996) 181.

86. *R. v. British Coal Corporation ex parte Vardy* [1993] ICR 720.

87. *London Underground Ltd. v. National Union of Rail, Maritime and Transport Workers* [1996] IRLR 636.

Lord Justice Millett expressed the remarkable view that balloting requirements had not been imposed for the protection of the employer or the public but were concerned exclusively with the relationship between the union and its members and were intended for the protection of members.

In *Middlebrook Mushrooms v. TGWU* union members were dismissed after industrial action. The union proposed to leaflet members of the public outside superstores urging a boycott of the employers' mushrooms. An injunction was sought to prevent this but the Court of Appeal held that the action, being directed to the public, did not interfere directly with the contractual relationship between employers and their employees, and was not unlawful.[88]

In a third case, the initiative came from the Equal Opportunities Commission, who challenged the validity under European Community law of UK legislation on redundancy pay and compensation for unfair dismissal for part-time workers, most of whom were women. The Law Lords decided in favour of the Commission and found that the Secretary of State had not shown that the existing discriminatory regulations resulted in the availability of more part-time work.[89]

In the opposite direction, various important decisions continued the restraints on trade union activities. In *Dimskal Shipping Co. v. ITWF* the workers' federation tried once again to force shipping employers to accord with internationally approved wages and conditions. The employers were a Panamanian company, managed from Greece and the ships were manned by Greeks and Filipinos. The ship berthed in Sweden and was blacked when documents setting out an agreement were not executed. Eventually the company paid $111,743 but later sued in the UK on grounds of economic duress. The Law Lords held the company was entitled to restitution notwithstanding that the blacking was lawful under Swedish law.[90]

88. *Middlebrook Mushrooms v. Transport and General Workers' Union* [1993] ICR 612.

89. *R. v. Secretary of State for Employment ex parte Equal Opportunities Commission* [1995] 1 AC 1.

90. *Dimskal Shipping v. International Transport Workers' Federation* [1992] IRLR 78.

In contrast with the *London Underground* decision (above), the Court of Appeal held that notices served on employers prior to industrial action describing those to be involved as 'all the union's members employed by your institution' were not sufficiently precise and that the union should have specifically named individuals. An interlocutory injunction restraining the union from taking action was granted. Lord Justice Steyn felt compelled to agree but recorded his 'unease about the consequences of a construction of this kind'.[91]

Lord Woolf has written recently of the strength of the common law which enables courts 'to vary the extent of their intervention to reflect current needs' and thus to 'maintain the delicate balance of a democratic society'.[92] Such creative flexibility was not favoured by Sir Donald Nicholls V–C in *Boddington v. Lawton*[93] where he was encouraged by counsel to remove the illegality attached to associations (not being trade unions enjoying statutory immunity) founded to negotiate collectively with employers. The Prison Officers' Association was such a body. The Vice–Chancellor insisted that it would be 'most undesirable for judges now to hold that, to reflect changes in social conditions, the common law in this field has developed and is now to the contrary effect of what has been established and acted on for so many years'. So the Prison Officers remained in unreasonable restraint of trade at common law, and a special declaration had to be made to enable them to finance their members in a dispute.

Also worthy of note is the view of Gibson LJ in *Ticehurst v. British Telecommunications*[94] that an employee may be in breach of her contract of employment if she 'evinces an intention' to withdraw the goodwill she owes to her employer.

But surpassing all these examples of the judicial attitude to organized labour was the remarkable decision in *Associated Newspapers Ltd. v. Wilson* and *Associated British Ports v.*

91. *Blackpool and the Fylde College v. National Association of Teachers in Further and Higher Education* [1994] IRLR 227.

92. 'Droit Public–English Style' in [1995] *Public Law* 58; and see pp. 331–3.

93. [1994] ICR 478.

94. [1992] IRLR 219 at 225.

Palmer.[95] Under section 23(1) of the relevant statute an employee had the 'right not to have action ... taken against him as an individual by his employer for the purpose of preventing or deterring him from being or seeking to become a member of an independent trade union or penalising him for doing so'. Section 153(1) provided, 'except so far as the context otherwise requires "action" includes omission and references to taking action shall be construed accordingly'.

The Associated Newspapers (publishers of the *Daily Mail*, the *Mail on Sunday* and the *Evening Standard*) and Associated British Ports (the two actions were taken together) both wished to replace collective bargaining with the union by individual contracts with employees. Employees willing to switch to individual contracts were offered a pay rise, which was not offered to those who chose to continue to have their rates of pay determined by collective bargaining. Both sets of employees were permitted to remain members of their union. Employees who rejected the offer complained to an industrial tribunal that the employers' action had infringed their statutory rights. Their complaints were upheld, but the Employment Appeal Tribunal reversed the decision. The employees' appeal to the Court of Appeal was upheld and the case went to the Law Lords where the employers were finally successful.

Two grounds were given. The first was held by Lords Keith, Bridge and Browne-Wilkinson (Lords Slynn and Lloyd dissenting). The majority concluded that the 'omission' to offer an employee a benefit conferred on another employee did not amount to 'action' taken against that first employee. But what about section 153(1)? It appears that at none of the lower levels in this litigation but only in the House of Lords was the point argued that section 153(1) was not relevant because a literal application produced grammatical ambiguity 'in that if the concept of taking action against a person was to embrace the concept of omitting to act, the omission had to be an omission to act in that person's favour without the circumstances in which the obligation to take action in favour of the employee was to arise being spelt out' (to quote the head note). Lord Lloyd (with whom Lord Slynn agreed) disposed of this sophis-

95. [1995] 2 WLR 354.

try. He accepted that the inclusion of omissions within section 23(1) meant that the phrase had to be substantially recast but argued that this had been foreseen by the draftsman when he provided that taking action was to be 'construed accordingly'.

The game of grammar and semantics (to which was added legislative history and the overruling of a Court of Appeal decision of 1987) became absurd when Lord Browne-Wilkinson found himself 'reluctantly forced' to come in on the side of the majority, reaching his conclusion 'with regret since, in my view, it leaves an undesirable lacuna in the legislation protecting employees against victimisation'. His Lordship was also unpersuaded by the view of the other four Law Lords on the second ground. This view was that it could not be said that the service, provided by the union, of collective bargaining with the employer was an essential union service or that membership of a union unable to offer that service was valueless or insignificant. Nor was derecognition of the union for collective bargaining capable of supporting a finding that the employers' purpose was to prevent or deter membership of the union.

Those who believed that the historical antagonism of the Law Lords to the collective power of employees expressed in their membership of trade unions was being mitigated in the post-Thatcher years received a firm reminder from this decision that old habits die hard, or not at all.

The best that can be made of the opinions of the Law Lords is that those who were strongest in the majority (Keith and Bridge) could be fairly described as old Tories, that the dissidents (Slynn and Lloyd) resembled new Labour, and that the reluctant middleman (Browne-Wilkinson) looked like a Liberal Democrat. So there may be some hope for the future.

4. The control of discretionary powers

The earlier cases

During the inter-war period, the courts showed little reluctance in overruling the decisions of ministers and local authorities especially where, as in slum clearance and compulsory purchase cases, property rights were interfered with. The exercise of statutory powers was closely scrutinized and any procedural or substantive defect was generally found to be sufficient to nullify a decision. Typical of this attitude was that of Swift J in *Re Bowman*:

> When an owner of property against whom an order has been made under the Act comes into this court and complains that there has been some irregularity in the proceedings, and that he is not liable to have his property taken away, it is right, I think, that his case should be entertained sympathetically and that a statute under which he is being deprived of his rights to property should be construed strictly against the local authority and favourably towards the interest of the applicant, in as much as he for the benefit of the community is undoubtedly suffering a substantial loss, which in my view must not be inflicted upon him unless it is quite clear that Parliament has intended that it shall.[1]

1 . [1932] 2 KB 261; and see *Carltona v. Commissioners of Works* [1943] 2 All ER 560, *Point of Ayr Collieries v. Lloyd George* [1943] 2 All ER 546, *Robinson v. Minister of Town and Country Planning* [1947] KB 702, *Franklin v. Minister of Town and Country Planning* [1948] AC 87.

Similarly in *Errington v. Minister of Health*,[2] Maugham LJ said:

> It seems to me a matter of the highest possible importance that where a quasi-judicial function is being exercised, under such circumstances as it had to be exercised here, with the result of depriving people of their property, especially if it is done without compensation, the persons concerned should be satisfied that nothing unfair has been done in the matter, and that *ex parte* statements have not been heard before the decision has been given without any chance for the person concerned to refute those statements.

Decisions such as these show that the courts inclined to the view that in a conflict between the common law property right of an individual and the statutory powers of a local authority to interfere with those rights, the benefit of any doubt in statute was to be given to the individual – and that this was particularly so if the statute gave less than full compensation to the individual. This is, indeed, often said to be a presumption to which judges should have regard in interpreting statutes. The idea that Parliament, in this field, was 'interfering' with the common law died hard.

The changes in attitude and the growth of interventionism

But during 1939–45 and for some years after the war, there was a marked change in judicial attitudes. The classic judgment was that in *Associated Provincial Picture Houses Ltd v. Wednesbury Corporation*.[3] On the one hand, Lord Greene MR indicated the strict limits on the powers of the courts to set aside an administrative decision where the public authority acted within its jurisdiction. On the other hand, such an authority must act in good faith, use the powers for the purpose for which they were given, take into account relevant matters

2 . [1935] 1 KB 249.
3 . [1948] 1 KB 223.

and disregard the irrelevant, and must not act in a way so unreasonable that no reasonable authority could have so acted. But it was no part of the courts' function to replace the discretionary decision of the public authority with one of its own.

The highest point in this reluctance to intervene with governmental activities was reached in the mid-1950s when the House of Lords interpreted a statutory provision, which limited the courts' jurisdiction to review a compulsory purchase order on land, so broadly that even fraud by public servants was held not to entitle the owner to bring an action.[4]

From the early 1960s, the courts reverted to their former attitude and became increasingly willing to review governmental activities on a variety of grounds; the reluctance of the 1940s and 1950s disappeared.

In *Ridge v. Baldwin*[5] the House of Lords held that a chief constable, who had been acquitted on a criminal charge but criticized for lack of leadership by the judge, was entitled, under the common law rules of natural justice, to a hearing before he could be dismissed by the local authority who employed him. This decision led the way to a general concept of the need for 'fairness' in the administrative process.

The earlier distinction between those matters which fell within ministerial or local authority discretion and those which were within the competence of the courts to adjudicate became increasingly blurred. Thus in *Padfield v. Minister of Agriculture, Fisheries and Food*[6] milk producers from the south-east asked the minister to appoint a committee of investigation, alleging that the price they were paid by the Milk Marketing Board was too low having regard to transport costs. The relevant statute empowered the minister to set up such a committee, but in this case he refused to do so on the ground that the complaint was unsuitable for investigation because it raised wide issues; that if the committee upheld the complaint he would be expected to make an order to give effect to the

4 . *Smith v. East Elloe RDC* [1956] AC 736; and see *Jones v. Department of Employment* [1988] 2 WLR 493.

5 . [1964] AC 40.

6 . [1968] AC 997. Contrast *British Oxygen v. Minister of Technology* [1971] AC 610, where the House of Lords refused to interfere with a ministerial discretion about investment grants.

committee's recommendations; and that the complaint should be dealt with by the board rather than by the committee of investigation. A majority of the House of Lords found these reasons insufficient and ordered the minister to set up the committee. They agreed that he had a discretion under the statute whether or not to do so, but said that he was not justified in refusing if the result was to frustrate the policy of the Act of Parliament. Lord Morris of Borth-y-Gest disagreed. In his view, the court could intervene only if the minister (a) failed or refused to apply his mind to or to consider the question whether to refer a complaint to the committee or (b) misinterpreted the law or proceeded on an erroneous view of the law or (c) based his decision on some wholly extraneous consideration or (d) failed to have regard to matters which he should have taken into account. And he held that none of these was the case. The view taken by the majority was surprising as the decision of the minister not to intervene was clearly one of policy with which the courts are usually reluctant to interfere.[7]

The decision of the House of Lords in *Anisminic Ltd v. Foreign Compensation Commission*[8] shows how, on occasion, the courts will resist the strongest efforts of the government to exclude them from reviewing executive discretion. The Foreign Compensation Commission was empowered by statute to deal with claims to compensation under agreements with foreign governments. The plaintiffs owned property in Egypt which they lost at the time of the Suez crisis in 1956. The Commission made a provisional determination that the plaintiffs had failed to establish a claim according to the rules laid down under the statute. The statute provided that: 'The determination by the Commission of any application made to them under this Act shall not be called in question in any court of law.'

Despite these last words the plaintiffs applied to the courts for an order declaring that the Commission had misconstrued the rules. The House of Lords, not for the first or for the last

7 . See, for example, *Bushell v. Secretary of State for the Environment* [1980] 3 WLR 22.
8 . [1969] 2 AC 147.

time, held that 'determination' should not be construed as including everything which purported to be a determination but was not, and so the court was not precluded from deciding that the order of the commission was a nullity. Looking at the way the commission had construed the rules, the House decided that the determination was a nullity.

Lord Morris of Borth-y-Gest again dissented. He agreed that the courts could intervene if the question was whether or not the commission had acted within its powers or its jurisdiction. But 'what is forbidden is to question the correctness of a decision or determination which it was within the area of their jurisdiction to make.'

This distinction has a long and respectable history. If an Act of Parliament says that A (who may be a minister or a commission or a local authority or an individual) shall be the person to settle certain specified questions and that there shall be neither appeal to nor review by any other body or person (including the courts), then A's decisions arc unchallengeable so long as (a) it is A, not another, who decides, (b) A decides those specified questions and not others and (c) A does not act in bad faith or with similar impropriety. The *Anisminic* decision goes much further than this and says in effect that A's decision can be set aside by the courts if they disagree with his interpretation of the rules which he is required to apply. In a later case Lord Denning MR said,

> So fine is the distinction that in truth the High Court has a choice before it whether to interfere with an inferior court on a point of law. If it chooses to interfere, it can formulate its decision in the words: 'The court below had no jurisdiction to decide this point wrongly as it did.' If it does not choose to interfere, it can say: 'The court had jurisdiction to decide it wrongly, and did so.' Softly be it stated, but that is the reason for the difference between the decision of the Court of Appeal in *Anisminic*. . . and the House of Lords.[9]

9 . *Pearlman v. Harrow School* [1978] 3 WLR 736, a decision of the Court of Appeal criticized by Lord Diplock in *Re Racal Communications Ltd* [1981] AC 374.

As Lord Diplock said in *Re Racal Communications Ltd*, 'The breakthrough made by *Anisminic* was that, as respected administrative tribunals and authorities, the old distinction between errors of law which went to jurisdiction and those which did not, was for practical purposes abolished.' In *Racal* the House of Lords held that where a statute provided that the decision of a High Court judge should 'not be appealable', it could not be reviewed or appealed from.

This extreme case of judicial interference with the powers of public authorities may be contrasted with the attitude of the Court of Appeal in *Secretary of State for Employment v. ASLEF*[10] *and Others (No. 2).*[11] The Secretary of State exercised his powers to apply to the NIRC under the Industrial Relations Act 1971 for an order requiring a ballot of trade union members to be held. This power existed where, as the statute provided, it appeared to him that there were reasons for doubting whether the trade union members, in taking part in industrial action, were acting in accordance with their own wishes. The trade union appealed against the order given by the NIRC. Lord Denning first considered how far the words 'if it appears to the Secretary of State' put his decision beyond judicial challenge. He said:

> In this case I would think that, if the minister does not act in good faith, or if he acts on extraneous considerations which ought not to influence him, or if he plainly misdirects himself in fact or in law, it may well be that a court would interfere; but when he honestly takes a view of the facts or the law which could reasonably be entertained, then his decision is not to be set aside simply because thereafter someone thinks that his view was wrong ... Of course it is to be remembered here that we are concerned with a grave threat to the national economy. The steps that are proposed do not imperil the liberty, livelihood or property of any man. The issue is simply: should a ballot be held of the railwaymen to ascertain their views?

10. Associated Society of Locomotive Engineers and Firemen.
11. [1972] 2 QB 455. The 'others' included the other railway unions.

Lord Denning then turned to the claim that the minister had acted improperly.

> It is said that it must 'appear' to the minister that there are 'reasons' for doubting whether the workers are behind their leaders: and that the minister has given no reasons. We have been referred to several recent cases, of which *Padfield v. Minister of Agriculture, Fisheries and Food* is the best example, in which the courts have stressed that in the ordinary way a minister should give reasons, and if he gives none the court may infer that he had no good reasons. Whilst I would apply that proposition completely in most cases, and particularly in cases which affect life, liberty or property, I do not think that it applies in all cases.

Lord Denning concluded that the proposition did not apply in this case and that there were reasons which a reasonable minister could entertain and so there was no ground on which the court could interfere with the minister's decision to ask for a ballot order. He was supported by the other members of the Court of Appeal. In the event the union leaders were wholly justified (as the result of the ballot showed) in their claim that there were no reasons for doubting that the industrial action was in accordance with the wishes of the workers.

In *Secretary of State for Education and Science v. Tameside Metropolitan Borough Council*[12] the minister acted under section 68 of the Education Act 1944 which provided:

> If the Secretary of State is satisfied . . . that any local education authority . . . have acted or are proposing to act unreasonably . . . he may . . . give such directions . . . as appear to him to be expedient.

In March 1975 the Labour-controlled Tameside Council put forward proposals to the Secretary of State for the reorganization of secondary education along comprehensive lines to come into effect in September 1976. The proposals were approved in November 1975. The council made many of the

12. [1976] 3 WLR 641.

necessary arrangements for the changeover and told pupils which schools they would be going to.

At the local elections in May 1976, the Conservatives won control of the council and on 7 June told the Secretary of State that they proposed not to implement the plans for the conversion of the five grammar schools into comprehensives and sixth-form colleges. On 11 June the Secretary of State gave the council a direction under section 68, requiring them to implement their predecessors' plans, and on 18 June the Divisional Court ordered the council to comply. On 26 July the Court of Appeal overruled the Divisional Court and on 2 August, moving with impressive speed, Lords Wilberforce, Diplock, Salmon, Russell and Dilhorne upheld the Court of Appeal.

The basis of their Lordships' decisions was that the minister could give a valid direction only if he was satisfied that no reasonable local authority could have decided as the Conservative majority did; and that he could not have been so satisfied.

A second case was that of Laker Airways. Under the Civil Aviation Act 1971, the Civil Aviation Authority was empowered to grant licences to those wishing to operate air transport lines. The authority granted a licence to Mr Freddy Laker for the period from 1973 to 1982 to operate a cheap passenger service known as 'Skytrain' between the United Kingdom and the USA. The Conservative government supported the project but in February 1976 the Labour government (which had previously supported Mr Laker) through its Secretary of State for Trade in a White Paper announced a change of civil aviation policy.

The Act of 1971 empowered the Secretary of State to 'give guidance' to the Authority with respect to their statutory functions. The White Paper purported to contain such guidance which, in accordance with the Act, was approved by a resolution of each House of Parliament. The crucial phrase in the White Paper guidance was that the authority should not license more than one British airline to serve the same route, with British Airways as the preferred airline to the USA. That prevented Skytrain from coming into operation.

The Court of Appeal held that the power of the Secretary of State to give guidance to the authority did not extend to such a discretion. Said Lord Denning MR, ' "Guidance" could only be used to explain, amplify or supplement the general objectives or provisions of the Act. If the Secretary of State went beyond the bounds of "guidance" he exceeded his powers; and the Civil Aviation Authority was under no obligation to obey him.' So Mr Laker succeeded in his action.[13]

These two cases while comparable are also dissimilar. In both cases two public authorities were in conflict. In *Laker*'s case the minister was seeking to require the Civil Aviation Authority to follow his policy but he chose a way of doing this which the Court of Appeal considered not to be within his powers. In *Tameside* the central department and the local authority were in direct conflict over a matter of administrative feasibility. The minister did not believe that Tameside Council could properly implement the change within the limited time available.

The decision in *Tameside* may be contrasted with *ASLEF (No. 2)*[14] where the trade union's complaint that the minister had no reason to believe that the members were not behind their leaders was not supported by the court. In *Tameside* the minister had sound administrative reasons for believing that the local authority was acting unreasonably, but it was held that merely to have such reasons was insufficient. A remarkable feature of this decision of the House of Lords was that it was based on almost no judicial authority at all. One of their Lordships referred to *ASLEF (No. 2)*, and to one other decision. The other three referred to none. Yet this is hardly an area where judicial pronouncements have been lacking. It concerns the whole matter of judicial control over ministerial discretion.

Professor de Smith[15] wrote that Parliament might purport to restrict judicial review by conferring powers in subjective terms, the public authority being entitled to act when it 'is satisfied' or when 'it appears' to it that, or when 'in its opinion', a prescribed state of affairs exists. Then the courts interpret

---

13. *Laker Airways Ltd v. Department of Trade* [1977] 2 WLR 234.
14. See p. 108.
15. *Judicial Review of Administrative Action* (3rd edn, 1973), pp. 318–20.

such phrases so as to give themselves more or less control as they wish. This depends on the judges' views of the merits of the case before them or (I would add) the direction their political inclinations lead them − what I call below their 'view of the public interest'.[16] If trade unions are being restricted by ministerial action (as in *ASLEF* (*No. 2*)) then statutory limitations on ministers' powers will be interpreted loosely. If ministers appear to the courts to be acting in a way which is arbitrary or unfair (as in *Padfield* and *Tameside* and *Laker*) then the limitations will be insisted on. Little attempt is made to treat like situations in a like manner or to act consistently within a framework of judicial analysis. And one is often left with a feeling that in this area of the law judges rely almost entirely on their own sense of justice or on their own personal conception of what is best.

Judicial review

The growth of intervention during the 1960s and 1970s was consolidated by a procedural change introduced in 1977 when the Supreme Court Rule Committee created a specific new remedy of judicial review. This brought together in a simplified form a number of remedies obtainable from a Divisional Court of the Queen's Bench Division consisting of two or three judges. The grounds on which this remedy could be sought were summarized by Lord Diplock in the GCHQ case[17] under the three headings of illegality, irrationality and procedural impropriety. These cover the situations where a public authority is alleged to be acting outside its statutory powers, to be acting in a grossly unreasonable way, or to be abusing the rules of natural justice governing procedure. So review is not an appeal on the merits of a decision but limited to those grounds. Sometimes the distinction between a fair procedure and a fair decision is very narrow. Since 1977 a case law has been built up to define the limits of the availability of this

16. See Chapter 9.
17. *In re the Council of Civil Service Unions* [1984] 3 All ER 935; see p. 156.

remedy, which proved very popular.[18] In early days the judiciary greatly encouraged litigants to use it and the House of Lords ruled in 1983 that those seeking redress for an infringement of public law rights must proceed by way of this remedy only.[19] More recently, the Law Lords have emphasized the need to retain flexibility between public and private law.[20]

An important limitation on the availability of judicial review arose when a senior nursing officer employed by a health authority was dismissed for misconduct. At the first hearing the judge held that the public was concerned to see that a great public service acted lawfully and fairly towards its officers and so judicial review was available. But the Court of Appeal, no doubt alarmed by the prospect of large numbers of public sector employees seeking similar review, held that such cases should be treated as ordinary master-and-servant situations governed by private law.[21] This principle was extended to civil servants who had the alternative remedy of taking their complaints to an industrial tribunal.[22] A similar reason was given for refusing the remedy to a convicted prisoner who brought an action against the Home Secretary and the prison governor requiring them to provide him with the necessary medical treatment in accordance with the Prison Rules.[23] But the remedy was made available by the House of Lords to a prisoner who alleged breaches of procedural rules by a deputy governor inquiring into disciplinary offences.[24]

As a preliminary step, an applicant seeking judicial review

18. See M. Sunkin, 'What is Happening to Applications for Judicial Review?', in 50 *Modern Law Review* 432 (1987).

19. *O'Reilly v. Mackman* [1983] 2 AC 237. For a recent example, see *R. v. Oldham Justices ex parte Crawley* [1996] 1 All ER 464 where habeas corpus was excluded; contrast *Re S-C* [1996] 1 All ER 532.

20. See *Mercury Communications Ltd. v. Director General of Telecommunications* [1996] 1 WLR 48.

21. *R. v. East Berkshire Health Authority ex parte Walsh* [1985] QB 152; and see *Roy v. Kensington and Chelsea and Westminster Family Practitioner Committee* [1992] 1 AC 624.

22. *R. v. Civil Service Appeal Board ex parte Bruce* [1988] ICR 649.

23. *R. v. Secretary of State for the Home Office ex parte Dew* [1987] 1 WLR 881.

24. *Leech v. Deputy Governor of Parkhurst Prison* [1988] 2 WLR 290. See p. 172.

of the decision or conduct of a public authority must first obtain from a judge of the High Court 'leave' to proceed to a full hearing. The purpose of this is to eliminate unmeritorious applications. The official statistics show the overall growth in the number of applications and of those which were allowed and refused leave or which were withdrawn. Between 1981 and 1994, the number of applications rose from 533 to 3208 but the proportion of those granted leave declined from a high 77 per cent in 1984 to 37 per cent in 1994. This decline in part reflects the numbers withdrawn, either before or after the decision on leave, and research[25] indicates that as many as 50 per cent of the total number of applications were withdrawn between 1981 and 1994. The significance of these figures is discussed later.[26] Of the applications which received full hearings over this period, on average 50 per cent were successful but the variations were considerable.

In addition to the requirements of obtaining leave, applicants must show that they have a sufficient interest in the subject matter of the application to be allowed to proceed. The problems have arisen in cases where the applicant is an organization, such as a pressure or public interest group, seeking to challenge a public authority. In 1990, the Rose Theatre Trust was denied the right to challenge a refusal by the Secretary of State for the Environment to make an order protecting the site of an Elizabethan theatre.[27] Recently the courts have taken a much more liberal approach and, amongst others, the Child Poverty Action Group, Greenpeace, the World Development Movement, and Save Our Railways[28] have been allowed to

25. The most informative account of the whole process is in Lee Bridges, George Meszaros and Maurice Sunkin, *Judicial Review in Perspective* (1995), to which I am indebted; see also Sunkin, 'The Problematical State of Access to Judicial Review', in B. Hadfield (ed.) *Judicial Review: A Thematic Approach* (1995).

26. See pp. 115–6, 143–5, 182, 185, 318.

27. *R. v. Secretary of State for the Environment ex parte Rose Theatre Trust* [1990] 2 WLR 186.

28. *R. v. Secretary of State for Social Services ex parte CPAG* [1989] 1 All ER 1047; *R. v. Inspectorate of Pollution ex parte Greenpeace (No.2)* [1994] 4 All ER 329; *R. v. Secretary of State for Foreign Affairs ex parte World Development Movement* [1995] 1 All ER 611; *R. v. Director of Passenger Rail Franchising ex parte Save Our Railways, The Times* 18 December 1995.

proceed against ministers. Even Lord Rees-Mogg was recognized as having a taxpayer's interest sufficient to enable him to attempt to derail the process of acceptance of the Maastricht Treaty.[29] Moreover, said Lloyd LJ, 'we accept without question that Lord Rees-Mogg brings the proceedings because of his sincere concern for constitutional issues,' though it is not clear whether that would be a sufficient interest for lesser mortals.

The grounds on which judicial review may be sought have been extended generously since Lord Diplock's threefold classification. Recently it was claimed: 'We now possess a jurisdiction in which every public body is in principle subject to the supervision of the court as regards every decision it makes', with the exception of the Queen in Parliament exercising the function of enacting primary legislation; and even that exception does not apply where the legislation is inconsistent with the law of the European Union.[30] Diplock's classification can be maintained only if his headings are widely defined so as to include, for example, the failure in a widening range of circumstances to give reasons for administrative actions.[31]

Although the jurisdiction is wide, most of the applications for judicial review in recent years have been made in a few areas.[32] In four of the six years 1981–86 immigration applications formed over 40 per cent of the caseload. After 1987, in which year immigration accounted for over 44 per cent of all applications, the annual percentages (to 1994) declined to between 22 per cent and 29 per cent. The second most significant subject area is housing, including homelessness. Housing in 1987, 1988 and 1989 accounted for 9 per cent, 13 per cent and 15 per cent of total applications for leave; homelessness considered separately accounted for 15 per cent in 1993 and 14 per cent in 1994.[33] Challenges concerning criminal matters

29. R. Rawlings, 'Legal Politics', in [1994] *Public Law* 367 on *R. v. Secretary of State for Foreign Affairs ex parte Rees-Mogg* [1994] 1 All ER 457. See pp. 121–2.

30. Sir John Laws, 'Law and Democracy' in [1995] *Public Law* 72 at 75.

31. See pp. 116–9.

32. For the figures that follow, see Bridges et al., Chapter 2 and Appendix 1.

33. Official statistics have distinguished homelessness cases only since the second six months of 1992.

accounted for between 10 per cent and 16 per cent in 1987–89 and 1991–94.[34]

Homelessness and immigration cases are discussed below.[35] In over twenty other subject areas, applications for leave have been made, but (with two exceptions)[36] each accounts for less than 4 per cent (most less than 1 per cent) of the total.

The high preponderance of judicial review cases concerning immigration and homelessness means that the Home Office and local housing authorities are those most proceeded against. During the period from 1 January 1987 to 31 March 1991, the Home Office attracted 1241 (74 per cent) applications for leave to seek judicial review, followed by the Department for the Environment with 121, and the Inland Revenue with 70. Thirty-five per cent of applications against local authorities concerned homelessness, 'other' housing 11 per cent with other subject areas following.[37]

The giving of reasons

Unless public authorities make known the reasons for their decisions, challenge by judicial review may often be difficult or even impossible. This is particularly so where the suspicion is that irrelevant considerations have been taken into account or relevant considerations disregarded. Increasingly the courts are insisting that reasons should be disclosed. In 1993 in *R. v. Secretary of State for the Home Department ex parte Doody*[38] Lord Mustill said, 'I accept without hesitation . . . that the law does not at present recognise a general duty to give reasons for administrative decisions. Nevertheless, it is equally beyond question that such a duty may in appropriate circumstances be implied.'

A person convicted of murder must be sentenced to life imprisonment. However, the Home Secretary may, after such a period of imprisonment as he thinks fit, refer the case to the

34. In 1990 the percentage rose to 29 because of a rise in challenges to certain drink-driving prosecutions.

35. Pp. 137–45, 182–90.

36. Town and country planning, and education.

37. Bridges et al., pp. 40–7.

38. [1993] 3 WLR 154.

Parole Board for review. If the board recommends release, the Home Secretary may, after consultation with the Lord Chief Justice and, if possible, the trial judge, release the prisoner on licence. Since 1983, the practice has been to consider that such sentences have a 'penal' element which reflects the seriousness of the offence, and a 'risk' element which reflects the possible danger to the public of releasing the prisoner on licence. Shortly after a person has received a mandatory life sentence, the Secretary of State sets the date for the first review by the Parole Board for releasing the prisoner on licence.

In *Doody*, the House of Lords held that a prisoner had a right to make representations to the Home Secretary, to know what the Home Secretary would take into account in fixing the penal element, and to be given the reasons for any departure by the Home Secretary from judicial recommendations.

In his judgment, Lord Mustill, speaking for the court, referred to the decision of the Court of Appeal in *R. v. Civil Service Appeal Board ex parte Cunningham*.[39] The applicant in this case was unfairly dismissed from a post in the prison department of the Home Office and so had to seek compensation from the Civil Service Appeal Board rather than from an industrial tribunal. The board awarded him compensation of £6500, giving no reasons. From an industrial tribunal he would have received about £15,000. Lord Donaldson MR in the Court of Appeal relied on the principle of fairness laid down by Lord Bridge in an earlier case[40] to require that reasons should have been given. The other members of the Court of Appeal agreed, taking no less broad a view of the obligation to give reasons.

Prisoners convicted of offences (other than murder) with 'discretionary' life sentences are similarly entitled. In *R. v. Parole Board ex parte Wilson* the Court of Appeal held that a prisoner convicted of buggery, who was, at the age of seventy-six, still in prison despite a number of reviews, was entitled to know the 'reasons, reports or facts adverse to his request for release'.[41]

39. [1991] 4 All ER 310.
40. *Lloyd v. McMahon* [1987] AC 625.
41. *R. v. Parole Board ex parte Wilson* [1992] QB 740; and see *R. v. Secretary of State for the Home Department ex parte Walsh, The Times*, 18 December 1991.

A number of convicted prisoners petitioned the Home Secretary to refer their cases to the Court of Appeal. The minister made inquiries and refused their application. It was held that the petitioners were entitled to have disclosed to them, before the minister made his decision, any fresh information revealed by the inquiries, and to have the opportunity to make representations about that material.[42] The administration of the prison service is controversial and highly publicized, and the courts have in recent years been anxious to ensure that its procedures directly affecting prisoners were seen to be fair and in accordance with universal human rights.

Other cases may receive different treatment. Sir Louis Blom-Cooper Q. C. was sitting as a deputy High Court judge in a case where a homeless woman with an invalid son refused accommodation as inadequate. Her appeal was dismissed by the local authority without reference to medical evidence and without giving reasons for its finding that the accommodation was suitable. Sir Louis adopted the broad principle laid down by Lord Mustill in *ex parte Doody* and held that there was a general duty to give reasons whenever the statutorily impregnated administrative process was infused with the concept of fair treatment; and that the decision of the local authority was not lawful.[43]

However, in a similar case of homelessness the Court of Appeal disagreed with Sir Louis and held that reasons were required to be given only in special circumstances, and that here the decision of the local authority was not prima facie aberrant and there was no obligation to specify the reasons.[44] Where, however, an applicant, refused housing, received no reasons or wholly deficient reasons, the Court of Appeal held he was entitled to have the decision quashed.[45]

So also in *R. v. Higher Education Funding Council ex parte*

42. *R. v. Secretary of State for the Home Department ex parte Hickey (No. 2)* [1995] 1 All ER 490. The petitioners included those convicted in 1979 of the murder of Carl Bridgewater whose cases were referred to the Court of Appeal, and the petitioners released.

43. *R. v. Lambeth LBC ex parte Walters* (1994) 26 HLR 170.

44. *R. v. Kensington and Chelsea LBC ex parte Grillo* (1995) 28 HLR 94.

45. *R. v. Westminster CC ex parte Ermakov* [1996] 2 All ER 302.

Institute of Dental Surgery,[46] the court found that academic judgments were not a class of case where giving reasons was a routine aspect of procedural fairness. It had to be shown that in the circumstances of the particular decision fairness required reasons to be given; and, although the court was highly critical of the exercise of academic evaluation conducted, there was no obligation to give reasons in this case. Ministers must act 'fairly' in considering applications for naturalization.[47]

In a group of recent cases, the courts have held that there was no general duty on the minister to disclose the specialist advice he received before deciding that a pupil with special educational needs could be catered for within a mainstream school;[48] that the Court of Aldermen of the City of London was under a duty to give reasons when deciding whether or not to ratify the election of an alderman;[49] that the chairman of a housing benefits review board was obliged to give reasons for the board's decision that a claimant's liability for rent had been created to take advantage of the housing benefits scheme;[50] that the Home Secretary should have explained his reasons for concluding that the head of the Unification Church should be refused entry to the UK.[51]

Ministerial policy

Challenges to government policy decisions are not often successful, the wisdom or unwisdom of the decisions being regarded by the courts as outside their jurisdiction.

46. [1994] 1 WLR 242.
47. *R. v. Secretary of State for the Home Department ex parte Al-Fayed*, *Independent*, 19 November 1996.
48. *R. v. Secretary of State for Education ex parte S*, *The Times*, 20 July 1994.
49. *R. v. Corporation of London ex parte Matson*, *The Times*, 20 October 1995.
50. *R. v. Solihull Metropolitan Council Housing Benefits Review Board ex parte Simpson* (1994) 92 LGR 719.
51. *R. v. Secretary of State for the Home Department ex parte Moon*, *The Times*, 8 December 1995.

Two attempted interventions by the Court of Appeal on major environmental decisions were reversed by the Law Lords in 1990–1. The Mappin and Webb building adjoins the Mansion House and the Bank of England. Proposals were put forward by the owners during the 1980s for the development of the site and were opposed by Save Britain's Heritage. The published policy of the Secretary of State was that he would not grant consent for the total or substantial demolition of a listed building unless he was satisfied that every effort had been made to continue the present use or find an alternative use. After an inquiry, the minister granted planning permission and listed building consent for the demolition of the building. The Court of Appeal held that this decision should be quashed because he had not adequately explained his reasons, particularly in failing to give his assessment of the merits of the existing building. But the Law Lords decided that the minister had adequately explained the special reasons justifying the overriding of his policy.[52]

When the Greater London Council was abolished in 1986, County Hall on the south bank of the Thames became vested in the London Residuary Body which applied for planning permission to use the main block for mixed hotel, residential and general office purposes unconnected with any local government functions. After an inquiry, the Secretary of State disagreed with his inspector and decided that these general office purposes should be permitted. The Court of Appeal held that this decision should be quashed because the minister had not applied the correct test of competing needs, in this case between those of local government and those of other office users. But the Law Lords unanimously decided that he was obliged to have regard only to 'material considerations', and that the amount of weight to be given to these was a matter for his judgment.[53]

Interpretation of statutory words led the minister into error when he told the Local Government Commission that he expected the result of its deliberations to be a substantial increase in the number of unitary authorities. This exceeded

52. *Save Britain's Heritage v. Number 1 Poultry Ltd.* [1991] 1 WLR 153.
53. *London Residuary Body v. Lambeth LBC* [1990] 1 WLR 744.

his power to give 'guidance' to the commission.[54] But he was entitled to modify the commission's recommendation of replacing a two-tier structure of seven councils in a county with five unitary authorities. He imposed six unitary authorities.[55]

A number of boroughs challenged the amended quotas for night flights at airports on the ground that the minister's expressed policy was to reduce the level of noise but that the new quotas would increase it. The court held that the minister in his decision was under an obligation to specify the maximum number of take-off and landing movements.[56]

The courts have accepted that, in certain circumstances, parties may have legitimate expectations of being consulted before public authorities take action. This claim was made by a company manufacturing oral snuff against the Secretary of State for Health when, after giving financial incentives to the company, he proposed to introduce regulations banning the product. The court held there was no legitimate expectation that there would be no ban but that the adopted process of consultation with the company was inadequate and the regulations should be quashed.[57] The right of ministers to change their policies was safeguarded, as it was in *R. v. Ministry of Agriculture, Fisheries and Food ex parte Hamble (Offshore) Fisheries Ltd*[58] where a moratorium was announced on certain licences to fish.

Much more ambitious as a challenge, and more blatantly a use of the courts for political propaganda was Lord Rees-Mogg's charge of the light brigade against the big guns.

On 7 February 1992, the twelve member States of the European Union entered into a Treaty commonly known by the

54. *R. v. Secretary of State for the Environment ex parte Lancashire CC* [1994] 4 All ER 165; see also for later proceedings, *The Times*, 9 December 1995.

55. *R. v. Secretary of State for the Environment ex parte Berkshire CC, Independent*, 31 January 1996.

56. *R. v. Secretary of State for Transport ex parte Richmond upon Thames LBC* [1994] 1 WLR 74; and see [1996] 1 WLR 1460.

57. *R. v. Secretary of State for Health ex parte United States International Inc.* [1992] QB 353.

58. [1995] 2 All ER 714; and see *R. v. British Coal Corporation ex parte Vardy* [1993] ICR 720.

town where they attached their signature: Maastricht. In the UK, treaties are not required to be approved by Parliament, only ratified by government. But those treaty provisions which are to be enforceable in the UK must be incorporated in a Bill and passed by Parliament. For this purpose the European Communities (Amendment) Bill, after long Parliament debate spread over fourteen months, received the Royal Assent on 20 July 1993. While the bill was being debated, Lord Rees-Mogg applied for judicial review of the government's proposed ratification of the treaty.[59]

The most substantive ground turned on Title V of the treaty, which established the machinery for a common security and foreign policy among member states. It was argued for the applicant that the Crown could not by such arrangements transfer or abandon its prerogative power in these fields without statutory authority. The court, however, held that the Title did not involve such transfer or abandonment, any more than occurred under other major treaties such as the North Atlantic Treaty Organization or the Charter of the United Nations. The court also rejected the other grounds put forward by the applicant.

In all this there was the possibility of a conflict between Parliament and the courts and the Speaker was moved to state that the House of Commons was entitled to expect that Article 9 of the Bill of Rights would be required to be fully respected by all those appearing before the court[60] – as indeed it was, by both counsel and judges. Certainly the court showed no signs of wanting to reach out to claim the status of an arbiter on grand constitutional issues.

Three remarkable decisions invalidating government policies were decided in 1995.

The entanglement of law with politics was strikingly shown in the decision of the Law Lords by a majority of 3 to 2, in *R. v. Secretary of State for the Home Department ex parte*

---

59. *R. v. Secretary of State for Foreign and Commonwealth Affairs ex parte Rees-Mogg* [1994] 1 All ER 457; [1994] 2 WLR 115; Rawlings (see next Note) says these law reports present a misleading picture of the litigation.

60. H.C. Deb. cols 353–4 (21 July 1993). See R. Rawlings, 'Legal Politics', in [1994] *Public Law*, 367–91; G. Marshall [1993] *Public Law*, 402–7.

Fire Brigades Union and others.[61] In 1964 the Criminal Injuries Compensation Scheme was set up under the prerogative,[62] not statute, to provide compensation for victims of crimes of violence by ex gratia payments calculated in the same way as common law damages. The amounts were assessed by a board of lawyers experienced in personal injuries cases. In 1988 this scheme was enacted in the Criminal Justice Act of that year, awards being assessed in each instance as before. The Act provided that the relevant sections were to come into force on a day to be appointed by the minister, until which time the non-statutory scheme continued. No date was appointed and in December 1993, government policy was announced in a White Paper[63] setting out details of a new scheme to be made under the prerogative. This provided a new method of assessment based on a flat rate 'tariff' according to categories of injury and not including specific loss of earnings or other special circumstances awardable under the old scheme. The government estimated that the annual cost of compensation under this new scheme would be halved by the year 2000. The White Paper stated the provisions of the 1988 Act would not be brought into force and would be repealed in due course.

Trade unions whose members were more than usually exposed to injuries from crimes of violence in the course of their work applied for judicial review by way of declarations that the decisions of the minister not to bring into force the provisions of the 1988 Act and to implement the tariff scheme were unlawful. The Law Lords held, first, that the minister was under no legally enforceable duty to bring into force the relevant provisions of the 1988 Act, this being a matter for his decision.[64] For the courts to seek to compel him to do so would be an interference with the parliamentary process. But secondly (Lords Keith and Mustill dissenting) the minister was required by the act to keep under review the question whether the statutory provisions should be brought into force, and it

61. [1995] 2 All ER 244; see G. Ganz, in 59 *Modern Law Review* (1996), 95.

62. See *R. v. Criminal Injuries Compensation Board ex parte Lain* [1967] 3 WLR 348; and *ex parte P* [1995] 1 WLR 845.

63. Cm 2434 (1993).

64. Lords Keith, Browne-Wilkinson, Mustill, Lloyd, Nicholls.

was an abuse or excess of power for him to exercise the prerogative power in a manner inconsistent with that duty. So his decision not to implement those provisions but to repeal them and instead to implement the tariff scheme was unlawful.

One of the factors which seems to have particularly influenced the majority of the Law Lords was the statement in the White Paper that the provisions in the 1988 Act 'will accordingly be repealed when a suitable legislative opportunity occurs'. It is, said Lord Browne-Wilkinson,

> for Parliament, not the executive, to repeal legislation. The constitutional history of this country is the history of the prerogative powers of the Crown being made subject to the overriding powers of the democratically elected legislature as the sovereign body.

The point may fall within the category called 'substantive formalism' by Robert Stevens,[65] given the political realities of the relationship between government and Parliament. But it is always dangerous for ministers to appear to arrogate to themselves practical powers which the theory of the Constitution denies them. Occasionally the form defeats the substance.

So also, for Lord Lloyd: 'It is the decision of the Home Secretary to renounce the statutory scheme and to surrender his power to implement it which constitutes the abuse of power.' And for Lord Nicholls the minister had 'disabled himself from properly discharging his statutory duty in the way Parliament intended'.

Lords Keith (briefly) and Mustill (at length), for the minority, rested their judgments on the general proposition that to declare the minister's decisions unlawful would be 'an unwarrantable intrusion by the court into the political field and a usurpation of the function of Parliament' and 'a penetration into Parliament's exclusive field of legislative activity far greater than any that has been contemplated even during the rapid expansion of judicial intervention during the past 20 years'. In rejecting the view of the majority of his colleagues, Lord Mustill accepted that 'Perhaps the Secretary of State has

---

65. See his *Law and Politics: The House of Lords as a Judicial Body 1800–1976*, (1979), Part 3.

laid himself open to attack more than he need have done by the tone of his announcement, but I cannot read him as having said that however much circumstances may change, he will never think again.'

Seven weeks after the decision of the Law Lords, the Secretary of State introduced the Criminal Injuries Compensation Bill to enable him to introduce the tariff scheme, modified however in some important respects. The bill received the Royal Assent on 8 November 1995.

The second decision concerned section 1(1) of the Overseas Development and Co-operation Act 1980 which provides:

> The Secretary of State shall have power, for the purpose of promoting the development or maintaining the economy of a country or territory outside the United Kingdom, or the welfare of its people, to furnish any person or body with assistance, whether financial, technical or of any other nature.

In 1991, the Foreign Secretary decided to make a grant to fund the Pergau Dam in Malaysia, and in 1994 refused to withhold outstanding payments. When the validity of his actions was challenged, the court held that the purpose of statute was to provide economically 'sound' development and that the evidence available to the minister was that there was no economic argument in favour of the grant; and that the decisions were unlawful.[66] Rose LJ added, 'It seems to me that if Parliament had intended to confer a power to disburse money for unsound developmental purposes, it could have been expected to say so expressly.' The grant money was supplied from other governmental sources. Given the wide generality of the statutory powers, the court's decision was remarkable.

Thirdly, in *R. v. Director of Passenger Rail Franchising ex parte Save Our Railways*[67] the question was whether, in specifying minimum service levels for railway passenger services about to be privatized, the director had complied with a statutory direction given to him by the Secretary of State for Trans-

---

66. *R. v. Secretary of State for Foreign Affairs ex parte World Development Movement Ltd.* [1995] 1 WLR 386.
67. *The Times*, 18 December 1995.

port. The direction was that the specifications were 'to be based on that being provided by British Rail immediately prior to franchising, taking into account the existence of and justification for seasonal variations in service schedules'.

The director issued Passenger Service Requirements (PSRs) which franchisees had to agree to provide. A number of applicants sought judicial review, including members of the travelling public whom the court recognized as 'plainly' having sufficient interest to apply.[68]

As Sir Thomas Bingham MR said in the Court of Appeal, 'based on' was not a term of art and permitted some latitude. It was obvious that not every train timetabled by British Rail need continue to run. But the changes must be 'marginal, not significant or substantial' and, in some of the PSRs before the court, this principle was infringed. The applicants pointed out, for example, that during weekday peak hours the minimum level of services at Thorpe Bay, Southend Central and Leigh on Sea were specified at, respectively, 55 per cent, 50 per cent and 41 per cent of the current BR service.

The Court of Appeal found that in some instances the director had failed to comply with the direction given him by the Secretary of State. In the event administrative changes were made by the minister which effectively reinstated the status quo.

The Fares Fair litigation ·

The decision of the House of Lords in *R v. Greater London Council ex parte Bromley London Borough Council* (1981),[69] confirming that of the Court of Appeal, has been widely regarded as a political decision, no doubt because it gave a ruling in an acutely political controversy. Both the ruling itself and the judicial reasoning adopted by the Court of Appeal and the House of Lords exemplify what is meant by the politics of the judiciary. The case is of great importance and interest because it illuminates the weaknesses inherent in the role of

68. See p. 114.
69. [1983] 1 AC 768; also known as *Bromley v. GLC.*

the judiciary when required to adjudicate in such matters.

In July 1981, the GLC passed a resolution implementing a commitment in the election manifesto of the Labour party to reduce fares charged by the London Transport Executive (LTE) by 25 per cent and to meet this cost (some £69m) issued a supplementary precept for rates of 6.1p in the £ to all London boroughs. In addition this policy resulted in the GLC losing some £50m of rate support grant from the government. Bromley London Borough Council applied to the High Court to quash the supplementary rate as *ultra vires*.

Under the Transport (London) Act 1969, the GLC was placed (by section 1) under the general duty to develop policies, and to encourage, organize and, where appropriate, to carry out measures, which would promote the provision of integrated, efficient and economic transport facilities and services for Greater London. The LTE consisted of persons appointed by the GLC with the function of implementing the policies of the GLC (section 4). The GLC was empowered by the Act to make grants to the LTE for any purpose (section 3), and the GLC intended in this way to reimburse the LTE for the revenue lost by the fares reduction and so enable the LTE to balance its books, this being an obligation placed on the LTE 'so far as practicable'. Subject to that obligation, the LTE was under a duty to exercise and perform its functions, in accordance with principles laid down or approved by the GLC, in such manner as, and with due regard to efficiency, economy and safety of operation, to provide or secure the provision of such public passenger transport services as best met the needs for the time being of Greater London (section 5). If the LTE accounts showed a deficit, the GLC was required to take such action as appeared necessary and appropriate to enable the LTE to balance its books (section 7(6)). Additionally the GLC was empowered to give the LTE general directions, and the approval of the GLC was required for the general level and structure of fares to be charged by the LTE (section 11).

The Divisional Court of the Queen's Bench Division which first heard the action refused Bromley's application, but the Court of Appeal and the House of Lords upheld it and quashed the precept and so the scheme.

The five Law Lords were Wilberforce, Diplock, Keith,

Scarman, and Brandon. All agreed that the GLC's power to make grants to the LTE included a large degree of discretion to supplement revenue received by the LTE from fares, including anticipated or prospective revenue deficits. But they put limitations on this discretion. All except Lord Diplock founded their decision on the ground that the LTE was under a general duty to run its operations on ordinary business principles and that this had been breached by the reduction of fares without regard to those principles. All except Lord Diplock (and in this he positively disagreed) held that the GLC had to have regard, when making a grant, to the LTE's obligation to run its operations so far as practicable on a break-even basis; so the GLC could make grants to the LTE only to make good unavoidable losses and not to further a particular social policy. All except Lord Keith also held that the GLC was under a fiduciary duty to its ratepayers which they had breached by the scheme, Lord Diplock particularly emphasizing the loss of rate support grant, and that they had acted thriftlessly.[70]

Much argument centred on the proper meanings to be attached to particular words such as 'economic' and on the recent history of transport legislation. But the concept of the fiduciary duty said to be owed by the GLC to its ratepayers was most widely emphasized by their Lordships. It is a judge-made concept and wholly imprecise. Lord Scarman, for example, rejected the GLC's interpretation of the 1969 Act on the ground that it 'would make mincemeat of the fiduciary duty owed to the ratepayers'. If Parliament had intended to depart from the break-even basis, he argued, this would have been enacted expressly in Part 1 of the Act where the general duties of the policy-maker, the GLC, were set; and added: 'But section 1(1) says nothing to suggest the exclusion of the fiduciary duty to the ratepayers.' The answer is, of course, that 'Parliament' never thought about the fiduciary duty at all. And this for the very good reason that the only relevant decision on the fiduciary duty – *Prescott v. Birmingham*[71] – had been immediately negatived by Parliament[72] in its application to the power of local transport authorities to fix the level of fares.

70. See M. Loughlin. *Legality and Locality* (1996) pp. 231–7.
71. [1955] Ch. 210.
72. By Public Service Vehicles (Travel Concessions) Act 1955.

The doctrine of the fiduciary duty, being judge-made, is capable of extended application as the courts please. In this case, the Law Lords chose to say that the GLC had not adequately taken into account the interests of the ratepayers and that the interests of the users of public transport had been unduly preferred.[73] Such an argument can logically be applied whenever public authorities spend the ratepayers' (or the taxpayers') money to further some statutory purpose. Particular public expenditure can always be criticized on the ground that it is excessive or wrongly directed, whether on defence or education or the building of motorways or any other public service. The constitutional reply is that public authorities, being directly or indirectly elected, are the representatives of the public interest and that their function is precisely that of making such decisions. The criticism is then seen as being political and if the electors of Greater London disapprove of what is done in their name by their representatives, the remedy lies in their hands at the next election. Nor is this merely constitutional or political theory, divorced from reality, for without doubt the election in 1985 for the GLC would have turned very largely on this issue and on the view taken of the controversial Labour administration at County Hall during its four years in office. It is surely no more the function of the judiciary to tell the GLC where the public interest lay in its spending of public money than it is the function of the judiciary to make similar judgments about spending by the departments of the central government. The application of the doctrine of the fiduciary duty in this case was gross interference by the judiciary in the exercise of political responsibility of an elected local authority.

There remains, however, the much more substantial argument that the GLC had exceeded its statutory powers as laid down in the Transport (London) Act 1969.

We may take Lord Wilberforce's argument as typical of the Lords' approach. He emphasized sections 5 and 7 as 'critical'. Section 5 provided that, subject always to section 7(3), it was the general duty of the LTE to exercise and perform their

73. *Cf. Pickwell v. Camden LBC* [1983] 1 All ER 602; *R. v. Greenwich LBC ex parte Cedar Transport, The Times*, 3 August 1983.

functions with due regard to efficiency, economy and safety of operation. He said that those last three sets of words 'point rather more clearly than does section 1 in the direction of running on business-like or commercial lines'. And, he said, the word 'economy' prevented the LTE from conducting its undertakings on other than economic considerations. He called the initial words of section 5 important as drawing attention to the 'paramount' financing provisions of section 7(3).

This section 7(3) required the LTE so to perform their functions as to ensure so far as practicable that at the end of each accounting period the aggregate of the net balance of the consolidated revenue account of the LTE and of their general reserve was such as might be approved by the GLC; and that if, at the end of any accounting period, the aggregate showed a deficit, the amount properly available to meet changes to revenue account in the next following accounting period should exceed those charges by at least the amount of that deficit. In other words, the LTE was to balance its books taking one year with the next. Further, under section 7(6), the GLC was required to have regard to section 7(3) and, where there was a deficit, the GLC was to take such action as appeared to the GLC necessary and appropriate to enable the LTE to comply with the requirements of section 7(3). As Lord Wilberforce said, the GLC might direct fares to be raised or services to be adjusted; or might make a grant to the LTE. Lord Wilberforce read this as meaning that the GLC could not exercise its powers 'unless and until' the LTE had carried out its duty. 'It appears to me clear', he said, 'that neither the LTE in making its proposals, nor the GLC in accepting them, could have power totally to disregard any responsibility for ensuring, so far as practicable, that outgoings are met by revenue, and that the LTE runs its business on economic lines.'

The alternative view is that 'revenue account' did not mean internally generated revenue only but included GLC grants. This is reinforced if the intention of Parliament in passing the act was that deficits on internally generated revenue would most likely be incurred, not merely casually, but deliberately as a consequence of treating transport as a social service. This view argued that section 7 was meant as an accounting section only and contained only a prohibition against annual accumulation deficits. The GLC was meant to be the dominant authority (see section 1), with the LTE as its instrument, and the power of the GLC to make grants to the LTE 'for any purpose' was strong evidence of this.

Lord Wilberforce answered this alternative view in these words:

> There is indeed, and has been for some years, discussion on the political level as to whether, and to what extent, public transport, particularly in capital cities, should be regarded, and financed, as a social service, out of taxation whether national or local. We cannot take any position in this argument; we must recognize that it exists. But I am unable to see, however carefully I reread the 1969 Act, that Parliament had in that year taken any clear stance on it.

The other Law Lords (Lord Diplock excepted) also placed great reliance on section 7(3) and correspondingly less on sections 1 and 3.

The GLC, bloody but unbowed, next produced a new scheme. This directed the LTE to reduce fares by 25 per cent and involved a grant to be made to the LTE to meet the resulting deficit on revenue account. The LTE objected to the direction on the ground that it failed to have regard to the LTE's financial duty under section 7(3) to break even so far as is practicable.[74]

Kerr L J said that some of the public comments on *Bromley v. GLC* gave the misleading impression that the judgments in the Court of Appeal and the House of Lords were designed to thwart the wishes of the majority on the GLC for political motives. 'Such reactions,' he said, 'whether based on ignorance or whatever, can only be described as utter rubbish ... It is to be hoped that nothing like that will happen again.'

All three judges in the Divisional Court (the others were Glidewell J and Nolan J) found the speeches of the Law Lords in *Bromley v. GLC* not easy to understand and impossible to reduce to agreed principles. As Mr George Cunningham MP

---

74. *R. v. LTE ex parte GLC* [1983] 1 QB 484.

said in the House of Commons on 22 December 1981, referring to those speeches:

> Each of the five judgments rambles over the territory in what can only be called a head-scratching way, making it impossible for the consumer of the judgment to know at the end just what the law is held to be, except negatively, and then only negatively on a few points. When one puts the five judgments together, the effect is chaos.[75]

The Divisional Court upheld the scheme adopted by the GLC but the ground on which they did so seemed to be no more than that 'since the LTE could exercise its function to balance its revenue account by a grant from the GLC, a policy that reduced fares by means of such a grant was not unlawful'. Those words are taken from the headnote in the Law Reports and seem a fair if wholly circular summary. To this was added the proviso that the GLC had not acted arbitrarily and had considered both its duties to the ratepayers and the statutory duties imposed by the 1969 Act on it and on the LTE.[76] This reinforces the view that what upset the Court of Appeal and the House of Lords in *Bromley v. GLC* was, above all, the way in which the Labour majority went about implementing their election promises rather than their statutory powers to do so. Local authorities would be well advised in future to preface all their decisions with the words: 'Having had regard to all relevant matters and having disregarded all irrelevant matters, and having considered the interests of all those likely to be affected, *resolved that*' etc.

When all this has been said, it is still very difficult to see how the Divisional Court in *R. v. LTE ex parte GLC* managed to come down in favour of the GLC in the face of the unanimous decision of the Law Lords. That decision was based primarily not on procedural defects but on interpretations of the words of the statute and on the notion of the fiduciary duty. The new scheme, upheld by the Divisional Court in the later case, was made under the same statute and did not appreciably

75. 15 HC Deb. col. 905.
76. See Transport Act 1983.

hold a different balance between ratepayers and transport users. The decision of the Divisional Court bears the marks of a rescue operation, seeking to save some sanity for transport policy in London.

Local policy

In *Wheeler v. Leicester City Council*, the City Council (which had adopted an anti-apartheid policy) banned the Leicester rugby club from using a council recreation ground because three members of the club had joined an English touring side to South Africa. The majority of the Court of Appeal held that the council was entitled to have regard to the need to promote good race relations under the Race Relations Act 1976. But the House of Lords held that in the absence of any infringement of the law or any improper conduct by the club the banning was unreasonable and a breach of the council's duty to act fairly, hence a procedural impropriety and a misuse of statutory powers.[77]

Similarly where a local authority, as owner of a pleasure ground, told the organizers of a community festival that 'no political activity whatsoever' was to take place, this was held to be so ill-defined as to be meaningless and incapable of reasonable compliance.[78]

Somerset County Council which had acquired land for the statutory purpose of the 'benefit, improvement or development of their area' decided on 4 August 1993 by 6 votes to 22: 'This Council, as landowners, with immediate effect, resolves to ban the hunting of deer with hounds on the County Council owned land at Over Stowey Customs Common.' The motive of the majority was to prevent what they considered to be a cruel sport. Mr Justice Laws held that the question of cruelty was irrelevant to a consideration of what was for the benefit of the area and quashed the council's decision. The majority

77. [1985] 3 WLR 335.
78. *R. v. Barnet LBC ex parte Johnson* (1980) 88 LGR 73; compare *R. v. Hammersmith and Fulham LBC ex parte Earls Court Ltd.*, *The Times*, 15 July 1993.

of the Court of Appeal upheld the judge's decision on the ground that the council had failed to appreciate that its powers were limited by the statutory purposes, though the cruelty argument was not necessarily irrelevant to a consideration of those purposes.[79]

Local government finance

During the 1980s the Thatcher administrations sought strictly to control spending by local authorities.[80] The introduction of the new block grant system under the Local Government, Planning and Land Act 1980 resulted in one hiccough for the minister when the Divisional Court held that he had not listened to further representations when he should have done.[81] But attempts in the Court of Appeal to set aside ministerial decisions on the payments of rate support grants on more precise grounds failed.[82]

A frontal attack by Hackney London Borough Council also failed when the court rejected the argument that restrictions on the council's expenditure meant it could no longer reasonably discharge its statutory duties.[83]

These cases forced the courts to consider where to draw the line between intervening in the public interest and effectively transferring the decision-making powers from local authorities to judges. In *R. v. Secretary of State for the Environment ex parte Nottinghamshire County Council*,[84] the Law Lords limited their jurisdiction in such matters of public financial administration to exceptional circumstances where the minister could be shown to have acted in bad faith or with an improper motive

79. *R. v. Somerset CC ex parte Fewings* [1995] 3 All ER 20.

80. See generally M. Loughlin, *Legality and Locality* (1996), a comprehensive survey of the role of law in central–local relations.

81. *R. v. Secretary of State for the Environment ex parte Brent LBC* [1982] 2 WLR 693.

82. *R. v. Secretary of State for the Environment ex parte Hackney LBC and Camden LBC* [1984] 1 All ER 956.

83. *R. v. Secretary of State for the Environment ex parte Hackney LBC*, *The Times*, 26 March 1984.

84. [1986] 2 WLR 1.

resulting in unfairness amounting to an abuse of power. But where a rating authority had a statutory power – but no duty – to refund rates overpaid by mistake, the Law Lords ordered repayment where the reasons given by the authority for its refusal to repay were held not to be valid.[85]

Restrictions on spending and on the raising of local revenue led to local authorities seeking ways around the legislation by embarking on 'creative accounting' to maximise their entitlement to government grants and to avoid financial penalties imposed for overspending. The London Borough of Hammersmith and Fulham, among many other local authorities, entered into a series of transactions with various banks in the swaps market in which two borrowers, one subject to a floating rate of interest and the other to a fixed rate, agree to exchange interest rate payments. By this means local authorities were able to turn a portion of their fixed-rate loans from the Public Works Loan Board into a floating rate debt and so avoid the complex rules limiting their borrowing power.[86] If their speculations were profitable, depending on the movements of interest rates, the exercise would generate more income. However, when interest rates began to rise in the late 1980s, profits turned into losses.

The question then arose whether these transactions were within the legal powers of local authorities. Put simply, one view was that the swaps were lawful provided they were part of a strategy of interest rate management but unlawful and beyond the powers of the local authority if the object was to trade for profit. The auditor for Hammersmith and Fulham in May 1989 applied to the Divisional Court seeking a declaration that certain items of account in Hammersmith's funds were unlawful. The declaration was granted but the Court of Appeal reversed the decision. The House of Lords reinstated the decision of the Divisional Court. Finally the question was whether, within the terms of section 111(1) of the Local Government Act 1972, a swap transaction was calculated to facilitate or was conducive or incidental to the discharge of

---

85. *R. v. Tower Hamlets LBC ex parte Chetnik Developments* [1988] 2 WLR 654.
86. See Loughlin (Note 80) chap. 6.

local authority functions. The Law Lords held it was not.[87]

The paradoxical consequence of such decisions on the financial position of local authorities who engage in such manoeuvres is best shown by the case of *Crédit Suisse v. Allerdale BC*.[88] The local authority wanted to borrow money to provide a leisure pool complex and related time-share accommodation in Keswick. A company was formed consisting of three members of the borough council to borrow £6 million, repayment being guaranteed by the council. In 1986, the bank Crédit Suisse agreed to advance the money which was to be wholly repayable by 1996. The sale of time-share units failed and the council could not make the repayments due to start in 1989. The company was put into voluntary liquidation and the bank sought repayment from the council. The council refused to honour its guarantee, contending that it had never had power to give the guarantee and so could not be held liable for its default.

The Court of Appeal agreed with the borough council. Although the council had statutory powers to provide swimming pools, the court held that the company was not the agent of the council; and that the time-share accommodation was not authorized by statute. So the council was able to avoid liability by pleading its own illegality.

In a parallel case, where the local authority established a property company to purchase properties to enable the local authority to discharge its statutory duty to house the homeless, the collapse of the property market meant that the local authority could not finance loan repayments to Crédit Suisse. Again it was held that the bank could not recover its loss.[89]

The Local Government Finance Act 1988 imposed a duty on local authorities to calculate how much they needed to raise by way of the poll tax. The Act empowered the Secretary of State to put a limit on the amount if in his opinion the amount proposed to be raised was 'excessive', according to principles which were to be the same for all authorities falling within

87. *Hazell v. Hammersmith and Fulham LBC* [1990] 2 WLR 17, 1038; [1991] 2 WLR 372.
88. [1996] 3 WLR 894.
89. *Crédit Suisse v. Waltham Forest LBC*, [1996] 3 WLR 943.

the same class. In June 1990, the minister proposed to 'cap' nineteen Labour authorities in this way. They argued that the principles he adopted had been politically motivated and should have had regard to the spending needs of each authority. The House of Lords rejected this and held that the minister was entitled to decide what was meant by 'excessive' and what principles to apply.[90] On the other hand, when Lambeth in March 1990 set its poll tax requirement on an assumption that 90 per cent of those liable would pay, and the minister fixed a lower requirement and the council set a revised charge but assumed that only 85 per cent would pay, the Court of Appeal held it was entitled to do this so long as it did so on the basis of the information it had in March.[91]

Homelessness

Under the Housing (Homeless Persons) Act 1977,[92] local authorities in certain circumstances become bound to provide accommodation where applicants have a priority need and have not become homeless intentionally. In *Cocks v. Thanet DC*,[93] the House of Lords made clear that those aggrieved by local authority decisions must proceed by way of judicial review and could not use procedures available in private law between landlord and tenant. This protected what Lord Bridge called the safeguards built into the judicial review procedure which protected from 'harassment' public authorities on whom Parliament imposed a duty. He referred particularly to the need, under judicial review procedure, to obtain leave to apply on the

90. *R. v. Secretary of State for the Environment ex parte Hammersmith and Fulham LBC* [1990] 3 WLR 898.

91. *R. v. Lambeth LBC ex parte Secretary of State for the Environment, The Times*, 9 October 1990.

92. Now the Housing Act 1985. For an account of the application of the provisions see Ian Loveland *Housing Homeless Persons* (1995), to which I am indebted.

93. [1982] 3 All ER 1135 following *O'Reilly v. Mackman* (above, Note 19). In *R. v. Northavon DC ex parte Palmer* (1995) 27 HLR 576, the Court of Appeal held that damages could not be awarded for breach of a local housing authority's duty under the homelessness provisions of the Housing Act 1985.

basis of sworn evidence, on the court's discretionary control of both discovery of documents and cross-examination, on the capacity of the court to act with the utmost speed when necessary and on the avoidance of the temptation for the court to substitute its own decision of fact for that of the housing authority. As early as 1979, Lord Widgery CJ was emphasizing the limits of judicial intervention in this field.[94]

The government issued a Code of Guidance which widened the provisions of the Act to the advantage of the homeless.[95] However Lord Denning was quick to point out that although local authorities had to have regard to the code, they could depart from it if they thought fit.[96]

As finally drafted, the statute presented the courts with considerable scope for interpretation. Its provisions were politically controversial, some of its opponents seeing the Act as a charter for 'the rent dodger, for the scrounger, and for the encouragement of the home leaver'.[97] The case law has been deep and wide, the decisions sometimes favouring the homeless and sometimes enabling local housing authorities to avoid 'harassment'.

A principal source of litigation arose from provisions designed to exclude from the benefits of the legislation any person who became homeless 'intentionally' by 'deliberately' acting or failing to act, as a consequence of which he ceased to occupy accommodation which was available for his occupation and which it would have been reasonable for him to continue to occupy. 'Deliberately' was interpreted to govern only the act or omission rather than to imply positive intention, so broadening the category of those held to have acted 'intentionally'[98] and this was supported by the Court of Appeal in *Devenport v. Salford CC.*[99] But a statutory provision which protected applicants acting 'in good faith' was to be interpreted

94. *R. v. Bristol City Council ex parte Browne* [1979] 1 WLR 1437.
95. See generally Lorraine Thompson, *An Act of Compromise* (1988).
96. *De Falco v. Crawley BC* [1980] QB 460.
97. Mr Rees-Davies MP 926 HC Deb. col. 972 (18 February 1977), cited in Lavender, *op. cit.*, p. 70.
98. *Robinson v. Torbay BC* [1982] 1 All ER 726.
99. (1983) 8 HLR 54.

broadly.[100] Failure to pay rent because of poverty was held by the Court of Appeal as not necessarily conclusive evidence of a deliberate act showing intentionality.[101]

In many of the cases arising out of homelessness, local authorities have sought to interpret their statutory obligations narrowly. Especially in London, the dimensions of the social problems far exceeded the available resources, both physical and financial. So the courts were called on to decide whether the authorities had correctly interpreted their duties. For example, in 1983 it was said that even where the husband had been violent, it might be reasonable for the wife to continue to reside in the matrimonial home and to seek a court order restraining his violence or barring him from the home, and in these circumstances the authority's duty would be to advise the applicant so to do, not to accommodate her as a homeless person.[102] So also, where an impoverished family left their accommodation on receipt of a distress warrant for rent arrears rather than wait for an eviction order, they were held by the House of Lords to have become homeless intentionally and this encouraged local housing authorities to require court orders before accepting such applicants as homeless.[103]

If 'intentional' homelessness, real or implied, was ascribed to one partner or spouse, was the other precluded from seeking accommodation? In *R. v. North Devon DC ex parte Lewis*[104] it was held that she was precluded when there was evidence that she had acquiesced in her partner's deliberate and intentional act. From the decision in *R. v. Swansea CC ex parte Thomas*,[105] it appears that there can be such acquiescence even when one of the couple is in prison.

100. *R. v. Hammersmith and Fulham LBC ex parte Lusi* (1991) 23 HLR 260; *R. v. Tower Hamlets LBC ex parte Rouf* (1991) 23 HLR 460; *R. v. Exeter CC ex parte Tranckle* (1993) 26 HLR 244.
101. *R. v. Wandsworth LBC ex parte Hawthorne* [1994] 1 WLR 1442.
102. *R. v. Wandsworth LBC ex parte Nimako-Boateng* (1983) 11 HLR 95; but see Housing Act 1985 s.58(3) and *R. v. Broxbourne BC ex parte Willmoth* (1989) 22 HLR 118.
103. *Din v. Wandsworth LBC* (1981) 1 HLR 73; but this did not require former licensees to continue in occupation as trespassers pending a court order: *R. v. Surrey Heath BC ex parte Li* (1984) 16 HLR 79.
104. [1981] 1 WLR 328.
105. (1983) 9 HLR 64.

Partly because of the controversies surrounding the Act – both during its passage through Parliament and later – and so of the need for compromises, terms were left undefined. Standards, both of existing accommodation and of that offered by local authorities, were left to be determined, or to depend on the locality. Amongst early cases was *ex parte Miles*[106] where a husband, pregnant wife and two children lived in a twenty-foot by ten-foot rat-infested hut with no mains services. The court found that this accommodation was 'on the borderline' of being suitable for human habitation but acceptable for the purposes of the Act until the third child was born, when it would not be reasonable to expect the family to remain. In *ex parte Fisher*[107] the applicant lived on a one-cabined boat, with her two children and two friends, without bath, shower, WC, electricity, hot water system or kitchen sink. The local authority's decision not to re-house the applicant was quashed.

A leading case in 1986 indicated a tightening of the requirements to be met by applicants under the legislation. In *Puhlhofer v. Hillingdon London Borough Council*,[108] a married couple with two young children lived in one room at a guesthouse. No cooking or laundry facilities were provided and no meals except breakfast. They applied to the local authority for accommodation as homeless persons, but were rejected on the ground that they had accommodation. At first instance, the judge held that the accommodation had to be appropriate and that no reasonable authority could have come to that conclusion in this case. But the Court of Appeal and the House of Lords supported the local authority. Lord Brightman considered that 'great restraint' should be exercised in giving leave to proceed by judicial review, and that he was troubled at 'the prolific use' of the procedure in these cases, saying:

> The plight of the homeless is a desperate one ... and commands the deepest sympathy. But it is not, in my opinion, appropriate that the remedy of judicial review, which is a discretionary remedy, should be made use of

106. *R. v. South Herefordshire DC ex parte Miles* (1983) 17 HLR 82.
107. *R. v. Preseli DC ex parte Fisher* (1984) 17 HLR 147; and see *R. v. Westminster CC ex parte Ali* (1983) 11 HLR 85.
108. [1986] 1 All ER 467.

to monitor the actions of local authorities under the Act
save in the exceptional case ... I express the hope that
there will be a lessening in the number of challenges
which are mounted against local authorities who are
endeavouring, in extremely difficult circumstances, to
perform their duties under the [Homeless Persons] Act
with due regard for all their other housing problems.

Lord Brightman said that the Act was intended to provide for
the homeless a lifeline of last resort, not to enable them to
make inroads into the local authority's waiting list of applicants
for housing. Some inroads there probably were bound to be,
but in the end the local authority would have to balance the
priority needs of the homeless on the one hand and the legitimate aspirations of those on their housing waiting list on the
other hand. Brightman limited judicial review in these cases
to abuse of power, e.g. bad faith, a mistake in construing the
limits of power, a procedural irregularity or 'unreasonableness
verging on absurdity'.

In 1986, it was provided that an applicant should not be
treated as having accommodation unless it was such that it
would be reasonable for him to continue to occupy it. In
determining what was reasonable, regard might be had to the
general housing circumstances prevailing in the local authority
to whom the application was made.[109] Where an applicant volun-
tarily left accommodation but had then acquired temporary
accommodation, the courts interpreted the legislation so as to
entitle the local authority to relate back to the first accommodation and so to find that he was intentionally homeless. And this
was applicable where the first accommodation was in another
country. So where Bangladeshis who spent periods of time in
the United Kingdom interspersed with periods in Bangladesh,
brought their families to the United Kingdom, took temporary
accommodation, and then applied to be treated as homeless
persons, it was held that the local authority was entitled to
refuse them. In considering whether it was reasonable for an
applicant to continue to occupy accommodation in another

109. Housing and Planning Act 1986 section 14 amending Housing Act
1985 s.58 by insertion of subs. (2A) and (2B); see *R. v. Kensington and
Chelsea RLBC ex parte Hammell* [1989] 2 WLR 90.

country, the local authority might take into account the custom and lifestyle in that country. The fact that the authority disregarded certain factors in that country (for example, the limited availability of welfare benefits or the poor prospects for employment) could not ground an application for judicial review as they were not factors which the authority was obliged to take into account. Lloyd LJ referred to Lord Brightman's concern in *Puhlhofer* at the 'prolific use of judicial review' in these homelessness cases. Despite the legislative amendments in 1986, that observation, he said, was 'as pertinent now as it ever was'. The Court of Appeal supported this view, Lord Justice Purchas saying that it was 'clearly established' that the circumstances in which the court would intervene by judicial review were 'severely circumscribed', though remitting the cases to the local authority for them to state correctly their reasons for determining that it was reasonable to expect the applicants to continue to occupy their settled accommodation in Bangladesh.[110]

In a remarkable case, very much of our times, the applicants lived in Belfast and had been guilty of criminal and anti-social activities. Their neighbours sought the help of the IRA (which adopted a vigilante role in the area), who told the applicants that unless they left Northern Ireland within seventy-two hours they would all be killed. They came to Hammersmith in London and applied for accommodation as homeless persons. The court held that they were intentionally homeless and so disqualified.[111]

The complexities of these situations are shown by the case of an applicant and his family who left what was described as an 'overcrowded tin or galvanised structure with no basic amenities' in Bangladesh and who were treated as intentionally homeless by one London borough (who considered that it was reasonable for them to continue to occupy that accommoda-

---

110. *R. v. Tower Hamlets LBC ex parte Monaf* (1987) 19 HLR 577 and (1988) 20 HLR 529; but the local authority must have a proper administrative system for considering applications: *R. v. Camden LBC ex parte Gillan* (1989) 21 HLR 114; and see *R. v. Kensington and Chelsea LBC ex parte Bayani* (1990) 22 HLR 406.

111. *R. v. Hammersmith and Fulham LBC ex parte P.* (1990) 22 HLR 21; *R. v. Newham LBC ex parte McIlroy* (1991) 23 HLR 570.

tion) but not intentionally homeless by a second London borough who referred the applicant back to the first.[112] The Court of Appeal found that the second authority's decision was deeply flawed by failing to take into account relevant matters, including the first authority's reasons for deciding that the applicant had become homeless intentionally; the referral was quashed.

In *ex parte Castelli* the two applicants were European Union nationals who had entered the UK lawfully looking for work or self-employment but who had become ill, being HIV positive. One of them had been told by the Home Office to make arrangements to leave the UK, but that he would not be forced to go; for the other no determination or other expression of view had been made by the Home Office. Neither had committed any offence and the Court of Appeal held that the local authority was obliged to offer them temporary accommodation under the Act.[113]

It had been the practice of local housing authorities to discharge their duty to the homeless by providing temporary accommodation pending an offer of suitable 'permanent' housing which was 'indefinite' in period.[114] The Code of Guidance from the department also spoke of a duty imposed on the local authority to secure 'permanent' accommodation. Other cases referred to 'settled' or 'long term' accommodation. In *Puhlhofer*[115] Lord Brightman summarized the duties as being to provide 'indefinite accommodation if not intentionally homeless, temporary if intentionally homeless'.

When homelessness legislation was introduced in 1977 it had been expected that only 'a tiny minority' would be served by it. In practice, said the government, 'as the courts have interpreted the legislation', the statutorily homeless received priority in the allocation of life-long tenancies over others on the waiting lists of local authorities, especially in some London boroughs. The government announced in June 1995 that it would introduce legislation to change the system, requiring

112. *R. v. Newham LBC ex parte Tower Hamlets LBC* (1990) 23 HLR 62.
113. *R. v. Westminster CC ex parte Castelli* (1996) 28 HLR 616.
114. *R. v. Camden LBC ex parte Wait* (1986) 18 HLR 434; also *R. v. Brent LBC ex parte Macwan* (1994) 26 HLR 528.
115. See p. 140.

local housing authorities to maintain registers and provide allocation schemes to ensure that houses went to those with the 'best claim', accommodation for the homeless being restricted to periods of not less than a year and reconsidered after two years.[116]

What happened next amounted to one of the most remarkable reversals of judicial precedent and accepted administrative practice in recent years, in effect implementing government future policy as announced in the White Paper of the previous month.

In July 1995, the Law Lords in *R. v. Brent LBC ex parte Awua*[117] reinterpreted the statute so as to produce a new set of rules. In 1991 Ms Awua applied to Tower Hamlets Borough Council for housing as a homeless person and was accepted as such. In January 1992 she was provided with temporary accommodation leased from a private landlord by the council, and in March was offered a permanent home which she refused. As a result, in accordance with declared council policy, she was given notice to quit her temporary accommodation. Ms Awua then applied to Brent Borough Council, but they concluded that she was intentionally homeless because of her refusal. They were supported by the Court of Appeal who held that a person remained homeless until acquiring a 'settled residence' or home; that temporary accommodation and settled residence were opposite sides of the same coin, but it was possible to have a settled residence without being in permanent accommodation.

On appeal, Lord Hoffman spoke for all five Law Lords in upholding the Court of Appeal. But his judgment radically changed the understanding of the statute and of the earlier decisions. Lord Hoffman began by observing that the relevant sections of the act referred to 'accommodation' only, which could not be construed as 'a settled home'. The 1986 amendments ensured that 'accommodation' had to be that which it was reasonable for the applicant to continue to occupy, regard being had to the general circumstances prevailing in the district. So the statutory duty of the local housing authority was

116. *Our Future Homes* (Cm 2901).
117. [1995] 3 All ER 493.

to provide such suitable accommodation, but that did not import any requirement of permanence.

Overnight, thousands of tenants who believed they had secure accommodation for as long as they fulfilled their contractual obligations found that the period of their occupancy was for the local council to decide. And those seeking accommodation as homeless persons learnt that even where they were successful, their tenure would be reviewable at regular intervals thereafter.[118]

Education

Cases arising out of the obligations of local education authorities have resulted in an increasing number of applications for judicial review. In *R. v. Secretary of State for Education and Science ex parte Avon County Council*, the minister approved an application from a school for grant-maintained status outside the jurisdiction of the local authority, which contended that this rendered the reorganization of their schools no longer viable. The court quashed the minister's decision on the ground that he should have considered the school's application in the wider context and not only as it affected the particular school. The judge ordered the minister to reconsider his decision; he did so and reaffirmed it.

In subsequent proceedings the Court of Appeal held that in such circumstances the court could grant a stay of the minister's decision. A differently composed Court of Appeal rejected an appeal by the local authority on the substantive questions.[119] Lord Justice Nichols said that an application to the court for judicial review of the minister's decision was not the appropriate means by which the council should seek to ventilate or pursue its differences of opinion with the minister.

In *R. v. Inner London Education Authority ex parte Ali*[120] a parent failed to persuade the court that he should be awarded damages for the failure of the respondents to fulfil their

118. See now Housing Act 1996 Pt.VII to similar effect.
119. (1990) 88 LGR 716, 737.
120. *Independent*, 21 February 1990.

statutory duty to provide sufficient schools. For a period of months, several hundred school children – mostly Bangladeshi in origin – in the London Borough of Tower Hamlets had been without places, but the court held this did not mean that the respondents were in breach of their duty if they were taking steps to remedy the situation.

Changes in the status of schools required special procedures which created problems for the courts. Failure to consult local authorities was held not to invalidate a ministerial decision because, it was held, no unfairness had resulted.[121] This is an example of the exercise of judicial discretion which is frustrating for those parties who have established wrongdoing but are left with no remedy. Where a local authority failed to consult school governors when developing a strategy for dealing with falling school numbers, this was considered sufficient to invalidate the decision.[122]

The role of the courts was also central to the decision in *R. v. Governors of the Bishop Challoner R. C. School ex parte Choudhury*.[123] The school had an admissions policy which gave priority first to Roman Catholics and then to other Christians. In November 1990, in accordance with the Education Act 1980, the parents of two children, one Hindu and one Muslim, expressed a preference for the school. Section 6(2)(3)(a) of the Act imposed a duty to comply with parental preference unless compliance would prejudice the provision of efficient education or the efficient use of resources. In the year beginning September 1991, the school had more applicants than it could accommodate without prejudicing the provision of efficient education. Lord Browne-Wilkinson said:

> Shortly stated, the main issue is whether a school which is over-subscribed so that it cannot accept all the applications for admission can adopt religious criteria (i.e. criteria intended to preserve the character of the school) in selecting the successful applicants for admission and

121. *R. v. Secretary of State for Education and Science ex parte Inner London Education Authority, The Times*, 17 May 1990.

122. *R. v. Tameside MBC ex parte Governors of Audenshawe High School, The Times*, 27 June 1990.

123. [1992] 3 WLR 99.

thereby exempt itself under section 6(3)(a) from the duty under section 2 to give effect to the preferences expressed by parents whose children do not meet such criteria.

The House of Lords held that the school could properly adopt such criteria.

Where under the Education Act 1981, a local education authority makes an assessment of the special educational needs of a child, an elaborate process ensues giving rights to the parent of making representations and of appealing to a local committee and then to the Secretary of State. Much litigation has followed.[124] But as Schiemann J said in *ex parte R* (below), courts are reluctant to grant judicial review in cases which are essentially concerned with professional judgments with a number of variables in play. This raises the question already considered of how far the advice of experts which informs the decisions should be revealed. In *ex parte S*[125] the Court of Appeal said that the concept of fairness in this context required disclosure only in the most exceptional circumstances.

There are many other cases which in different ways touch on the education or care of children giving rise to possible applications for judicial review.[126] In this context, private law actions in tort were brought for breach of statutory duty and negligence in carrying out by or on behalf of local authorities functions relating to children.[127] One authority was alleged to have failed to identify the plaintiffs as being in need. In other cases a psychiatrist and a social worker were alleged to have misidentified a child abuser; the local council was alleged to have wrongly advised parents; a headmaster was alleged to have failed to use proper care in ascertaining a child's learning difficulties. In yet another, a wrong placement in special schools was alleged.

In such cases, the Law Lords are extremely reluctant to hold

124. More recently, see, for example, *R. v. Newham LBC ex parte R* [1995] ELR 156, *R. v. Hackney LBC ex parte GC* [1995] ELR 144, *R. v. Secretary of State for Education ex parte S* [1995] ELR 71.

125. See previous note.

126. See Paul Meredith, 'Judicial Review and Education', in B. Hadfield (ed.), *Judicial Review: A Thematic Approach* (1995).

127. *X v. Bedfordshire CC* [1995] 3 WLR 152.

the local authorities liable or to interfere with the exercise of statutory powers, especially where questions of policy arise.

Social services

The decision in *Lambeth LBC v. Secretary of State for Social Services*,[128] where Woolf J struck down the minister's decision to use his statutory powers to suspend the members of an area health authority and to appoint commissioners in their place, was strongly interventionist. The power of the minister arises under the National Health Service Act 1977 if he considers that by reason of an emergency it is necessary for a specified period to transfer functions from one body to another. The disagreement between the minister and the area health authority was caused by the overspending by the authority and its unwillingness to make economies. The court held that such a power could not be used, where there was no particular crisis and no specified power, so as to control the authority's financial affairs. The minister had a separate power, which he did not use, to issue directions to the authority. Woolf J referred to the *Tameside* decision[129] and to *ASLEF (No. 2)*.[130] 'There can be no question', he said, 'of my substituting my view of the facts for that of the Secretary of State.' He seems nevertheless to have come very close to substituting his view of the statutory power and the discretions within it for that of the minister.

In *R. v. Wandsworth LBC ex parte Beckwith*[131] a group of pensioners resisted the decision of the local authority to close old people's homes. The High Court judge held that the authority had a duty to provide at least one home for the elderly in need of care. But the Court of Appeal and the Law Lords disagreed and found that the authority was entitled to make arrangements under which all old people in its homes were

128. (1981) 79 LGR 61.
129. See pp. 109–10.
130. See p. 108.
131. [1996] 1 WLR 60. On the effect and status of ministerial 'guidance', see *R. v. Islington LBC ex parte Rixon, The Times*, 17 April 1996.

transferred to private homes. Section 7 of the Local Authority Social Services Act 1970 provides, 'Local authorities shall, in the exercise of their social service functions, including the exercise of any discretion conferred by any relevant enactment, act under the general guidance of the Secretary of State.' One piece of such guidance was, 'It is the view of the Department that the amendments introduced by the Act of 1948 by section of the Community Care (Residential Accommodation) Act 1992 will require authorities to make some provision for residential care.' Lord Hoffman disposed of this by saying, 'The opinion of the Department is entitled to respect, particularly since I assume that the Act was drafted upon its instructions. But in my view this statement is simply wrong.'

Under the Chronically Sick and Disabled Persons Act 1970, where a local authority was satisfied that it was necessary to meet the needs of a person, it was under a duty to make arrangements to do so. In *ex parte Mahfood*,[132] the Divisional Court held that a local authority when faced with governmental cuts in financial resources could not withdraw or fail to provide services to meet those needs simply on financial grounds. But in *ex parte Barry*[133] the Law Lords reversed this ruling and held that a local authority could take into account its financial resources when determining needs.[134]

Social security

The complexity of the social security regulations and the attempts, during the 1980s, by ministers to limit their applicability resulted in a series of judicial decisions. In 1985 regulations were held to be void as having no statutory authority where their purpose was to force able-bodied young people who lived on supplementary benefit to move from one area to

132. *R. v. Gloucestershire CC ex parte Mahfood, The Times*, 21 June 1995.
133. *R. v. Gloucestershire CC ex parte Barry, The Times*, 21 March 1997.
134. See also *R v. Cambridge Health Authority ex parte B* [1995] 2 All ER 129; p. 274.

another in search of employment.[135] But where thousands of claimants did not receive repayments to which they were entitled because of errors of local officials, the Court of Appeal held that the minister was not obliged to carry out a fullscale review of files.[136] Nor was he under a duty to appoint a sufficient number of adjudication officers to handle applications within a statutory period.[137]

The Social Security Act 1986 radically changed the law by requiring special or emergency needs, which had previously been dealt with at the discretion of local officers, to be met out of the Social Fund under directions and guidance from the minister who allocated funds to local offices. The minister purported to give guidance, the effect of which was that social fund officers must not make payments which would result in the budget being exceeded. The court held that the guidance was defective because it was couched in mandatory terms, and inconsistent with the intended flexible nature of the scheme. The court quashed decisions not to give furniture grants in two cases. But, in a third case, the court upheld a ministerial direction that no money was to be paid out for domestic assistance and the Court of Appeal confirmed this decision.[138]

A provision in the Act of 1986 required the minister to consult certain organizations before making regulations relating to housing benefit, unless the urgency of the matter made this inexpedient. The Law Lords found that the minister delayed consultation and that this had created the urgency for action. The minister was not entitled to rely on self-induced urgency.[139]

Another provision in that Act enabled overpayments to be

135. *R. v. Secretary of State for Social Services ex parte Cotton, The Times,* 5 August 1985 and 14 December 1985.

136. *R. v. Secretary of State for Social Services ex parte Child Poverty Action Group, The Times,* 8 August 1985.

137. *R. v. Secretary of State for Social Services ex parte Child Poverty Action Group* [1989] 1 All ER 1047.

138. *R. v. Social Security Fund Inspector ex parte Sherwin, Stitt and Roberts, The Times,* 23 February 1990; *R. v. Secretary of State for Social Services ex parte Stitt, Independent,* 6 July 1990.

139. *R. v. Secretary of State for Social Security ex parte Association of Metropolitan Authorities, The Times,* 23 July 1992.

recovered out of certain benefits to be prescribed. Ministerial regulations made under the act modified the statutory provision and extended its scope, but the Law Lords concluded that the modification was 'not so radical' as to be regarded as an excess of power by the minister.[140] Lord Keith justified what he called 'undoubtedly an innovation' by saying it was 'reasonable to suppose that Parliament was informed of the intention' and, if it was not, 'the matter would surely have been raised when the regulations were laid before Parliament under the negative resolution procedure'. On such shaky assumptions are some statutory interpretations based.

In *Chief Adjudication Officer v. Foster*,[141] a severely disabled single woman had claimed to be entitled to receive a premium payment, and argued that a regulation excluding this payment because she lived at home with her parents was invalid. An adjudicator and the local tribunal refused her claim but the Social Security Commissioner allowed her appeal on the ground that the regulation was ultra vires. The House of Lords, overruling the Court of Appeal, held that the commissioner had jurisdiction but, after recourse to Hansard, that the regulation was valid. The effect of the Court of Appeal's decision would have required the claimant to proceed by judicial review which would, as Lord Bridge said, have added to the already overburdened list of proceedings awaiting decision in the Divisional Court.

In 1996 regulations preventing asylum seekers from qualifying for benefit were invalidated by the Court of Appeal.[142]

---

140. *R. v. Secretary of State for Social Security ex parte Britnell* [1991] 1 WLR 198.

141. [1993] 1 All ER 705.

142. *R. v. Secretary of State for Social Security ex parte JCWI* (see p. 203).

5. Personal rights

Individual freedom

Traditionally, judges are thought of as the defenders of the rights of individuals from attack by public authorities. In recent years this tradition has been upheld only spasmodically.

In 1939 the government took powers by Defence Regulations to detain persons without trial but these powers were expressed in those regulations to be exercisable only 'if the Secretary of State has reasonable cause to believe' that a person had hostile associations. The use of the limiting adjective, one would have thought, clearly empowered the courts to review the reasonableness of the 'cause'. But the House of Lords in *Liversidge v. Anderson*[1] held otherwise. This was a considerable abdication by the courts, in circumstances of national emergency, of their controlling jurisdiction.

Yet this decision was also a rallying ground for those who believed that, especially where a man's personal freedom was involved, the powers of the executive should be strictly interpreted. For this was the case in which Lord Atkin, alone against such powerful colleagues as Lords Maugham, Macmillan, Wright and Romer, delivered the most highly influential minority opinion in the English courts of the twentieth century. In the course of his judgment he said:

> I view with apprehension the attitude of judges who on a mere question of construction when face to face with claims involving the liberty of the subject show themselves more executive minded than the executive. Their

---

1 . [1942] AC 206. See also *Greene v. The Secretary of State for Home Affairs* [1942] AC 284.

function is to give words their natural meaning, not, perhaps, in wartime leaning towards liberty, but following the dictum of Pollock CB in *Bowditch v. Balchin*[2] cited with approval by my noble and learned friend Lord Wright in *Barnard v. Gorman:*[3] 'In a case in which the liberty of the subject is concerned, we cannot go beyond the natural construction of the statute.' In this country, amid the clash of arms, the laws are not silent. They may be changed, but they speak the same language in war as in peace. It has always been one of the pillars of freedom, one of the principles of liberty for which on recent authority we are now fighting, that the judges are no respecters of persons and stand between the subject and any attempted encroachments on his liberty by the executive, alert to see that any coercive action is justified in law. In this case I have listened to arguments which might have been addressed acceptably to the Court of King's Bench in the time of Charles I.

Liversidge v. Anderson was a wartime case, and the powers of detention without trial (internment) were conferred on the executive under an express statutory provision which authorized the making of regulations 'for the detention of persons whose detention appears to the Secretary of State to be expedient in the interests of public safety or the defence of the realm'.[4] The comparable legislation passed for the purposes of the 1914—18 war contained no express powers authorizing internment but in *R. v. Halliday*[5] the majority in the House of Lords held that general words in the Defence of the Realm Act 1914 were sufficient, a view from which Lord Shaw dissented. In contrast, it was later held by Mr Justice Salter that a similar exercise of powers, this time to take property without payment of full compensation was illegal.[6] Here, as elsewhere, the courts seemed to be more concerned to protect property rights than

2 . (1850) 5 Ex. 378.
3 . [1941] AC 378, 393.
4 . Emergency Powers (Defence) Act 1939, section 1(2)(a). See R. J. Sharpe, *The Law of Habeas Corpus* (1976), especially pp. 89—124.
5 . [1917] AC 260.
6 . *National Breweries v. The King* [1920] 1 KB 854.

rights of personal freedom. In *R. v. Governor of Wormwood Scrubs Prison*[7] it was held by the Divisional Court that the internment powers extended to cover the situation in Ireland even after the war was over.

The decision of the majority in *Liversidge v. Anderson* effectively meant that the minister's order authorizing internment could not be questioned because the minister could not be required to show on what basis his order had been made. The general principle that this is the proper interpretation of the words 'If the minister has reasonable cause to believe' has been doubted[8] and two recent decisions in Northern Ireland courts have suggested that improper arrest or a failure to provide the internee with a statement of the material on which the internment was based is sufficient for the internment order to be set aside.[9]

However the majority decisions in *R. v. Halliday* and *Liversidge v. Anderson* were referred to with approval by Lord Denning in *R. v. Secretary of State for Home Affairs ex parte Hosenball*[10] in 1977, where an American journalist lost his appeal against deportation under the Immigration Act 1971. The decision to deport was challenged in the Court of Appeal on the ground that there had been a breach of the rules of natural justice in that the Home Secretary had refused to tell the appellant any of the details on the basis of which the Home Secretary had decided that the appellant was a security risk.

In a remarkable passage Lord Denning MR seemed to accept that the courts had no part to play because the government never erred. He said:

There is a conflict between the interests of national security on the one hand and the freedom of the individual on the other. The balance between these two is not for a court of law. It is for the Home Secretary. He is the person entrusted by Parliament with the task. In some parts of the world national security has on occasion been

7 . [1920] 2 KB 305.
8 . E.g., in *Nakkuda Ali v. Jayaratne* [1951] AC 66 and *Ridge v. Baldwin* [1964] AC 40.
9 . *Re McElduff* [1971] 23 NILQ 112; *Re Mackay* [1972] 23 NILQ 113.
10. [1977] 1 WLR 166.

used as an excuse for all sorts of infringements of individual liberty. But not in England. Both during the wars and after them successive ministers have discharged their duties to the complete satisfaction of the people at large. They have set up advisory committees to help them, usually with a chairman who has done everything he can to ensure that justice is done. They have never interfered with the liberty or the freedom of movement of any individual except where it is absolutely necessary for the safety of the state.

It is well known that unlawful detention may be challenged by means of an application for habeas corpus but the courts sometimes withhold that remedy for political reasons.

Dr Sharpe summarizes his extensive examination of the authorities on habeas corpus and other remedies thus:

This review of the authorities demonstrates that habeas corpus can be an effective remedy to control the exercise of the discretionary power, but that policy considerations may often make the courts reluctant to act. There are several habeas corpus cases which illustrate the ordinary rule of the reviewability of executive action and, most recently, the law of immigration has provided examples. On the other hand it is submitted that the cases which involve emergency powers indicate a reluctance on the part of the courts to use the remedy of habeas corpus to its full potential. Judicial innovation would not have been required to justify intervention in *Halliday* or in *Greene* and *Liversidge v. Anderson*. In each case, accepted principles of constitutional and administrative law were available and applicable. In *Halliday*, and almost certainly in *Greene* and in *Liversidge v. Anderson*, the legal arguments weighed against the result reached, and the judges acted on policy grounds.[11]

When it is remembered that habeas corpus is not a discretionary remedy, this amounts to saying that the judiciary, despite all the rhetoric which they pour out in praise of this ancient writ, are willing to deny it to an imprisoned applicant, who in law

11. R. J. Sharpe, *op. cit.*, pp. 123–4.

should be set free, because they consider that the politics of the situation entitle them to do so. This is not what is generally understood to be the function of the courts.

The great weight attached by the courts to claims of national security was shown in the unanimous decision of the House of Lords in *In re the Council of Civil Service Unions* (1984).[12] This was the GCHQ (Government Communications Headquarters) case where the government, without consulting the unions, introduced with immediate effect new conditions for civil servants at GCHO, the result of which was that they were no longer permitted to belong to national trade unions. The Law Lords held that normally the unions had a legitimate expectation that there would be prior consultations before such a change was made but that the requirements of national security overrode this. The argument first advanced by the Crown before Glidewell J was that previous disruptions caused by trade union activity made the change necessary, although there had been no such disruption during the twenty months preceding the change. The judge ruled in favour of the unions. Before the Court of Appeal, however, the Crown claimed that there had been no consultation because to have consulted would have made disruption more likely. The Law Lords were willing to accept that the Crown had to show there was some evidence to support the claim that the interests of national security must prevail. But it was apparent that they were willing also to accept very slight, even contradictory, evidence for this purpose. In 1987, the Divisional Court decided that it was not competent to set aside the Secretary of State's exclusion order made under the Prevention of Terrorism (Temporary Provisions) Act 1976, where he had refused to give his reasons for not revoking the order.[13]

The right to a jury selected at random has been under recent judicial scrutiny. In *R. v. Crown Court at Sheffield ex parte Brownlow*[14] two police officers were charged and committed

12. [1984] 3 All ER 935; compare *Secretary of State for Defence v. Guardian Newspapers Ltd* [1984] 3 WLR 986, see p. 253; *R. v. Secretary of State for Transport ex parte Greater London Council* [1985] 3 WLR 574.

13. *R. v. Secretary of State for the Home Department ex parte Stitt, Independent*, 3 February 1987.

14. [1980] 2 All ER 444.

for trial on counts of assault occasioning bodily harm. On an application by the prosecution, the Crown Court judge ordered that a copy of the panel from which the jury for the hearing would be drawn be supplied to the chief constable and that he supply the accused's solicitors and the prosecution with full details of criminal convictions recorded against any member of the panel. This might have included offences which would not normally disqualify a juror from service. In the Court of Appeal, Lord Denning MR strongly condemned this practice of jury vetting and called it 'unconstitutional'. Shaw L J echoed this opinion. The majority of the Court of Appeal held, however, that they had no jurisdiction to revoke the judge's order and when the chief constable applied to the judge for revocation, the judge declined to do so but amended his order only so as to exclude spent convictions.

Three months later, in *R. v. Mason*,[15] a differently composed Court of Appeal expressed very different views. Lawton L. J. said that if, when a panel was scrutinized, convictions were revealed which did not amount to disqualifications, 'there was no reason why information about such convictions should not be passed to prosecuting counsel' (but not to the defence), who could then ensure that that juror would not be selected to hear the case. 'The practice of the past was founded on common sense. Any juror might be qualified to sit on juries generally but might not be suitable to try a particular case.'

In 1996, it was reported that the son of an usher at the Crown Court had been called five or six times to serve as a juror to fill a vacancy. This was held to conflict with the principle of random selection and an appeal against conviction was allowed.[16]

The abolition of the right of peremptory challenge has made more difficult the selection of multi-racial juries. And the Lord Chief Justice has ruled that judges have no power to interfere with selection to that end.[17]

15. [1980] 3 WLR 617.
16. *R. v. Salt, The Times*, 1 February 1996.
17. *R. v. Ford* [1989] 3 All ER 445.

Police powers

The earlier cases

Police powers and their exercise frequently result in the judiciary drawing and re-drawing the lines of what they consider to be permissible and impermissible conduct. In *Thomas v. Sawkins*,[18] the court held that a police sergeant was entitled to enter private premises to attend a meeting called to protest against the Incitement to Disaffection Bill then before Parliament and to demand the dismissal of the chief constable of Glamorgan. It was sufficient that the sergeant had reasonable grounds for believing an offence was imminent and likely to be committed. So it is possible on the flimsiest of evidence to be found guilty of obstructing the police if it can be shown that there was a reasonable apprehension of a breach of the peace.[19]

The difficulty and danger of such decisions is that so much discretion resides in the police and neither the courts nor the legislature are willing to lay down any guidelines. This gives rise to suspicion that the police will prosecute one person advocating one set of views while not prosecuting another advocating a different set of views. Certainly this was the impression conveyed when Pat Arrowsmith was convicted of obstructing the highway when addressing a meeting at a place where such meetings were frequently held and where previously no prosecutions had followed. 'That,' said the Lord Chief Justice, speaking without apparent irony, 'of course, has nothing to do with this court. The sole question here is whether the defendant had contravened section 121(1) of the Highways Act 1959.'[20]

Charges relating to conduct likely to cause a breach of the peace, obstruction of the highway, and other trivial offences can be used to impede freedom of speech and of association. Arrest for the purpose of encouraging the making of confessions has been upheld by the Law Lords though it may

18. [1935] 2 KB 249.
19. *Duncan v. Jones* [1936] 1 KB 218.
20. *Arrowsmith v. Jenkins* [1963] 2 QB 561.

often be indistinguishable from legalizing an arrest for the purpose of questioning.[21]

Elias v. Pasmore[22] is a leading case on search and seizure. The plaintiffs were the lessees of the headquarters of the National Unemployed Workers' Movement. Walter Hannington (one of the plaintiffs) made a speech in Trafalgar Square, in consequence of which a warrant for his arrest was issued. The defendant police inspectors entered the headquarters, arrested Hannington, and seized a number of documents, some of which were used at the trial of the plaintiff Elias on a charge of inciting Hannington to commit the crime of sedition. The plaintiffs claimed the return of those documents, and the question was whether their seizure was lawful, since they had no relevance to the charge against Hannington and no search warrant had or would have been obtained. The court decided that, though the original seizure of the documents was 'improper', it was 'justified' because they were capable of being used, and were used, as evidence in the trial of Elias.

In 1969 police officers enquiring into the disappearance of a woman they believed to have been murdered, searched (without a warrant) the house of her father-in-law. At their request he handed them the passports of himself, his wife and daughter. Subsequently these persons, being Pakistanis and wishing to visit Pakistan, asked for the return of the passports but the police refused. The court ordered their return but in the course of his judgment Lord Denning, summarizing the law where police officers enter a man's home without a warrant, said:

> I take it to be settled law ... that the officers are entitled to take any goods which they find in his possession or in his house which they reasonably believe to be material evidence in relation to the crime ... for which they enter. If in the course of their search they come upon any other goods which show him to be implicated in some other crime they may take them provided

21. *Mohammed-Holgate v. Duke* [1984] 2 WLR 666.
22. [1934] 2 KB 164.

they act reasonably and detain them no longer than is necessary.[23]

Two years later in another case, police officers, armed with a warrant authorizing them to enter premises to search for explosives, found none but seized a large number of leaflets and posters, contending that these were evidence of a crime such as conspiracy to pervert the course of justice or to commit contempt of court. The police claimed further that they needed to retain the documents for comparison with other documents purporting to emanate from a criminal organization responsible for causing explosions. The court held that the police were entitled to seize the documents and that they had established they were acting reasonably and were detaining the documents no longer than necessary.[24]

In 1977, the defendant was arrested by officers of the drug squad for stealing a sandwich from a public house. They then searched his lodgings where they found cannabis, and he was charged with possession of the drug. The court held that the entry and search were unlawful but nevertheless that the evidence was admissible.[25] In another case it was confirmed that, save with regard to admissions and confessions and generally to evidence obtained from the accused after the commission of the offence, judges have no discretion to refuse to admit relevant admissible evidence on the ground that it was obtained by improper or unfair means, for example, through the activities of an *agent provocateur*.[26]

Some statutes confer very wide powers on judges or magistrates to issue search warrants and seize documents so that it may be difficult for the courts to control their exercise in particular cases.[27] The general trend of these cases is alarming. It comes very close to giving the police a right to search and

23. *Ghani v. Jones* [1970] 1 QB 693. Cp. *Frank Truman Export v. Commissioner of Police for the Metropolis* [1977] 3 All ER 431.

24. *Garfinkel v. Metropolitan Police Commissioner*, *The Times*, 4 September 1971.

25. *Jeffrey v. Black* [1977] 3 WLR 895.

26. *R. v. Sang* [1979] 3 WLR 263. Cp. *Morris v. Beardmore* [1980] 2 All ER 753.

27. See, for example, *R. v. Inland Revenue Commissioners ex parte Rossminster Ltd.* [1980] AC 952.

to seize documents which have nothing to do either with the warrant (if they have one) or with the original purpose of their investigations. It is an old tradition that general warrants to arrest unspecified persons and to search property at large are illegal and are not justifiable on the ground of the public interest. The tradition is beginning to look less strong than it did. The danger of placing so sharp a weapon in the hands of the government and of the police is very obvious.

John Cox was a member both of the Campaign for Nuclear Disarmament and of the Communist Party of Great Britain. In 1983, Cathy Massiter, then a member of MI5, was authorized by a warrant of the Home Secretary to tap Mr Cox's telephone on a regular basis. When she later revealed this, during a television programme, he and two other members of the CND (Joan Ruddock and Bruce Kent) sought judicial review of the decision to issue the warrant on the ground that it did not accord with the published criteria for warrants. Counsel for the Home Secretary argued that as it was never admitted, for security reasons, whether or not a particular warrant had been issued, the court should decline jurisdiction and not allow the action to proceed. However, Taylor J would not go so far in the absence of any evidence that to proceed would damage national security. But he found there was no evidence that the Home Secretary had flouted the published criteria, nor any bad faith, nor any grossly unreasonable conduct on the part of the Home Secretary.[28]

The Interception of Communications Act 1985 empowered the Home Secretary to issue a warrant authorizing interceptions of postal or telephonic communications described in the warrant, in the interests of national security, for the purpose of preventing or detecting serious crime, or safeguarding the economic wellbeing of the United Kingdom. Subject to this, interception is made a criminal offence. In any proceedings before a court or tribunal, no evidence may be adduced and no question in cross-examination asked which tends to suggest that a warrant has been issued. In *R. v. Preston*[29] the Law

28. *R. v. Secretary of State for the Home Department ex parte Ruddock* [1987] 2 All ER 518.
29. [1993] 3 WLR 891.

Lords held that this prohibition against adducing evidence was insufficient reason for an investigating authority to refuse to disclose information which might assist a defendant; but, in accordance with the Act, material obtained by interception must be destroyed and did not have to be retained until trial for disclosure to the defence.

The Police and Criminal Evidence Act 1984

The exercise by the police of their powers of arrest, search and seizure, interrogation and charge may be challenged in the courts and so faces the judges with a constantly recurring dilemma posed by the difficulty of their being, at one and the same time, the protectors of personal rights and preservers of law and order. Until recently the courts have consistently, though not in every case, lent their support to the police rather than to the individual. Especially in the numerous minor situations where police and public clash, on marches, demonstrations and protests, police evidence has been preferred and the charges of obstruction of the highway or of the police, or of assault on the police, or of other more serious offences, upheld. Also on more important occasions, allegations that the police have fabricated evidence or concealed evidence helpful to the defence have not been believed.

In the last few years the attitude of judges and of juries has changed. So many cases have been disclosed of police misconduct, even corruption, that the reputation of the police for objectivity and fairness has greatly declined. Following a royal commission which reported in 1981,[30] the Police and Criminal Evidence Act 1984 was passed and came into effect on 1 January 1986. This act, known as PACE, tried to strike a balance between police powers and individual rights. Its provisions and those in the accompanying Codes of Practice made more clear, in particular, many aspects of the relationship between police and suspect in the police station, including the individual's rights of access to lawyers and to family. The act also sought to clarify important questions relating to the admissibility of evidence in court proceedings. While the police have obtained wider statutory powers, they have also

30. Report of the Royal Commission on Criminal Procedure (Cmnd 8092).

been placed under stricter statutory procedures.[31] What follows concerns a few of the areas where the courts have been required to respond during the first years of the act's operation.

R. v. Samuel[32] was an important case. The appellant was arrested on suspicion of robbery and burglary. He asked to see his solicitor but this was refused. Section 58 of the Act provides that such refusal can be justified if based on the reasonable belief that the exercise of this right '*will* lead to interference with or harm to evidence' or '*will* lead to the alerting of other persons suspected' or '*will* hinder the recovery of any property obtained as a result of such offence'. After further questioning the appellant confessed to the burglaries and was charged. But he was still denied access to legal advice. Later he confessed to the robbery, was charged, and then allowed to see his solicitor. The Court of Appeal held that the refusal of access was unjustified and stressed that the use of the word 'will' (which I have emphasized above) must be taken to be deliberately restrictive, thus making it difficult for the police to establish the belief necessary to justify refusal. The conviction was quashed.

This principle was accepted by the Court of Appeal in *R. v. Alladice*[33] but, although there had been a breach of section 58 procedures, the conviction was upheld because there was no suggestion that the confession might have been obtained as a result of the refusal of access to a solicitor and no reason to believe that that fact was likely in all the circumstances to render the confession unreliable. So the confession was admissible. Similarly in *R. v. Dunford*, evidence was admitted, despite a breach, when the accused had previous experience of arrest and detention and a solicitor's advice would have added nothing to his knowledge of his rights.[34] In *R. v. Parris*[35]

31. For a critical review of the 'PACE regime' see A. Sanders and R. Young, in 66 *The Political Quarterly* (1995) p. 126. See generally R. Reiner and L. Leigh, 'Police Power', in C. McCrudden and G. Chambers (eds), *Individual Rights and the Law in Britain*, Chapter 3; P. Osborne, 'Judicial Review and the Criminal Process', in B. Hadfield (ed.) *Judicial Review: A Thematic Approach*, Chapter 5.

32. [1988] 2 All ER 135.

33. (1988) 87 Cr.App.R. 380.

34. (1990) 91 Cr.App.R. 150.

35. [1989] 89 Cr.App.R. 68; compare *R. v. Quayson* [1989] Crim.LR 218.

it was said that, although a breach in the required procedures did not necessarily mean that any subsequent statement by a defendant should be excluded, in this case the trial judge had erroneously concluded there was no breach and so never directed his mind to the adverse effect the admission of evidence might have had, consequent on the refusal to allow access to a solicitor.[36] More recently, in *R. v. Khan (Sultan)* the police, in accordance with Home Office guidelines, installed on the outside of a house, without the knowledge or consent of the owner or occupier, an electronic listening device from which a tape recording was made. The Crown conceded that this involved civil trespass and an intrusion on privacy. The Law Lords held that the recording was admissible as evidence although it arguably constituted a breach of the European Convention for the Protection of Human Rights.[37]

Another group of cases concerns the conduct of police 'interviews'. In *R. v. Absolam*[38] the appellant, who was on bail for possession of cannabis, was arrested for a different offence and taken to the police station where he was required to report. When the appellant had emptied his pockets, the custody officer asked him to produce any drugs in his possession whereupon he handed over some cannabis which he admitted he was selling. The court decided that these events constituted an interview and that the appellant had been wrongly questioned before being informed of his right to legal advice. His appeal against conviction of supplying cannabis was allowed and a conviction for simple possession was substituted. However, in *R. v. Maguire*,[39] where a juvenile was questioned in a police car following his arrest for attempted burglary and gave incrim-

36. For other cases where refusal of access to legal advice led to statements being ruled inadmissible, see *R. v. Paul Deacon* [1987] Crim.LR 404, *R. v. Vernon* [1988] Crim.LR 445, *R. v. Davison* [1988] Crim.LR 442; contrast *R. v. Hughes* [1988] Crim.LR 519, where the accused agreed to be interviewed in the absence of a solicitor having been wrongly informed that no duty solicitor was available. The conviction was upheld.

37. [1996] 3 WLR 162.

38. [1989] 88 Cr.App.R. 332; see also *R. v. Kingsley Brown* [1989] Crim.LR 500; and contrast *R. v. Parchment* [1989] Crim.LR 290; *R. v. Sparks, Guardian,* 13 September 1990.

39. [1989] Crim.LR 815.

inating replies, the Court of Appeal decided this was not an interview and so the absence of an appropriate adult (as required by the Code) was not a breach and the statements were admissible. This was an unfortunate decision, especially as there have been allegations that police sometimes deliberately interrogate outside the police station where they can more easily avoid being bound by the rules governing interviews.

The effect of a breach of the rules governing interviews varies according to the circumstances and to the view taken by judges of its significance. Thus in *R. v. Delaney*,[40] a seventeen-year-old educationally sub-normal youth, charged with indecent assault, eventually confessed after lengthy questioning. The interview was not recorded at the time, as it should have been. Nevertheless the judge admitted the statements made by the accused. But the Court of Appeal, speaking of 'flagrant and serious breaches of the Code', struck down the conviction. But in *R. v. Doolan*,[41] the failure to caution and to make a proper record of the interview, while sufficient to have statements excluded, did not vitiate the jury's verdict of guilt, the Court of Appeal finding that the remainder of the evidence was more than enough to justify it.

In *R. v. Fulling*,[42] it was alleged that the police told the accused that her boyfriend, also a suspect, had been having an affair with another woman and that, being distressed by this news, the accused had confessed in order to get out of prison. The Court of Appeal allowed the confession to stand saying: 'We do not consider that the policeman's remark was likely to make unreliable any confession of the appellant's own criminal activities.' One wonders how any court could come to such a conclusion with any degree of certainty.[43]

In *R. v. Mason*,[44] the accused confessed after he and his solicitor had been falsely told by the police that his fingerprints had been found on a bottle used in starting a fire. The Court

40. [1989] 88 Cr.App.R. 338; and see *R. v. Foster* [1987] Crim.LR 821.
41. [1988] Crim.LR 747.
42. [1987] 2 WLR 923.
43. Compare *R. v. Harvey* [1988] Crim.LR 241.
44. [1987] Crim.LR 757. But entrapment by police officers posing as private citizens does not necessarily exclude evidence, *DPP v. Marshall* [1988] 3 All ER 683.

of Appeal held that although it was not for the court to discipline the police for misbehaviour, the judge should have excluded the confession.

These and other examples suggest that the courts are anxious to insist that the police act in accordance with PACE and the Codes of Practice as the price they pay for additional powers given by the legislation. In *R. v. Canale*, police notes not made at the time of the interview, made on the wrong form, and not shown to the accused to read and sign, were allowed in evidence by the trial judge exercising his discretion to do so. The Lord Chief Justice, allowing the appeal, said that two police officers had engaged in a flagrant, deliberate and cynical breach of the rules. 'If,' he said, 'which we find it hard to believe, police officers still do not appreciate the importance of [PACE] and the accompanying Code, then it is time they did.' It was reported that, as a result, all Scotland Yard officers had been warned by their seniors of the need to abide by the rules.[45]

Under PACE greater powers are given to the police under new provisions relating to search warrants. Some material held in confidence by journalists may be protected but much may be demanded under statutory special procedure. Where photographers from an agency took photographs during communal riots in Bristol, the police demanded their production as likely to be of substantial value to their investigations. This was challenged on the ground that particular photographs were not specified and it was not known whether photographs would be of any use. But the court overruled this objection.[46] So also, after a demonstration of between 10,000 and 15,000 people at Wapping, an investigation was conducted by the police, supervised by the Police Complaints Authority, into allegations and complaints about police behaviour. The investigating officer sought access to films, photographs and other journalistic material. Those who refused argued that they held the material as a result of the operation of the free independent press which would be undermined if they were required to disclose the material. But the judge held that 'there was nothing to put in

45. [1990] 2 All ER 187.
46. [1990] 2 All ER 187; *R. v. Bristol Crown Court ex parte Bristol Press and Picture Agency Ltd.* [1987] 85 Cr.App.R. 190.

the scales in the balancing act to weigh against the undoubted benefit likely to accrue to the investigation if the material was obtained'. Accordingly 'it was in the public interest that the material be produced or that access to it should be given'.[47]

But in August 1989, Judge Mohat Singh at Southwark Crown Court refused an application by the police for an order requiring the BBC to hand over a film on alleged rioting by sections of the Bengali community in London's East End.[48] After the demonstrations in and around Trafalgar Square which resulted in violence in March 1990, many newspapers and television companies were ordered by courts to hand over to the police all their published and unpublished film footage and photographs.

Under PACE, protection from search and seizure extends to certain communications between solicitor and client and may embrace others where legal proceedings are contemplated. But this legal privilege does not attach to documents or other items passed to a solicitor for his advice, though it would attach to the advice given.[49] Moreover 'items held with the intention of furthering a criminal purpose are not items subject to legal privilege.' The police applied for an order against a firm of solicitors requiring the production of all files relating to the purchase of certain property involving a client who was a member of the suspect's family. The police believed this was part of a laundering exercise whereby the suspect, accused of drug trafficking, was trying to dispose of his assets. The solicitors had no criminal purpose though the client allegedly had. The House of Lords by a majority held that the files were not privileged because the 'intention' did not have to be that of the person holding the documents.[50]

The Wapping demonstration on 24 January 1987 has already

47. *Re an application under section 9 of the Police and Criminal Evidence Act 1984, Independent*, 27 May 1988.

48. *Independent*, 19 August 1989.

49. *R. v. Crown Court at Inner London Sessions ex parte Baines and Baines* [1987] 3 All ER 1025. The police must set out in their notice of application a description of the material sought: *R. v. Central Criminal Court ex parte Adegbesan* [1987] 3 All ER 113.

50. *R. v. Central Criminal Court ex parte Francis and Francis* [1988] 3 All ER 775.

been referred to. It took place to mark the first anniversary of the strike of employees of News International. As a result of the inquiry, a number of police officers were alleged to have conspired to pervert the course of justice. The Crown had all the evidence by June 1987 but decided to wait until all the necessary evidence had been collected in the inquiry as a whole before interviewing officers involved in individual incidents. The detailed allegations were served on the officers in February 1988; on 12 October 1988 their files were sent to the Crown Prosecution Service and on 12 January 1989 they were summoned to appear before a magistrate. Police (Discipline) Regulations required the investigating officer 'as soon as is practicable' in writing to inform the officer subject to investigation of the report, allegation or complaint and to give him a written analysis.

A stipendiary magistrate declined to proceed with the committal for trial of these officers on the ground that they had been prejudiced by the delay and that to proceed further would be an abuse of process. The Divisional Court upheld this decision.[51] Subsequently the cases against other officers were dropped on the same ground. In March 1990 an application by the Crown Prosecution Service to certify that the decisions raised matters of national importance requiring a clarification by the Law Lords was rejected.

In two recent cases, the courts have held that the police are in general immune from liability for negligent failure to fulfil their duties. Common to both is the view that this immunity is based on public policy. In *Hill v. Chief Constable of West Yorkshire*,[52] the unsuccessful plaintiff was the mother of the last victim of the murderer Peter Sutcliffe; she alleged negligence in criminal investigation. Lord Keith said:

The general sense of public duty which motivates police

51. *R. v. Bow Street Stipendiary Magistrate ex parte Director of Public Prosecutions* (1989) 91 Cr.App.R. 283.
52. [1989] 1 A.C. 53. But in *Swinney v. Chief Constable of Northumbria* [1996] 3 All ER 449, the Court of Appeal held that public policy might be outweighed by other considerations such as protecting the identity of informers. Not so in *Silcott v. Commissioner for Metropolitan Police*, *The Times*, 9 July 1996.

forces is unlikely to be appreciably reinforced by the imposition of such liability [which] in some instances ... may lead to the exercise of a function being carried on in a detrimentally defensive frame of mind ...

A great deal of police time, trouble and expense might be expected to have to be put into the preparation of the defence to the action and the attendance of witnesses at the trial.

So the plaintiff's statement of claim should be struck out as disclosing no cause of action.

In *Osman v. Ferguson*,[53] a teacher became obsessed with one of his pupils. He harassed the family and was interviewed by the police whom he told he might do something criminally insane. The police were aware of many other incidents. Eventually, he obtained a shotgun, injured the pupil and killed the pupil's father. The pupil and his mother sued the police. Again the action was dismissed on the ground that it would be against public policy to impose a duty of care.

PACE contains detailed provisions governing the periods for which an arrested person may be kept in police detention without being charged. Section 43 provides for further detention on a warrant granted by a magistrates' court. Application for such a warrant must be made within specified periods and these must be adhered to.[54]

A person held in custody in cells at a courthouse has a common law right, on request, to be permitted to consult a solicitor as soon as is practicable. A chief constable operated a policy which authorized officers at the cells to refuse access to a solicitor on the sole ground that the request was made after 10 a.m. A failure by officers in charge at 3.15 p.m. to permit a prisoner to consult his solicitor was held to be unlawful, as interfering with his fundamental right of access to legal advice.[55]

---

53. [1993] 4 All ER 344. But police officers may be personally liable for unlawful discrimination under Race Relations Act 1976: *Farah v. Commissioner for Metropolitan Police*, *The Times*, 10 October 1996.

54. See *R. v. Slough Justices ex parte Stirling* [1987] Crim.LR 576.

55. *R. v. Chief Constable of South Wales ex parte Merrick* [1994] 2 All ER 560. The common law right is in addition to any such right he may have under section 58 of PACE.

Sections 15 and 16 of PACE govern the obtaining and the execution of search warrants. Lack of clarity in drafting and some inherent vagueness (such as a requirement that a warrant shall identify 'so far as is practicable' the articles or persons to be sought) has inevitably resulted in litigation.[56]

In the particular conditions in Northern Ireland since 1969, the role of the courts has been politically significant, and the procedural safeguards for suspects and defendants have assumed greater importance. The record of British courts according to one experienced commentator 'has been remarkable for its total and consistent deference to executive authority'. Dr Conor Gearty lists the six major challenges which have reached the Law Lords, all of which have been unsuccessful.[57] In *McEldowney v. Forde*,[58] statutory regulations provided that all 'republican clubs' or 'any like organisation howsoever described' were unlawful associations. Despite the vagueness of this description, the regulations were upheld. In *Murray v. Ministry of Defence*, failure to inform a person of her arrest was held not to support an action for false imprisonment.[59] *Ex parte Brind* was decided in 1991 and is discussed below.[60] The allegations of a 'shoot to kill' policy adopted by the security forces surfaced in three cases involving killings by those forces.[61] In these and other cases, it has proved very difficult to obtain a conviction or civil remedy against members of the armed forces or public authorities. The preservation of law and order, as seen by the State, has been accorded overriding importance.

A different analysis of thirteen cases (including Gearty's six) showed that the Law Lords found for the government in all but two cases. The author concluded:

56. See, for example *R. v. Reading Justices ex parte South West Meat Ltd.* and *R. v. Central Criminal Court ex parte AJD Holdings* [1992] Crim.LR 672, 669.

57. 'Political Violence and Civil Liberties', in McCrudden and Chambers (see Note 31).

58. [1971] AC 632.

59. [1988] 1 WLR 692.

60. See pp. 247–8.

61. *Attorney General for Northern Ireland's Reference (No. 1 of 1975)* [1976] 3 WLR 235; *Farrell v. Secretary of State for Defence* [1980] 1 WLR 172; *McKerr v. Armagh Coroner* [1990] 1 WLR 649.

Such judicial reluctance to intervene may well please those who endorse a philosophy of judicial restraint. However, the record in the Northern Ireland cases can hardly be encouraging to those who advocate a Bill of Rights in the United Kingdom, especially if they see the courts as its ultimate guarantor.[62]

Part V of the Criminal Justice and Public Order Act 1994 creates many new criminal offences relating to gatherings of people on land, which previously gave rise to civil actions only. These include an offence of aggravated trespass and powers to enable local authorities to direct unauthorized campers to leave land, while the duty to provide sites for gypsies is repealed.

It has been held that local authorities in exercising these powers must have regard to considerations of common humanity, including the various statutory provisions for the protection of children. Failure to take such considerations into account could invalidate actions taken.[63]

Prisoners

Twenty-five years ago, Lord Denning MR stated that the courts would not entertain claims of judicial review from 'disgruntled prisoners' and that judicial oversight of internal proceedings could not be allowed.[64] The judicial attitude was that the management of prisons was, like the armed forces, a matter of discipline for the authorities and not to be interfered with. Prisoners had no right to legal representation.[65]

Partly because of pressure from the decisions of the European Commission and Court of Human Rights, more recent decisions have seen judicial recognition of prisoners' rights.

62. Stephen Livingstone, 'The House of Lords and the Northern Ireland Conflict', in 57 *Modern Law Review* (1994) 333.

63. *R. v. Wealden District Council ex parte Wales*, *Independent*, 3 October 1995. *R. v. Wolverhampton MBC ex parte Dunne*, *The Times*, 2 January 1997.

64. *Becker v. Home Office* [1972] 2 QB 407.

65. *Fraser v. Mudge* [1975] 3 All ER 78.

In 1976 a riot took place at Hull prison and proceedings were taken against a number of prisoners under the internal disciplinary procedure. The prison's board of visitors heard the cases acting under the statutory Prison Rules 1964 and the prisoners were convicted. They sought judicial review for breach of the rules of natural justice. On the evidence, many of the board's findings were quashed on grounds including the improper refusal of the board to call witnesses and the manner in which the board handled the hearsay evidence. The case established the principle that a prisoner had a right to a fair hearing.[66]

In *Raymond v. Honey*[67] and *R. v. Secretary of State for Home Affairs ex parte Anderson*[68] it was established that prisoners had a right of access to the courts, interference with which by the prison authorities was contempt of court; and that this included access to legal advisers. But while applications from prisoners for legal representation before internal disciplinary proceedings must be considered in each case, no right has been accorded.

On matters classified as relating to internal prison management, the courts have proved reluctant to grant judicial review.[69]

In *ex parte Hague*[70] the Law Lords held that a prisoner could not challenge the physical conditions of his or her imprisonment, though Ackner LJ in the Court of Appeal had appeared to consider that detention was unlawful if, for example, the cell 'became and remained seriously flooded or contained a fractured gas pipe allowing gas to escape into the cell'.[71] This

66. *R. v. Hull Prison Board of Visitors ex parte St Germain (No. 2)* [1979] 3 All ER 545.

67. [1983] 1 AC 1.

68. [1984] QB 778; and see *R. v. Secretary of State for the Home Department ex parte Leech* [1993] 4 All ER 539.

69. See generally Stephen Livingstone, 'The Impact of Judicial Review on Prisons', in B. Hadfield (ed.), 173; Genevra Richardson, 'Prisoners and the Law,' in McCrudden and Chambers, 179.

70. *R. v. Deputy Governor Parkhurst Prison ex parte Hague* [1992] 1 AC 58.

71. *Middleweek v. Chief Constable of Merseyside Police* [1990] 3 All ER 662. On lower standards of medical care, see *Knight v. Home Office* [1990] 3 All ER 237.

judicial reluctance has extended to powers to classify prisoners,[72] search them and their cells, remove them from association with others, transfer them to other prisons. The nearest to a statutory requirement is the prohibition of 'cruell and unusuall' punishments in the Bill of Rights 1689. In *ex parte Herbage*[73] the court expressed great reluctance to exercise control over a prison governor in the implementation of his responsibilities for management. But, on the second hearing of the case, two members of the Court of Appeal said that the right under the Bill of Rights was fundamental and went beyond the ambit of the Prison Rules.[74]

On a conviction for murder, the judge must impose the so-called mandatory 'life' sentence. For some other serious offences, a 'life' sentence may be imposed; this is called discretionary.

In *ex parte Doody* the prisoners had been sentenced to mandatory life imprisonment and sought review of the procedure adopted by the Home Secretary for their release on licence. The Law Lords held that the Home Secretary was not obliged to follow the judicial view of the tariff period to be served for retribution and deterrence, but that the prisoners had the right to make representations to the Home Secretary, to know what he took into account in fixing the tariff period, and to be given reasons for the Home Secretary's departure from any recommendations by the judiciary.[75] In a policy statement, the Home Secretary accepted these findings. He added that a prisoner would not necessarily be released at the end of the tariff period even if considered no longer to be a risk, as the Home Secretary would still have to consider the public acceptability of release.[76]

In *ex parte Pierson*, the judiciary recommended a penal

72. However, in *R. v. Secretary of State for the Home Department ex parte Duggan* [1994] 3 All ER 277, the Court of Appeal held that the prisoner was entitled to know the reasons why his classification had not been reduced.

73. *R. v. Secretary of State for the Home Department ex parte Herbage* [1987] QB 872.

74. See [1987] 1 All ER 324.

75. *R. v. Secretary of State for the Home Department ex parte Doody* [1993] 3 WLR 154.

76. 229 HC Deb. col. 863–4 (27 July 1993).

tariff term of fifteen years on a mandatory conviction, but the Home Secretary in 1988 fixed the term at twenty years. After *Doody*, the prisoner in 1993 was told that the decision was because of aggravating features. In 1994 a new Home Secretary adhered to twenty years though conceding that those features were absent. The Court of Appeal held that the adherence was not irrational and that the decision to increase the tariff to twenty years was lawful.[77]

Children convicted of murder are subjected to detention at Her Majesty's pleasure. In the case of the ten-year-olds who murdered James Bulger in 1993, the trial judge recommended a tariff of eight years, increased by the Lord Chief Justice to ten years. The Home Secretary set the term at fifteen years after a flood of public petitions urging an increase. The Court of Appeal held that the Home Secretary's decision was unfair and illegal in taking petitions into account at this stage and in a way impossible for the applicants to test.[78]

Following a decision by the European Court of Human Rights, the Criminal Justice Act 1991 empowered the Parole Board (which is independent of government) to direct the release of a prisoner after the expiry of his tariff period. In *ex parte Norney*, five members of the Provisional IRA were in 1976 convicted of various offences and given discretionary life sentences. In 1992 they were told that the Home Secretary, in accordance with advice from the Lord Chief Justice, had fixed their tariff periods at twenty years, due to expire early in July 1995. In March 1995 the Home Secretary was asked to refer their cases to the Parole Board forthwith so that the board might give consideration to their release on the expiry date. The Home Secretary, in accordance with his normal practice, decided to refer the cases on, but not before, the expiry date, and the Parole Board set the date for consideration at 11 December 1995. In September 1995 the court held the Home Secretary's decision was unlawful as irrational because it resulted in prolonging by at least twenty-three weeks the deten-

77. *R. v. Secretary of State for the Home Department ex parte Pierson* [1996] 1 All ER 837.
78. *R. v. Secretary of State for the Home Department ex parte Venables*, *The Times*, 7 August 1996; affirmed by Law Lords, 12 June 1997.

tion of prisoners no longer dangerous. But in practical terms the board had to accept the referrals when they were made.[79] In December 1995, the Home Office stated that its practice had been changed.[80]

Race relations

The earlier cases
In 1965 the Race Relations Act was passed making discrimination on the ground of colour, race, ethnic or national origins unlawful in certain circumstances. These provisions were expanded by the Race Relations Act 1968. In 1972 came the first of a series of leading cases.

Stanislaw Zesko was born and bred a Polish national and joined the Polish Air Force. In November 1939, after the Nazi invasion of Poland, he escaped to France, came to the United Kingdom, enlisted in the Royal Air Force, and completed three operational tours in Bomber Command. After the war he remained in the United Kingdom, married and for fourteen years lived in the borough of Ealing in conditions of great hardship. He was, said the judge who first heard the case, 'a man of perfect character and integrity and a wholly admirable person'. In 1966, and again in 1968, Mr Zesko applied to be placed on the housing waiting list of Ealing Borough Council. His applications were refused under a council rule that an applicant had to be 'a British subject within the meaning of the British Nationality Act 1948'. A complaint was made to the Race Relations Board which, after investigation, notified the council that its action was one of unlawful discrimination because the Race Relations Act 1968 made unlawful the special treatment of a person on the ground of his national origins. The council applied to the courts for a declaration that its rule was not unlawful. The House of Lords, by a majority of four to one, decided in favour of the council on the ground that

79. R. v. *Secretary of State for Home Department ex parte Norney*, *Independent*, 4 October 1995.
80. 567 HL Deb. col. 83 (6 December 1995).

'national origins' did not mean 'nationality' which was what the council's rule was concerned with.[81]

The approach of the majority was linguistic and formalistic. Viscount Dilhorne argued that Parliament could have used the word 'nationality' and the failure to do so indicated that discrimination on the ground of nationality was meant to be excluded from the Act. It was also argued that to interpret national origins so as to include nationality would extend its meaning in a different context and enlarge the scope of the criminal offence of stirring up hatred under the Act of 1965.

More serious because affecting more people were two decisions about clubs which the House of Lords decided in 1973 and 1974.

In the first, Mr Amarjit Singh Shah was refused membership of the East Ham South Conservative Club because of his colour. The Law Lords rejected a complaint from the Racc Relations Board on the ground that club members were not 'a section of the public'.[82] In the second case, associate members of some 4000 dockers' clubs were held by the Law Lords not to comprise 'a section of the public'.[83] In both cases the Law Lords overrode the Court of Appeal.

How did it come about that the judges who sat in the Court of Appeal and the House of Lords differed so markedly? The answer seems to be that they took different political views.

The conservative view is that Parliament should intervene as little as possible in matters about which people differ in large numbers,[84] and that statutes should be so interpreted. No doubt motives are mixed when intervention to control racial discrimination is discouraged. But Lord Diplock in the *Dockers' Club* case put it thus, referring to the Race Relations Act:

This is a statute which, however admirable its motives, restricts the liberty which the citizen has previously

81. *Ealing LBC v. Race Relations Board* [1972] AC 342.
82. *Charter v. Race Relations Board* [1973] AC 868.
83. *Dockers' Labour Club v. Race Relations Board* [1974] 3 WLR 533.
84. In *Race Relations Board v. Applin* [1975] AC 259 the House of Lords held that foster parents were concerned with the provision of facilities or services to a section of the public, i.e. the children.

enjoyed at common law to differentiate between one person and another in entering or declining to enter into transactions with them ... The arrival in this country within recent years of many immigrants from disparate and distant lands has brought a new dimension to the problem of the legal right to discriminate against the stranger. If everyone were rational and humane – or, for that matter, Christian – no legal sanctions would be needed to prevent one man being treated by his fellow men less favourably than another *simply upon the ground of his colour, race or ethnic or national origins*. But in the field of domestic or social intercourse differentiation in treatment of individuals is unavoidable ... Thus, in discouraging the intrusion of coercion by legal process in the fields of domestic or social intercourse, the principle of effectiveness joins force with the broader principle of freedom to order one's private life as one chooses. [Italics in the original.]

This view begins with the private rights of the individual, including the right to discriminate on the ground of the colour of a man's skin. In interpreting an Act of Parliament, it assumes that those rights are to be diminished to the extent necessary to make sense of the legislation but no further. Therefore within the spectrum of happenings which range from the way a family makes provision for its friends within the home to the conduct of an open market, the definition of 'a section of the public' must be restricted as tightly as possible.

The alternative view does not found itself on this individualist position, does not think primarily of private rights. It makes other assumptions. It seeks to interpret the Race Relations Act in a way which will extend its operation and not restrict it, while recognizing that the act clearly means to avoid intervention in the domestic sphere and in other private gatherings (certainly including some clubs). It regards racial discrimination not as an individual right but as a social wrong.[85]

One of the most remarkable decisions was *ex parte Selvara-*

85. On the 'club' cases, see now Race Relations Act 1976.

jan[86] where a college lecturer was denied promotion in circumstances which strongly suggested racial discrimination. The Race Relations Board rejected the lecturer's application after following procedures which were flagrantly in breach of the rules of natural justice. But the Court of Appeal, presided over by Lord Denning, refused to interfere.

The CRE cases

The Commission for Racial Equality (CRE) was established by the Race Relations Act 1976 to replace the Race Relations Board and the Community Relations Commission. The statutory duties of the CRE are (a) to work towards the elimination of discrimination, (b) to promote equality of opportunity, and good relations, between persons of different racial groups generally, and (c) to keep under review the working of the act.

Several attempts have been made in the courts to frustrate investigations instituted by the CRE. As the CRE reported in 1983:

> There have been legal challenges over investigations on such *highly technical procedural matters* as whether terms of reference are too wide; whether the Commission can investigate named persons without a belief that they are acting unlawfully; whether it is reasonable to embark on an investigation; whether natural justice applies as well as the statutory requirements to hear representations; whether the right to make representations under s.49(4) of the Act applies during the course of an investigation if the Commission forms a belief as to unlawful acts; whether it is reasonable to change from a strategic investigation to one based on a belief that unlawful acts have occurred . . . None of these matters actually touch on the fundamental question whether discrimination has occurred and what should be done about it . . . Yet, all this has happened in a system which was itself designed

86. *R. v. Race Relations Board ex parte Selvarajan* [1975] 1 WLR 1686. Cp. *Ward v. Bradford Corporation* [1972] 70 LGR 27.

to give the person investigated every opportunity to make representation.[87]

Three decisions in particular have seriously diminished the scope of investigations by the CRE. In each of these cases,[88] the courts interpreted the statutory provisions in ways which enabled those complained against to use the procedures to defeat the purposes of the legislation, Lord Denning MR in the first case saying that the CRE had been 'caught up in a spider's web spun by Parliament from which there is little hope of their escaping'. Certainly he gave them no assistance. The decision of the Law Lords in the *Prestige* case, treating a procedural safeguard as a substantive limitation, and so preventing the commission from embarking on a formal investigation, was probably not intended by Parliament.

Lord Denning MR further castigated the CRE in *Mandla v. Dowell Lee*.[89] This was the case where a headmaster refused to admit a Sikh as a pupil unless he cut his hair and ceased to wear a turban. The question was whether Sikhs were a 'racial group' defined by reference to 'ethnic origins' within the meaning of the Race Relations Act 1976. The CRE, said Lord Denning, 'pursued the headmaster relentlessly'. And he expressed 'some regret that the CRE thought it right to take up this case against the headmaster . . . The statutes . . . should not be used so as to interfere with the discretion of schools and colleges in the proper management of their affairs.' And Kerr LJ thought that all the CRE had achieved in this case was 'to create racial discord where there was none before', and referred to notes of an interview between the headmaster and an official of the CRE which he said read in part 'more like an inquisition than an interview' and which he regarded as harassment of the headmaster. Oliver LJ suggested that the machinery of the act had operated against the headmaster as

87. Commission for Racial Equality: *The Race Relations Act 1976 – Time for a Change?* (July 1983). See also G. Appleby and E. Ellis, 'Formal Investigations by the CRE and EOC', in [1984] *Public Law* 236. In 1992 the Commission published a Second Review of the 1976 Act.

88. *CRE v. Amari Plastics Ltd.* [1982] 2 All ER 499; *R. v. CRE ex parte Hillingdon LBC* [1982] AC 779; *CRE v. Prestige Group plc* [1984] 1 WLR 335.

89. [1982] 3 WLR 932.

'an engine of oppression'. The House of Lords overruled the Court of Appeal, found that Sikhs were a racial group and that there had been unlawful discrimination. Lord Fraser said that he thought the Court of Appeal's strictures on the CRE and its officials were 'entirely unjustified'. Lord Templeman agreed that the CRE had not acted oppressively. Lords Edmund-Davies, Roskill and Brandon concurred in their decision.[90]

But Sikhs have often been unsuccessful in claims of discrimination because they were bearded or wore turbans, as employers have been able to 'justify' special requirements or conditions on grounds of health or safety.

In *Commission for Racial Equality v. Dutton*[91] gypsies were recognized as a racial group, being an identifiable minority with long-shared history, common geographical origin and distinctive cultural features. But Rastafarians have failed this test.[92]

In *Ojutiku v. Manpower Services Commission*[93] Eveleigh LJ said that if a person produced reasons for doing something, which would be acceptable to right-thinking people as sound and tolerable reasons for so doing, then he had 'justified' his conduct. But this highly subjective approach was replaced in *Hampson v. Department of Education and Science*[94] by the need for an objective balance to be made between the discriminatory effect of the requirement or condition imposed and the reasonable needs of the person imposing it. This still falls far short of requiring the employer to show that the requirement or condition he has imposed is necessary.

Two other cases suggest that in this context, as in others, the courts are more willing than hitherto to grant judicial review against public bodies.[95] In *R. v. Army Board of the Defence Council ex parte Anderson*,[96] the court was particularly

90. [1983] 2 WLR 620.
91. [1989] QB 783.
92. *Dawkins v. Department of the Environment* [1993] IRLR 284.
93. [1982] ICR 661.
94. [1990] 2 All ER 25; endorsed by the Law Lords in *Webb v. EMO Air Cargo (UK) Ltd.* [1992] 4 All ER 929.
95. For the effects of the adoption of general policies relating to redeployment and redundancy, see *R. v. Hammersmith and Fulham LBC ex parte NALGO* [1991] IRLR 249.
96. [1991] IRLR 425.

severe on the failure of the army authorities to deal properly with a complaint of racial discrimination brought by a soldier; and in another case was critical of the failure of the Department of Health to disclose documents to an internal investigation into a complaint by a medical doctor of Indian origin.[97]

Direct evidence of discrimination is seldom available. Inferences have to be drawn from the primary facts. In *Baker v. Cornwall CC*,[98] the Court of Appeal approved the approach adopted by the Employment Appeal Tribunal in *Khanna v. Ministry of Defence*.[99]

> If the primary facts indicate there has been discrimination of some kind, the employer is called on to give an explanation and, failing clear and specific explanation being given by the employer to the satisfaction of the Industrial Tribunal, an inference of unlawful discrimination from the primary facts will mean the complaint succeeds.

This was elaborated by the Court of Appeal in *King v. The Great Britain-China Centre*[100] where the complainant failed to gain promotion. The majority of the Industrial Tribunal members concluded that they were entitled to draw the conclusion that the complainant had been discriminated against because she did not come from the 'same, essentially British academic, background as the existing staff'. The Appeal Tribunal reversed this on the ground that the majority had wrongly approached the case on the basis that there was a burden on the employers to disprove racial discrimination. The Court of Appeal restored the decision of the Industrial Tribunal following the approach adopted in *Baker*.

---

97. *R. v. Department of Health ex parte Gandhi* [1991] IRLR 431; compare *R. v. General Medical Council ex parte Virik*, [1996] ICR 433.
98. [1990] IRLR 194.
99. [1981] ICR 653.
100 [1991] IRLR 513.

Immigration

The law is to be found primarily in the Immigration Act 1971[101] which empowers immigration officers to refuse admission to the United Kingdom (or to admit only on conditions including limitation on length of stay and on employment) to citizens of countries outside the European Community. Since 1962, Commonwealth citizens have been subject to this control.

Immigrants constitute by far the most numerous group seeking judicial review.[102] Among the reasons for the large numbers was that until 1993 there was no right of appeal from the Immigration Appeal Tribunal to the courts;[103] that from many decisions by immigration officers adverse to immigrants, an appeal can be made only from outside the United Kingdom; and that from such decisions (such as some exclusions deemed conducive to the public good by the Secretary of State), there are no rights of appeal at all. So judicial review, even on the limited grounds for which it is available, may be the only way of having a rejection looked at again.

In *Zamir v. Secretary of State for the Home Department*[104] an applicant for habeas corpus was a Pakistani on whose behalf in December 1972 (he was then aged fifteen) an entry certificate was sought so that he might join his father who had been settled in England since 1962. The certificate was eventually granted, in November 1975, on the basis that the applicant was unmarried and dependent on his father. In February 1976 he married in Pakistan. In March 1976 he arrived at Heathrow airport in London, was asked no questions and volunteered no information. He was granted leave to enter for an indefinite period. In August 1978 he was questioned by the immigration authorities and in October 1978 he was detained as an illegal

101 As amended by British Nationality Act 1981, Immigration Act 1988, Asylum and Immigration Appeals Act 1993; and supplemented by Immigration Rules.

102 See p. 115.

103 The Asylum and Immigration Appeals Act 1993 gives such a right but its impact on numbers seeking judicial review is not yet clear.

104 [1980] 2 All ER 768.

immigrant with a view to his removal from the United Kingdom.

In the House of Lords, Lord Wilberforce, with whom the other Law Lords agreed, said that an applicant for entry to the United Kingdom owed a positive duty of candour on all material facts which denoted a change of circumstances since the issue of the entry clearance. Lord Wilberforce managed to suggest that perhaps the applicant had obtained entry clearance on the basis of a forged birth certificate, though he admitted that this matter had 'not been adjudicated on'. It was, said Lord Wilberforce, for the applicant to show that his detention was unlawful. But this the applicant could not do unless he could show either that there were no grounds on which the immigration officer could legally have detained him or that no reasonable person could have decided as the immigration officer did. To prove these negatives is, of course, virtually impossible. For immigrants the great writ of habeas corpus, which is supposed to stand between the imprisoned individual and the powers of the State, had been effectively neutralized by the judiciary.

Within three years, the House of Lords in a remarkable turnabout reversed its own decision in *Zamir*. The appellant Bohar Singh Khera was born in India in 1956. In 1972 his father was granted leave to enter the United Kingdom for settlement and applied for entry certificates for the appellant and the appellant's mother. In August 1972 they were interviewed by the entry clearance officer in New Delhi. On 5 June 1973, unknown to the UK immigration authorities, the appellant married in India. In December 1974, the appellant and his mother were granted entry certificates. They arrived in the UK in January 1975 and were granted indefinite leave to enter. In November 1978, the appellant's wife applied to join her husband together with two children of the marriage. Enquiries were made, the marriage came to light, and in November 1978 an immigration officer made an order detaining the appellant as an illegal entrant, pending summary removal. The appellant applied to the court for a declaration that he was lawfully in the United Kingdom and had indefinite leave to enter and remain.

It was argued on behalf of the immigration authorities that

on one occasion, after the appellant had reached the age of eighteen, he had falsely told a medical officer of the immigration authorities that he was not married and so was guilty of deception on a fact which was material because, as with Zamir, only if he were unmarried and dependent on his father, was he entitled to be admitted for settlement.

The appellant denied that he had made this statement and it appeared that the immigration officer who made the order detaining him had not relied on this evidence and that there was no other evidence outstanding against the appellant.

Lord Fraser, who, with Lord Wilberforce, had also participated in *Zamir*, remarked that the notice of the immigration officer's decision began: 'Having considered all the information available to me, I am satisfied that there are reasonable grounds to conclude that you are an illegal entrant' and he, with Lords Bridge and Scarman, held that this indicated the immigration officer had applied the wrong test. The officer was entitled to order the detention and removal of a person who had entered the country by virtue of an ex facie valid permission only if that person *was* an illegal entrant and in these cases the degree of probability required that this was so on the evidence was high. The Law Lords also agreed that there was no positive duty of candour although silence was capable of amounting to deception.[105]

In February 1986, the Court of Appeal delivered judgment in *R. v. Secretary of State for the Home Department ex parte Swati*.[106] The applicant sought permission to enter the United Kingdom as a visitor for one week. The immigration officer refused, saying: 'I am not satisfied that you are genuinely seeking entry only for this limited period.' Leave to apply for judicial review was sought on the ground that this statement was not a sufficient reason, as required by the regulations, and was itself irrational. The court rejected these arguments but also ruled that those refused entry on the ground that they were

105 *R. v. Secretary of State for the Home Department ex parte Khawaja and Khera* [1983] 2 WLR 321; and see *Ali v. Secretary of State for the Home Department* [1984] 1 All ER 1009 and *R. v. Secretary of State for the Home Department ex parte Awa, The Times*, 12 March 1983.

106 [1986] 1 All ER 717.

not genuine visitors must normally use their statutory right of appeal (available only after they have left the United Kingdom) and not use judicial review. At the same time the government was seeking to limit the opportunities for Members of Parliament to make representations to ministers on behalf of those refused entry. This decision in *ex parte Swati* was almost certainly the reason for a sharp decline in the number of applications for judicial review from immigrants in 1986. The number fell from the high point of 516 in 1985 to 409 in 1986.

The decision in *Swati* was reinforced by the Court of Appeal in *Davendranath Doorga v. Secretary of State for the Home Department*.[107] The applicant was refused entry as a student although he had written evidence that the course fees had been paid, that his brother (resident in the UK) would maintain him, and that his employers in Mauritius had given him a year's leave for study. The court held that there was no evidence to suggest that the decision to exclude was unreasonable on *Wednesbury* grounds. Again, it is clear that the courts are taking a very restricted attitude to their powers of judicial review in these cases and are refusing to consider general questions of the fairness of decisions.

In *ex parte Zakrocki* a husband and wife were given leave to enter the United Kingdom to visit her mother. The mother died leaving a dependent son incapable of looking after himself. The couple were refused extensions of leave. The court held that there was no evidential basis to support the minister's assertion that arrangements could be made to look after the son, that the decision was unreasonable and should be quashed.[108]

It would seem that where a person is prosecuted for an offence, the courts apply the stricter standards of proof of criminal liability. So where the accused were involved in providing false passports, they could not be convicted of facilitating the entry of illegal entrants when the travellers made no attempt to go through immigration control or to use the passports.[109] Nor were possessors of valid work permits to be treated

107 [1990] IAT 98.

108 *R. v. Secretary of State for the Home Department ex parte Zakrocki*, *The Times*, 3 April 1996.

109 *R. v. Naillie* [1993] 2 WLR 927.

as illegal immigrants when, unknown to them, the permits had been issued to them by an official acting contrary to departmental instructions.[110]

Once British governments had decided on strict immigration control, the categories of those to be allowed entry, either temporarily or permanently, fell to be determined. These were governed by Immigration Rules supplementing the immigration statutes and statutory instruments. One situation has resulted in considerable case law.

Typically, a woman who is a British citizen settled in the United Kingdom, with full rights of nationality and citizenship, wishes to sponsor the entry of a man from a non-European country either because he is her husband or because he is her fiancé. Vinod Bhatia[111] was such a fiancé and he applied for entry clearance in Delhi in February 1981. Two years later the entry clearance officer (ECO) rejected his application and one year later his appeal to an adjudicator was dismissed. So he appealed to the Immigration Appeal Tribunal (IAT) which decided against him, by a majority, in October 1984. He applied for judicial review of this decision and his case came before the Court of Appeal in London, in July 1985. Because of the facts, some 200 other cases were said to be awaiting the outcome of his appeal.

Under the Rules, entry clearance is to be refused unless the ECO is satisfied under the following sub-paras: (a) that it is not the primary purpose of the intended marriage to obtain admission to the United Kingdom and (b) that there is an intention that the parties to the marriage should live together permanently as man and wife and (c) that the parties to the proposed marriage have met.

Mr Bhatia's intended wife was Vijay Kumari. She came to the United Kingdom in 1970, married, had a child in 1971 and obtained a divorce in 1978 with custody of the child. Back in Delhi, her parents advertised for a husband and Vinod was selected. Vijay met him in Delhi in 1980. Later Vinod said he

110 *R. v. Secretary of State for Home Department ex parte Ku* [1995] 2 WLR 589.
111 *R. v. Immigration Appeal Tribunal ex parte Vinod Bhatia* [1985] Imm. AR 50.

did not think his father would have agreed to the marriage had Vijay not been settled in Britain. Vijay herself said she was not prepared to live in India because she wanted her child to be educated in the United Kingdom.

The IAT and the Court of Appeal held that the onus was on the applicant to establish on a balance of probabilities that the three requirements of the Rules under sub-paras (a) (b) and (c) set out above were fulfilled. In this case, there was no dispute about (b) and (c). But the IAT took the view that the rules presume that the primary purpose is to obtain admission to the United Kingdom and that it is for the applicant to satisfy the ECO that this is not so. The applicant argued that once the genuineness of the intended marriage (that is (b)) was accepted, that was also conclusive of the primary purpose. The Court of Appeal agreed that an applicant who satisfied the ECO on sub-paras (b) and (c) was better placed to satisfy him on (a) also but that it was still possible for the ECO and the IAT to conclude that the primary purpose of the marriage was to gain entry for the applicant. So the Court of Appeal held that the IAT had not misdirected itself in law and that the refusal of Mr Bhatia's application was justified. It is obvious that this gives a wide and subjective discretion to the ECO and it is argued that the requirement that a marriage is genuine (under (b)) is a sufficient safeguard against abuse.

In 1986 *Bhatia* was followed by *Kumar*.[112] In this case, there had been a marriage in India in 1982, the wife being already settled in the United Kingdom. In January 1984, she returned to this country, being pregnant. In February her husband was interviewed in Delhi by an ECO who refused his application for entry. A few days later the wife had a miscarriage. She visited her husband again in India for some time in early 1985 and returned to the United Kingdom where a child was born to her in October. Meanwhile an adjudicator, following or purporting to follow *Bhatia*, dismissed an appeal by Mr Kumar and the IAT refused leave to appeal against that decision. So the matter came to the Court of Appeal for judicial review, which was granted.

The rules for an application by a husband are substantially

112 *R. v. IAT ex parte Arun Kumar* [1986] Imm.AR 446.

the same as those for a fiancé save that, for a husband, the ECO must look at the circumstances obtaining when the marriage was entered into, and the events since marriage, such as continuing devotion, may be material as evidence of purpose. In both these cases the marriage or proposed marriage had been arranged by the parents.

In *Kumar* the adjudicator emphasized the arranged nature of the marriage and suggested that this might give rise to an 'ulterior primary reason' to gain admission to the United Kingdom. He also was concerned to separate the requirements of sub-para (a) from (b) and not to 'blur' the distinction between them. The Court of Appeal criticized him on both these points and emphasized the inter-relationship between, in particular, the requirements of those two sub-paragraphs. As the Master of the Rolls said: 'Evidence bearing on one question will often cast a flood of light on the other.'

Both *Bhatia* and *Kumar* were reviewed extensively by the Court of Appeal in *Hoque and Singh*.[113] Both these respondents were husbands of wives settled in the United Kingdom. Mr Hoque was refused leave to remain in this country, and Mr Singh was refused leave to enter, on the grounds of primary purpose. Lord Justice Slade put forward ten propositions of which the most important were those which reinforced the criticisms of the Court of Appeal in *Kumar*. The Court also warned of the danger of treating an admission by the applicant that he sought to obtain admission to or remain in the United Kingdom as evidence that this was the primary purpose of the marriage. On the other hand they disagreed strongly with the view of the judge below in *Hoque* who suggested, on the supposed authority of the Master of the Rolls in *Kumar*, that once it was found that a 'very genuine and soundly based marriage' existed, the requirement in sub-para (a) as well as that in sub-para (b) was satisfied. This, they said, was going too far. Similarly they distanced themselves from similar words used by the judge below in *Singh*. So they reiterated the need for both (a) and (b) requirements to be satisfied.

In both *Hoque* and *Singh* the Court of Appeal ruled that the

---

113 *R. v. IAT ex parte Hoque and Singh* [1988] Imm. AR 216. See, similarly, *Choudhury v. IAT* [1990] Imm. AR 211.

adjudicator had misdirected himself by not taking into account that the existence of an apparently happy and stable marriage, which had already resulted in the birth of a child, might well throw light on the intentions of the parties when they entered into the marriage. So the cases were returned to the IAT for reconsideration.

In the event, therefore, the Court of Appeal emphasized that if an applicant satisfied the ECO or the adjudicator of the genuineness of the marriage or proposed marriage (that is of the intentions of the two parties to live together permanently as man and wife) this must have an important bearing on the question of primary purpose.[114]

Sumeina Masood, a British citizen by birth, sought entry clearance for her husband who was a national of Pakistan. They had married during a visit she made to Pakistan. She made it entirely clear that she had no intention of living in Pakistan. The court held that the adjudicator was correct to look at the intentions of both parties. The husband's intention to live with his wife, no doubt based on a sincere wish to do so, was itself contingent on his obtaining an entry clearance. From this it was a short step, said the Court of Appeal, to conclude that the marriage was entered into primarily to obtain admission to the UK.[115]

On the other hand, when Mohammed Saftar, seeking entry to marry a British citizen settled in the UK, made abundantly clear his strong wish to leave Pakistan (married or not), Lord Prosser considered that his statements did not necessarily show that the primary purpose was to secure settlement in the UK. He said that the rules 'are not merely granting a right or privilege to the appellant in question. They are protecting or preserving for the sponsor, a UK citizen, the ability to marry and live permanently with the man that she wants to marry and live with, without being forced to leave the UK in order to do so.'[116]

But although the burden of proof lies with the applicant to

114 See also *R. v. IAT ex parte Khatab* [1989] Imm.AR 313.

115 *Masood v. Immigration Appeal Tribunal* [1992] Imm.AR 69.

116 *Saftar v. Secretary of State for the Home Department* [1992] Imm.AR 1 (Outer House of the Court of Session).

show that the primary purpose of the marriage is not to gain entry, the adjudicator must show what the facts are on which his conclusion is based.[117]

Deportation, asylum, extradition and exclusion

Any person who does not have the right of abode in the United Kingdom is liable to deportation if (a) having limited leave to enter or remain he/she does not observe this limitation or (b) the Secretary of State deems his/her deportation to be conducive to the public good or (c) another person to whose family he/she belongs is or has been ordered to be deported. The reasons for deportation vary from almost any deception of the authorities to conduct damaging governmental relationships with other states, or threatening national security.

The high moral ground was taken by the Court of Appeal in *R. v. IAT ex parte Cheema*.[118] The deportation order was upheld by the Court of Appeal where a marriage was shown to be not genuine but had as its primary purpose the obtaining of admission to the United Kingdom. Lord Lane CJ said:

> Marriage is still, like it or not, one of the cornerstones of our society, despite recent trends of behaviour. If a person chooses to use a ceremony of marriage or the status simply as a dishonest and deceitful way of avoiding the law . . . then I consider it properly open to the Secretary of State to come to the conclusion that that person's continued presence in this country is not conducive to the public good.

In *Khawaja*,[119] Lord Bridge said: 'I cannot suppose that this power [of the Secretary of State] was ever intended to be involved as a means of deporting a perfectly respectable established resident on grounds arising from the circumstances of his original entry'. It had been argued that the Secretary of

117 *R. v. Immigration Appeal Tribunal ex parte Iqbal* [1993] Imm.AR 270.

118 [1982] Imm.AR 124.

119 See pp. 183–4.

State's power was meant to cover only highly undesirable persons. The decision in *Cheema* rejected this. So did the Court of Appeal in *Owusu-Sekyere*,[120] where Lloyd LJ said there was no reason why the Secretary of State should not deem it conducive to the public good that an immigrant who had deceived the immigration authorities and thereby abused the system should be deported *pour encourager les autres*.

In 1988, the House of Lords decided *R. v. IAT ex parte Patel*.[121] The applicant had been admitted for 'settlement accompanying parents' but had falsely represented that he was unmarried. When this was discovered, he was put on notice that he was liable to be deported. He obtained a re-entry visa when he left to visit India but was refused re-entry on his return on the ground that his exclusion was conducive to the public good. In the lower courts this refusal was quashed because by virtue of *Khawaja* the original deception on entry could not of itself be sufficient. But the House of Lords refused to follow *Khawaja* in this, Lord Bridge eating his words:

> I am happily free of any obligation to decide whether what I said in Khawaja was part of the *ratio decidendi* or merely *obiter*. Still less need I attempt to plumb the mystery of precisely what I meant by what I said. I am at liberty, with the concurrence I believe of all your Lordships, to resort to the more direct and satisfactory expedient, not available in the courts below, of recognising that the opinion I expressed was simply mistaken.

Generally the courts, especially the House of Lords, are much more reluctant to support challenges to the exercise of the Secretary of State's powers to deport than to the exercise of the appellate powers of the immigration authorities. In *Secretary of State for the Home Department v. Zalife Huseyin*,[122] Lord Donaldson MR expressed his reluctance, but held that the wife of a Commonwealth citizen settled in the UK on 1 January

120 *R. v. IAT ex parte Owusu-Sekyere* [1987] Imm.AR 425.
121 [1988] 2 WLR 1165.
122 [1988] Imm.AR 129; see now Immigration Act 1988.

1973 could not be deported even if the marriage was one of convenience.

This reluctance shows itself in the emphasis which courts put, in deportation and asylum cases, on the inherent limitations of judicial review. This is one of the games played by judges, extending and restricting the scope of judicial review like Procrustes fitting victims to his bed. For instance in *Budgaycay*,[123] where three Turkish subjects gave reasons, which were untrue, to obtain entry but later sought asylum on political grounds, it was argued that they could not be deported unless and until the courts had rejected their claims to be refugees. But the House of Lords did not accept this, saying that all questions of fact on which the discretionary decision to grant or withhold leave to enter or remain depended must necessarily be determined by the immigration officer or the Secretary of State. Judicial review was strictly limited to *Wednesbury* principles.[124] But their Lordships did accept jurisdiction when the question was whether the minister had adequately considered what were the consequences of deportation, and Lord Templeman spoke of 'a defect in the decision-making process'.[125]

The House of Lords adopted the harder line of interpretation, overruling the Court of Appeal, in *R. v. Secretary of State for the Home Department ex parte Sivakumaran*,[126] where six Tamils from Sri Lanka were refused political asylum. The question was whether they had 'a well-founded fear' of being persecuted for reasons of race if they were returned to Sri Lanka. The Court of Appeal held that each had merely to establish that he had what appeared to him to be a well-founded fear, but the House of Lords rejected this subjective test and said that he had to demonstrate 'a reasonable degree of likelihood that he would be persecuted', and the Secretary of State could take into account facts and circumstances possibly unknown to the refugee in order to determine whether his fear was objectively justified. On their return to Sri Lanka, two of the Tamils

123 *R. v. Secretary of State for the Home Department ex parte Budgaycay* [1987] AC 514.

124 See pp. 104–5.

125 *Re Musisi* [1987] AC at 537.

126 [1988] 1 All ER 193.

appealed and the adjudicator held that they should be treated as political refugees and granted asylum. The Secretary of State applied for judicial review on the ground that the adjudicator lacked jurisdiction but the Court of Appeal rejected the application.[127]

Early in 1990, six Lebanese nationals obtained from the Brazilian embassy in Beirut tourist visas to enter Brazil. They landed in the United Kingdom and claimed political asylum. The six had obtained Brazilian visas by deception, never intending to go to Brazil, and they claimed that when this was realized the Brazilian authorities would return them to the United Kingdom. The minister took the view that Brazil was the country which should accept asylum responsibility and directed that they be removed to Brazil. He refused to consider their applications for asylum. They applied for judicial review. Schiemann J said that while it was possible (though doubtful) that the minister's belief that Brazil was responsible was one to which he was entitled to come, no reason had been suggested for him to believe that the Brazilians would share his view and admit the six. It was therefore a belief to which the minister could not lawfully come. His decisions and directions should be quashed.[128] The government decided not to appeal.

The Secretary of State has powers of deportation under the Immigration Act 1971 which also confers many powers on immigration officers. He authorized certain officials in the immigration department of the Home Office to exercise his powers to deport. It was argued successfully before Lord Justice Woolf that this delegation was not authorized by the Act. But the Court of Appeal, after taking new evidence, held that the immigration officials were not authorized to act 'as such'

127 *R. v. IAT ex parte Secretary of State for the Home Department* [1990] 1 WLR 1126. In August 1990, the European Commission of Human Rights held that the United Kingdom had violated article 13 of the European Convention in requiring the applicants to pursue their remedies in Sri Lanka (*Guardian*, 7 August 1990).

128 *R. v. Secretary of State for the Home Department ex parte Yassine* [1990] Imm.AR 354.

and were to be regarded simply as ordinary civil servants acting on their minister's behalf.[129]

The Court of Appeal has accepted the principle that an asylum seeker who has had his claim rejected may, in special circumstances, make a fresh claim. But this must not be in effect a repeat of the first claim, even if other ingredients are added; nor must it rely on evidence available but not advanced at the time of the earlier claim. The new claim had to be 'sufficiently different from the earlier claim to admit of a realistic prospect that a favourable view could be taken of the new claim despite the unfavourable conclusion reached on the earlier claim'.[130] Clearly, it will not be easy to establish the ground on which a second application will be entertained as a fresh claim. In addition, the Court held that the Home Secretary's refusal to recognize a second claim, in the absence of any challenge on the ground of irrationality, was unassailable.

The impact on international relations with other states sometimes seems to be a determining factor in judicial decisions affecting individuals. We have already seen that the civil war in Sri Lanka resulted in young Tamil men seeking asylum in the UK.[131] Some had been arrested and tortured in the past after round-ups by security forces in Colombo; but their claims were rejected by the Home Secretary, the adjudicator and the Appeal Tribunal. Staughton LJ said in the Court of Appeal

> We should not seek to discriminate too nicely as to what is and what is not the appropriate response of the forces of law and order in such circumstances. Persecution must at least be persistent and serious ill-treatment without just cause by the state or from which the state can provide protection but chooses not to do so.

The Court also decided that the relevant situation in the country

129 *R. v. Secretary of State for the Home Department ex parte Oladehinde* [1990] 2 WLR 1195; confirmed by the House of Lords [1990] 3 WLR 797. See C. Vincenzi, 'Extra-statutory Ministerial discretion in immigration law', in [1992] *Public Law* 300, for the wider context.

130 *R. v. Secretary of State for the Home Department ex parte Onibiyo* [1996] 2 WLR 490.

131 See Bridges et al, *op. cit.*, pp. 19–22; Sunkin, in [1991] *Public Law*, pp. 493–4.

from which the asylum seekers had fled was that prevailing at the time of the court's hearing, not the date of the Home Secretary's decision.[132] But the Home Secretary erred in not considering renewed applications based on recent evidence.

Abdullai Conteh had close links with this country, being a graduate of London and Cambridge Universities and a member of the English Bar, with two children having rights of abode, and a house in the United Kingdom to which he made regular visits from Sierra Leone. In that country of his origin he had held very high ministerial appointments until forced to flee via Guinea and (very briefly) Belgium to the UK, where he obtained leave to enter by misrepresentation. Because of his stay in Belgium, his application for asylum, despite these links, was not considered on its merits. The Court of Appeal referred to 'compelling humanitarian reasons for granting asylum', but nevertheless held that the Home Secretary was entitled to deport him on the ground that he 'had a long-standing and close involvement with a regime [in Sierra Leone] that had seriously unsavoury aspects'.[133]

In *T v. Immigration Officer*,[134] an illegal immigrant from Algeria claimed asylum as a refugee. There was no doubt that he would be persecuted for his political opinions if he were returned to Algeria and this would entitle him to asylum under the international Convention on the Status of Refugees of 1951,[135] the Immigration Act 1971 and the Asylum and Refugees Act 1993, unless there were reasons for considering that he had committed a serious non-political crime outside the United Kingdom. T had played a part in the detonation of a bomb at an airport in Algeria in which ten people were killed. He had participated as a member of a political group which, according to evidence given on his behalf, had been cheated of success in a democratic election and had recourse to violent means aimed at displacing the ruling powers. The Law Lords held that the bombing was an act of terrorism, being an act striking

132 *Sandralingam v. Secretary of State for the Home Department* [1996] Imm.AR 97.
133 *Abdullai Conteh v. Secretary of State for the Home Department* [1992] Imm.LR 594.
134 [1996] 2 All ER 865.
135 Cmd. 9171.

not at tyrannical opponents but at people to whom the terrorist was indifferent, and who existed only as a means to inspire terror at large. The means used were indiscriminate, and the link between the crime and the political object which T was seeking to achieve was too remote. So T failed to establish his claim to asylum. However, the court also seemed to characterize an attack on a military barracks as 'terrorist', thus excluding from international protection anyone committing such an act by seeming to deny any distinction between political and non-political acts.

In *ex parte Abdi*,[136] two Somali nationals claimed asylum in the UK, having stayed en route for a few days in Spain. The Home Secretary proposed to return them to Spain having 'no reason to believe' that Spain was not a safe country and would not comply with its obligations under the international Convention on the Status of Refugees. Lord Mustill considered this was an insufficient ground and had a 'distant echo' of *Liversidge v. Anderson*.[137] But he was in a minority. Lord Slynn went further in dissent and considered that the special adjudicator, who reviewed the Home Secretary's decision on whether the third country was 'safe', should be provided with documents supporting the applicants' as well as the Home Secretary's contentions.[138] But the majority found otherwise on both matters.

National security continued to be put forward by the executive as justification for its actions, and the courts continued to refuse to consider the validity or the extent of this claim. At the beginning of the Gulf war, Mr Cheblak along with many others was served with a notice of deportation. He immediately sought both a writ of habeas corpus and judicial review.[139] The Court of Appeal followed Denning's approach in *Hosenball*.[140]

136 *R. v. Secretary of State for the Home Department ex parte Abdi* [1996] 1 WLR 298.

137 See pp.152–3.

138 See also *R. v. Secretary of State for the Home Department ex parte Mehari* [1994] 2 WLR 349.

139 *R. v. Secretary of State for the Home Department ex parte Cheblak* [1991] 2 All ER 219.

140 See p.154–5.

Later the Home Secretary decided not to confirm the deportation orders.

The remedies of habeas corpus and judicial review were further considered in *ex parte Muboyayi*,[141] an asylum case where M's claim was refused on the ground that he had travelled from Zaire through France where his claim should have been considered. His successful application for a writ of habeas corpus was set aside by the Court of Appeal on the ground that the proper procedure in such cases was by way of judicial review (which was also refused). Lord Donaldson MR took the view that, on an application for habeas corpus, the only challenge could be to the power or jurisdiction of the detaining authority, not to the reasons for the decision to detain. This seems to be contrary to the view of Lord Wilberforce in *Khawaja*;[142] and to that of others.[143]

In *ex parte Khan*[144] the judge held that habeas corpus should issue to release illegal immigrants from detention, pending the hearing of their application for asylum. But the Court of Appeal reversed this decision, holding that the statutory provisions prevented only the giving of directions for their deportation, not the giving of directions for detention.

Karamjit Singh Chahal, a prominent supporter of Sikh separatism, has been detained in custody since 14 August 1990, his claims for asylum being rejected. He was granted indefinite leave to remain in the UK in 1974. He was tortured by the Indian security forces during a visit in 1984. In 1995 the Court of Appeal held that involvement in Sikh nationalism was not a threat to national security in the UK but refused to review the evidence on which the Home Secretary was basing his deportation order. The European Court of Human Rights condemned the actions of the Home Secretary and Mr Chahal was released from detention.[145]

141 *R. v. Secretary of State for the Home Department ex parte Muboyayi* [1991] 3 WLR 442.

142 See p.183−4.

143 For a defence of habeas corpus see M. Shrimpton, in [1993] *Public Law* 24.

144 *R. v. Secretary of State for the Home Department ex parte Khan* [1995] 2 All ER 540.

145 *R. v. Secretary of State for the Home Department ex parte Chahal* [1995] 1 WLR 526; *Chahal v. United Kingdom, Independent,* 20 November 1996.

In *Jahromi v. Secretary of State for the Home Department*,[146] the reason given for the decision to deport, on the usual ground that J's continued presence would not be conducive to the public good, was 'the likelihood of your involvement in terrorist activities'. The Court of Appeal found that the reason was not in itself adequate, but upheld the order because of other undisclosed reasons which were before the court in affidavits. Reference was made to *Hosenball*, *Budgaycay* and *Cheblak*.[147]

Akin to immigration control but exercisable to control movement within the UK are the powers of the Home Secretary under the Prevention of Terrorism Act 1989. He may make an 'exclusion order' prohibiting any person from entering Great Britain where it appears to him to be expedient to prevent acts of terrorism. The Home Secretary must be satisfied that the person to be excluded is or has been concerned with acts of terrorism connected with the affairs of Northern Ireland or is attempting to enter Great Britain with a view to being so concerned. In September 1993, Tony Benn MP invited Gerry Adams, the president of Sinn Fein, to address a meeting at the House of Commons on the developing peace process. The Home Secretary made an order excluding Adams from entry.

A challenge to the validity of this order was dismissed,[148] following a decision of the Court of Appeal in *ex parte Gallagher*[149] that the Home Secretary was not under any obligation to give reasons for his decision to make such an order, because reasons to be meaningful would usually have to reveal sensitive intelligence information which it would be contrary to the public interest to disclose. The court said:

> We can readily accept that the exclusion order made against Mr Adams may have had the effect of saving the Government from political embarrassment . . . Without access to the information available to the Home Secretary

146 [1996] Imm.A.R.20.

147 See pp. 154–5, 192, 196.

148 *R. v. Secretary of State for the Home Department ex parte Adams*, *Independent*, 27 July 1994.

149 *R. v. Secretary of State for the Home Department ex parte Gallagher*, unreported; see also *R. v. Secretary of State for the Home Department ex parte McQuillan* [1995] 4 All ER 400.

we cannot form any judgment that would enable us to conclude that the Secretary of State acted for an improper purpose in the *Padfield* sense or that his decision was unreasonable in the *Wednesbury* sense.

Behind this lay the suggestion that the government had made the order to ensure that the Ulster Unionists supported the government in a crucial vote on the Maastricht Treaty. The court referred other questions to the European Court of Justice.

However, when entry clearance to the United Kingdom was refused to the founder of thc Unification Church because the Home Secretary considered the exclusion conducive to the public good, it was held that there being 'no perceptible reason' in the letter conveying the decision, this departed from 'the ground rule' that there was an obligation to listen fairly to both sides. So the decision was unlawful by reason of procedural unfairness and reasons should be given.[150]

Bennett was a New Zealand citizen wanted for criminal offences allegedly committed in England. He was traced to South Africa, with which country the United Kingdom had no extradition treaty nor any exceptional extradition arrangements. The South African police put him on a London-bound aircraft and he was arrested in London. He deposed that his forcible return to England resulted from collusion between Britain and South African police and was a form of disguised extradition or kidnapping. The Law Lords, with one dissentient, held that if this were shown to be what happened the Divisional Court could stay the prosecution and release the accused. The case was remitted to the High Court for further consideration.[151] On 1 April 1994, the Divisional Court considered the remitted case and held that in a case involving the liberty of the subject a high burden of proof was required that the applicant was lawfully available for arrest in the United Kingdom; that this had not been discharged and that Bennett's committal for trial should be quashed.[152] Bennett was held in

---

150 *R. v. Secretary of State for the Home Department ex parte Moon*, *Independent*, 2 November 1995.

151 *R. v. Horseferry Road Magistrates' Court ex parte Bennett* [1993] 3 WLR 90.

152 Ibid., *The Times*, 1 April 1994.

custody from February 1991 to July 1993. Following the decisions in his favour, he claimed damages from the Police Commissioner of the Metropolis. But the court held that there was no evidence of an intent to injure on the part of the commissioner and that the claim failed.[153]

Bennett's case, on the issue of extradition, was considered in *ex parte Schmidt*. He was wanted in Germany on drug charges and was known to be in the Irish Republic and to travel frequently to the UK using false passports. He was persuaded by the Metropolitan Police to come to London, allegedly so that he could be eliminated from currency fraud investigations. When he arrived, he was arrested and extradition proceedings were started. Authority to proceed was given by a minister who was ignorant of how he had come to be in the UK. There was expert evidence that the police action had infringed the law of the Irish Republic. Schmidt sought his release by habeas corpus and also judicial review of the authority to proceed. The Divisional Court held that the principle in *Bennett*'s case did not apply to extradition from the UK, although Sedley J thought that had the court been free to decide otherwise, the behaviour of the police was sufficiently reprehensible for the principle to have been invoked. The Law Lords upheld the decision.[154]

In *ex parte Launder*[155] the Governor of Hong Kong in 1993 requested the extradition of the applicant to face trial on charges of corruption (the receipt of bribes totalling some £4.5 million) over the period October 1980 to June 1982. On 31 July 1995, the Home Secretary agreed to the request. This decision was challenged by the applicant on the ground that any trial in Hong Kong (and any sentence imposed) would take place after the transfer of sovereignty to China on 30 June 1997, and that there was a risk of such a trial being unfair or being followed by inhumane or inappropriate punishment.

The Home Secretary and the government of Hong Kong

153 *Bennett v. Commissioner of Police for the Metropolis* [1995] 1 WLR 488.

154 *R. v. Secretary of State for the Home Department ex parte Schmidt* [1994] 2 All ER 784; [1994] 3 WLR 228.

155 *R. v. Secretary of State for the Home Department ex parte Launder*, *The Times*, 29 October 1996, 26 May 1997; *Independent*, 3 June 1997.

argued that the applicant's rights were protected by a treaty entered into with China in 1984 which aimed to preserve the present way of life in Hong Kong for a period of fifty years from July 1997, and specifically provided that the laws currently in force in Hong Kong would 'remain basically unchanged'. Further, the People's Congress in China in April 1990 invested Hong Kong with independent judicial power and the right to a fair trial without delay. Evidence was given on behalf of the applicant suggesting that China had a bad human rights record and that there was a risk that the terms of the treaty might not be adhered to. The Home Secretary argued that such matters were not justiciable, being founded on a political judgment taken by the Home Secretary: 'On an issue of this kind it is vital that the Crown speaks with a single voice, and that the judicial branch of government defer to the position rightly assumed by the executive touching this area of the executive's prerogative, namely the conduct of relations with another sovereign state and the implementation of treaty obligations with that state.'

The Divisional Court rejected this formulation and asserted its jurisdiction. The court further noted that the Home Secretary's decision was 'dictated by a collective Cabinet decision and not his individual decision' and proceeded on the basis that the terms of the treaty would be kept by China. But the Law Lords concluded that the question was whether the respondent would be exposed to the risk of injustice or oppression if he were returned to Hong Kong to face trial and that the Home Secretary had not failed to address that question.

In *ex parte Patel* the Minister of State sanctioned the extradition to the USA of Patel, to stand trial for offences of theft which were alleged to have occurred nine to twelve years previously. The court held that all the culpable delay was the fault of the United States authorities and the minister had misdirected himself.[156]

Despite the caution habitually observed by the courts in matters affecting governmental powers in these cases, the

---

156 *R. v. Secretary of State for the Home Department ex parte Patel* [1995] Admin. LR 56.

courts may resist where there is any suggestion that court orders are being flouted.

M, a national of Zaire, was refused asylum and denied judicial review of that refusal. Shortly before he was due to be deported, a fresh application was made to the duty judge who understood he was given an undertaking by counsel from the Home Office that M's departure would be postponed over-night pending consideration. No such undertaking was intended to be given and M's departure was not prevented. The duty judge made a mandatory order directed to the Home Secretary (Kenneth Baker) requiring M's return. This order was not complied with. The Court of Appeal held that ministers and civil servants were liable to be proceeded against and that the Home Secretary was personally guilty of serious contempt, but because he had acted within a very short time and on legal advice that the mandatory order was not valid, no penalty was imposed.[157]

The Law Lords held that injunctions were available against officers of the Crown and that breach of the order was a contempt actionable against the Home Secretary in his official capacity.[158] The decision has been viewed as a considerable breakthrough towards ensuring that remedies are available against Crown servants while stopping short of subjecting indi-vidual ministers in their personal capacity to the full rigours of the law. But, given the development of judicial review in so many directions, the case is of less significance than is claimed for it. Nevertheless, it reinforces the constitutional principle that it is for the courts to determine, according to law, what are the limits of governmental powers.

This principle, though not its practical effectiveness, was demonstrated strikingly when the government sought to dis-courage asylum seekers. Early in 1996 regulations made by the Secretary of State for Social Security came into force pre-venting asylum seekers from qualifying for income support or housing benefit unless they applied for asylum immediately on arrival in the United Kingdom. The Joint Council for the Welfare of Immigrants obtained leave to apply for judicial

157 *M. v. Home Office* [1992] 2 WLR 73.
158 [1993] 3 WLR 433.

review to challenge the validity of the regulations. The Divisional Court, while expressing concern at the 'drastic and unwelcome consequences' this policy would have on claimants so placed 'in a penurious or perilous condition', rejected the application but gave leave to appeal. The Court of Appeal, by a majority, declared the regulations invalid. They had been made under the Social Security (Contributions and Benefits) Act 1992.

The court held that Parliament had clearly demonstrated by the Asylum and Immigration Appeals Act 1993 a full commitment to the Convention on the Status of Refugees, but these regulations, for some genuine asylum seekers at least, rendered nugatory their rights under that act. Either that 'or the regulations necessarily contemplated for some a life so destitute that no civilised nation could tolerate it'. The regulations were 'so draconian in effect that they must be held to be ultra vires'.[159]

The Asylum and Immigration Bill of 1996 was at that time being debated in the House of Lords where the government successfully moved a new clause to negate the decision of the Court of Appeal. The Lords passed an amendment giving asylum seekers three days within which to make application for asylum after their arrival.[160] This was rejected by the government majority in the House of Commons,[161] and the new clause was approved.

At the same time, London boroughs refused asylum seekers emergency housing accommodation. Section 59 of the Housing Act 1985 included as having a priority need a person who was vulnerable as a result of old age, mental illness or handicap or physical disability 'or other special reason'. The Court of Appeal held that this last phrase permitted an examination of all the personal circumstances of an applicant for accommodation, and that certain asylum seekers were so vulnerable, being without money or friends, that they were to be treated as having priority need.[162] But local authorities are entitled to investigate

159 *R. v. Secretary of State for Social Security ex parte JCWI* [1997] 1 WLR 275.

160 573 HL Deb. col. 1220–66 (1 July 1996).

161 281 HC Deb. col 844–87 (15 July 1996).

162 *R. v. Kensington and Chelsea LBC ex parte Kihara; Independent*, 3 July 1996; similarly *R. v. Hammersmith and Fulham LBC ex parte A, Independent*, 26 February 1997.

the status of immigrants applying for housing with priority needs and to decide whether applicants are illegal entrants by deception.[163] On the other hand where an immigrant, who had not misled the local authority, was granted a lawful tenancy, his unlawful residence did not entitle the authority to evict him.[164]

Miscarriages of justice

Recent cases, especially those arising out of bombings on the mainland by the IRA, have raised serious questions about the processes of the criminal law. Convictions have been set aside, often after long periods of imprisonment, and doubts have been raised not only about police methods but about the role of the courts in remedying miscarriages of justice.

Under the Criminal Appeal Act 1968, appeals against conviction on serious offences lay to the Court of Appeal (Criminal Division), usually after leave had been obtained. The court was required by statute to allow an appeal if it thought (a) that the conviction should be set aside on the ground that under all the circumstances of the case it was unsafe or unsatisfactory or (b) that the judgment of the court of trial should be set aside on the ground of a wrong decision or any question of law or (c) that there was a material irregularity in the court of the trial. In any other case the court must dismiss the appeal and might do so, in any event, if it considered that no miscarriage of justice had actually occurred. Where the court allowed an appeal, it might direct the trial court to enter a verdict of acquittal or it might order a retrial. In addition the Secretary of State might, if he thought fit, at any time refer a case to the Court of Appeal to be there treated as an appeal.[165] He might

163 *R. v. Secretary of State for the Environment ex parte Tower Hamlets LBC* [1993] QB 632.

164 *Akinbolu v. Hackney LBC, The Times*, 13 May 1996. The housing situation of asylum seekers, as of others who are homeless, has been worsened by the provisions of Pt.VII of the Housing Act 1996.

165 Criminal Appeal Act 1968 section 2, 17. But see below, pp. 212–3, for the reforms introduced under the Criminal Appeal Act 1995. In the 8 years 1988–1995, 71 cases involving 99 defendants were referred to the Court of Appeal (269 HC Deb. col. *374*).

also recommend the Queen to grant a pardon or to remit all or part of the penalty imposed.

In 1969, Widgery LJ in the Court of Appeal said that, in the case before him, no one criticized the summing-up of the trial judge, every issue was before the jury, the jury was properly instructed and so the court would be 'very reluctant indeed' to intervene. However, the court was now required to consider whether the decision was 'unsafe or unsatisfactory'. That means, he said, that 'in cases of this kind the court must in the end ask itself a subjective question, whether we are content to let the matter stand as it is, or whether there is not some lurking doubt in our minds which makes us wonder whether an injustice has been done.'[166] It is doubtful whether this view is now prevalent. The more common approach seems to be that where the summing-up is impeccable and there are no mistakes of law, the Court of Appeal will not substitute its own opinion for that of the jury in the trial court.

The Court of Appeal may hear fresh evidence where there is a reasonable explanation for this not having been adduced at the trial. In *Stafford v. DPP*,[167] the House of Lords was confronted with two views of how it should consider such evidence. Counsel for the appellant said that the Court of Appeal had asked the wrong question in that they took as the test the effect of the fresh evidence on their minds and not the effect that that evidence would have had on the mind of the jury. Counsel for the respondent said that there was nothing in the act or in the cases which supported the view that the Court of Appeal should allow the appeal when they did not themselves think that the verdict was unsafe or unsatisfactory, or when they were themselves convinced of the guilt of the appellant but considered that some hypothetical jury might have thought otherwise. Their Lordships decided unanimously in favour of this second view.

Lord Devlin has argued strongly against this decision, saying that it meant a person might be convicted of a serious offence

166 *R. v. Cooper* [1969] 1 QB 267; see *Miscarriages of Justice* (1989), a report by Justice.
167 [1974] AC 878.

without having been found guilty by a jury which had heard substantially all the relevant evidence.[168]

We have seen that the Secretary of State might refer a case to the Court of Appeal. In the case of the murder of the Luton sub-postmaster in 1969 he did so on four occasions. On the first occasion, the Court of Appeal quashed the conviction of one of the accused but not of the other two whose convictions the court refused consistently to reject. Eventually the Secretary of State released the two by remitting the remainder of their sentences in 1980. Of one of the hearings, the Court of Appeal said of the evidence given by the principal witness (Matthews): 'Each of us watched him closely while he was giving evidence. The conclusion which each of us independently has reached in this Court on the vital part of his story is that he was clearly telling the truth.' On this Devlin wrote:

> What was wanted from the Court of Appeal was not confirmation that Matthews appeared from his demeanour to be a truthful witness, whether on essentials or on the whole. What was wanted was an answer, based on a more comprehensive view of the case than the jury could have as well as a more detached one, to the question whether, however convincing Matthews might sound, it was safe to act upon the evidence of an habitual liar, who even at the trial had not come clean, who was an accomplice almost uncorroborated, and who had turned Queen's evidence in the hands of a police officer who was not above suspicion.[169]

Under the Act of 1968, the Court of Appeal had a limited power to order a retrial. Since the Criminal Justice Act 1988, the court may so order whenever satisfied that it is in the interests of justice to do so. But if the case is very old, this may not be a realistic course.

On 5 October 1974, bombs exploded in two public houses in Guildford killing five people and injuring over sixty. This was followed by bombings in Woolwich on 7 November, when two died. Other bombings occurred in London.

168 Patrick Devlin, *The Judge* (1979), pp. 148–76.
169 Ibid., pp. 170–1.

Three men and a woman – known as the Guildford Four – were charged with the murder of those killed in the Guildford bombings, two of the men being also charged with the murders at Woolwich. In September 1975, all were convicted on the basis of confessions they had made while in police custody and which they retracted in court alleging that the confessions had been extorted. In December 1975, four IRA members were surrounded in a flat in Balcombe Street, London, and when arrested admitted to having been responsible for bombings in and around London over the past year. Subsequently, statements were made by those IRA members that they had been responsible for the Guildford and Woolwich bombings and that the Guildford Four had no connection with those events.

In 1977, the Guildford Four applied unsuccessfully for leave to appeal. The Court of Appeal, said Lord Roskill, 'wholly rejected as unworthy of credence' the evidence of the IRA members that they did not know the applicants and that IRA members alone took part in the Guildford bombings. So, said the court, the new evidence 'therefore gives rise to no lurking doubts whatever in our minds'.

As the result of statements made by two of the Guildford Four, seven other persons were convicted in 1976 of unlawfully handling nitroglycerine. Six were of or related to the Maguire family and one was a friend of the family. The evidence was almost entirely based on traces which were said to be found on their hands or gloves. Two were sentenced to 14 years' imprisonment, three (of whom one died in prison) to 12 years' and one to 5 years'. The youngest (aged 14) was sentenced to 4 years in youth custody. All applied unsuccessfully for leave to appeal in 1977. The decision was that no member of the Court of Appeal saw any reason for disturbing any of the convictions, either on the basis that any of them was unsafe or unsatisfactory or that the learned judge was guilty of any non-direction or misdirection or that his summing-up in any way was unbalanced.[170]

Doubts about the rightness of the convictions of these eleven

170 The fullest accounts of the trials and the events concerning the Guildford Four and the Maguire Seven are to be found in Robert Kee, *Trial and Error* (2nd edn 1989).

persons persisted, and the Cardinal Archbishop of West-minster, Basil Hume, raised the matter with Mrs Thatcher in 1979. When in 1986 Robert Kee published his book on the case,[171] he found that his doubts were shared by two former Law Lords (Devlin and Scarman) and two former Home Secretaries (Roy Jenkins and Merlyn Rees). They tried to persuade the Home Office to refer the cases to the Court of Appeal. In November 1986, the matter was raised in the Lords by Baron-ess Ewart-Biggs, Lord Fitt and Lord Scarman, but the govern-ment refused on the ground that there was no factor other than the evidence already examined. In January 1987, the Home Secretary, Douglas Hurd, told the House of Commons that he could see no grounds for referral. In July 1987, Cardinal Hume, the two former Law Lords and the two former Home Secre-taries went as a deputation to see Mr Hurd. In the following month, the Avon and Somerset police were appointed to under-take an enquiry. In April 1988, the first report of that enquiry did not, it is believed, encourage the Home Secretary to refer the case to the Court of Appeal but, after further pressure from the Hume deputation, he did so in January 1989, on the basis of new evidence about the effects of drugs on the confession statement of one of those convicted and of new alibi evidence. This by itself might well have proved insufficient. But, at this point, according to Robert Kee, the Crown Prosecution Service pressed the Avon and Somerset police to make more inquiries, as a result of which documents were found at Guildford which led to the conclusion of police fabrication.

On 19 October 1989, counsel for the Director of Public Prosecutions told the Lord Chief Justice (Lord Lane) and two Lord Justices in the Court of Appeal that the confessions in the Guildford case had been found to be the product of fabrica-tions on the part of the Surrey constabulary and that it would be wrong for the Crown to seek to sustain the convictions.

Counsel said there was 'clear prima facie evidence that a total of five police officers seriously misled the court in relation to two of the four appellants'. Notes and records of crucial interviews had been rewritten, altered and suppressed. Lord Lane said of the officers: 'They must have lied'. The evidence

171 See last note.

of the fabrication by the police was found unexpectedly among the police files at Guildford. The convictions were quashed and the Four were freed.

It was perhaps significant that the Home Secretary decided to pre-empt the consideration by the Court of Appeal. He also set up an enquiry[172] under a former Lord Justice of Appeal (Sir John May) with lay assessors into matters arising from the freeing of the Guildford Four, and into aspects of the Maguire Seven, six of whom had by this time served their sentences, the seventh having died in prison. In June 1990, the Director of Public Prosecutions accepted that the convictions of the Maguire Seven were unsafe and unsatisfactory and could not be upheld.[173] In July 1990, Sir John May published his interim report on the Maguire case. His conclusion was that the convictions were unsound.[174] They were so declared by the Court of Appeal.

On 21 November 1974, two bomb explosions took place at public houses in Birmingham. Twenty-one people were killed and more than 160 injured. This followed a series of ten or eleven IRA bombings in the West Midlands. At one of those earlier incidents the bomb had exploded prematurely, killing James McDade who was planting it. On the evening of 21 November, six men were arrested, five of them on their way from Birmingham to Belfast to attend McDade's funeral. The sixth man was arrested in Birmingham. According to police evidence, all six made statements admitting they had taken part in planting the bombs on 21 November, the statements of four being in writing, two being orally made. Those statements which the accused alleged had been forced out of them by the police under torture, violence, threats and intimidation were the foundation of the prosecution case. There was also some disputed scientific evidence. All six were convicted in November 1975 of the murder of the twenty-one who died.

In March 1976, the Six applied for leave to appeal on the grounds that the trial judge displayed excessive hostility to

172 158 HC Deb. col. 271 (19 December 1989).
173 See 174 HC Deb. col. 454 (14 June 1990) for the Home Secretary's statement.
174 HC 556 of 1989–90.

their case, overstepped the bounds of his judicial function in criticism of certain defence witnesses, wrongly allowed certain witnesses to be called by the prosecution in rebuttal, and did not sum up fairly. The applications were refused.

In 1987, following television broadcasts on their case and statements by an ex-police constable that he had seen the Six being ill-treated by the police on 22–3 November 1974, an enquiry was ordered by the Home Office and carried out by the Devon and Cornwall police. Subsequently the Home Secretary referred the case to the Court of Appeal to consider whether any of the convictions should be regarded as unsafe or unsatisfactory. The Court of Appeal (Lord Lane LCJ, Lords Justices Stephen Brown and O'Connor) reported in January 1988: 'The longer the hearing has gone on the more convinced this Court has become that the verdict of the jury was correct. We have no doubt that these convictions were both safe and satisfactory.'

Early in 1990, following the abandonment of the convictions of the Guildford Four, a police investigation was set up into the Birmingham convictions.[175] In August, the Home Secretary referred the case back to the Court of Appeal for the second time. On 14 March 1991 the court set the six men free.

Three persons had their convictions overturned by the Court of Appeal in April 1990. They had been charged with conspiracy to murder the then Secretary of State for Northern Ireland (Mr Tom King). At their trial, each of the accused chose not to give evidence, but when their counsel was addressing the jury, the Secretary of State announced the government's intention to change the law so as to limit the right to silence. The Secretary of State said on television that this change should increase convictions among terrorists. Also, the former Master of the Rolls, Lord Denning, said that the right to silence was a help to the guilty while the innocent would want to give evidence and be cleared. The three were convicted.

The Court of Appeal held that these statements constituted a real risk that the jury might have been influenced and that the judge should have ordered a retrial. At the time when the appellants' notices for leave to appeal were given, the Court

---

175 See generally Chris Mullin, *Error of Judgment*.

of Appeal had no power to order a retrial. So the convictions were quashed and the appellants set free.[176]

Judith Ward was given a life sentence in 1974 for the murder of twelve people who died when a bomb exploded in a coach on the M62 motorway. At her trial she made admissions and confessions, some of which were clearly false. Some of the evidence against her was given by the Home Office forensic scientist whose evidence in the case of the Birmingham Six had been declared unreliable. In 1992 the Court of Appeal found that there had been a 'grave miscarriage of justice' when West Yorkshire police officers failed to disclose evidence to the defence. The court also found that some members of the staff of the Director of Public Prosecutions and counsel who advised them failed to carry out their basic duty to seek to ensure a fair trial.[177] Two of the scientists were investigated, but there was insufficient evidence to justify criminal proceedings.[178]

Other miscarriages of justice include the Tottenham Three, arising out of a riot on Broadwater Farm Estate in 1985 during which a police officer was murdered. Winston Silcott, Engin Raghip and Mark Braithwaite were convicted. Their first appeal was rejected, but a reference to the Court of Appeal resulted in the quashing of the conviction in 1991. Amongst other reasons, it appeared that police interview notes on Silcott had been altered, that evidence of the psychological condition of Raghip would have been admissible, and that interviews with Braithwaite took place after he had been denied access to a solicitor contrary to PACE.[179]

Also involving miscarriages of justice were the Arms to Iraq scandals, three of which are discussed below.[180]

These and other cases emphasize the difficulties the courts face in evaluating evidence. Forensic evidence has been critically unreliable, raising suspicions that scientists, like the police, may fail to disclose the results of tests that favour the accused. The Home Office Forensic Science Service is now

176 *R. v. Cullen and others, Independent*, 1 May 1990.
177 *R. v. Ward* [1993] 1 WLR 619.
178 See Paul Foot, 'Still it goes on', in *London Review of Books*, 4 November 1993, p.11.
179 See p. 163; *R. v. Alladice* (1988) 87 Cr. App.R 380.
180 See pp. 239–44.

an independent agency, charging the police for use, and this may further distort its evidentiary value. More broadly, the quality of the techniques used is sometimes suspect, including the application of DNA analysis. Confessions are notoriously unreliable, partly because they may be extracted by duress and partly because some people are highly suggestible. It is at best highly doubtful whether the adversarial criminal trial is suited to discover the truth in such cases.[181]

After the release of the Guildford Four in 1989, three Surrey police officers were charged with conspiring to pervert the course of justice by giving perjured evidence at the trial where they claimed that a document was a contemporaneous record of a confession of one of the Four. This and other documents were discovered in May 1989, but the officers did not stand trial until April 1993. On a majority verdict the officers were found not guilty.[182]

Three West Midlands police officers were similarly charged after the release of the Birmingham Six. Their trial was abandoned when the judge concluded that they could not get a fair trial because of the volume and intensity of the publicity surrounding the affair.[183] By the end of 1993, twenty or more people had had their convictions quashed in cases involving that force. '*Not one* police officer accused of malpractice arising from the many miscarriages of justice put right by the Court of Appeal since 1989 has been convicted of a criminal offence.'[184] Considerable sums of money have been paid out by police authorities as compensation or in damages to victims of miscarriages of justice.

The Criminal Appeal Act 1995 was based, in part, on the recommendations of the Royal Commission on Criminal Justice.[185] The Court of Appeal is required to allow an appeal

181 See John Jackson, 'Due Process', in McCrudden and Chambers, *op.cit.*, pp. 130−5.

182 For a detailed criticism of the way the judge conducted the hearing, see the article by Alastair Logan (solicitor to one of the Four) in *London Review of Books*, 4 November 1993, p. 9.

183 Ibid.

184 David Rose, *In the Name of the Law* (1996), p. 296 (emphasis in original).

185 Cm 2263 (chairman: Viscount Runciman).

on the simpler ground that the conviction is unsafe. The Act establishes the Criminal Cases Review Commission, consisting of not less than eleven members, at least one-third of whom are legally qualified; and two-thirds are persons having knowledge or experience of the criminal justice system. Petitions for review are no longer made to the Home Secretary but to the Review Commission, which supervises investigations and reports to the Court of Appeal.

Since 1994, the Home Secretary has been obliged to disclose to the petitioner any fresh material he obtained as a result of inquiries he made when considering a petition. This is an all-important provision; the disclosure must take place before the Home Secretary makes his decision and the petitioner must have a specific opportunity to make effective representations on the material.[186]

---

186 *R. v. Secretary of State for the Home Department ex parte Hickey No.2*) [1995] 1 WLR 734 (the Bridgewater case). See p.118.

6. Contempt, confidentiality and censorship

The meaning of contempt

A report stated that the law relating to contempt of court had developed over the centuries as a means whereby the courts might act to prevent or punish conduct which tended to obstruct, prejudice or abuse the administration of justice.[1] Such conduct may take place, in relation to any particular case, before, during or after the trial. Most obviously, if the court makes an order which is disregarded, that is contempt, as happened when trade unions were fined for failing to obey orders of the National Industrial Relations Court; or as happens in matrimonial cases where parties disobey orders not to molest or invade the privacy of other parties.

But, less usually, there may be positive disruption as when, in 1970, a group of Welsh students invaded a court in the Royal Courts of Justice in London and broke up the hearing of a case by striding into the well of the court, shouting slogans, scattering pamphlets and singing. They did this to demonstrate for the preservation of the Welsh language, and those who refused to apologize to the judge were instantly committed by him to three months' imprisonment. On appeal they were bound over for twelve months to be of good behaviour. The members of the Court of Appeal emphasized that the right to

1 . Report of the Committee on Contempt of Court (Cmnd 5794) para. 1; and see discussion paper Cmnd 7145; and see 948 HC Deb. col. 1340–50 (25 April 1978). For a rare example of ministerial contempt, see *M. v. Home Office*, p. 202.

protest must be executed within the law. But their judgments also establish, despite statutory law which seemed, as applicable to these students, to require that their sentences should be suspended, that the High Court still had power at common law to commit instantly to prison for such contempt.[2]

Section 8(1) of the Contempt of Court Act 1981 prohibits the disclosure of information about proceedings of a jury. The Law Lords held that this includes disclosure not only by individual jurors but by others including the media.[3] But in another case it was held that no contempt had been established when nine months had elapsed between publication (in a single broadcast and in newspapers of limited circulation) and the trial.[4]

Prejudicial statements

Clearly the position of an accused person may be adversely and unfairly affected if, before his trial is concluded, publicity about him appears in the press. This may well create prejudice, not least in the mind of any member of the jury. So for a newspaper to describe an accused person of having had an unedifying career as brothel-keeper, procurer and property racketeer is a serious contempt of court – and when this happened in 1967 the *Sunday Times* was fined £5000.[5] In February 1988, News Group Newspapers was fined £75,000 for contempt of court in publishing articles in the *Sun* (one of the group) about a doctor subsequently privately prosecuted (with finance provided by the *Sun*) and acquitted.[6]

Between 1959 and 1961 a company made and marketed under licence a drug containing thalidomide, as a result of which about 450 children were born with gross deformities.[7] In 1968 and subsequently actions were begun by the issue of writs against the company and some of these were settled out

2 . *Morris v. Crown Office* [1970] 2 QB 114.
3 . *A-G v. Associated Newspapers Ltd.* [1994] 2 WLR 277.
4 . *A-G v. Independent Television News Ltd.* [1995] 2 All ER 370.
5 . *R. v. Thomson Newspapers* [1968] 1 WLR 1.
6 . *A-G v. News Group Newspapers* [1988] 3 WLR 163.
7 . *A-G v. Times Newspapers* [1974] AC 273.

of court. For others, negotiations continued and in September 1972 the *Sunday Times* published the first of a series of articles to draw attention to the plight of the children. The company complained to the Attorney-General that the article was a contempt of court because some actions were still pending. The editor justified the articles and at the same time sent to the Attorney and to the company for comment a second article in draft (for which he claimed complete factual accuracy) on the testing, manufacture and marketing of the drug. The Attorney-General asked the courts to grant an injunction to prevent the publication of this second article on the ground that it was a contempt. The Divisional Court granted the injunction but the Court of Appeal refused it. The House of Lords allowed the company's appeal and granted the injunction.

Essentially, the view of the Court of Appeal[8] was that in the unique circumstances of a national tragedy where the public interest required that the issues should be discussed, where the legal proceedings had been dormant for years, and where there appeared no possibility of any action coming to trial, the public interest in fair comment outweighed the possible prejudice to a party. The House of Lords decided against the *Sunday Times* on the ground that the second article might be prejudicial to a subsequent trial. The public interest in proper discussion in the circumstances of this case and the weakness of the parents' situation, unless they could be championed by the press, appeared to carry very little weight with their Lordships whose decision was unnecessary in law and deplorable in practice.[9]

The issue was then taken to the European Court of Human Rights on the ground that the injunction violated Article 10 of the European Convention which protects the right to freedom of expression. The court concluded, by eleven votes to nine, that the injunction did not correspond to a social need sufficiently pressing to outweigh the public interest in freedom of expression and therefore was not 'necessary in a democratic society' for maintaining the authority of the judiciary; and accordingly, was in violation of Article 10.

8 . [1973] 1 QB 710.
9 . The report of the Committee on Contempt of Court in 1974 (Cmnd 5794) was highly critical of this approach adopted by the House of Lords.

In response to this finding, the government introduced a bill which became the Contempt of Court Act 1981. Section 5 provided:

> A publication made as or as part of a discussion in good faith of public affairs or other matters of general public interest is not to be treated as a contempt of court under the strict liability rule if the risk of impediment or prejudice to particular legal proceedings is merely incidental to the discussion.

The Act also provided in section 2 that the strict liability rule — which meant liability although there was no intention to interfere with the course of justice — applied only to a publication which created a substantial risk that the course of justice would be seriously impeded or prejudiced.[10]

On 15 October 1980 the *Daily Mail* published an article by Mr Malcolm Muggeridge entitled 'The vision of life that wins my vote' in support of an independent 'pro-life' candidate at a parliamentary by-election. She was supported by the Society for the Protection of Unborn Children and took as a main plank in her campaign the stopping of the practice that she asserted was developing in some British hospitals of killing new-born handicapped babies.

The date of publication was also the third day of the trial in the Crown Court at Leicester of a well known paediatrician on a charge of murdering a three-day-old mongoloid baby by giving instructions that it should be treated with a drug which caused it to die of starvation. The newspaper article made no mention of the trial but it contained the words 'Today the chances of such a baby surviving would be very small indeed. Someone would surely recommend letting her die of starvation or otherwise disposing of her.'

Lord Diplock said that 'substantial' and 'seriously' in section 2 were intended to exclude a risk that was only remote; that the article was clearly capable of prejudicing the jury against the accused; and that it satisfied the criterion in that section. He held, however, that section 5 applied, that the risk of prejudice was merely incidental to the public discussion

10. *A-G v. News Group Newspapers Ltd* [1986] 2 All ER 833.

about the rights and wrongs of the alleged practice of letting deformed babies die, and that the prosecution for contempt therefore failed. The other Law Lords agreed.[11]

However Lord Diplock also commented that the article in this case was 'nearly in all respects the antithesis of the article which the House of Lords had held to be a contempt of court in *Attorney-General v. Times Newspapers Ltd* (the thalidomide case). In that case, he said, the whole subject of the article was the pending civil actions against the drugs company and the whole purpose of the article was to put pressure on the company in the lawful conduct of their defence in those actions.

Lord Diplock's words make clear that, in his opinion, section 5 of the Contempt of Court Act 1981 does not bring English law into conformity with the European Convention. But indeed his judgment seems to go further. His findings that the article was clearly capable of creating a substantial risk that the course of justice would be seriously impeded or prejudiced reflects a poor view of the independence, fair-mindedness and intelligence of jurors. Moreover, Lord Diplock's emphasis on 'the whole purpose' of the article in the thalidomide case suggests that, in his view, the limitations in the Act on the strict liability rule might not in any event have availed the *Sunday Times*. Those limitations, including section 5, apply only to unintentional contempts, while 'whole purpose' suggests intention. In the result the Contempt of Court Act 1981, as interpreted by Lord Diplock, may well have made further inroads on the freedom of the press and of publications generally.

An unusual case arose in 1989 when the House of Lords was about to hear argument on an application for judicial review of decisions by the Secretary of State for Trade and Industry to defer publication of an inspector's report and not to refer the matter to the Monopolies and Mergers Commission. While appeal to the Lords was pending, the chief executive of the applicant company (Lonrho) came into possession of a copy of the report, and extracts from it were published in a special mid-week edition of the *Observer* newspaper (a wholly owned subsidiary of Lonrho) which also contained a front-page

11. *A-G v. English* [1982] 3 WLR 278; and see *A-G v. TVS Television Ltd., Independent*, 7 July 1989.

editorial alleging bad faith on the part of the Secretary of State. The Secretary of State obtained an injunction to prevent publication but too late to stop copies which had been sent to certain persons including (by mistake) four of the five Law Lords due to hear the appeal. The Lords heard and dismissed the appeal and a differently constituted Appellate Committee of the Lords considered whether the *Observer* publication was a contempt of court. That committee decided that, under Section 2 of Contempt of Court Act 1981 (see above) it was not a contempt because the publication did not in the circumstances create any risk that the course of justice in the appellate proceedings would be impeded or prejudiced.[12] Lord Keith, referring to the decision in the thalidomide case, said:

> How far these passages from the speeches of their Lordships may still be relied upon as accurate expressions of the law is extremely doubtful, certainly in relation to the kind of contempt which is the subject matter of the strict liability rule in sections 1 and 2 of the Act of 1981 ... Whether the course of justice in particular proceedings will be impeded or prejudiced by a publication must depend primarily on whether the publication will bring influence to bear which is likely to divert the proceedings in some way from the course which they would otherwise have followed.

Two sisters were convicted of murder. A witness who provided the main identification evidence at the trial had made a previous inconsistent statement which the police sergeant in charge of the case did not disclose to the prosecution. The Court of Appeal held that this was a material irregularity and also that the press coverage of the trial was unremitting, extensive, sensational, inaccurate and misleading. The convictions were quashed.[13]

12. *In re Lonrho plc* [1989] 3 WLR 535.
13. *R. v. Taylor* (1994) 98 Cr.App.R.361.

Confidentiality

Over the last twenty years the courts have developed rules to protect statements made in confidence. This particularly relates to trade secrets, personal relationships, and government secrets. The courts have been willing to issue injunctions preventing disclosure, as well as giving damages for breach of confidence.

R. H. S. Crossman kept a diary during the six years from 1964 to 1970 when he was a member of the Cabinet. Thereafter he began to collate his records and had completed and handed to his publishers the first volume before his death in April 1974. On 10 May 1974, one of the publishers, who was also a literary executor of Mr Crossman, sent a copy of the type-script of this volume (which dealt with the period 1964–6) to the Cabinet Secretary asking for 'a reasonably quick reading' as publication was planned for that autumn. On 22 June the Secretary said that he could not agree to publication of this volume. He said there were two complementary principles. The first was the collective responsibility of the Cabinet and the need to maintain secrecy to ensure completely frank discussion within the Cabinet and its committees. The second was the personal responsibility of individual ministers. Further correspondence followed and the *Sunday Times* published some extracts from the diaries, not all of which had been 'cleared' by the Cabinet Secretary. Then, in June 1975, the Attorney-General brought two actions for injunctions to prevent the publication of the first volume and of further extracts by the *Sunday Times*. The Attorney-General argued that the courts should forbid publication as being contrary to the public interest. He also argued that there was a principle of law that no one should profit from the wrongful publication of information received in confidence. This principle had been recognized as a ground for restraining the unfair use of commercial secrets transmitted in confidence. And in *Argyll v. Argyll*[14] the same

14. [1967] Ch. 302. In *Fraser v. Evans* [1969] 1 QB 349 the confidential report of the plaintiff, who was a public relations consultant to the Greek government, came into the hands of the *Sunday Times*. The Court of Appeal refused to issue an injunction to prevent its publication on the ground that the person to whom the confidential duty was owed (i.e. the Greek government) was not seeking the protection of the court.

principle was applied to domestic secrets passing between husband and wife during marriage. On the basis of the decision in that case, the Lord Chief Justice concluded that when a Cabinet minister received information in confidence the improper publication of such information could be restrained by the courts. In particular, he said: 'The expression of individual opinions by cabinet ministers in the course of cabinet discussions are matters of confidence, the publication of which can be restrained by the court when this is clearly necessary in the public interest.'

This was a new principle or, at least, the considerable extension of an older principle. When the Lord Chief Justice came to apply this to the case before him, he decided that in view of the lapse of time (nearly ten years since the end of the period covered by the first volume of the diaries) he would not issue the injunctions asked for because he could not believe that publication would inhibit free discussion of the cabinet in 1975.[15]

In the event, therefore, the first volume of the Crossman diaries was published. But more important was the establishment of the new rule of law that the courts have jurisdiction to determine when the public interest requires that ministers shall not be permitted to disclose information. I am not suggesting that there should be no constraints on such publication. But hitherto the constraints, if they have not been imposed by the Official Secrets Acts, have been political. The principle established by this case enables the courts to determine what is in the public interest on a matter which is at the heart of the political system.

In 1981 the majority of the Court of Appeal in *Schering Chemicals Ltd v. Falkman Ltd* upheld the granting of an injunction restraining Thames Television Ltd from showing a film about the Primodos drug used in pregnancy testing. Two actions by mothers of deformed children claiming compensation against the manufacturers were due to start some nine months later. This was not a decision on contempt of court but on whether there had been breach of confidence by the

15. *A-G v. Jonathan Cape Ltd; A-G v. Times Newspapers Ltd* [1975] 3 All ER 484.

producer of the film in respect of confidential information. Shaw LJ, for the majority, said: 'The law of England was indeed, as Blackstone declared, a law of liberty; but the freedoms it recognized did not include a licence for the mercenary betrayal of business confidences.'[16] Lord Denning MR, dissenting, said that he stood as ever for the freedom of the press, including television, except where that freedom was abused as, he said, it was in the *Granada* case. Even if there were abuse in this present case, it was not such as to warrant an injunction operating as a prior restraint.

In *Francome v. Mirror Group Newspapers*,[17] the plaintiffs were man and wife, he being the champion National Hunt jockey. Unknown persons tapped telephone conversations to and from the plaintiffs' home and offered the tapes for sale to the *Daily Mirror*, alleging that they revealed breaches by the jockey of the rules of racing. The plaintiffs brought an action for breach of confidence against the *Daily Mirror*, and the Court of Appeal, pending trial, made an order that the newspaper be restrained from publishing any article based on the tapes, that there be a speedy trial and that the newspaper disclose the identity of the unknown persons. On appeal, this order was varied so that disclosure of the identity was not required at this stage.

Ten days later, a differently composed Court of Appeal considered a case where the plaintiff company marketed an electronic computerized instrument known as the Lion Intoximeter 3000, and 60 per cent of their sales were to police authorities for measuring intoxication by alcohol. Two of their former employees leaked copies of the plaintiffs' internal correspondence to the *Daily Express* and the plaintiffs sought an injunction to prevent publication. A conflict of public interests arose because the allegation was that the instrument was not accurate. The court allowed the publication of some of the documents.[18]

Such cases of breach of confidence or of copyright frequently give rise to such conflicts and the courts determine

16. [1982] QB 1; for the *Granada* case, see pp. 252–3.
17. [1984] 1 WLR 892.
18. *Lion Laboratories v. Evans* [1984] 3 WLR 539.

whether the private rights or the public interest should prevail. In *Francome* Sir John Donaldson MR said:

> The 'media' ... are an essential foundation of any democracy. In exposing crime, antisocial behaviour and hypocrisy and in campaigning for reform and propagating the view of minorities, they perform an invaluable function. However, they are peculiarly vulnerable to the error of confusing the public interest with their own interest. Usually these interests march hand in hand, but not always. In the instant case, pending a trial, it is impossible to see what public interest would be served by publishing the contents of the tapes which would not equally be served by giving them to the police or to the Jockey Club. Any wider publication could only serve the interests of the *Daily Mirror*.

The most famous cases where the protection of confidentiality was claimed deserve a section to themselves.

The Spycatcher cases

The story is complicated and the litigation was conducted over a period of more than four years in Australia, the United Kingdom, Hong Kong and New Zealand.[19] Here, I will concentrate on the hearings in the United Kingdom.

Peter Maurice Wright was a member of the internal security service known as MI5 from 1955 to the beginning of 1976. From 1964, he was in the counter-espionage branch and on the staff of the Director-General as a senior officer. When he retired, he lived in Tasmania and became an Australian citizen. There he wrote his memoirs, entitled *Spycatcher*, to be published in Australia by Heinemann. The material in the book was not less than ten years old. It included allegations of a plot by members of MI5 to destabilize the Wilson government of the United Kingdom in 1974–6; of a plan by MI6 (the security service concerned with activities outside the United

19. The most useful collection is Michael Fysh (ed.), *The Spycatcher Cases* (1989) cited as FSR.

Kingdom) to assassinate President Nasser of Egypt; of regular bugging of foreign embassies, including the French, in London. Wright also alleged that Sir Roger Hollis, one-time Director-General of MI5, was a Soviet spy.

In September 1985, the Attorney-General of the United Kingdom, having discovered that Wright intended to publish his memoirs in Australia, began proceedings in the Supreme Court of New South Wales seeking to restrain publication. The ground on which the order was sought was that, in making disclosures, Wright would be in breach of the terms of his employment and in particular in breach of his duty of lifelong confidentiality imposed on him by the Official Secrets Act 1911 and declarations which he had signed. On 10 September 1985, the Attorney-General obtained an *ex parte* order in Australia from a court in Australia pending the litigation, and on 16 September the defendant publishers and Wright gave undertakings not to publish until the case had been decided.

On 22 and 23 June 1986, two British newspapers, the *Guardian* and the *Observer*, published articles outlining allegations to be made in *Spycatcher* but denied having seen the manuscript of the book or copies of it. They said the allegations were not new and had been published before. But they wished to be able to publish information in the future deriving directly or indirectly from Wright. The newspapers also argued that breach of confidentiality was permissible if it disclosed wrongdoing and that they should not be restrained from publication, save exceptionally, when the information was of legitimate public interest. On 27 June, the Attorney-General obtained *ex parte* injunctions and on 11 July these were upheld by Millett J pending the full trial. The judge added a proviso that the defendants should be free to publish matters disclosed in open court in Australia. The newspapers appealed but on 25 July the Court of Appeal upheld the Millett injunction citing, amongst other cases, *American Cyanamid v. Ethicon*,[20] *British Steel Corporation v. Granada Television*,[21] *Francome v. Mirror*

20. See p. 91.
21. See pp. 252–3.

Group,[22] *Fraser v. Evans,*[23] *Lion Laboratories v. Evans.*[24] Sir John Donaldson MR said:

> Given the special nature of the confidentiality which applies to any aspect of the security service, such publication could not possibly be justified on the evidence at present available and I regard it as in the highest degree unlikely that it could be justified on further evidence which may be available at the trial.[25]

In November and December of 1986, the Attorney-General's application for injunctions in Australia was heard, but on 13 March 1987 it was rejected by Powell J in the Supreme Court of New South Wales.

On 27 April 1987, the *Independent* newspaper published an article referring to information in *Spycatcher*, having received a manuscript copy. Two other London papers copied, in part. The Attorney-General moved for contempt of court and this was heard by the Vice Chancellor (Sir Nicolas Browne-Wilkinson) on 20–22 May. On 2 June, the motion was dismissed on a preliminary point of law of great importance. The parties agreed that it had first to be decided:

> Whether a publication made in the knowledge of an outstanding injunction against another party and which if made by that other party would be in breach thereof constitutes a criminal contempt of court upon the footing that it assaults or interferes with the process of justice in relation to the said injunction.

In other words, while publication in the *Independent* and the other newspapers was not a breach of the Millett injunction against the *Guardian* and the *Observer*, the Attorney-General argued that nevertheless the publication was one of contempt as it frustrated or impeded the due administration of justice. The newspapers argued that this was to widen the law of contempt and offended the basic principles of natural justice.

22. See pp. 222–3.
23. See p. 220.
24. See p. 18.
25. *A-G v. Guardian Newspapers Ltd and The Observer* (1986) [1989] 2 FSR 23.

The Court of Appeal on 15 July accepted the Attorney-General's argument. Sir John Donaldson MR said:

> I should like to re-emphasize with all the power at my command that this case is not primarily about national security or official secrets. It is about the right of private citizens and public authorities to seek and obtain the protection of the courts for confidential information which they claim to be their property.

The duty of confidentiality (in these cases, that owed by Wright to the Crown) could be opposed by a claim of a right to publish, whether on grounds of the public interest or otherwise but, pending the trial of the action, 'the balance will normally come down in favour of preserving confidentiality, for the very obvious reason that, if this is not done and publication is permitted, there will be nothing left to have a trial about.'

So the preliminary point of law was decided in favour of the Attorney-General and the case was remitted to the High Court. We return to this below.

Three days before the conclusion of the hearing before the Court of Appeal in July 1987, the *Sunday Times* published extracts from *Spycatcher* and two days before, on 13 July, the book was published in the United States of America, and became available in the United Kingdom. On 18 July, the Attorney-General was granted an injunction, in contempt of court proceedings, against the *Sunday Times* to restrain it from continuing its serialization of *Spycatcher*.[26]

On 20 July, the *Guardian* and the *Observer* applied for the Millett injunction against them to be discharged on the ground that there had been a material change of circumstance, particularly the availability of *Spycatcher* in the United Kingdom and the earlier failure of the Attorney-General's application in New South Wales. It was agreed that if the Millett injunction were discharged, the Attorney General's action against the *Sunday Times* would also fail. So the order against the *Sunday Times* was continued to await the decision on the Millett injunction.

Sir Nicolas Browne-Wilkinson V-C on 22 July discharged

26. For these and subsequent proceedings, see *A-G v. Guardian Newspapers Ltd and others* [1987] 1 All ER 1248.

the injunction against the *Guardian* and the *Observer*. He observed:

> It is frequently said that the law is an ass. I, of course, do not agree. But there is a limit to what can be achieved by orders of the court. If the courts were to make orders manifestly incapable of achieving their avowed purpose, such as to prevent the dissemination of information which is already disseminated the law would to my mind indeed be an ass.

At this point, if the drama were being enacted on stage, the curtain would surely fall for the interval. Once *Spycatcher* was published in the United States, and then made available in the United Kingdom, how could publication of articles or extracts be denied? The United Kingdom government did not seek to prevent publication in the United States, no doubt because they had been advised that the First Amendment to the Constitution of the USA protecting freedom of speech would have precluded the possibility of success in that country. As the audience took their drinks and ate their ice-cream they would have wondered how the dramatist could develop his story in the second act.

But the Court of Appeal revived the drama by immediately allowing an appeal. They agreed that the Millett injunction could not continue in its present form but the Vice Chancellor had made the mistake of not considering some modification of the order. Peter Wright was still in breach of his duty of confidentiality. The common law showed its virility in the words of the Master of the Rolls. Sir John Donaldson said:

> I accept that to the extent that these publications have been read, the information to which they relate has become public knowledge, but not that it has entered the public domain, so losing the seal of confidentiality, because that only occurs when information not only becomes a matter of public knowledge, but also public property.

So Sir John rewrote the injunction to prevent publication of any passage of *Spycatcher* or any words of Peter Wright which 'concerned the British Security Service or its activities or any other security service or its activities' provided that the order should 'not prevent the publication of a summary in very general terms of the allegations made by Mr Wright'.

Off then, posthaste, to the House of Lords, for a hearing at the end of July. Both sides agreed that the modified injunction 'could not be supported in law and was unworkable in practice', not to say daft. There was much speculation which way their Lordships would jump: to restore the Millett injunction or to take the view of the Vice Chancellor? Would the government's pursuit of Peter Wright and the enforcement of his duty of confidentiality be temporarily successful? Or would the Law Lords bring the chase to an end, now that *Spycatcher* was being read by anyone who went to the trouble of obtaining a copy? In the majority, Lords Brandon, Templeman and Ackner came down on the government's side, with Lords Bridge and Oliver in the minority. The proviso to the Millett injunction permitting the publication of material disclosed in the proceedings in New South Wales was deleted.

For the majority view Lords Brandon and Ackner emphasized that the injunction was temporary, awaiting the full trial of the issues and that the Attorney-General should not be deprived of having the case properly adjudicated. Lords Templeman and Ackner said there was a substantial public interest in maintaining the efficiency of the security service; that the publication of *Spycatcher* would cause grievous harm to individuals and deal a blow to the morale of the service; and that there was ample justification for the continuance of the Millett injunction. Lord Templeman added that if the injunction were discharged an immutable precedent would be created.[27]

Lord Oliver, dissenting, said that as the Vice Chancellor had properly exercised his discretion in discharging the injunction, appellate courts should not interfere. He also questioned 'both the effectiveness and the appropriateness' of seeking to protect the security service by continuing against the newspaper 'a fetter on disclosure of information which, for good or ill, is now freely obtainable and disclosable by other members of

27. In October 1989, the European Commission of Human Rights admitted applications from the *Guardian*, the *Observer* and the *Sunday Times*, alleging that this decision infringed the European Convention on Human ~hts.

the public'. He added: 'I cannot help but feel that your Lordships are being asked in the light of what has now occurred to beat the air and to interfere with an essential freedom for the preservation of a confidentiality that has already been lost beyond recall.'

These were strong words but Lord Bridge, the other dissentient, went even further. To him the crucial facts were the publication of *Spycatcher* in the United States and the government's decision not to try to prevent the importation of the book. As the case for maintaining the injunctions could not be any stronger at the trial, the real question was whether the Attorney-General could sustain a claim for permanent injunctions. Lord Bridge questioned whether there was any remaining interest of national security which the Millett injunctions were capable of protecting. Then he said:

> Freedom of speech is always the first casualty under a totalitarian régime. Such a régime cannot afford to allow the free circulation of information and ideas among its citizens. Censorship is the indispensable tool to regulate what the public may and what they may not know. The present attempt to insulate the public in this country from information which is freely available elsewhere is a significant step down that very dangerous road.

On 24 September 1987, the appeal from Powell J's decision in New South Wales was dismissed.

At last in November and December 1987, the full trial of the Attorney-General's case against the *Guardian*, the *Observer* and the *Sunday Times* was heard at first instance, by Scott J.[28] At the end of a long judgment, he refused injunctive relief in the three actions. It must be remembered that the Attorney-General was arguing that it was essential for the future of the security service that the lifelong confidentiality of officers of that service should be enforced; that the newspapers knew that Peter Wright had this duty not to disclose information obtained when he was an officer; that they were therefore under a comparable duty not to disclose. Scott J held

28. *A-G v. Guardian Newspapers Ltd and others (No. 2)* [1988] 2 WLR 805.

that the *Guardian* and *Observer* articles reporting the court action in Australia and disclosing other allegations in *Spycatcher*, such as the plot to assassinate President Nasser of Egypt and to destabilize the government of Harold Wilson in the 1960s, were justified as being in the public interest. The wide publication of *Spycatcher* meant that there was no longer any duty of confidence lying on the newspapers.

The Court of Appeal dismissed the Attorney-General's appeal while stressing, as had Scott J, that, depending on the facts of the case, third parties (such as the newspapers) might be bound to respect the confidentiality of information coming into their possession.[29] Certainly the government had an enforceable right to the maintenance of confidentiality by its confidant. But when information had been generally communicated to the public, the duty of confidentiality could no longer be sustained. The Court of Appeal also accepted that breach of confidence might be justified by countervailing public interests. The Attorney-General appealed and the *Sunday Times* cross-appealed. And so, once again, to the House of Lords, where the case was argued in June 1988 and opinions were delivered in October. The appeal and the cross-appeal were dismissed.[30]

On the main issue, the Law Lords held that for the Crown to obtain an injunction to prevent the disclosure of confidential information, damage to the public interest, or a likelihood thereof, must be shown. General publication of *Spycatcher* would not bring any significant further damage to the public interest and so the Millett injunction must be discharged. A third party who comes into possession of confidential information may be under a duty not to disclose it, but this depends on the particular circumstances. The articles in the *Guardian* and the *Observer* had not contained information damaging to the public interest (Lord Griffiths dissenting on this point).

Lord Keith of Kinkel said:

The Crown's argument in the present case would go the length that in all circumstances where the original disclosure has been made by a Crown servant in breach

29. See last note.
30. [1988] 3 WLR 776.

of his obligation of confidence any person to whose knowledge the information comes and who is aware of the breach comes under an equitable duty binding his conscience not to communicate the information to anyone else irrespective of the circumstances under which he acquired the knowledge. In my opinion that general proposition is untenable and impracticable, in addition to being unsupported by any authority . . . A communication about some aspect of government activity which does no harm to the interests of the nation cannot, even where the original disclosure has been made in breach of confidence, be restrained on the ground of a nebulous equitable duty of conscience serving no useful practical purpose.

And he referred to the Crossman diaries case where Lord Widgery CJ allowed publication on the ground that it would do no harm to the public interest.

It was, however, held that the *Sunday Times* was in breach of its duty of confidence in publishing its first serialised extract from *Spycatcher* on 12 July 1987; that it was not protected by either the defence of prior publication or the disclosure of iniquity; that imminent publication of the book in the USA did not amount to a justification; and that, accordingly, the *Sunday Times* was liable to account for the profits resulting from that breach.

In May 1989 the remitted case against the *Independent* and others, including the *Sunday Times*, was heard by Mr Justice Morritt. He found them guilty of contempt of court and fined each of the publishers £50,000. The Court of Appeal, in February 1990, dismissed the appeals but discharged the fines. This decision confirmed that it is a contempt of court, as interfering with the course of justice, for a newspaper editor to publish information which he knows is the subject of an injunction against another newspaper.[31]

Several newspapers brought proceedings against the United Kingdom before the European Court of Human Rights. A majority of the court upheld the injunctions issued by Millett

---

31. *A-G. v. Newspaper Publishing plc and others* [1989] FSR 457.

J as not infringing freedom of expression (Article 10 of the Convention), but found that their continuance in July 1987 after the publication of the book in the United States did infringe the Article.[32]

Disclosure of documents

Official secrets may be protected by the courts under a rule which provides that the Crown may claim that certain documents should not be disclosed to a party engaged in litigation on the ground that the public interest would be harmed by their production.[33] In the leading case of *Duncan v. Cammell Laird*[34] the plaintiffs were the legal representatives or dependants of some of the ninety-nine men who lost their lives when the submarine *Thetis* sank during tests in Liverpool Bay. The defendants were those who had built the submarine. The plaintiffs called for the disclosure of plans, specifications and other documents relating to the construction of the submarine and the First Lord of the Admiralty objected. The objection was upheld by the House of Lords. That the rule applied to a great variety of cases is shown by the decision of the Court of Appeal in *Wednesbury Corporation v. Ministry of Housing and Local Government*[35] when an objection was upheld to the disclosure of departmental briefs for the guidance of, and correspondence with, ministerial inspectors who had held a local enquiry into a proposal by the Local Government Commission that five local authorities should be extinguished and included in larger county boroughs.

As a result of these and other cases, it had come to be assumed that the affidavit of the minister concerned which claimed non-disclosure, so long as it was properly executed, could not be challenged in the courts. If he said that disclosure was not in the public interest, that was the end of the matter.

32. See [1992] *Public Law* 156, 200−8.
33. For the historical background, see J. M. Jacob, 'From privileged Crown to interested public', in [1993] *Public Law* 121−50; also Jacob, *The Republican Crown* (1996).
34. [1942] AC 624.
35. [1965] 1 WLR 261.

But in *Conway v. Rimmer*[36] the House of Lords held that there might be a clash between the public interest that harm should not be done to the nation or the public service by the disclosure of certain documents, and the public interest in the proper administration of justice. If this were so, the court could inspect the documents and might override the minister's claim — though if the minister's reasons were beyond the competence of the court to assess, the minister's view would have to prevail. The action in the case was brought by a former probationary police constable against his former superintendent for malicious prosecution, and the documents included reports made by the defendant on the plaintiff. In the light of the later decision on the Crossman diaries, Lord Reid's comments at one point in his judgment are interesting and left no doubt where his sympathies lay in the perennial conflict between the secretiveness of governments and people's wish to know what is being done in their name:

> Virtually everyone agrees that cabinet minutes and the like ought not to be disclosed until such time as they are only of historical interest. But I do not think that many people would give as the reason that premature disclosure would prevent candour in the cabinet. To my mind the most important reason is that such disclosure would create or fan ill-informed or captious public or political criticism. The business of government is difficult enough as it is, and no government could contemplate with equanimity the inner workings of the government machine being exposed to the gaze of those ready to criticize without adequate knowledge of the background and perhaps with some axe to grind.

One result of this decision may have been that the Crown's claim to non-disclosure is less frequently made than in the past. Recent cases involving disclosures of documents held by Customs and Excise have been decided in opposite directions,[37]

36. [1968] AC 910; and see *Burmah Oil Co. Ltd v. Bank of England* [1980] AC 1198.
37. See *Norwich Pharmacal v. Customs & Excise* [1974] AC 133 and *A. Crompton Ltd v. Customs & Excise (No 2)* [1974] AC 405.

but one decision of more public interest is disturbing. Under the Gaming Act 1968, certificates of consent have to be obtained from the Gaming Board for the running of bingo halls. R applied and the Gaming Board made certain enquiries with the police. The assistant chief constable of Sussex replied in a letter, a copy of which came into the possession of R, who laid an information against him alleging criminal libel. As a result the chief constable of Sussex and the secretary of the Gaming Board were both summoned to produce this letter. The Home Secretary objected to its disclosure. The House of Lords held

> that the public interest required that the letters should not be produced, since, if the information given to the Board was liable to be disclosed, it might be withheld and they would thereby be hampered in the discharge of the duty imposed on them by statute to identify and exclude persons of dubious character and reputation from the privilege of obtaining a licence to conduct a gaming establishment.

The argument of the House of Lords was based widely on the public interest, not on the particular position of the Crown. Lord Reid said: 'It must always be open to any person interested to raise the question' of the public interest and it was said that Parliament in passing the Gaming Act must have expected that the Gaming Board would be obliged to receive certain documents which no one would contemplate they had to divulge.[38] The problem in all this is, of course, that such decisions make it extremely difficult, often impossible, for a private citizen to challenge a 'confidential' report made about him by the police or other public authority. The 'proper functioning of the public service' can be bought at too high a price.

A similar reflection inevitably arises from considerations of the grounds given by Lord Denning MR for the decision of the Court of Appeal in *Home Office v. Harman* (1981).[39] Harriet Harman, a solicitor and legal officer of the National Council for Civil Liberties, was acting for a convicted prisoner in his

---

38. *R. v. Lewes JJ ex parte Home Secretary* [1973] AC 388.
39. [1981] 2 WLR 310; *Williams v. Home Office* [1981] 1 All ER 1551.

action against the Home Office arising out of his treatment in prison in an experimental 'control unit'. She sought certain documents from the Home Office, the disclosure of which was refused on the ground of public interest. But a judge ordered their disclosure. In the action brought by the prisoner against the Home Office, several of these documents were read out in court. Subsequently Ms Harman allowed a journalist to see them. The Home Office brought an action against her for contempt on the ground that documents are disclosed only for the purposes of the specific litigation and that she had no right to show them to a journalist even though they had been made public in court.

In words reminiscent of Lord Reid in *Conway v. Rimmer* (see above) Lord Denning said:

> It was in the public interest that these documents should be kept confidential. They should not be exposed to the ravages of outsiders. I regard the use made by the journalists in this case of these documents to be highly detrimental to the good ordering of our society ... The danger of disclosure is that critics − of one political colour or another − will seize on this confidential information so as to seek changes in governmental policy, or to condemn it. So the machinery of government will be hampered or even thwarted.

The Court of Appeal upheld the decision of the judge at first instance that Ms Harman was guilty of contempt. The court was obviously influenced by the fact that the journalist had used the documents to write an article condemning the Home Office for what he called 'internal bureaucratic intrigue' surrounding the setting up of the control units.

Ms Harman appealed to the House of Lords which upheld the Court of Appeal but only by the decisions of three Law Lords against two. Lord Diplock, who was joined in the majority by Lords Keith and Roskill, began with a stylistic mannerism of which some of the senior judiciary are apparently fond.[40]

---

40. [1982] 2 WLR 338; cf. Lord Wilberforce in *British Steel Corporation v. Granada Television* [1980] 3 WLR at 821: 'This case does not touch upon the freedom of the press even at its periphery.' And see p. 226 above.

He insisted that the case was *not* about freedom of speech, freedom of the press, openness of justice or documents coming into 'the public domain'; nor did it call for consideration of any of those human rights and fundamental freedoms contained in the European Convention on Human Rights. To Lord Diplock the case was only about 'an aspect of the law of discovery of documents in civil actions in the High Court', and he saw discovery as 'an inroad' upon the right of the individual 'to keep his own documents to himself'. So seen, the obligation not to use a disclosed document for any purpose other than of the litigation did *not* terminate at the moment the document was read out in court. Lord Keith spoke similarly of discovery constituting 'a very serious invasion of the privacy and confidentiality of a litigant's affairs'.

Lord Scarman, joined by Lord Simon in the minority, took a broader view by reference to the European Convention and American law. And he noted that the Home Office took no steps to prevent the documents from being made public once the judge had ordered their disclosure. The Home Office had not appealed against that order or renewed their objection at the trial. So once the documents were read out in open court, in Lord Scarman's opinion, the obligation binding the litigant and his solicitor ceased.

The majority seemed to be unmoved by the manifest absurdities of the position they took up (though Lord Roskill was more hesitant than his colleagues). The journalist could have obtained a transcript of the proceedings in court and so have had legitimate access to the documents. Moreover, only the litigant and his solicitor could be bound by the limitations imposed. Anyone could have taken a shorthand note of the documents when they were read out in court and used the information so acquired as he wished.

Two connected facts seem to have been most influential in the minds of the majority. The first was that these were government documents and governments must not be unduly embarrassed in such circumstances. And the second was the use made by the journalist in attacking the activities of a government department. None of the majority was so explicit as Lord Denning in the Court of Appeal but Lord Keith noted: 'It would be unrealistic not to recognize that (Ms Harman) must have been activated by a desire to advance some aspect of the causes espoused by the National Council for Civil Liberties, which employed her as a legal officer.' It must be very doubtful whether any action for contempt would have been brought by the Home Office had the journalist's article not been critical of the department.

After the decision, Ms Harman, the *Guardian* newspaper and the National Council for Civil Liberties applied to the European Commission of Human Rights alleging breach of the Convention. In 1986, after the Commission had decided that the complaint was admissible, a friendly settlement was reached and the government made new provision under the Rules of the Supreme Court. This reads:

> Any undertaking, whether express or implied, not to use a document for any purposes other than those of the proceedings in which it is disclosed shall cease to apply to such document after it has been read to or by the Court, or referred to, in open court, unless the Court for special reasons has otherwise ordered on the application of a party or of the person to whom the document belongs.

This falls short of a ringing declaration in support of the principle that proceedings in open court are public property.[41]

This conflict between the public interest in the proper administration of justice and the protection of documents from disclosure has been the subject of more and more litigation in recent years. In *Neilson v. Laugharne*[42] the plaintiff's house was searched by the police while he was on holiday, on suspicion of drug offences, but nothing was found. During the search the police noticed that his electricity meter appeared to have been tampered with and, on his return, he was arrested but not charged. He complained to the chief constable who instituted the complaints procedure under the Police Act 1964, which resulted in a decision that there were no grounds for proceedings against the police officers involved. The plaintiff com-

41. See *Bibby Bulk Carriers v. Consulex Ltd* [1988] 2 All ER 820.
42. [1981] 2 WLR 537; and see *Hehir v. Commissioner of Police for Metropolis* [1982] 1 WLR 715.

menced proceedings against the chief constable who refused to disclose statements made during the course of the enquiry into the complaints on the ground that they were covered by legal professional privilege. The Court of Appeal upheld the refusal. Lord Denning MR said, 'Legal aid is being used by complaining persons to harass innocent folk who have only been doing their duty. The complainants make all sorts of allegations – often quite unjustifiable – and then use legal machinery to try to manufacture a case. We should come down firmly against such tactics. We should refuse to order production.' Oliver LJ rested his decision on the ground that disclosures would inhibit the proper conduct of the enquiry procedure and that the public interest required that the documents should be protected as a class.

The facts in *Williams v. Home Office*[43] are set out above.[44] The prisoner sought documents from the Home Office, some of which were refused on the ground that they came within the class of documents relating to the formulation of government policy and that their production would inhibit freedom of expression between ministers and inhibit officials from giving full advice to ministers. McNeill J ordered the disclosure of some of these documents and, citing the authority of Law Lords in an earlier case, rejected the argument about the need to preserve candour between ministers and public servants. But in *Air Canada v. Secretary of State for Trade (No. 2)*[45] a group of airlines which wished to challenge the defendant's approval of substantial increases in landing charges at Heathrow airport were refused disclosure of documents concerned with the formulation of government policy. Three members of the House of Lords upheld this refusal on the ground that the plaintiffs had to show that the information sought was likely to help their case or damage their adversary's in the sense that there was a reasonable probability and not just a mere speculative belief that it would do so; and that the plaintiffs had failed to establish this. The other two Law Lords, while

43. [1981] 1 All ER 1151.
44. See pp. 234–5.
45. [1983] 1 All ER 910; see also *Campbell v. Tameside Metropolitan BC* [1982] 3 WLR 74.

agreeing in the result, held that the court should consider disclosures whenever this was necessary for a just determination of the case.

In the Court of Appeal, Lord Denning MR had referred to *Williams v. Home Office*, and to the judge's overruling of the department's objections to disclosure. Lord Denning said:

> He thought that there was a safeguard in that they could only be used for the purpose of the action . . . His decision was claimed by the advocates of 'open government' to be a 'legal milestone'. But the safeguard proved to be no safeguard at all. The documents were used by a journalist to make severe criticisms of ministers and of higher civil servants who could not answer back. When this was brought to our attention, I said, 'The "legal milestone" will have to be taken up and set back a bit,' see *Home Office v. Harman*. That case is a good illustration of the need for keeping high-level documents secret. Once they are let out of the bag, untold mischief may be done. It is no use relying on safeguards. The documents must not be let out of the bag at all. I trust that today we are setting back the 'legal milestone' to the place where it was before.[46]

Arms to Iraq

We have already referred to the setting up in November 1992 of an inquiry, under the chairmanship of Sir Richard Scott, into the export of defence equipment and dual-use goods to Iraq, the prosecution of senior executives of Matrix Churchill, and the circumstances of the acquittal of the company executives.[47]

Four ministers had, in the days preceding the trial, signed public interest immunity (PII) certificates claiming that the production of certain documents held by the Crown would be contrary to the public interest. Mr Justice Smedley overruled

46. [1983] 1 All ER 161.
47. See p. 37. For the report of the inquiry, see HC115 of 1995–96.

their claims in part and ordered the release of documents. The claims led to accusations that, amongst other things, the ministers were prepared to put the company executives at risk of conviction and imprisonment rather than disclose documents which might embarrass the government.

A dispute arose about the obligations of ministers in relation to PII certificates, the Attorney-General asserting that ministers had a duty to claim immunity for documents the production of which would be contrary to the public interest; and that this duty could not be waived.[48] The four ministers who claimed immunity for documents in the Matrix Churchill case were told by the Attorney-General that they had no choice but to sign, though one of them (Mr Heseltine) protested and insisted on certain reservations.

Sir Richard Scott examined this question at length.[49] The most frequently cited passage for the Attorney-General's assertion is by Lord Justice Bingham in *Makanjuola v. Metropolitan Police Commissioner*[50] where he said, 'Where a litigant asserts that documents are immune from production on disclosure on public interest grounds he is not (if the claim is well founded) claiming a right but observing a duty.' In particular the Attorney-General asserted that ministers must sign certificates which claimed immunity for documents falling within a class (such as advice to ministers) for which immunity is habitually claimed. Indeed, it was asserted that in such cases a minister's signature testified only that the document fell within such a class, not that the document itself should be kept from disclosure in the public interest.

Sir Richard disagreed with the Attorney-General's assertion saying that Lord Justice Bingham's statement 'nowhere states or implies that a Minister is under a duty to claim PII for documents that he does not think the public interest requires to be withheld from the defendant. The duty to claim PII arises

48. 213 HC Deb. col. 743 (10 November 1992); other ministers, including the Prime Minister, supported this assertion. See 272 HC Deb. col. 303–5 (22 February 1996).

49. See his report, volume III Section G, chapter 18; for further discussion of the cases, see G. Ganz, 56 *Modern Law Review* (1993) 564; A. Tomkins, [1993] *Public Law* 650; Simon Brown L. J. [1994] *Public Law* 579.

50. [1992] 3 All ER 617.

if the Minister is of the opinion that the disclosure of the documents to the defendant would be damaging to the public interest.'[51]

In the ensuing debate, senior members of the judiciary spoke for or against the Attorney-General's interpretation of ministerial obligation. Lord Fraser of Carmyllie, government spokesman in the House of Lords, claimed support for the Attorney-General's view from 'a current Lord of Appeal in Ordinary, the Master of the Rolls, Lord Alexander of Weedon, a number of distinguished judges who were Treasury Counsel, prominent Silks who advised the Attorney-General at the time and three of the counsel who represented the defendants in the Matrix Churchill trial'.[52] Lord Jenkins of Hillhead spoke of 'the spectacle of half the Bar – perhaps not quite half but a large part of it – and some of the judiciary lining up to say Scott is wrong on PIIs; and the other half and other judges indicating the reverse'.[53] Lord Lloyd of Berwick (perhaps the Law Lord referred to by Lord Carmyllie) treated Sir Richard Scott's detailed review of the cases as if hearing an appeal from the court below, quoted Scott's opinion that the Attorney-General's view was based on a 'fundamental misconception', disagreed, added the usual tribute ('a judge for whom I and all my fellow judges have the greatest admiration') and ended with a direct insult ('possibly he allowed his strong views as to what the law ought to be, to colour his view as to what the law actually was'). Lord Hailsham supported the Attorney-General; so did Lord Simon of Glaisdale; so, somewhat less enthusiastically, did Lord Slynn, another Law Lord. Other distinguished lawyers and former Law Lords expressed their views. Lord Thomson of Monifieth, not a lawyer, said the way the legal profession rallied round the Attorney-General rather reminded him 'of the boilermakers' union in the old days dealing with somebody who had been victimised on the shop floor'.[54]

Before the Scott Report was published the Law Lords

51. See Note 49, para. G18.60.
52. 569 HL Deb. col. 1232 (26 February 1996).
53. See last note at col. 1243.
54. At col. 1344.

decided *ex parte Wiley*.[55] The Court of Appeal had held, following *Neilson v. Laugharne*[56] and *Makanjuola*,[57] that documents produced for the investigation of a complaint against the police belonged to a class which enjoyed public interest immunity. The Law Lords overruled this line of authority. They held that, in the absence of any clear and compelling evidence, there was no justification for imposing a general class public interest immunity on all documents generated by such an investigation.

Lord Lester asked the government whether in the light of the opinion of Lord Woolf expressed in *ex parte Wiley*, the government accepted that the President of the Board of Trade was incorrectly advised by the Attorney-General that public interest immunity required that documents relevant to criminal proceedings concerning the Matrix Churchill affair could not be disclosed to the defence (as the President wished) without the permission of the criminal courts. The Lord Chancellor replied that the speech of Lord Woolf gave fresh guidance, which served to define the approach to be adopted towards certain aspects of public interest immunity; and that guidance would be given full weight in any future advice by the Law Officers on public interest immunity.[58] Translated out of Whitehall language into English, the answer to Lord Lester's question would appear to be Yes. Some, but not all, of their Lordships seemed to favour the strict curtailment, if not the abolition, of public interest immunity based on the 'class' claim.

The Scott Report contained analyses of many cases. Two more examples may be given.

Ordnance Technologies Ltd. (Ordtec) specialized in the design and supply of artillery fuses and propellant charges. Paul Grecian performed the role of managing director. In 1990 he and three others were prosecuted by Customs for illegally exporting components to Iraq. They pleaded guilty. Three were given suspended sentences and one was fined.

55. *R. v. Chief Constable of the West Midlands Police ex parte Wiley* [1994] 3 WLR 433. See also *R. v. Keane* [1994] 2 All ER 478.

56. See p. 237.

57. See p. 240.

58. 557 HL Deb. col. 62 (25 July 1994); See 287 HC Deb. col. 949 (18 December 1996).

Paul Grecian, like Paul Henderson in Matrix Churchill, provided information to the intelligence agencies relating, amongst other matters, to the development by the Iraqis of the Babylon Project (the Supergun).

PII certificates were signed by Mr Lilley (Secretary of State for the DTI) and Mr Baker (Home Secretary) for the trial. In January 1993, the four convicted persons applied for leave to appeal, this being prompted mainly by the disclosure of the documents for which a PII claim had been made in the Matrix Churchill prosecution. On 7 November 1995 the Court of Appeal, headed by the Lord Chief Justice, allowed the appeals principally on the ground that relevant documents had not been disclosed to the defence. The Court of Appeal said they were satisfied that the documents which were now before the court ought to have been made available before the trial. The defence contended that the authorities had 'turned a blind eye' to what they were doing. The documents might at least have left a jury in doubt as to whether the appellant's conduct was condoned by one or more limbs of the executive.[59]

In February 1983 a shipment from a United Kingdom company of 200 Sterling sub-machine guns was seized by Customs at London Docks. The destination was Jordan according to the documents but Customs believed the guns were destined for Iraq. In 1985 the marketing director (Mr Dunk) and the company consultant pleaded guilty to illegally exporting the guns; they were fined. As a result of new evidence that emerged during the course of the Scott inquiry, they appealed in 1994. The director's solicitor had been given assurances by the Iraqi and Jordanian embassies in London that the consignments were presents from Iraq to Jordan and that embassy officials would give evidence in court to this effect. But these promises were withdrawn shortly before the trial and the defence collapsed.

It appeared that Foreign Office and Customs officials had persuaded the embassy officials not to appear in court. The Court of Appeal finding was:

The machinations in this case to prevent witnesses for

59. See HC 115 of 1995—96 volume 2, Section E, Chapter 10 and volume 4 Section J, Chapter 5, 6; *R. v. Grecian* [1996] 1 Cr.App.R. 326.

the defence being available, coupled with the non-disclosure of what had been done, constituted such an interference with the justice process as to amount to an abuse of it.

The appeal was successful and the convictions were quashed.

Restrictions on freedom of expression

In recent years the courts have been particularly severe on local authorities which seek to use their powers to combat action taken against their members and employees by national newspapers. Certain local authorities in London decided to stop taking in their libraries publications of Times Newspapers Ltd, as a gesture of support for employees dismissed by the company during an industrial dispute. The Divisional Court held that this was an abuse of their powers and quashed the decisions. The court held that the ban had been imposed by the local authorities for an ulterior object being inspired by political views which had moved them to use their statutory powers to interfere in an industrial dispute. Lord Justice Watkins said:

> It cannot be other than to all sensible and right-minded people alarming, I think, to see such irresponsible behaviour by persons elected to serve their interest according to clearly stated law and in defiance of impeccably correct advice. There could hardly be a clearer manifestation of an abuse of power, the remedy for which it is for the court and not the Minister to provide.[60]

So also, a Labour-controlled council was held to have abused its powers when it decided to ban the advertising of teaching posts in the *Times Educational Supplement*, in order to punish the proprietors for publishing, in the *Sunday Times*, allegedly libellous articles about the council's leader. Costs at the highest level were awarded against the council because of its 'blatant

60. *R. v. Ealing BC ex parte Times Newspapers Ltd.* [1986] 85 LGR 316.

abuse of power' and a 'gross attempt to deceive the court'.[61]

Subsequently, in *Derbyshire County Council v. Times News-papers*[62] the House of Lords decided that the local authority could not sue for libels said to be contained in two articles in the *Sunday Times* in September 1989 questioning the propriety of certain investments made by the authority with specific references to the Leader of the Council, Mr David Bookbinder. Lord Keith (with whom the other Law Lords agreed) based the decision on the principle that it was of the highest public importance that a democratically elected governmental body, or indeed any governmental body, should be open to uninhibited public criticism; and that the threat of a civil action for defamation must inevitably have an inhibiting effect on freedom of speech. It was contrary to the public interest that such a body should be able to sue.

How broadly this principle may be extended is uncertain but it is not clear why it should be limited to statements made by governmental institutions and officials. In the USA, 'public figures' generally are similarly limited in their right to sue. Commercial tycoons and prominent businessmen, even newspaper proprietors, have been known to use the threat of libel actions to quieten public criticism. But supporters of the general principle in the UK do not favour its application to such persons.[63]

A separate action brought by Mr Bookbinder against Times Newspapers was settled in May 1996, the defendants paying the plaintiff a substantial sum by way of damages and indemnifying him in respect of his legal costs. The defendants also cleared Derbyshire County Council Pension Fund of any allegations of dealings of a corrupt nature.

The BBC's programmes under the title of *Rough Justice* were designed to express doubts about convictions in criminal cases. They aroused the wrath of some judges. In January 1986, the BBC suspended two journalists after the Lord Chief

61. *R. v. Derbyshire CC ex parte Times Supplement Ltd, Independent*, 19 July 1990.

62. [1993] AC 534.

63. See, for example, Lord Lester QC in [1995] *Public Law* 3 ('a line has to be drawn somewhere').

Justice (Lord Lane) had accused them of 'outrageous' behaviour and 'investigation by menaces' in putting together a programme about a man found subsequently to have been wrongly convicted. A year later, as the result of a similar programme (*Out of Court*), the BBC was accused by Lord Lane of broadcasting 'a deliberate attack on the integrity and reliability of the system of criminal justice in this country'.

In 1986 the BBC prepared a series of television programmes called *The Secret Society*, the purpose of which, according to its principal author Duncan Campbell, was to examine how government concealed from Parliament and the public expenditure which should have been disclosed. Under government pressure, the BBC withdrew the programmes, the first of which concerned a defence project, code-named Zircon. On 21 January 1987, the Attorney-General obtained an injunction restraining Mr Campbell and others from disclosing or publishing any information about or included in the programmes. Some Members of Parliament proposed to show the *Zircon* programme in a room in the House of Commons and on 22 January the Attorney-General sought another injunction against them. But the judge refused this on the ground that it was for the House to regulate its own proceedings. So the Speaker issued a direction that the film should not be shown in any room in the House, until the House could decide the matter. On 22 January, the *New Statesman* published an article on the Zircon affair. On 27 January, after debate,[64] the House referred the Speaker's ruling to the Committee of Privileges, on the understanding that it should continue in force until the injunction was lifted or the House decided otherwise. A few days later the police, under warrants, searched the premises of the BBC and the premises of Mr Campbell and others and the *New Statesman* offices in Glasgow and London, and removed films, videotapes and other material.[65] The *Zircon* programme

---

64. 109 HC Deb. col. 206–74. In May 1987, the Committee, by a majority, concluded that the Speaker had acted 'wholly correctly'; the minority wished to record that his action was unconstitutional (see HC 365 of 1986–7.)

65. On 25 February 1987, Mr Campbell gave a detailed undertaking to the High Court and the injunction was discharged.

was eventually shown in September 1988. No prosecutions were brought.

Eleven months later, the procedure was repeated. On 3 December 1987, the government obtained *ex parte* an injunction preventing the BBC from broadcasting a three-part series on Radio 4 on the role of the British security service.

The injunction prevented the BBC from

> broadcasting or causing or permitting to be broadcast, parts of a radio programme *My Country: Right or Wrong* or in any other way whatsoever, any interviews with, or information derived from, current or former members of the security or intelligence services in the UK relating to any aspect of the work of the said services, including their identity as current or former members.

Unlike *The Secret Society* programmes, *My Country* was the responsibility of permanent current affairs producers and editors at the heart of the BBC. The basis of thc application for the injunction was that former and serving security service personnel who were to speak on the programme owed the government a duty of confidentiality. A fortnight later the judge, after a hearing, continued the injunction. Subsequently, after the government had obtained access to the documents, the injunction was discharged by consent. The programmes were transmitted in 1988. Again there were no prosecutions.

During the hearing of appeals (by persons convicted of IRA bombing) in which the possibility of retrials was argued, the Court granted an injunction to prohibit the broadcast of a television programme in which actors would represent some of those in court and which would be based on excerpts from the appeal proceedings.[66]

On 19 October 1988, the Home Secretary announced[67] that he had issued instructions to the British Broadcasting Corporation and the Independent Broadcasting Authority requiring them not to broadcast material which included any words spoken by a representative of an organization proscribed in Northern Ireland and of Sinn Fein, Republican Sinn Fein and

66. *A-G v. Channel 4 Television Co.* [1988] Crim. LR 237.
67. 138 HC Deb. col. 893.

the Ulster Defence Organization. Excluded were words spoken in the course of proceedings in Parliament or by or in support of a candidate at a parliamentary, European parliamentary or local election. The three named organizations are lawful bodies and Sinn Fein had an elected Member of the House of Commons.

The direction to the BBC was issued under clause 13(4) of the Licence and Agreement and that to the IBA under section 29(3) of the Broadcasting Act 1981, both of which authorize the Home Secretary to require the two bodies to refrain from broadcasting specified matters. Neither the BBC nor the IBA challenged the legal validity of the ban but an action was brought by broadcasters and a member of the public and backed by the National Union of Journalists.[68]

The Law Lords appeared unperturbed at the interference with freedom of speech of Sinn Fein, a legitimate political party with elected representatives in the House of Commons and on local councils. Lord Bridge indeed said it was perhaps surprising that the restriction imposed was of such limited scope, there being no restriction on the matter to be broadcast, only on its manner.

Equally short shrift was accorded to the European Convention when Amnesty International sought to place advertisements on radio, drawing attention to the distress of victims of human rights violations in Rwanda and Burundi. The objects of Amnesty were held by the Court of Appeal to be 'mainly of a political nature', and so the advertisements were excluded under the Broadcasting Act 1991.[69]

The National Council for One-Parent Families complained to the Broadcasting Complaints Commission about a BBC programme called *Babies on Benefit*. The Commission found the programme 'misleading unjust and unfair', and the court held that the National Council did not have a sufficiently 'direct interest' to complain.[70] But a parish council was held to have

68. *R. v. Secretary of State for the Home Department ex parte Brind* [1991] AC 696.

69. *R. v. Radio Authority ex parte Bull, The Times* 21 January 1997.

70. *R. v. Broadcasting Complaints Commission ex parte British Broadcasting Corporation, The Times*, 24 February 1995; see also *R. v Central Independent Television* [1994] 3 WLR 20.

such an interest when making a complaint about a programme purporting to show racism in a Derbyshire village.[71] These two cases posit acutely the conflict of two public interests: freedom of expression and the protection of minorities.

In April 1995 a major row erupted when a Scottish judge upheld an order banning the screening of an interview with the Prime Minister until local polling stations north of the border had closed, on the ground that otherwise the impartiality of the BBC would have been breached.

In *R. v. Chief Metropolitan Magistrate ex parte Choudhury*,[72] an unsuccessful attempt was made to prosecute Salman Rushdie for blasphemy in *The Satanic Verses*, the court deciding that in this country the offence concerned Christianity only and could not be extended to Islam. The case was taken to Strasbourg but the European Commission on Human Rights refused to entertain it. The Law Commission recommended the abolition of the offence but no action was taken. A second ground was that the author and publishers had published a seditious libel but this failed on the ground that intention to incite violence or create public disorder had to be shown.

Article 9 of the Bill of Rights 1689 asserted that the freedom of speech and debates or proceedings in Parliament ought not to be impeached or questioned in any court or place out of Parliament. Words spoken in the House cannot be the cause of legal action. Until 1980 the Commons required that leave of the House be obtained before reference was made, in court, to the official debates. This requirement was waived, but it was still not clear for what purposes evidence might be given of what a Member said in Parliament and leave to introduce such evidence has been refused.[73]

In *Prebble v. Television New Zealand*,[74] a former minister sued the defendants for libel. They pleaded justification, relying partly on allegations that he had made misleading state-

---

71. *R. v. Broadcasting Complaints Commission ex parte Channel Four Television Corporation, The Times*, 4 January 1995.

72. [1991] QB 429.

73. *Church of Scientology of California v. Johnson-Smith* [1972] 1 QB 522; *R. v. Secretary of State for Trade ex parte Anderson Strathclyde* [1983] 2 All ER 233; *Rost v. Edwards* [1990] 2 WLR 1280.

74. [1994] 3 All ER 407 PC.

ments in the New Zealand Parliament. The Privileges Committee of the House of Representatives held that the privilege under Article 9 (adopted by the New Zealand Parliament) could not be waived, so that no evidence of those statements could be given. The Privy Council held that no statement could be made in court to suggest that words spoken in Parliament were lies or intended to mislead. But the action was allowed to proceed because the case substantially turned on acts done outside Parliament. Had the whole subject matter of the libel related to the plaintiffs' conduct in the House, the action would not have been allowed to proceed.[75]

In *Allason v. Haines*,[76] a Member of the House of Commons brought a libel action against a journalist and a newspaper editor who pleaded that certain early day motions in the House were at least inspired by improper motives or activated upon improper behaviour. The action was struck out since the defendants could not bring the evidence, drawn from parliamentary proceedings, in their support. Similarly, in *Hamilton v. The Guardian* the plaintiff MP was prevented from suing for libel concerning allegations of parliamentary misbehaviour.

On 7 May 1996, a majority of peers passed an amendment to the Defamation Bill,[77] subsequently supported by a majority in the Commons,[78] enabling MPs to waive the privilege conferred by Article 9 of the Bill of Rights 1689 so that they could sue for defamation. Section 13(1) of the Defamation Act 1996 now provides:

> Where the conduct of a person in or in relation to proceedings in Parliament is in issue in defamation proceedings, he may waive for the purpose of those proceedings, so far as concerns him, the protection of any enactment or rule of law which prevents proceedings in Parliament being impeached or questioned in any court or place out of Parliament.

The amendment was put down by Lord Hoffman, a Law Lord.

75. See G. Marshall in [1994] *Public Law* 509.
76. *The Times*, 25 July 1995.
77. 572 HL Deb. col. 24–54.
78. 280 HC Deb. col. 54–75, 123–6 (24 June 1996).

Although, as we have seen (p. 38), there is nothing unusual in Law Lords speaking in the upper chamber on matters of law reform (and sometimes on other matters also), involvement in politically controversial debates is generally regarded as unwise. The Lord Chancellor asked Lord Hoffman to move the amendment to enable discussion to take place in the Lords. Later Lord Hoffman appears to have realized the party political implications and he abstained on the vote.

Mr Hamilton subsequently exercised his waiver but on the eve of the trial withdrew, and proceedings were discontinued. The allegations of parliamentary misbehaviour were then conducted by the relevant bodies in the House of Commons.

The founder of 'Child Line', a charitable service for sexually abused children, was awarded £250,000 damages for a libel published in *The People*. The Court of Appeal reduced this to £110,000, saying that where damages were excessive the legislation should be construed in a manner not inconsistent with the European Convention on Human Rights; and in future such awards should be more carefully scrutinized by the court.[79]

The protection of sources

Journalists have long insisted on their need to be able to protect their sources and not to be required by the courts to disclose the names of those who have provided them with information. In 1963, two journalists who gave evidence to a tribunal of enquiry investigating breaches of security by an Admiralty clerk refused to disclose the sources of the information they published. This tribunal was by statute in a position similar to the High Court, where to refuse to answer proper questions is a contempt of court. The Court of Appeal upheld sentences of six and three months' imprisonment.[80]

In 1982, a journalist who refused to reveal the source of his information (which had resulted in the exposure of illegality and corruption at Ladbroke's casinos) was found not guilty of

79. *Rantzen v. Mirror Group Newspapers* [1993] 3 WLR 953.
80. *A-G v. Mulholland* [1963] 2 QB 477.

contempt of court because to reveal the source would have served no useful purpose.[81]

The principles governing these cases were reviewed in *British Steel Corporation v. Granada Television Ltd* (1980).[82] An employee of BSC, without the permission of BSC, supplied Granada with confidential documents, the property of BSC. These documents were used by Granada in a televised interview with the chairman of BSC. Subsequently BSC sought an order from the courts requiring Granada to tell BSC who had supplied the information. Granada argued that they should not be obliged to do so, principally because it was desirable in the public interest that press and television journalists should be entitled to protect their sources of information. In the Court of Appeal, Lord Denning MR, who with his colleagues upheld the Vice Chancellor in ordering disclosure of the name, recognized the interest of journalists. But he found against Granada because he decided that in the circumstances they had not acted 'with a due sense of responsibility'. A majority of the Law Lords agreed with the Court of Appeal. Lord Wilberforce noted that Granada had not disputed that to supply the information was a wrongful act in law. He agreed that journalists had an interest in protecting their sources but the court had to decide, in the particular circumstances, whether that interest was outweighed by other interests to which the law attached importance. He held that BSC had suffered 'a grievous wrong' and to deny them the opportunity of a remedy against their employee would be 'a significant denial of justice'.

Lord Salmon alone dissented. He emphasized that BSC was losing large sums of taxpayers' money and that the employee considered it to be his public duty to reveal the information in the documents. Lord Salmon thought that Granada were right to consider that they had a public duty to disclose any information which exposed the faults and mistakes of BSC. He concluded:

There are no circumstances in this case which have ever before deprived or ever should deprive the press of its

81. *A-G v. Lundin* 75 Cr. App. Rep. 90.
82. [1980] 3 WLR 774.

immunity against revealing its sources of information. The freedom of the press depends upon this immunity. Were it to disappear so would the sources from which its information is obtained; and the public be deprived of much of the information to which the public of a free nation is entitled.

In *Secretary of State for Defence v. Guardian Newspapers Ltd*,[83] a copy of a 'secret' document was passed anonymously to the editor of the *Guardian*. This document was a minute of 20 October 1983, from the Minister of Defence to the Prime Minister. It dealt with parliamentary and public statements to be made on 1 November about, and contemporaneously with, the delivery of Cruise missiles from the USA to Greenham Common. Six other copies were sent, five to ministers and one to the Secretary of the Cabinet. On 31 October, the *Guardian* published this minute in full. Not until 11 November – eleven days later – did the Treasury Solicitor write to the editor of the *Guardian* asking for the return of the document, and on 22 November he issued a writ claiming delivery of the document from the newspaper. It was accompanied by a notice of motion claiming, as interlocutory relief, immediate delivery of the document. On 15 December, Scott J ordered the return of the document. This was affirmed by the Court of Appeal the next day and complied with. As a result of a study of the markings on the document, the leak was traced to Miss Sarah Tisdall, a clerk in the private office of the Foreign Secretary and she was subsequently convicted and sentenced to six months' imprisonment. From the decision of the Court of Appeal, the *Guardian* appealed to the House of Lords on the ground that section 10 of the Contempt of Court Act 1981 protected them from being obliged to return the document.

Section 10 provides:

No court may require a person to disclose, nor is any person guilty of contempt of court for refusing to disclose, the source of information contained in a publication for which he is responsible, unless it be established to the satisfaction of the court that disclosure is necessary

83. [1984] 3 WLR 986.

in the interests of justice or national security or for the
prevention of disorder or crime.

The evidence put forward on behalf of the Secretary of State for
Defence was on affidavit, sworn by the principal establishment
officer of the department. And the question was whether the
facts stated in the affidavit were sufficient to establish that the
delivery up of the document was necessary in the interests of
national security, it being accepted that the markings on the
copy would probably lead to identification of the person who
had leaked the document. In the event, three Law Lords thought
the facts stated were sufficient and two Law Lords thought
they were insufficient.

The majority, faced with an affidavit which did not contain
the evidence required to show that disclosure was 'necessary'
in the interests of national security, managed to infer facts
which could satisfy them. The minority quite sharply found
this course impossible. That is hardly a firm basis on which
to found the freedom of the Press.

In 1985, a takeover bid of a brewery company was referred
to the Monopolies and Mergers Commission. On 8 November,
The Times published an article by a financial journalist which
said that the report of the commission would recommend that
the bid would be allowed without any conditions. This proved
to be correct. In October 1986, the *Independent* published an
article by the same journalist which accurately forecast that a
different bid would be referred to the commission because the
Director-General of Fair Trading was 'understood to have been
impressed' by the arguments in favour of a reference and
would so advise the Secretary of State. This also proved to be
correct. In December 1986, inspectors were appointed under
the Financial Services Act 1986 to investigate criminal insider
dealings resulting from suspected leaks from the Office of Fair
Trading, the Commission or the Department of Trade and
Industry. In February 1987, the financial journalist was
required to attend before the inspectors and was asked questions about the nature and sources of the information on which
the two articles had been based. He refused to answer. Under
section 178(2) of the act, the question for the court was whether
his refusal was 'without reasonable excuse'. If so, he could be

punished as if he had been guilty of contempt of court. His defence was that his refusal was justified by section 10 of the Contempt of Court Act 1981 or the public interest in the protection of journalists' sources of information.

The House of Lords held that the inspectors had produced sufficient evidence that it was 'necessary for the prevention of crime' that they should know the journalist's sources of information and that the journalist did not have a reasonable excuse to refuse to reveal them.[84] The journalist was fined £20,000, paid by the *Independent*.

In 1989, while a company was negotiating for a large bank loan, a copy of its draft business plan for the loan disappeared. The next day a journalist was telephoned and given information about the company and the loan. The company applied to the court for an order requiring the publishers of the magazine for whom the journalist worked to reveal the source (known only to the journalist) of the information which could be discovered from the journalist's notes. The publishers were ordered to disclose the notes but the journalist refused to make them available. An order was then made, the effect of which was that the journalist should communicate with the source who could deliver the file without identifying himself. The journalist refused to communicate the order. The Court of Appeal gave the journalist the option of handing over the notes in a sealed envelope pending an appeal. The journalist did not accept this. The company sought to commit him to prison for contempt of court.

In the mean time, the publishers appealed against the order requiring them to disclose the notes. This appeal was dismissed, the Master of the Rolls saying that the 'interests of justice' referred to in section 10 of the Contempt of Court Act 1981 meant 'the interests in the administration of justice' generally, and in those interests disclosure was necessary in this case. The House of Lords agreed, saying that it was in the 'interests of justice' that persons should be enabled to exercise important legal rights and to protect themselves from serious legal wrongs, whether or not resort to legal proceedings

84. *Re an Inquiry under the Company Securities (Insider Dealing) Act 1985* [1988] 2 WLR 33.

in a court of law were necessary to attain those objectives.

Lord Bridge made heavy weather of the position taken by the publishers and the journalist whom he thought might be acting 'under the misguided influence of some members of his profession who see his predicament as providing the opportunity for some kind of an ideological confrontation with the courts'. Lord Bridge's 'unease' was increased by the knowledge that the journalist's litigation costs were being paid by 'another undisclosed source'. He was clearly incensed by the prospect of a journalist being willing, if necessary, to go to prison rather than reveal his sources, and rested his interpretation of section 10 and his decision on the highest principles, referring to undermining 'the rule of law . . . wholly unacceptable in a democratic society . . . sovereignty of the Queen in Parliament . . . [and] of the Queen's courts . . . abdication of the role of Parliament . . . tantamount to conferring an absolute privilege against disclosure . . . paradoxical that a serious challenge to the rule of law should be mounted by responsible journalists' and much else beside. It was held that the potential damage to the plaintiff's business was very substantial and so the necessity for disclosure was established. In the event Mr Goodwin was not sent to prison but was fined £5,000.[85] He was ordered to pay costs said to exceed £100,000. His employer was believed to have backed the case.

In March 1996 the European Court of Human Rights ruled in favour of the journalist that the exercise of the statutory power to order disclosure of sources 'in the interests of justice' was not 'necessary in a democratic society'.[86]

Official Secrets

Until 1989, the principal statute was the Official Secrets Act 1911. Section 1 (which is still in force) is concerned with spying, but the words are wide enough to cover lesser activities such as demonstrations in 'prohibited places'.[87] Section 2 was

85. *X Ltd. v. Morgan Grampian (Publishers) Ltd* [1990] 2 WLR 1000.
86. And see *Broadmoor Hospital v. Hyde, Independent*, 4 March 1994.
87. *Chandler v. DPP* (see pp. 266–7).

so wide that it had been called a 'catch-all' section. It created offences where almost all that needed to be proved was the unauthorized communication or receipt of official information. In 1971, the section was used to prosecute the editor and a journalist of the *Sunday Telegraph* for publishing material from a report on the Nigerian civil war.[88] The defendants were acquitted after the judge, in his summing-up to the jury, had suggested that section 2 had reached retirement age and should be pensioned off.

In 1978 when two journalists interviewed a former soldier about the operations of army intelligence seven and more years before, all three were charged under sections 1 and 2. But the judge expressed his view that the use of section 1 in a case not concerned with spying was oppressive and those charges were dropped. The accused were convicted on less serious charges under section 2, but none of them was sent to prison. The whole proceedings reflected judicial dissatisfaction with prosecutions under the Official Secrets Acts.[89] Yet one is left with serious doubts whether the Court of Appeal or the House of Lords would have taken a similar view. These cases are a reminder that not all judges act the same way on all occasions.

In May 1982, an Argentine cruiser, the *General Belgrano*, was sunk by a British submarine during the Falklands conflict. This gave rise to political controversy in the United Kingdom. In July 1984, the Foreign Affairs Committee of the House of Commons began an investigation into the surrounding events. Clive Ponting, who was an Assistant Secretary in the Ministry of Defence, decided that Parliament was being deliberately misled by ministers and so sent copies of two internal ministry documents to Tam Dalyell MP who passed them to the chairman of the Committee who returned them to the ministry.

88. *R. v. Cairns, Aitken and Roberts*; and see J. Aitken, *Officially Secret* (1971).

89. *R. v. Aubrey, Berry and Campbell*. See Andrew Nicol, 'Official Secrets and Jury Vetting' in the *Criminal Law Review*, May 1979, p. 281. The soldier John Berry had given the information because he was disturbed at the deportation of Hosenball. This was also the case where 'Colonel B' made his appearance and where jury vetting was first, in recent times, disclosed (p. 157). See Crispin Aubrey, *Who's Watching You?* (1981). See p. 154.

Subsequently, Clive Ponting was charged under section 2 of the Official Secrets Act.[90]

Section 2 provided that it was an offence for a civil servant to communicate official information to any person other than a person to whom he was authorized to communicate it 'or a person to whom it is in the interest of the State his duty to communicate it'. The prosecution argued that this duty could mean only official duty and that the interest of the State meant what was in the interest of the State according to its recognized organs of government and the policies as expounded by the particular government of the day. The judge indicated that he agreed with the prosecution and so would have to direct the jury to convict. At this point, the prosecution protested that they wanted a jury verdict, not a direction, and obtained a short adjournment after which the judge withdrew his proposal to direct. The judge summed up strongly in favour of the prosecution but the jury acquitted the accused.

Section 2 was repealed and replaced by the provisions of the Official Secrets Act 1989. It was sought to include in the bill a general defence that the disclosure was in the public interest, particularly where it revealed criminal activity or other serious misbehaviour by public officials. But this was unsuccessful. However, the Act did require that in certain circumstances disclosure had to be shown to be 'damaging'. In *Lord Advocate v. Scotsman Publications*,[91] a former member of the security services was refused authorization for publication of a book of memoirs. He had 500 copies printed at his own expense and distributed 279 to private individuals before undertaking not to distribute more. One of the recipients handed his copy to a Scottish newspaper, which published an article including some information from the book. The Lord Advocate sought to restrain the newspaper. He argued that, although the book and the article did not contain any information the disclosure of which was capable of damaging national security, any unauthorized disclosure of the work of a member of the secret service was against the public interest. The House of Lords held the prosecution had failed to advance

90. *R. v. Ponting* [1985] Crim. LR 318.
91. [1989] 3 WLR 358.

a good arguable case. Lord Templeman said that, although the Official Secrets Act 1989 was not in force at the time of the publication, the courts should exercise their discretion on the principles of that act including that of the need to show damage. The prosecution failed.

The reaction of the jury in the Ponting case was paralleled when four women were acquitted of damaging a Hawk warplane bound for despatch to the Indonesian air force. They defended themselves on the ground that they had used force to prevent crime under the Genocide Act.[92]

In *Attorney General v. Blake*[93] B was convicted of spying for the Soviet Union, sentenced to forty-two years' imprisonment but escaped. In 1989 he wrote his autobiography, based in part on information obtained while he was a member of the British intelligence service from 1944 to 1961, and was to be paid substantial sums by a publisher. The Crown sought an account of profits. The court held that he owed the Crown a lifelong duty not to disclose confidential information, but by 1989 none of the information was any longer confidential; the duty on B went no further than was reasonably necessary for the protection of the interests of the service; the law did not impose an unreasonable restraint on his ability to earn his living or exercise his right of freedom of speech; to grant relief would entail an infringement of B's rights under the European Convention on Human Rights; the submission of the manuscript constituted an offence under section 1 of the Official Secrets Act 1911, but this did not give rise to the civil remedies sought by the Crown.

92. *Guardian*, 31 July 1996.
93. [1996] 3 WLR 741.

7. The moral maze

Moral behaviour

The Street Offences Act 1959 made it an offence, punishable by fine and, after more than one previous conviction, by imprisonment, for a prostitute to loiter or solicit in a street or public place for the purposes of prostitution. The effect of this statute was to prevent prostitutes soliciting in public. The accused published a booklet, the *Ladies Directory*, in which prostitutes inserted advertisements which they paid for. He was charged with, firstly, conspiracy to corrupt public morals; secondly, living on the earnings of prostitution; and thirdly, publishing an obscene article. His conviction on all three counts was upheld by the House of Lords.

With one dissentient the Law Lords held, against the vigorous denial by counsel for the accused, that there was an offence known to the common law of conspiracy to corrupt public morals. Viscount Simonds said:

> I entertain no doubt that there remains in the courts of law a residual power to enforce the supreme and fundamental purpose of the law, to conserve not only the safety and order but also the moral welfare of the State, and that it is their duty to guard it against attacks which may be the more insidious because they are novel and unprepared for. That is the broad head (call it public policy if you wish) within which the present indictment falls. It matters little what label is given to the offending act. To one of your Lordships it may appear an affront to public decency, to another considering that it may succeed in its obvious intention of provoking libidinous desires, it will seem a corruption of public morals. Yet others may

deem it aptly described as the creation of a public mischief or the undermining of public conduct. The same act will not in all ages be regarded in the same way. The law must be related to the changing standards of life, not yielding to every shifting impulse of the popular will but having regard to fundamental assessments of human values and the purposes of society. Today a denial of the fundamental Christian doctrine, which in past centuries would have been regarded by the ecclesiastical courts as heresy and by the common law as blasphemy, will no longer be an offence if the decencies of controversy are observed. When Lord Mansfield, speaking long after the Star Chamber had been abolished, said that the Court of King's Bench was the *custos morum* of the people and had the superintendency of offences *contra bonos mores*, he was asserting, as I now assert, that there is in that court a residual power, where no statute has yet intervened to supersede the common law, to superintend those offences which are prejudicial to the public welfare.[1]

This now famous statement was not universally applauded, many of those who disliked it being of the opinion that Law Lords were not necessarily the most appropriate persons to prescribe codes of moral behaviour (and to make them into rules of law also) for the rest of the community. Lord Reid's dissent was based on an examination of the history of criminal conspiracy (from its origins in the Star Chamber) and on 'the broad general principles which have generally been thought to underlie our system of law and government and in particular our system of criminal law'. He concluded that there was 'no such general offence known to the law as conspiracy to corrupt morals'.

The judgments in the House of Lords were delivered on 4 May 1961. No further prosecutions for conspiracy to corrupt morals were brought until 1965 in which year seventy-seven persons were convicted and this was followed in 1966 by a further forty-five convictions. In 1972, the Lord Chancellor said that most of the thirty-two cases (involving 134 individual

1. *Shaw v. DPP* [1961] 2 WLR 897.

convictions) between 1961 and 1971 were for 'blue' films which could not be proceeded against for obscenity unless shown in a private home.[2] So the conspiracy charge was used.

In 1971 three editors of *Oz* were charged with conspiracy to corrupt public morals by producing a magazine containing obscene articles, cartoons, drawings and illustrations; and with contravening the Obscene Publications Act 1964 and the Post Office Act 1953. On the conspiracy charge the jury acquitted them, not being satisfied that they intended to corrupt public morals. On other charges they were convicted and sentenced to imprisonment of fifteen, twelve and nine months. On appeal these convictions were quashed except for that relating to the Post Office Act, the sentence for which was automatically suspended. The appeals succeeded because it was held that the judge had misdirected the jury about the meaning of obscene in the Obscene Publications Act.[3] The addition of a conspiracy charge enables the whole lifestyle of the accused to be brought before the court[4] and the jury, so that the case becomes politically charged in the sense that the accused can be subjected by prosecution counsel to such allegations as advocating dropping out of society, living off the state, and regarding sex as something to be worshipped for itself.

The next year saw the prosecution of another magazine, *International Times*. Three directors were convicted of conspiracy (1) to corrupt public morals and (2) to outrage public decency, because they had published advertisements inviting readers to meet the advertisers for the purpose of homosexual practices. The House of Lords (with one dissentient) upheld the convictions on the first count, on the grounds either that the *Shaw* case was rightly decided, or that even if it were wrongly decided it should stand until altered by Act of Parliament. The Lords (with one dissentient) allowed the appeal on the second count, two of them on the ground that the offence of conspiracy to outrage public decency was an offence unknown to the law, and two of them on the ground that there

2. See 333 HL Deb. col. 1569; and 839 HC Deb. col. 263–4, 427–8. See also *The Law Commission*, Working Paper no. 57, pp. 35–9.

3. *R. v. Anderson* [1971] 3 WLR 939.

4. See Geoff Robertson, 'Whose Conspiracy?' (NCCL, 1974)

had been misdirection by the judge; those latter two and the dissentient agreed that there was an offence of that nature.[5]

Lords Morris and Reid took part in the decisions of both *Shaw* and *Knuller*. Lord Reid had dissented in *Shaw* and had held there was no offence to corrupt public morals; but he was not willing to participate in overruling that decision when the same point arose in *Knuller*. He did, however, hold in *Knuller* that there was no offence of conspiracy to outrage public decency. Lord Morris had been with the majority in *Shaw* when upholding the conviction. And in *Knuller* he was the dissentient to allowing the appeal on the second count.

In the event, therefore, the decision in *Knuller* reinforced that in *Shaw*. But Lord Diplock in the former case was strongly critical of *Shaw*, saying bluntly of that decision that he thought it was wrong and should not be followed. He said that Viscount Simonds's reasoning in *Shaw* had been anticipated in 1591 in Lambard:[6]

> Is it not meet and just, that when the wicked sort of men have excogitated anything with great labour of wit and cunning, so as it may seem they have drawn a quintessence of mischief, and set the same abroach, to the remedilesse hurt of the good and quiet subject; Is it not meet (I say) that authoritie itself also ... should straine the line of justice beyond the ordinarie length and wonted measure and thereby take exquisite avengement upon them for it? Yea is it not right necessarie, that the most godly, honourable, wise, and learned persons of the land, should be appealed unto, that may apply new remedies for these new diseases?

It was not, said Lord Diplock, compatible with the development of English constitutional and criminal law over the past century that the House of Lords in its judicial capacity should assume the role of 'the most godly' etc. persons and take 'exquisite avengement' on those whose conduct was regarded as particularly reprehensible when Parliament had not found it necessary

5 . *R. v. Knuller (Publishing etc.) Ltd* [1972] 3 WLR 143; and see *R. v. Gibson* [1990] 2QB 619.

6 . *Lambard Archeion* (1635 edn), pp. 86, 87.

to proscribe that conduct and no previous precedent for punishing it could be found. As a result of *Shaw*'s case, he said, it would seem that any conduct of any kind which conflicted with widely held prejudices as to what was immoral or indecent, at any rate if at least two persons were in any way concerned with it, might *ex post facto* be held to have been a crime.

In a case in 1973, twenty-one persons were charged with forty-three separate specific offences relating to drugs. And then the forty-fourth count alleged a conspiracy to corrupt public morals in that persons conspired together with other persons unknown to corrupt the morals of such persons as might consume heroin by procuring quantities of heroin and supplying the same to members of the public in, and in the vicinity of, Gerrard Street, London, W.1.[7] So it would seem that conspiracy to corrupt public morals may extend, as an offence, beyond the areas of sexual conduct and be used as a net to catch those who may be acquitted on other kinds of substantive charges. It should be added that if persons are convicted of a number of substantive offences the penalties can be severe because made cumulative; and that under the Misuse of Drugs Act 1971 the maximum punishment for the more serious offences (of which there are fourteen) is fourteen years' imprisonment. So it cannot be argued that the conspiracy charge is necessary to ensure that the penalties are severe.

The Independent Broadcasting Authority is under a duty to satisfy themselves that, so far as possible, the programmes broadcast do not offend against good taste or decency and are not offensive to public feeling. Mrs Mary Whitehouse sought judicial review of the manner of the exercise of this duty in relation to the showing of the film *Scum*, which portrayed life in borstal institutions. Watkins LJ held that the director-general of the IBA had committed a grave error of judgment in failing to refer the film to all the members of the IBA before authorizing its showing. The judge said that, had the decision been his, he would have been opposed to showing the film. Taylor J agreed that the film was shocking but did not accept Mrs Whitehouse's assertion that it was gratuitous exploitation of

7 . See *New Statesman*, 23 February 1973.

sadistic violence for its own sake, and he would have permitted transmission. Nevertheless he agreed that the director-general should not have taken it upon himself to make the decision. He thought that Mrs Whitehouse's more general accusations against the IBA were extravagant and unwarranted.[8] The director-general might well have replied that how he exercised his judgment, within the law, was not a matter which the court had any competence to assess. In this respect it presents a nice contrast to the more ambivalent attitude of the Court of Appeal to the exercise of police judgment.

In 1993 the Law Lords were set a problem in jurisprudence they would no doubt sooner have avoided. Members of a group of sado-masochistic homosexuals had over a ten year period willingly participated in acts of violence, including genital torture for sexual pleasure, against each other. They were tried on various charges and sentenced to imprisonment. On appeal their defence was that each had consented to the violence inflicted on him. The Law Lords held by a majority of three to two that public policy required that society be protected against a cult which contained the danger of proselytization and the corruption of young men. Lord Mustill, dissenting, said that these were matters of private morality and that the only question was whether the acts were offences against the existing law of violence. He held they were not and was supported by Lord Slynn, insisting that such matters were for the legislature.[9]

In 1994 the Ministry of Defence decided that homosexuality was incompatible with service in the armed forces and dismissed three men and one woman.[10] All had exemplary service records. Lip service was paid by the Court of Appeal to individual rights, with reference to *Budgaycay*[11] and *Brind*[12] but, amid expressions of hesitation and regret, the court held that the ministerial decision could not be held irrational and should

8 . *R. v. Independent Broadcasting Authority ex parte Whitehouse, The Times*, 14 April 1984.

9 . *R. v. Brown* [1993] 2 All ER 75.

10. *R. v. Ministry of Defence ex parte Smith* [1996] 2 WLR 305.

11. See p. 192.

12. See pp. 247–8.

not be interfered with. An extraordinary standard was set up by Lord Justice Simon Brown in the Divisional Court:

> Only if it were plain beyond sensible agreement that no conceivable damage could be done to the armed services as a fighting unit would it be appropriate for this court now to remove the issue entirely from the hands both of the military and of the government.

This was supported by a cop-out argument used from time to time when the judiciary want to wash their hands in public. Sir Thomas Bingham MR in the Court of Appeal said,

> The greater the policy content of a decision, and the more remote the subject matter of a decision from ordinary judicial experience, the more hesitant the court must necessarily be in holding a decision to be irrational. That is good law and, like most good law, common sense. Where decisions of a policy-laden, esoteric or security-based nature are in issue even greater caution than normal must be shown in applying the [Wednesbury] test, but the test itself is sufficiently flexible to cover all situations.

Demonstrations and protests

In 1961, members of the Committee of 100 who sought to further the aims of the Campaign for Nuclear Disarmament took part in organizing a demonstration at an airfield which was a 'prohibited place' within the meaning of the Official Secrets Act 1911 and which was occupied by the US airforce. The plan was that some people would sit outside the entrances to the airfield while others would sit on the runway to prevent aircraft from taking off. The six accused were charged with conspiring to commit and to incite others to commit a breach of the Official Secrets Act, namely, 'for a purpose prejudicial to the safety or interests of the State' to enter the airfield. Their counsel was not allowed to cross-examine or call evidence as to their belief that their acts would benefit the State or to show that their purpose was not in fact prejudicial to the safety or interests of the State. They were all convicted, five of them being sentenced to eighteen months' and one to twelve months' imprisonment. The Court of Appeal and the House of Lords upheld the conviction and sentences.[13]

The accused were not charged with any substantive offence, such as breach of the Official Secrets Acts (approaching or entering a prohibited place). No doubt, proof of conspiracy was easier.

In July 1972, Peter Hain appeared on charges of conspiracy to interrupt visits of South African sporting teams to Britain. The prosecution was brought by a private individual. He was convicted on one of the four counts, and fined £200. The count concerned his running on to a tennis court in Bristol during a Davis Cup match and distributing anti-apartheid leaflets.[14] It is not clear how far the conviction amounted to trespass (see below) but that was not the basis of the decision. It may be that any action which is 'a matter of public concern' can found an action for conspiracy. If so 'the agreement to commit an unlawful act' which is the definition of conspiracy may have been extended further.[15]

At present, however, another extension is of greater importance because it was created by a decision of the House of Lords as a deliberate statement of new law. The case concerned some students from Sierra Leone who occupied for a few hours part of the premises of the High Commission of Sierra Leone in London. They brandished an imitation gun and locked some ten members of the staff in a room. No blows were struck. Lord Hailsham said, delivering the opinion of the House of Lords, that the students

appear to have been reasonably careful to see that no one was seriously harmed, and their motives were *not necessarily* contemptible. They acted from a genuine sense of grievance. The father of at least one of them

13. *Chandler v. DPP* [1962] 3 WLR 694.
14. *Hain v. DPP, The Times*, 28 July–22 August 1972, Robertson, *op. cit.*, p. 16, and Derek Humphry, *The Cricket Conspiracy* (1975).
15. In *Cozens v. Brutus* [1973] AC 854, the House of Lords held that running on to the Centre Court at Wimbledon during a tennis match and distributing anti-apartheid leaflets was not 'insulting behaviour within the meaning of the Public Order Act 1936'.

was, we were told, under sentence of death at the time of the alleged offence, and all appear to have believed that the government in power in their country, *though recognized by Her Majesty's Government here*, was arbitrary, tyrannical and unconstitutional [my italics].

The students were convicted of conspiring with other persons to enter the premises as trespassers.[16]

Sit-ins and occupations, by students and factory workers, had for some time been troubling the courts and the legislators. As forms of protest, these were in varying degrees effective, especially if they received publicity and caused embarrassment. Normally they gave rise to no criminal action and the police were reluctant to intervene in what was seen as a private dispute on private property. From the beginning of student activity, however, there had been some who urged the introduction of legislation to enable such demonstrations to be dealt with as criminal.

Lord Hailsham was a Lord Chancellor who chose to sit as a judge more frequently than is usual. On this occasion, he delivered the leading judgment with which two other Law Lords concurred (adding nothing) and the fourth concurred with a brief speech. Lord Hailsham was a highly political Lord Chancellor well known for his flamboyance and overstrained rhetoric. He lumped together in his political speeches:

The war in Bangladesh, Cyprus, the Middle East, Black September, Black Power, the Angry Brigade, the Kennedy murders, Northern Ireland, bombs in Whitehall and the Old Bailey, the Welsh Language Society, the massacre in the Sudan, the mugging in the Tube, gas strikes, hospital strikes, go-slows, sit-ins, the Icelandic cod war.

The new rule of law he set forth in this case was:

Trespass or any other form of tort can, if intended, form the element of illegality necessary in conspiracy. But in my view, more is needed. Either (1) execution of the combination must invade the domain of the public, as, for instance, when the trespass involves the invasion of

16. *Kamara v. DPP* [1973] 3 WLR 198.

a building such as the embassy of a friendly country or a publicly owned building, or (of course) where it infringes the criminal law as by breaching the statutes of forcible entry and detainer, the Criminal Damage Act 1891, or the laws affecting criminal assaults to the person. Alternatively (2) a combination to trespass becomes indictable if the execution of the combination necessarily involves and is known and intended to involve the infliction on its victim of something more than purely nominal damage. This must necessarily be the case where the intention is to occupy the premises to the exclusion of the owner's right, either by expelling him altogether . . . or otherwise effectively preventing him from enjoying his property.

By a simple but considerable extension of the existing law, Lord Hailsham brought within the definition of criminal conspiracy, with its vagueness, and with its almost limitless powers of punishment, demonstrations of all kinds which involved either any entry into a public building or any use of property, whether public or private, which interfered (to however small an extent for however short a time) with an owner's enjoyment of any part of his property. Such an owner would be entitled to call on the police to enter the premises and make any arrests they thought appropriate because a criminal offence would be in the course of commission once two or more people appeared to be combining in such a demonstration. This decision is remarkable even for these authoritarian middle decades of the twentieth century. It also provides a very strong weapon for dealing as criminals with those who squat in empty buildings. In the same case, the only other judge to speak (other than to concur) was Lord Cross. He went further even than Lord Hailsham, saying that an agreement by several to commit acts, which if done by one would amount only to a civil wrong, might constitute a criminal conspiracy if the public had a sufficient interest. Such vagueness could lead almost anywhere.

The right to protest was further limited in *Hubbard v. Pitt*[17] in 1975. Lord Denning MR said that, some years before, Isling-

17. [1975] 3 WLR 201.

ton was 'run down in the world', with houses in a dilapidated condition, tenanted by many poor families. Then property developers stepped in, bought up houses, persuaded tenants to leave, did up the houses and sold them at a profit. Now they were occupied by well-to-do families. A group of social workers who deplored this development conducted a campaign. They accused the developers of harassing tenants and trying to make them leave. The social workers submitted various demands to local estate agents which, said Lord Denning, if tenants had been subjected to undue pressure, seemed reasonable enough. In the course of the campaign the social workers picketed the offices of Prebble & Co. About four to eight men and women stood on the pavement in front of Prebble's offices for about three hours on Saturday mornings, carrying placards saying 'Tenants Watch Out Prebble's About' and 'If Prebble's In — You're Out', and handing out leaflets. They behaved in an orderly and peaceful manner and with the full knowledge and agreement of the local police. Prebble & Co. brought an action to stop these activities and Forbes J granted an interim injunction from which the defendants appealed. In the Court of Appeal, two of the Lord Justices rejected the appeal on the technical ground that the interim injunction should be continued until the case was fully heard. As these cases are normally decided on the availability or otherwise of interim injunctions, this was an unrealistic view of the matter. Lord Denning, however, dissented from his two brethren, saying,

Here we have to consider the right to demonstrate and the right to protest on matters of public concern. These are rights which it is in the public interest individuals should possess; and, indeed, that they should exercise without impediment so long as no wrongful act is done. It is often the only means by which grievances can be brought to the knowledge of those in authority — at any rate with such impact as to gain a remedy. Our history is full of warnings against suppression of these rights. Most notable was the demonstration at St Peter's Field, Manchester, in 1819 in support of universal suffrage. The magistrates sought to stop it. At least twelve were killed and hundreds injured. Afterwards the Court of Common

Council of London affirmed 'the undoubted right of Englishmen to assemble together for the purpose of deliberating upon public grievances' ... The courts ... should not interfere by interlocutory injunctions with the right of free speech; provided that everything is done peaceably and in good order.

This is the voice of freedom under law. But on a technicality it was overridden by the other two members of the Court of Appeal.

The Central Electricity Generating Board were considering possible sites for a nuclear power station in southwest England and were obstructed, first by farmers and later by protestors preventing them from surveying a site. The chief constable refused to remove the protestors since there was no actual or apprehended breach of the peace nor an unlawful assembly. The Board sought an order from the court requiring the chief constable to instruct police officers or agents to act. The Court of Appeal refused the order. Lord Denning MR, while deploring the activities of the protestors, and expressing the hope that the police would help the Board, said it was of the first importance that the police should decide on their own responsibility what action should be taken in any particular situation and that the decision of the chief constable not to intervene was a policy decision with which the courts should not interfere.[18]

The anti-nuclear protest by women camping near the United States Air Force base at Greenham Common in Berkshire continued over several years. Under the Military Lands Act 1892, the minister was empowered to make byelaws regulating the use of land appropriated for military purposes and prohibiting entry. But no byelaw should authorize the minister 'to take away or prejudicially affect any right of common'. The byelaw made for Greenham Common failed to make any saving for commoners having rights over the land. The defendants entered the land and were convicted under the byelaw. They were not commoners, but the Law Lords quashed their convictions on the ground that the byelaw was invalid.[19]

18. *R. v. Chief Constable of Devon and Cornwall ex parte Central Electricity Generating Board* [1981] 3 WLR 967.
19. *DPP v. Hutchinson* [1990] 3 WLR 196.

Following public protests, a local authority suspended flights out of a city airport by a company exporting livestock. Under an Air Navigation Order the airport was 'to be available to all persons on equal terms and conditions'. In similar circumstances, a harbour authority decided not to permit cross-channel services for export of live animals. The relevant statute required the port to be 'open to all persons for the shipping and unshipping of goods'. It was held that the public authorities concerned had no general discretion to distinguish between lawful trades and should not respond to unlawful protest and threats.[20]

In the Divisional Court, Lord Justice Simon Brown said:

> One thread runs consistently throughout all case law: the recognition that public authorities must beware of surrendering to the dictates of unlawful pressure groups. The implications of such surrender for the rule of law can hardly be exaggerated ... None of [the authorities] it appears gave the least thought to the awesome implications for the rule of law of doing what they propose ... We confirm that it will indeed be for the chief constable to decide upon the measures necessary and that all concerned should co-operate fully with him.

This last piece of advice might not have proved effective. The Chief Constable of Sussex was concerned that the financial and manpower resources he was deploying, to deal with protestors at Shoreham who were seeking to prevent the export of livestock, were interfering with the efficient and effective policing of the county. So he decided to reduce the level of policing at Shoreham.[21] On the days when no cover was to be provided, the police would turn back livestock vehicles if it was thought that a breach of the peace might otherwise occur. This decision was challenged by some exporters. The Divisional Court held that the decision was a proper exercise of the chief constable's discretion under domestic law; but that

20. *R. v. Coventry City Council ex parte Phoenix Aviation* [1995] 3 All ER 37.

21. *R. v. Chief Constable of Sussex ex parte International Trader's Ferry Ltd.* [1995] 3 WLR 802. Reversed on appeal, *Independent* 31 January 1997.

it infringed article 34(1) of the European Community Treaty which provided that quantitative restrictions on exports, and all measures having equivalent effect, should be prohibited between member states. Article 36 provided that such restrictions were not precluded if justified on the grounds of public policy. But the court rejected this defence because the chief constable had not approached the Home Office for a special grant, even though the court accepted, in the light of known Home Office policy, that this would not have been forthcoming. The Court of Appeal reversed this decision saying that the chief constable could rely on Article 36.

The Criminal Justice and Public Order Act 1994 created a new offence of trespassory assembly. On 23 January 1997 the Divisional Court in *DPP v. Jones* held that a peaceful assembly of 20 or more persons which did not obstruct the highway at Stonehenge nevertheless committed the statutory offence.

Matters of life and death

In 1985, the Law Lords were required to decide between the rights of a parent and the professional obligations of doctors. The Department of Health issued a memorandum of guidance to area health authorities to the effect that in exceptional circumstances it was for a doctor exercising his clinical judgment to determine whether to prescribe contraceptive advice and treatment to a girl under the age of sixteen years. The mother of five girls under that age sought assurance from the area authority that no such action would be taken without her knowledge and consent. The Law Lords by a majority of three to two held that the guidance was lawful and that a doctor so acting, without such parental authority, would not be guilty of a criminal offence or acting contrary to public policy.[22]

In *Airedale NHS Trust v. Bland*,[23] a man aged seventeen was severely injured in the Hillsborough stadium disaster. For three years he remained in a persistent vegetative state in which he

22. *Gillick v. West Norfolk and Wisbech Area Health Authority* [1985] 3 WLR 830.
23. [1993] 2 WLR 316.

had permanently lost all higher brain functions. The hospital authorities, supported by his parents, sought declarations that they might allow him to die peacefully, with the greatest dignity and with the least pain, suffering and distress. The Law Lords, with considerable doubts about the desirability of judges, rather than Parliament, having to decide what were the principles to be applied in such cases, agreed to the granting of the declarations.

In *ex parte B*,[24] a girl had developed leukemia at the age of five. After chemotherapy and a bone marrow transplant she went into remission. She suffered a relapse in 1995 and was given six to eight weeks to live. Her health authority doctors said she should receive only palliative treatment. B's father obtained another medical opinion that a particular combination of drugs might result in a complete remission so that a second bone marrow transplant might then be possible. The cost would be £75,000, with a 10–20 per cent chance of success. When the health authority refused to allocate the necessary funds, B's father applied for a judicial review of the decision. Sir John Laws in the lower court quashed the decision because the wishes of the parents had not been taken into account, the proposed treatment had been wrongly described as 'experimental', the evidence about cost was not specific but consisted only of grave and well-rounded generalities, the health authority had wrongly assessed the problem as one of spending £75,000 whereas, in the first instance, the treatment involved the expenditure of only £15,000. The Court of Appeal disagreed with the judge on all these matters and found that there were no grounds on which the health authority's decision could be set aside. The courts could not express opinions on the likely effectiveness of medical treatment or the merits of medical judgment.

In *Re T*,[25] the unanimous medical prognosis was that an eighteen-month-old child would not live beyond the age of 2½ years without a liver transplantation. The unanimous clinical opinion of the consultants was that it was in the child's interests to undergo the operation. The parents, both trained as health

24. *R. v. Cambridge Health Authority ex parte B* [1995] 2 All ER 129.
25. [1997] 1 WLR 242.

care professionals and experienced in the care of young sick children, refused consent to the operation. Underlying the mother's objections was a deep seated concern as to the benefits to the child of major invasive surgery and post-operative treatment, the dangers of failure long term as well as short term, the possibility of the need for further transplants, the likely length of life, and the effect on the child of all these concerns.

The Court of Appeal considered that the welfare of the child was the paramount consideration. The court's concern was whether it was in the child's best interests for the court in effect to direct the mother to take on this total commitment where she did not agree with the course proposed. The court held that the best interests of the child required that his future treatment should be left in the hands of his devoted parents.

It is difficult to see how the Court could have decided otherwise. But the decision was made easier by the apparent character, status and suitability of the parents to bear the responsibility of their decision and provide the means to fulfil it. Had they not been able to convince the court that they had these qualities, on what considerations could the court have come to its decision?

Part Three

Policy

The courts hold justly a high, and I think, unequalled pre-eminence in the respect of the world in criminal cases, and in civil cases between man and man, no doubt, they deserve and command the respect and admiration of all classes of the community, but where class issues are involved, it is impossible to pretend that the courts command the same degree of general confidence. On the contrary, they do not, and a very large number of our population have been led to the opinion that they are, unconsciously, no doubt, biased. [Hon. Members: 'No, no', 'Withdraw' and interruption.]

The Secretary of State for the Home Department (Mr W. S. Churchill) on the second reading of the Trade Unions (No. 2) Bill, 1911 (26 HC Deb. col. 1022).

The habits you are trained in, the people with whom you mix, lead to your having a certain class of ideas of such a nature that, when you have to deal with other ideas, you do not give as sound and accurate judgments as you would wish. This is one of the great difficulties at present with Labour. Labour says 'Where are your impartial Judges? They all move in the same circle as the employers, and they are all educated and nursed in the same ideas as the employers. How can a labour man or a trade unionist get impartial justice?' It is very difficult

> sometimes to be sure that you have put yourself
> into a thoroughly impartial position between two
> disputants, one of your own class and one not
> of your class.

Lord Justice Scrutton in an address delivered to
the University of Cambridge Law Society on 18
November 1920 (1 *Cambridge Law Journal*,
p. 8).

> *I know that over 300 years ago Hobart C J said
> the 'Public policy is an unruly horse'. It has
> often been repeated since. So unruly is the horse,
> it is said (per Burrough J in* Richardson v.
> Mellish *[1924]) that no judge should ever try to
> mount it lest it run away with him. I disagree.
> With a good man in the saddle, the unruly horse
> can be kept in control. It can jump over
> obstacles. It can leap the fences put up by fictions
> and come down on the side of justice* . . .

Lord Denning MR in *Enderby Town Football
Club v. Football Association Ltd* [1971] 1 Ch.
591.

> *So far as this country is concerned, hitherto
> every judge on his appointment discards all poli-
> tics and all prejudices. The judges of England
> have always in the past — and I hope always will
> — be vigilant in guarding our freedoms. Someone
> must be trusted. Let it be the judges.*

Lord Denning MR in the Richard Dimbleby Lecture, 1980.

> *The call today is for more 'open government'.
> It is voiced mainly by newsmen and critics and
> oppositions. They want to know all about the
> discussions that go on in the inner circles of*

government. They feel that policy-making is the concern of everyone. So everyone should be told about it.

Lord Denning MR in *Air Canada v. Secretary of State for Trade (No. 2)* [1983] 1 All ER 161.

When I started in practice one of the qualities that many of the judges had was eccentricity; it was part of their character. But we are now so leavened into a mould of similarity that eccentricity no longer exists.

Lord Ackner during the committee stage of the Courts and Legal Services Bill on 29 January 1990 (515 HL Deb. col. 96).

For [Lord Denning] judicial review was not a matter merely of mechanistically applying a value-free ultra vires *rule to a decision. There were substantive values and principles in public law. But, regrettably in my view, the Denning approach fell out of favour in the 1980s, largely due to the climate of scepticism about judges that was fostered by the publication of John Griffith's* Politics of the Judiciary.

Dawn Oliver, professor of Constitutional Law in the University of London [1994] *Public Law* p. 249.

. . . the attempt to overturn Scott by weight of letters to The Times *is surely a most extraordinary procedure for judicial gentlemen to engage in.*

Lord Jenkins of Hillhead during the debate in the House of Lords on the Scott report on 26 February 1996 (569 HL Deb. col. 1243).

8. Judicial creativity

In the first chapter I referred to the importance of the creative function which judges perform both in the development of the common law and in the interpretation of statutes. All the cases in this book are examples, greater or smaller, of this function.

It was common at one time for judges to deny that they had any creative function at all or, more precisely and more positively, to assert that, in the development of the common law, all they did was to declare it. Lord Rcid, one of the outstanding Law Lords of this century, has said:

> Those with a taste for fairy tales seem to have thought that in some Aladdin's cave there is hidden the Common Law in all its splendour and that on a judge's appointment there descends on him knowledge of the magic words Open Sesame. Bad decisions are given when the judge has muddled the password and the wrong door opens. But we do not believe in fairy tales any more.[1]

Nowadays, however, the argument still persists in relation to the interpretation of statutes. When a particular interpretation – for example of the Race Relations Acts – is objected to, it is common for the interpretation to be defended on the ground that all the judges can do is to apply the law as made by Parliament and not to improve it.

But if the statute is open to more than one interpretation, then the judges are supposed to discover, by looking at the

---

1. 'The Judge as Law Maker' in 12JSPTL 22 (1972). And see Lord Devlin, 'Judges and Lawmakers', in 39 *Modern Law Review* (1976) 1; Lord Diplock, 'The Courts as Legislators' (1965 *Holdsworth Club*); Anthony Lester, 'English Judges as Lawmakers' [1993] *Public Law* 269.

whole of the law on the matter, including the statute itself, what was the intention of Parliament and to interpret accordingly. At this point strong disagreement may arise, even within the court itself. If the court decided that, for example, it was the intention of Parliament to exclude Conservative clubs or dockers' clubs from the operation of the Race Relations Act 1968, some critics will say that so widespread an exception, applying to clubs with such extensive membership, is wholly contrary to the spirit and the intention of that statute. And they will go on to say that the courts are showing a restrictive attitude on a matter of social policy and politics.

On the other hand there will be those who say that the Race Relations Acts mark a serious intervention and a considerable regulation of personal relationships. Therefore, they will argue, such regulation should be kept to a minimum and Parliament should be assumed to have intended that the intervention should not be extended beyond the most explicit provision.[2]

A similar division of opinion can be seen where other forms of regulation arise – for example, in the interpretation of the legislation about the control of the use of land. Wherever private rights are regulated, whether of property or of persons, there will be those who say that the regulation should be kept to a minimum and those who say that it must not be so restricted as to weaken its application.

But the difficulty lies deeper than disagreements about the so-called 'intention of Parliament'. First, if particular judges or particular courts consistently interpret certain types of legislation either widely or narrowly they will gain the reputation either of being 'liberal', 'progressive', 'socialist' et cetera, or of being 'restrictive', 'reactionary', 'conservative' et cetera. Secondly, many people will simply disbelieve the judges who say that they are concerned only with ascertaining the intention of Parliament. And this disbelief is strengthened when judges express opinions, in the course of their judgments, which seem to show where their sympathies lie.

Similarly Lord Diplock drew attention to the way the law of conspiracy had developed because 'what was proved against the defendant at the trial was that he had done something of

2 . Cp. Lord Diplock in the *Dockers' Club* case; see p. 176.

which the judge and jury strongly disapproved' although he had done nothing illegal or, if he had, was not charged with it.[3]

Lord Denning has said:

It is plain that Parliament intended that the Supplementary Benefit Act 1966 should be administered with as little technicality as possible. It should not become the happy hunting ground for lawyers. The courts should hesitate long before interfering by certiorari with the decision of the appeal tribunals ... The courts should not enter into a meticulous discussion of the meaning of this or that word in the Act. They should leave the tribunals to interpret the Act in a broad reasonable way, according to the spirit and not to the letter: especially as Parliament has given them a way of alleviating any hardship. The courts should only interfere when the decision of the tribunal is unreasonable in the sense that no tribunal acquainted with the ordinary use of language could reasonably reach that decision.[4]

The discussion about how creative judges should be, how far the approach to statutes should be literal and semantic, or seeking 'the intention' of Parliament, and other variants on the same theme, has been continuing for many years. Yet it has been and is a somewhat unreal discussion. While in certain circumstances and on some specific issues particular judges can be shown, from the record of their decisions, to belong more to the creative or more to the conservative school, it is very doubtful whether either tendency follows from one or other general judicial position. Lord Diplock is not regarded as a more creative judge than was Lord Reid, and Lord Devlin was thought of by some as a more creative judge than either.[5]

All this leads to the conclusion that, as one might expect, judges, like the rest of us, are not all of a piece, that they

3 . *R. v. Withers* [1974] 3 WLR 751.
4 . *Ex parte Moore* [1975] 1 WLR 624. Cp. *R. v. Ebbw Vale and Merthyr Tydfil S. B. Appeal Tribunal ex parte Lewis* [1981] 1 WLR 131.
5 . Lord Devlin retired from the bench in 1964 at the age of fifty-eight.

are liable to be swayed by emotional prejudices, that their 'inarticulate major premises' are strong and not only inarticulate but sometimes unknown to themselves. The judges seldom give the impression of strong silent men wedded only to a sanctified impartiality. They frequently appear – and speak – as men with weighty, even passionate, views of the nature of society and the content of law and of their partial responsibility for its future development.

Individualistic strains could, of course, exist alongside a consistent attitude to creativity or its opposite. What is lacking however is any clear and consistent relationship between the general pronouncement of judges on this matter of creativity and the way they conduct themselves in court. Lord Simonds was Lord Chancellor in 1951–4 and is often quoted as the exemplar of the conservative view. Thus in one case he said that he would not 'easily be led by an undiscerning zeal for some abstract kind of justice or ignore our first duty, which is established for us by Act of Parliament or the binding authority of precedent'.[6] Yet it was he who in the previous year had discovered that there was an offence known to the common law of conspiracy to corrupt public morals, a view which caused no little surprise in legal and political circles.[7]

For a time Lord Simonds and Lord Denning carried on a public dispute, the latter making a strong plea for the creative function. Lord Denning, like Lord Simonds, is a reminder that creativity is neither good nor bad but that thinking makes it so. When he supported the action of the college governors in changing the rules of discipline to enable them to dismiss the woman student who was found to have a man in her room, he was certainly acting 'creatively'.[8] When he sought to protect the rights of demonstrators to protest outside the offices of the estate agents in *Hubbard v. Pitt*, he was refusing to be bound by an earlier procedural decision which his colleagues on the bench thought binding on them. And he did so on strong liberal principles. The view taken by Lord Denning can be seen as either creative (refusing to be bound by the earlier decision)

6 . *Scruttons Ltd v. Midland Silicones* [1962] AC 446.
7 . *Shaw v. DPP*; see pp. 260–1.
8 . *Ward v. Bradford Corporation* [1972] 70 LGR 27.

or conservative (maintaining the traditional right of individuals to 'free speech', as he put it).

I am arguing that the public position adopted by judges in the controversy about creativity is not consistently reflected in their judgments, and that more important are their reactions to the moral, political and social issues in the cases that come before them.

The law reports abound with references to the duty of the courts to abide by the provisions of Acts of Parliament. But that does not help in deciding how to deal with ambiguities or obscurities. In *Chandler v. DPP*,[9] Lord Reid said:

> Of course we are bound by the words which Parliament has used in the Act. If those words necessarily lead to that conclusion then it is no answer that it is inconceivable that Parliament can have so intended. The remedy is to amend the Act. But we must be clear that the words of the Act are not reasonably capable of any other interpretation.

The 'conclusion' referred to was that Parliament in passing the Official Secrets Act in 1911 intended that a person who deliberately interfered with vital dispositions of the armed forces should be entitled to submit to a jury that government policy was wrong and that what he did was really in the best interests of the country. Lord Reid continued:

> The question whether it is beneficial to use the armed forces in a particular way or prejudicial to interfere with that use would be a political question − a question of opinion on which anyone actively interested in politics, including jurymen, might consider his own opinion as good as that of anyone else. Our criminal system is not devised to deal with issues of that kind. The question therefore is whether the Act can reasonably be read in such a way as to avoid the raising of such issues.

Lord Reid concluded that it could be read 'in such a way' and that the submissions about government policy were rightly excluded.

9 . [1962] 3 WLR 694; see p. 266, and cp. *R. v. Ponting*, pp. 257−9.

The problem in *Charter* (the Conservative Club case) and the *Dockers' Club* case[10] was where to draw the line between 'public' and 'private' in interpreting the Race Relations Act of 1968. In both cases Lord Reid extended the notion of what was private far beyond the domestic sphere. And he said in *Charter*:

> I would infer from the Act as a whole that the legislature thought all discrimination on racial grounds deplorable but thought it unwise or unpracticable to attempt to apply legal sanctions in situations of a purely private character.

The three members of the Court of Appeal and one member of the House of Lords disagreed with Lord Reid and with the majority in the Lords. It is difficult to believe that the judges in these cases did not consider the effect their views would have on race relations. It is difficult to believe that such considerations would be regarded as improper by the ordinary layman. It was, after all, what the Act of Parliament was concerned with.

Similarly, are we expected to assume that the House of Lords did not take into account or were ignorant of the effect of their decision in *Rookes v. Barnard?*[11] The realities were referred to by Lord Devlin. He said:

> But there is one argument, or at least one consideration, that remains to be noticed. It is that the strike weapon is now so generally sanctioned that it cannot really be regarded as an unlawful weapon of intimidation; and so there must be something wrong with a conclusion that treats it as such. This thought plainly influenced quite strongly the judgments in the Court of Appeal ... I see the force of this consideration. But your Lordships can, in my opinion, give effect to it only if you are prepared either to hobble the common law in all classes of disputes lest its range is too wide to suit industrial disputes or to give the statute a wider scope than it was ever intended to have.

10. See p. 176–7.
11. See p. 70.

The Court of Appeal had held that the tort of intimidation did not include a threat to break a contract. The Law Lords, including Lords Devlin and Reid, held that it did. And so a crucial section of the Act of 1906 received an interpretation nearly sixty years later which challenged the right to strike and had to be corrected by another statute.[12] Lord Devlin warned their Lordships of the dangers of the courts interfering in 'matters of policy' in this branch of the law, although this was certainly the consequence of their decision and one which Devlin himself strongly supported.

Thirty years later, the same sense of unease re-surfaces. Are these conflicts between employers and trade unions, or between one union and another, matters where judicial creativity is to be encouraged? Whatever may have been the motive of the decision of Associated Newspapers to seek to persuade employees to abandon collective bargaining in 1995, the effect was to weaken the unions. As Lord Browne-Wilkinson said it left 'an undesirable lacuna in the legislation protecting employees against victimisation'. Surely the other Law Lords recognized this. Whichever way they decided, the political consequences were considerable. It is difficult to believe that they thought their tortuous interpretation of the legislation to be what the legislators intended.[13]

The considerable conflict that surfaced in late 1979 and early 1980 between the Court of Appeal and the House of Lords over the interpretation of industrial relations law flowed from differing views about the creative function of the judiciary and not from differing views about the undesirability of that law. The Court of Appeal pursued its policy of interpreting the legislation restrictively so as further to control and curtail the activities of trade unionists. But the House of Lords refused to adopt a similar role and began to emphasize the danger to the administration of justice of so positive and so political a stance.[14] At the same time, some of them made no secret of their distaste for the legislation.

The conflict became acute when the Court of Appeal held

12. Trades Disputes Act 1965.
13. *Associated Newspapers Ltd. v. Wilson* [1995] 2 WLR 354; see p. 100.
14. See pp. 79–84.

in *Duport Steels v. Sirs* that the extension of the steel strike to the private sector was not 'in furtherance' of a trade dispute. In view of the recent decision of the House of Lords in *Express Newspapers v. McShane*, the Court of Appeal's interpretation of the phrase was positively perverse, and was a challenge which their Lordships could not ignore. Nor did they. Lord Diplock said:

> When the meaning of the statutory words is plain and unambiguous it is not for the judges to invent fancied ambiguities as an excuse for failing to give effect to its plain meaning because they themselves consider that the consequence of doing so would be inexpedient or even unjust or immoral . . . It endangers continued public confidence in the political impartiality of the judiciary, which is essential to the continuance of the rule of law, if judges, under the guise of interpretation, provide their own preferred amendments to statutes which experience of their operation has shown to have had consequences that members of the court before whom the matter comes consider to be injurious to the public interest.

The prose may be convoluted but the meaning is clear. Lord Scarman said:

> My basic criticism of all three judgments in the Court of Appeal is that in their desire to do justice the court failed to do justice according to law. Legal systems differ in the width of the discretionary power granted to judges but in developed societies limits are invariably set, beyond which the judges may not go. Justice in such societies is not left to the unguided, even if experienced, sage sitting under the spreading oak tree.

Lord Scarman then distinguished common law where society has been content to allow the judges to formulate and develop the law. Even in this, their 'very own field of creative endeavour', the judges bound themselves by the doctrine of precedents. But in the field of statute law 'the judge must be obedient to the will of Parliament in its enactments'. And in the *Express Newspapers* case Lord Scarman said: 'It would need very clear language to persuade me that Parliament intended to allow the courts to act as some sort of backseat driver in trade disputes.'

This is to put the matter boldly – deliberately so, no doubt, to make the argument stick. In practice, judges are often most reluctant to be creative in the development of the common law, though it is precisely there that Lord Denning had been at his most creative during his long judicial life. And judges are often not reluctant at all to interpret statutes in a way which Parliament could not have intended. But I think Lord Scarman is here rebuking Lord Denning for applying his common law instinct for creative developments to statute law where, according to Lord Scarman, it has much less justification.[15] The distinction is a valuable contribution to the debate (which will continue as long as the present system lasts) about the proper limits of judicial creativity.

15. 'The choice', Lord Denning has said on statutory interpretation, 'is a matter of policy for the law: which gives the more sensible result? It is not a semantic or linguistic exercise.' (*R. v. Crown Court Sheffield ex parte Brownlow* [1980] 2 All ER 444 at 451.)

9. The political role

The traditional view

In the traditional view, the function of the judiciary[1] is to decide disputes in accordance with the law and with impartiality. The law is thought of as an established body of principles which prescribes rights and duties. Impartiality means not merely an absence of personal bias or prejudice in the judge but also the exclusion of 'irrelevant' considerations such as his political or religious views. Individual litigants expect to be heard fairly and fully and to receive justice. Essentially, this view rests on an assumption of judicial 'neutrality'.

This neutrality is regarded as more than impartiality between the parties. It means, also, that the judge should not advert to matters which go beyond those necessary for decisions in the case before him. On this view the judge is not to take into account any consequences which might flow from his decision and which are wider than the direct interests of the parties. He must act like a political, economic, and social eunuch, and have no interest in the world outside his court when he comes to judgment.

Where the issues are simple and the dispute limited to the interests of the two parties, the judge may fulfil his traditional function. Divorce, the meaning of a contract between businessmen, a personal claim for injury sustained in a road accident, the buying and selling of a house – for these the traditional view often suffices. But less simple issues can easily emerge. If there are children of the marriage which is to be

---

1 . As in the foregoing parts of this book, I am speaking in this part primarily of judges of the High Court, the Court of Appeal and the House of Lords.

dissolved, if the purpose of the contract is contrary to public policy, if the accident was caused by dangerous driving, if the seller is a bankrupt, then other persons and even the State itself may be involved. And their interests may have to be taken into account.

Moreover, these are all civil cases. But if the proceedings are for alleged crimes, then the State is almost always directly concerned and considerations again arise which go beyond the individuals themselves.

A more sophisticated version of this traditional view sees the judiciary as one of the principal organs of a democratic society without whom government could be carried on only with great difficulty. The essence of their function is the maintenance of law and order and the judges are seen as a mediating influence. Democracy requires that some group of persons acts as an arbiter not only between individuals but also between governmental power and the individual. In criminal matters this governmental power will be exercised through the police and the prosecution service to bring a wrongdoer before the court. It will ensure that the order of the court is enforced, that prisons are provided, that fines are paid. But there must be some body, other than the government, which hears the case, makes the decision, and decides the sentence. By this means the daily use, by the government and its agencies, of *force* is legitimated and so made acceptable to society at large.

Judges then, in this view, operate as an essential part of the democratic machinery of administration. They take their place alongside the other two great institutions of Government and Parliament, more passive than they, but indispensable. No doubt there is something of a dilemma in the judiciary's position as both upholders of law and order and protectors of the individual against a powerful executive. But this is explained in terms of checks and balances or countervailing power, and so what might be an inherent contradiction dissolves in a cloud of words which nevertheless, be it noted, defines the function of the judiciary in *political* terms.

In these terms, therefore, the judiciary may come into conflict with the government of the day. Formally, this conflict can arise only where the government acts 'illegally'. But it is the judges who, particularly in their creative and interpretative function, determine whether governments or their agents have so acted. Thus they set limits to the discretionary powers of governments and to the rights of individuals, especially when these two forces conflict. Where and how they set those limits has been the theme of this book.

Governments have extensive powers and, with adequate parliamentary majorities, can add to them without too much difficulty. This being so, it is well that judges should be willing to ensure that government bodies do not seek to act beyond those powers. And no doubt the existence of the courts and of opportunities to bring before them dubious exercises of governmental power is some deterrent to any public servants who may be inclined to stretch their powers beyond legal limits. So also where statutes lay down procedures to be followed before powers are exercised, the courts should insist that those procedures are followed and may even add their own gloss to ensure that governmental bodies do not act unfairly or in bad faith. How far beyond those elementary propositions of principle the judges should go, how far they should exercise their own wide powers further to control governmental activity, is the crucial political question.

The myth of neutrality

I have said that, traditionally, impartiality is thought of as part of a wide, judicial neutrality. Judges are seen essentially as arbiters in conflicts – whether between individuals or between individuals and the State – and as having no position of their own, no policy even in the narrowest sense of that word.

In denying such neutrality, I am not concerned to argue that judges, like other people, have their own personal political convictions and, with more or less enthusiasm, privately support one or other of the political parties and may vote accordingly. That, no doubt, is true but political partisanship in that sense is not important. What matters is the function they perform and the role they perceive themselves as fulfilling in the political structure.

Neither impartiality nor independence necessarily involves neutrality. Judges are part of the machinery of authority within the State and as such cannot avoid the making of political decisions. What is important is to know the bases on which these decisions are made.

Lord Devlin put this most clearly when he wrote immediately after the industrial dispute of 1972 and when the five dockers had just been released from prison (see p. 75). He made a distinction between consensus and non-consensus law, by consensus meaning a result which people generally were 'prepared to put up with'. 'Most law', said Lord Devlin, 'is in fact based on this sort of consensus. It is what gives the law its stability and saves it from change after every swing of the pendulum.' The Industrial Relations Act 1971, continued Lord Devlin, was not based on consensus, and he asked what was the position of the courts with regard to such law. Lord Devlin then said:

> The question would not need to be asked if in Britain the role of the courts was in accordance with theory. In theory the judiciary is the neutral force between government and the governed. The judge interprets and applies the law without favour to either and its application in a particular case is embodied in an order which is passed to the executive to enforce. It is not the judge's personal order; it is substantially the product of the law and only marginally of the judicial mind. If its enforcement is resisted or evaded, the judge is no more concerned than if he were an arbitrator.
>
> British judges have never practised such detachment. The reason may lie in their origin as servants of the Crown or perhaps in the fact that for a long time the law they administered was what they had made themselves. A mixture of the two has left the High Court with the power to enforce its order in civil cases by treating disobedience as contempt itself.
>
> In the criminal law the judges regard themselves as at least as much concerned as the executive with the preservation of law and order. Then there is what can best be described as the expatiatory power. Whereas under most systems the judgment is formal, brief and to the legal point, the British judge may expatiate on what

he is doing and why he is doing it, and its consequences; and because of his prestige he is listened to.

These high powers make the British judiciary more than just a neutral arbitral force. On the whole their wise and cautious deployment has enabled the judiciary to use its reputation for impartiality and independence for the public good. But it is imperative that the high powers should not be used except in support of consensus law. If the judges are to do more than decide what the law means, if they are also to speak for it, their voice must be the voice of the community; it must never be taken for the voice of the government or the voice of the majority.

So, he argued, non-consensus law should not be enforceable by the courts and he criticized the way the Industrial Relations Act involved the courts in making orders for the enforcement of strike ballots and cooling-off orders. 'The prestige of the judiciary,' concluded Lord Devlin, 'their reputation for stark impartiality to be kept up in appearance as well as in fact, is not at the disposal of any government: it is an asset that belongs to the whole nation.'[2]

The distinction drawn between consensus and non-consensus law is not easy to sustain. Every government passes a number of politically controversial statutes – commonly about ten in each session – which contain much that is objected to by a large section of the electorate. Tax provisions, privatization, police powers, local government finance, industrial relations, education reform, race relations, all these are obvious recent examples. If Lord Devlin meant to limit non-consensus legislation only to those measures which people generally were not 'prepared to put up with', then his list would be very short indeed. If he meant to extend it to include those major areas of controversy just exemplified then the list would be much longer. Was he saying that the enforcement procedures of the courts should not be used where, for example, council tenants refuse to pay rents, or councillors refuse to pay sums surcharged on them after an auditor's examination, or a member of the National Front refuses to remove a sign from his property

2. *Sunday Times*, 6 August 1972.

which is in breach of the Race Relations Act, or a parent keeps his child away from a comprehensive school, or Welsh students disrupt court proceedings?

Surely Lord Devlin was trying to have it both ways. If the judiciary is more than 'a neutral arbitral force' – and I agree that it is – then it is most obviously so in controversial matters where its 'deployment' of power is highlighted. When the public interest is involved, judges become active and cannot suddenly become coy about enforcing laws – if necessary by their own procedures – which they believe to be politically controversial. Judges are in the business of upholding the law and that means they are part of the machinery for enforcing party political law as much as other 'consensus' legislation. Moreover, Lord Devlin was wrong if he believed that trade union distrust of the judiciary flowed from the fact that the enforcement of the order for committal to prison of the dockers was effected by court officials rather than by other public servants. It was the order of the court that mattered, not the method of its enforcement.

Nevertheless, when all this is said, the importance of Lord Devlin's analysis rests in his denial of the neutrality of the judiciary in matters like the criminal law and, I would add, inevitably whenever judges set limits, as they frequently do, to governmental powers and individual rights in circumstances where statutes and common law give guidance which is inadequate or imprecise or where they decide they should intervene in the public interest.

The public interest and its application

The higher judiciary comprises some hundred and fifty persons, but the truly effective number of policy-makers in the Divisional Court, the Court of Appeal and the House of Lords is about sixty-five. *These judges have by their education and training and the pursuit of their profession as barristers, acquired a strikingly homogeneous collection of attitudes, beliefs and principles, which to them represent the public interest.* They do not always express it as such. But it is the lodestar by which they navigate.

I use 'the public interest' because that is the phrase most used by the judges themselves when they choose to be explicit. Sometimes they speak of 'the interests of the State', but this carries a somewhat narrower meaning and suggests either the interests of the United Kingdom internationally or the interests of good government. 'The national interest' is synonymous, in judicial usage, with State interests. I take 'the public interest' to embrace both these other phrases but also to include the interest of the people at large, especially when contrasted with the interests of sections of the people.

What is or is not in the public interest is a political question which admits of a great variety of answers. On important issues, especially where there are only two or three possible alternative courses of action, personal opinions easily become part of group opinions. Indeed, as conventional rhetoric, political parties always claim that their policies, and not those of their opponents, best serve the public interest. Another truism is that I will be inclined to identify my interests with those of the public. If I am chairman of General Motors I will be inclined to think that what is good for General Motors is good for the nation. But my own interests, as I see them, will not be limited to my obvious economic interests. They may include, for instance, the continuing stability of the society in which I live, or the continuance of those surrounding circumstances which may give my life meaning.

Clearly then, what the government proposes to do may, or may not, in my opinion, promote the public interest. To accuse the government of not acting in the public interest is the oldest political criticism.

Judges in the United Kingdom are not beholden politically to the government of the day. And they have longer professional lives than most ministers. They, like civil servants, see governments come like water and go with the wind. They owe no loyalty to ministers, not even that temporary loyalty which civil servants owe. Coke said that Bracton said that the King ought to be under no man but under God and the law.[3] Judges are also lions under the throne but that seat is occupied in their eyes not by the Prime Minister but by the law and by

3 . *Prohibitions del Roy* (1607) 12 Co.Rep.63

their conception of the public interest. It is to that law and to that conception that they owe allegiance. In that lies their strength and their weakness, their value and their threat.

By allegiance to 'the law' judges mean the whole body of law, much of which has its origins in the judge-made common law. 'The law' also means the rule of law and here the allegiance is to the philosophical ideal that we should be ruled by laws and not by men. If that means that power should not be exercised arbitrarily or on the whim of rulers and their officials but should be dependent on and flow from properly constituted authority and from rules written down and approved by some form of representative assembly, it is an admirable and necessary, if partial, safeguard against tyranny. The proposition can hardly be taken further because, in modern industrial society, it is impossible to avoid vesting considerable discretionary power in public officials if only because laws cannot be adequately framed to cover every eventuality.

The judicial conception of the public interest, seen in the cases discussed in this book, is threefold. It concerns, firstly, the interests of the State; secondly, the preservation of law and order, broadly interpreted; and thirdly, the judges' views on social and political issues of the day.

The interests of the State

It is unusual for claims based on fundamental 'rights' to be upheld in the courts when challenged by arguments based on State interests. The civil liberty cases like *Liversidge v. Anderson*, *Greene*, *Halliday* and others (above, pp. 152–7) are examples, and it is significant that the so-called libertarian principles which are said to lie behind habeas corpus and other such remedies have seldom proved strong enough to prevail over the interests of the State. The decisions of the House of Lords in the *Guardian Newspapers* and the *GCHQ* cases of 1984 show how difficult it is to rebut overriding claims by ministers that actions are necessary in the interests of national security (pp. 156, 253).

But the interests of the State, or the national interests, are invoked more widely as the basis for judicial policies. The exercise of judicial legerdemain which sprang the five dockers from prison in 1972 was certainly motivated by the imminence of a probable general strike (see p. 75). So also the national interest in the administration of justice was the reason given by the Law Lords when they decided to stifle further discussion in the *Sunday Times* of the thalidomide tragedy (p. 215). Indeed, freedom of expression is frequently a major casualty when the national interest is invoked (chapter 6), or in the judicial attacks on television programmes seeking to uncover miscarriages of justice (pp. 204–13). The judges' view was summarized by Lord Wilberforce when he said that there was 'a wide difference between what is interesting to the public and what it is in the public interest to make known'.[4]

Above all these cases, towers the *Spycatcher* saga (pp. 223–32). Here the claim was essentially that of confidentiality, the government not being prepared to put to the test the opposing arguments of any threat to national security. And for many months the courts in the UK suppressed publication in the press on this ground. The crucial decision was that of the majority of the House of Lords on the continuation of the interim injunction, and we have seen how the minority as well as the majority expressed themselves. Those who put their faith in the incorporation into UK law of the European Convention on Human Rights, should read Lord Templeman's view. It was put to him that the question for the House was whether interference with the freedom of expression constituted by the continuation of the injunctions was, in the words of the Convention, 'necessary in a democratic society in the interests of national security, for protecting the reputation or rights of others, for preventing the disclosure of information received in confidence, or for maintaining the authority or impartiality of the judiciary'. Lord Templeman said that the continuance of the injunctions 'appears to be necessary for all these purposes'.[5] Publication was eventually allowed only when the book was so widely available that further restraint had become absurd.

The *Spycatcher* litigation exposed the political bias of some of the most senior members of the judiciary in the most blatant

4 . *British Steel Corporation v. Granada Television* [1980] 3 WLR 774 (p. 252).

5 . *A-G v. Guardian Newspapers Ltd* [1987] 3 All ER 316.

way. The case was pursued by the government with great vigour both in this country and in Australia long after any useful purpose could be achieved. Before it was concluded, the action had become an abuse of the judicial process. And for much of the time a majority of the judges sitting in the Court of Appeal and the House of Lords gave support to the government in circumstances which grossly interfered with the right and duty of the national press to report matters of the greatest public concern.

The serious charge to be laid against the judiciary is that they rarely do more than pay lip service to freedom of expression.[6] That is why the outburst by Lord Bridge in *Spycatcher* when he spoke of totalitarianism (p. 229) seemed so remarkable. For once an English judge hit the table hard, almost as if he were one of the great liberal judges of the Supreme Court of the United States. The shock was considerable; but the mood passed and the impulse died.

More recently, *ex parte Brind* was a particularly outrageous decision (p. 248). In a parliamentary democracy, it is essential that freedom of expression is officially afforded to all recognized political parties on an equal basis. The playing field is not in practice level because access through the press is controlled by newspaper owners and editors who are politically committed in varying degrees to one or other side in the political contest. The situation in Northern Ireland is such that governments have been empowered to proscribe certain political parties, to make criminal the membership and attendance at meetings of such parties, and other forms of support. Sinn Fein is not proscribed. Members of Sinn Fein stand at local and parliamentary elections with success at different times and in different places. To interfere with the freedom of expression of its members so as to reduce the participation in the political process in a way not applied to the other main parties and to do so expressly to prevent them from promoting their political aims is indistinguishable from the actions of totalitarian regimes the world over. The Law Lords were required to decide whether the general words in the statute and Licence and

6 . See in general, K. D. Ewing and C. A. Gearty, *Freedom under Thatcher* (1990).

Agreement authorized the restraints imposed. They did so, and expressed surprise at the moderation shown by the UK government. Throughout his judgment, Lord Bridge identified Sinn Fein with terrorism and terrorists. In the absence of proscription, Sinn Fein was constitutionally entitled to the same opportunities as other parties and the Law Lords would have had no difficulty, had they so chosen, in concluding that general words could not have been intended to deprive Sinn Fein of such fundamental and democratic rights.

For some reason, the decision in *Derbyshire County Council v. Times Newspapers* (p. 245) is regarded by libertarians as a step forward in the movement for greater freedom of expression. A powerful newspaper conglomerate chose to make serious defamatory statements about the leader of a local authority, in his official capacity, and about those who managed its pension fund. In the name of democracy, the courts denied those defamed the right to challenge those statements. It is difficult enough for individual citizens to obtain redress for false statements made in the national press without risking their livelihood. Now it seems that locally elected bodies are also to be denied protection.

Paradoxically, Members of Parliament have been made free to sue newspapers criticizing their activities at Westminster, following the amendment inserted in the Defamation Bill (p. 250). The privilege accorded to Members by article 9 of the Bill of Rights 1689, which was intended to ensure that they could not be proceeded against for words spoken in Parliament, remains, though a High Court judge has suggested that it should be amended (see below, p. 333). If elected Members may sue, why should not elected bodies, when defamed by the mass media?

The interests of the State are invoked when government claims that documents should not be disclosed. *Conway v. Rimmer, Burmah Oil, Air Canada* (pp. 232–9) and later cases were all reviewed by Sir Richard Scott during his inquiry into the arms for Iraq affair (pp. 239–44), and we have seen how this threw him into conflict not only with the government but with his fellow judges. Here the reputation, even the continued existence, of the government was in issue. As Sir Richard said, 'In forming his view as to what the public interest requires, the minister will, obviously, take into account the contents of the documents in question and also, in appropriate cases, the class of documents into which the documents in question fall.' He added that all the ministers who signed the PII certificates were advised by their departmental lawyers that it was not permissible for ministers to take into account any administration of justice factors in favour of disclosure of the documents.[7] This advice, said Sir Richard, was wrong, but because of this advice the charges that the ministers were seeking to deprive the defendants in a criminal trial of the means by which to clear themselves were not well founded.[8]

Because of the number of cases in the courts where judges in recent years have been critical of ministers, especially the Home Secretary, and have struck down their decisions, there has arisen a general image of a judiciary united against this particular government at this particular time. It is important to remember that in this controversy when ministers and civil servants were considered by Sir Richard Scott to be seriously at fault in seeking to withhold documents which benefited those charged with criminal conduct, many Law Lords and former Law Lords, supported by the present Lord Chief Justice, joined to disagree publicly with Sir Richard. There can be no doubt that during the tumultuous days which followed the publication of the Scott Report the speeches of those eminent judges were of the greatest help to ministers in their attempts to establish that they were under a legal obligation to sign the PII certificates.

Law and order

The public interest is seen as a reflection of social discipline. Lord Devlin said, in the passage already quoted (p. 293), 'the judges regard themselves as at least as much concerned as the executive with the preservation of law and order.' One of the greatest political myths is that the courts in this country are alert to protect the individual against the power of the State. Sometimes, it is true, they will intervene to help the

7 . HC 115 of 1995–96 para. G 18.65.
8 . *Ibid.*, para. G18.106.

weakest, as some of the immigration cases show. But minority groups, especially if they demonstrate or protest in ways which cause difficulty or embarrassment, are not likely to find that the courts support their claims to free speech or free assembly. The judges see themselves as occupying a key position in the struggle to enforce the law, and are always conscious of the dangers which they believe will follow if they do not support the powers of the police.

Demonstrations, if properly organized and controlled by the police, are acceptable by the judiciary as being within the framework of law and order. But individual demonstrators are always likely to be viewed with considerable disfavour by the courts. Although very different in kind, two of the most repressive decisions handed down in recent years were those in *Kamara* (pp. 268–9) and in *Hubbard v. Pitt* (pp. 269–70). Lord Hailsham's extension of the criminal law to cover peaceful sit-ins and occupations as a method of demonstration in the first of these cases, and the Court of Appeal's finding for the estate agents against peaceful demonstrators in the second, mark once more the willingness of the judiciary to extend the rather special judicial conception of where the public interest lies into the areas of political controversy. We have seen that angry but non-violent demonstrators had injunctions issued against them during the miners' strike.[9]

Action taken by public authorities responding to public protestations against the export of live cattle became, in the view of the courts,[10] surrendering to the dictates of unlawful pressure groups' with 'awesome implications for the rule of law' which could 'hardly be exaggerated'. Such extravagant language shows the depth of judicial reaction which inspired headlines like *Public bodies must not bow to mob rule.*[11] And when the chief constable for Sussex used his discretionary powers to reduce police cover, the court absurdly concluded that he was in breach of article 34 of the Treaty of Rome which prohibited quantitative restrictions on exports between member states,

9 . *Thomas v. NUM (South Wales area)*: see p. 92.
10. *R. v. Coventry ex parte Phoenix* [1995] 3 All ER 37; see p. 272.
11. *Independent,* 13 April 1995.

especially as he had not 'sought to increase the financial resources available to him'.[12]

The independence of the judiciary is not enhanced when protests on the streets by those seeking to prevent cruelty to animals are defeated in the courts on the ground that they threaten the foundations of the State and infringe the principles of free trade. Once again the judges, faced with the realities of a genuine political conflict, retreated hastily behind the barricades of legal and constitutional formalism.

To these cases must now be added the decision of the Court of Appeal in *ex parte Al-Fayed* (p. 119). The upsetting of the Home Secretary's decision to refuse the application for naturalization was remarkable. Section 44(2) of the British Nationality Act provided

> The Secretary of State . . . shall not be required to assign any reason for the grant or refusal of any application under this Act the decision on which is at his discretion; and [his] decision . . . shall not be subject to appeal to, or review in, any court.

The Court of Appeal held that fairness required that the applicants should be told what aspects of their applications had given rise to difficulties or reservations; that they should have an opportunity to be heard; that the statutory words did not relieve the minister of his obligation to be fair; and that his decisions must be quashed so that they could be taken in a manner which was fair.

The decision of the court seems to make considerable inroads into the hitherto apparently absolute discretion of the minister in such cases, so long as he had no regard to the race, colour or religion of the applicant.

But by far the most important aspects of law and order are the powers of the police and the exercise of those powers. Today, as we have seen (above, pp. 162–71), many of the problems have centred around the Police and Criminal Evidence Act 1984. Before 1 January 1986, when the act came into operation, the judges' Rules laid down what was the proper

---

12. *R. v. Chief Constable of Sussex ex parte International Traders' Ferry Ltd.* [1995] 3 WLR 802; but see p. 273.

practice for the police to follow when dealing with suspects. The rules had not the force of law, though breach of them might have legal consequences for the prosecution. They were not always followed and often the courts seemed not to be assiduous in their enforcement. When PACE came into operation with its statutory rules and code of practice, it seems that the police did not fully appreciate that they were now operating under a new dispensation. It also took the courts some time to decide what the rules and the code meant when applied to particular situations. The decision in *Samuel* (p. 163) showed that failure to allow access to legal advice could be fatal to the conviction, but *Alladice* (p. 163) in effect went the other way. Moreover, the disregard by the police of the rules did not mean that they were guilty of an offence; so the 'rights' were not directly enforceable. The Lord Chief Justice presided over the Court of Appeal in *Alladice* and some attributed the difference to him, but the act itself had left the issue open by not conferring a positive right to legal advice.

Nor were the police happy, being uncertain of their rights and the limits of their investigatory powers. Some resorted to various devices to avoid the rules. So, for example, suspects were questioned at times and in circumstances which might avoid the procedures applicable to 'interviews'; arrests were delayed to avoid the full protection of the act; detainees were not always told of the existence of duty solicitors; the existence of statutory rights was communicated too quickly, incomprehensibly or incompletely. Then in *Canale* as we have seen (p. 166) the Lord Chief Justice sought to impose his authority.

The courts claim that it is no part of their function to discipline the police for misbehaviour (see p. 166). But it is clear that the failure of the police to apply the procedures provided in PACE and the code has forced a revision of this judicial attitude. The judges' criticism, sometimes heavy, of police practice has no doubt had consequences within the force. How far these will result in better observance by individual police officers remains to be seen. Continuous pressure from the courts may well be essential.

PACE itself does not seem adequately to protect confidential material. Judicial interpretation has to some extent undermined the efficacy of the new safeguards. It is surprising that the courts ruled there was no implied contractual duty on the bank in *Taylor's* case to inform its client that information about his account had been passed to the police.[13] And the courts seem to have assumed, almost without question, that all police demands for press photographs should be met even though this may amount to general unspecific search warrants. The requirement that the material sought by the police must be shown to be 'of substantial value' to the investigation has proved to be no safeguard — so easily have the courts been satisfied. The decision in *Francis and Francis* (p. 167) has been criticized as interfering with the privileged relationship between solicitor and client. Other increases of police powers on arrest and road blocks seem to have led to a large increase in arrests, followed by the release of a third of these without charge or caution. On the other hand, the taping of interviews, where it takes place, may result in an improvement in the relationships between police and public.

If, as has been said, *Samuel* 'sent shock waves through the police',[14] eight years later *Khan (Sultan)* (p. 164) looked set to go to the European Court of Human Rights. The conflict between police effectiveness and procedural fairness is no doubt set to continue and will probably next develop over the extent to which those charged are required to disclose their defence in advance of the hearing.

We have seen that Stephen Livingstone's analysis of thirteen cases in Northern Ireland shows that the Law Lords found for the government in all but two cases.[15] The Court of Appeal in Northern Ireland found against the government in four cases out of twelve (*ex parte Brind*[16] being the one that did not emanate from Northern Ireland). Livingstone asks what are the common features of the Law Lords' judgments and whether they indicate any views which might predispose the judges to favour the executive. Apart from the first two cases, in 1969

13. *Barclays Bank v. Taylor* [1989] 3 All ER 563; and see *Criminal Law Review* of July 1990.

14. Reiner and Leigh, in *McCrudden and Chambers, op. cit.*, p. 100.

15. 'The House of Lords and the Northern Ireland conflict', in 57 *Modern Law Review* (1994) 333.

16. See p. 170.

and 1975, the Law Lords were unanimous. The first feature is the brevity of the judgments, the small amount of authority cited, and the swift dismissal of arguments based on human rights. Secondly, the judgments strive to indicate that the cases are not particularly 'about' Northern Ireland, with little reference to the local circumstances. Where determinations of 'reasonableness' are called for or whether there should be 'exceptions' to established principles, the Law Lords appeared to construct the context from the perspective of the security forces and the dangers they faced. To maintain order, on this view the security forces were to be accorded wide powers and 'should be largely relieved from the burden of judicial supervision'. In an emergency situation, Livingstone argues, 'the role of the judiciary is to scrutinise more closely both the nature and operation of such powers, in order to ensure that citizens' rights are only derogated from to the extent clearly mandated by Parliament.' This was not a perspective applied by the Law Lords. 'By consistently upholding government action in Northern Ireland, the House of Lords has ruled itself out of playing a role in the conflict.'

In many procedural ways, the courts have intervened to improve prison administration, ensuring prisoners access to courts, reforming the quasi-criminal process of disciplinary proceedings and the quasi-sentencing function of life sentence release. But they have had little impact on prisoners' living and working conditions, perhaps because litigation on such matters is very difficult to mount, though the revelations in *Williams v. Home Office* (p. 234) about the control unit regime ultimately led to its disbandment.[17]

The appalling miscarriages of justice which were revealed in the late 1980s and early 1990s were a serious blow to the whole system of criminal investigation and trial (pp. 204–13).

David Rose has written that the old regime in criminal justice was destroyed when, on 19 October 1989, Lord Lane C J said at the Old Bailey, speaking of the Surrey police detectives who had elicited 'confessions' from the Guildford Four, 'the officers must have lied'. These words 'exploded like a depth

17. Stephen Livingstone, 'The Impact of Judicial Review on Prisons', in B. Hadfield (ed.) *Judicial Review: A Thematic Approach*, pp. 180–3.

charge in a placid lake', and Rose writes of the 'horror and cold fury' of the Lord Chief Justice.[18] From that time, the general view of law-abiding members of the public that police evidence was to be relied on, despite the occasional fall from grace, was seriously damaged.

Perhaps the institution of the Criminal Cases Review Commission will improve the situation. Under the present system, it has been difficult to persuade the Home Secretary to have the case re-opened by referring it back to the Court of Appeal. The overriding reason for this reluctance is, once again, because to allow re-opening is to question the validity of the system. So the Home Secretary has to be firmly convinced that there is some fresh information or consideration of substance which might suggest that the conviction is unsafe or unsatisfactory. If all that can be shown is that, on reflection, the trial and appeal courts probably made a mistake in coming to their decision, a reference is not likely to be made. In the past the Home Office has sometimes seemed unduly sensitive to the known distaste of the senior judiciary for the referral procedure.

It is also clear that the Court of Appeal is traditionally most reluctant to quash a conviction, or order a retrial, on a referral. The court seems to believe that the general public will be likely to lose faith in a system that admits any errors. But of course when the error is made manifest, as in the case of the Guildford Four, the failure to rectify the error earlier is seen as a far greater condemnation of the system.

The danger of admitting the possibility of error has been written firmly into English jurisprudence by the infamous words of Lord Denning when rejecting civil proceedings sought by the Birmingham Six:

> If the six men win it will mean that the police were guilty of perjury, that they were guilty of violence and threats, that the confessions were involuntary and were improperly admitted in evidence and that the convictions were erroneous. That would mean the Home Secretary would either have to recommend they be pardoned or he

18. David Rose, *In the Name of the Law* (1996), p. 1.

would have to remit the case to the Court of Appeal.
This is such an appalling vista that every sensible person
in the land would say: 'It cannot be right that these
actions should go any further'.

In the most difficult and most political cases of IRA bombings,
especially those on the mainland where public opinion runs so
strongly, the judicial system is put under strain. The police are
under great pressure to show that they can make arrests and
obtain convictions. Ministers want results. And the judicial
system is not expected to impede the process. For the police
this means that any leads which look at all promising will be
pursued vigorously. (It has been suggested that the Special
Branch drew the attention of the police to one of the Guildford
Four as a possible suspect.) Interrogations follow and confessions are obtained. The police may become convinced they
have the culprits and then fabricate evidence; or they may do
so anyway. The prosecution lawyers will act on the evidence
put before them by the police. They will not do so slavishly
and they will draw attention to the weaknesses of what they
are expected to present. But, under the adversarial system, it
is their job to present the case against the accused as strongly
(one hopes, also, as fairly) as possible.

Robert Kee in his book[19] on the trial of the Guildford Four,
seems to me to indicate strongly that Mr Justice Donaldson
(as he then was, Lord Donaldson MR as he became) summed
up impeccably but unfairly in favour of the prosecution. What
he said could not be faulted but there was much that he could
have said, favourable to the accused, which he did not. Surprisingly, Donaldson J. was also the judge at the trial of the Maguire Seven. And Robert Kee, it seems to me, makes the same
criticism of him in that case.

In his interim report on the Maguire case (p. 209) Sir John
May was critical of the conduct of the trial under Sir John
Donaldson. Sir John May said he did not think that the jury
were adequately directed about the effect of an exhibit which
cast doubt on the Crown's argument that the scientific tests
showed the accused must have handled nitroglycerine. Sir John

19. *Trial and Error* (2nd edn, 1989); see p. 207.

May added that in his opinion certain Crown evidence on the results of tests was inadmissible.

On the Maguire appeals, Kee is more direct in his opinion. 'Lord Justice Roskill', he says, 'seemed almost to go out of his way to give Mr Justice Donaldson the benefit of any doubt ... His judgment in fact reads more like an opportunity seized to reinforce the case against the Maguire Seven than a balanced hearing of the appellants' complaints.' Roskill L J also presided over the appeal of the Guildford Four. Robert Kee found him unduly dismissive of evidence which favoured the accused.

When to Lord Denning's words, rejecting civil proceedings brought by the Birmingham Six, are added those of the Court of Appeal – 'the longer the hearing has gone on the more convinced this Court has become that the verdict of the jury was correct', (p. 210) – confidence in the judiciary is badly shaken.

Behind this lies a deeper consideration. In the trials both of the Guildford Four and of the Maguire Seven, three men were appointed under the judicial system to prosecute and adjudicate: Sir Michael Havers, later to be Conservative Attorney-General and then Lord Chancellor; Mr Justice Donaldson, later to be Lord Donaldson and the Master of the Rolls; and Lord Justice Roskill, later to be Lord Roskill.

To the accused at these two trials, these three must have appeared as a formidable team before whom they were unlikely to have a fair and impartial hearing. Much was said about the two trials being separate and distinct, but it must have seemed to the Maguires in particular that their case was wholly prejudiced by the previous trial of the Guildford Four. It was Anne Maguire's nephew who, as one of the Guildford Four, had allegedly implicated her, and she was originally charged with murder until it was realized that there was no evidence to support this. But the Maguire Seven were from the beginning inevitably associated with the Guildford Four and their trial. Any expectation they had of the prosecution objectively presenting facts and legal argument and of the judges as independent arbiters being alert to ensure that proof of guilt was clearly established beyond reasonable doubt must have been difficult to sustain.

Social and political issues

Historically, the longest running political conflict between whole sections of the public and the judges has been in industrial relations. We have seen (pp. 64–7) that the prevailing view of the senior judiciary in the late nineteenth and early twentieth centuries was, in conflict with much of the governmental view of the time, that the growing power of the trade unions should be strictly controlled by law. The judges were seeking to undo some of the effects of earlier legislation and Lord Halsbury, as Lord Chancellor, led them to some success in this attempt. When, over half a century later, the judges and the unions once more came into conflict, the government had adopted the judicial view which was shown in the picketing cases, *Rookes v. Barnard*, and the culmination in *Heaton*'s case and the imprisonment by the NIRC of the five dockers (pp. 73–4). Nor is the view unpopular. But when the economic consequences of the continued detention of the dockers and the threat of a general strike became clear, then what was in 'the public interest' was seen to have changed dramatically, and the dockers were released. The president of the NIRC imprisoned the dockers expressly in defence of the rule of law, when to ignore their challenge would be to 'imperil all law and order' on which 'our whole way of life' was based. A few days later he released them – also, expressly, in defence of the rule of law – having been provided by the House of Lords with a flimsy justification for so doing (p. 75).

So the National Industrial Relations Court in 1972 forced the judiciary to take up a position on the government's side of industrial disputes which divided the country (see pp. 72–9). But, especially here, the distinction must be observed between the interests of the government of the day and the judiciary's view of the public interest. Certainly, the two interests coincided, for the judges enabled the government to escape from a situation which would probably have brought it down and would have presented the trade union movement with a considerable political victory. The judges, we may assume, were not concerned to save that particular Conservative government. They were concerned, however, both to preserve the authority of governments and to avoid economic chaos. That was where they saw the public interest to lie. The price they paid was the increase in distrust between themselves and the trade union movement. So they may have mistaken the public interest. But that is a political comment about a political choice.

In the conflict between the Court of Appeal and the House of Lords in 1979–80 (pp. 79–84) the difference in views of the law, as I have said, did not reflect any difference about its undesirability. In *NWL Ltd v. Woods*, Lord Diplock talked of the possibility of wage demands bringing down 'the fabric of the present economic system'. In *Express Newspapers v. McShane* he said that the consequences of applying the subjective test in interpreting 'furtherance of a trade dispute' 'not surprisingly have tended to stick in judicial gorges',[20] and in *Duport Steels v. Sirs* he said that the immunity given to trade unionists was

> intrinsically repugnant to anyone who has spent his life in the practice of law or the administration of justice . . . It involves granting to trade unions a power, which has no other limits than their own self-interest, to inflict by means which are contrary to the general law, untold harm to industrial enterprises unconcerned with the particular dispute, to the employees of such enterprises, to members of the public and to the nation itself . . .[21]

even though the 'immunity' was, as Lord Scarman said, in substance that given by the legislation of 1906.

In the same case Lord Edmund-Davies called the outcome of the statute 'unpalatable to many', and Lord Keith referred to trade unionists as 'privileged persons' who could 'bring about disastrous consequences with legal impunity'.[22]

Similarly, Lord Denning MR in the Court of Appeal said:

> There is evidence of the disastrous effect which the action will have, not only on all the companies in the private sector, but on much of British industry itself . . . our competitors will clap their hands . . . there is a residual

20. [1980] 2 WLR at 97.
21. [1980] 1 All ER at 541; and see Wedderburn's article referred to below at Note 50.
22. Ibid. at 548, 550.

discretion in the courts to grant an injunction restraining such action as in this case, where it is such as to cause grave danger to the economy and the life of the country, and puts the whole nation and its welfare at risk.[23]

Why, then, did the House of Lords not support the Court of Appeal? To have done so in *Express Newspapers v. McShane* would not have been difficult. It is not manifestly absurd to interpret 'in furtherance of a trade dispute' as implying an objective test and the gap between Lord Wilberforce's approach and that of Lord Denning (see pp. 80–1) is not large. To have supported the Court of Appeal would certainly have brought the judiciary into even sharper confrontation with the trade unions and would have further diminished in certain quarters what Lord Diplock in *Duport Steels* called 'that voluntary respect for the law as laid down and applied by courts of justice'. Lords Keith and Scarman expressed similar fears.

Moreover, these decisions were taken at a time when the newly elected Conservative government were embarking on their legislative reforms of trade union law, the Employment Bill being published at the beginning of December 1979. Their Lordships may well have concluded that it would be wiser to leave such highly contentious political matters to the professional politicians. At the same time, some of their Lordships did not hesitate to push the Conservative government in what they saw as the right direction. Their criticism of the powers which the existing legislation gave to trade unionists could hardly have been stronger and Lords Diplock, Salmon and Edmund-Davies in *Duport Steels* made quite clear that they hoped the law would be changed. To the layman it must have seemed that members of the senior judiciary were publicly throwing their weight behind the Conservative government.

The Law Lords were, in these cases, moving sharply and clearly to restrain Lord Denning and the Court of Appeal from developing a policy of restricting trade union activity. The Law Lords saw the need, in the public interest, of avoiding an open conflict between the courts and the trade unions. The disagreement between the Court of Appeal and the House of

23. Ibid. at 535, 536, 538.

Lords presented a clear difference of tactics. Both courts were agreed that trade union power should be curbed, and in this their political position was identical. But on the question of how far the courts should intervene, the Law Lords preferred discretion to valour. But they knew the Employment Bill would do the job for them.

During the 1980s, the Thatcher government continued to develop anti-union legislation, making illegal a number of union practices. The courts, as we have seen (p. 92), became deeply involved in the miners' strike of 1984 and the punitive effect of injunctions, fines and sequestration of assets became severe. The attitude of the courts even to those demonstrations and picketing which did not result in violence was to seek to curtail union activity. Certainly there was violence by both strikers and the police. Later, during the dispute over the National Dock Labour Scheme, the Court of Appeal went beyond previous limits in granting an interim injunction, so that what it called a difficult question of law could be considered subsequently at the full trial. Had this question been decided in favour of the employers, it would have meant that since 1947 dock workers had had no sanction to strike. The House of Lords prevented what would have been a manifest injustice and a display of political bias remarkable even in the context of industrial relations. Nevertheless the consequences were negligible as the government bill abolishing the scheme was passed before further action could be taken. So the Lords' decision was no great blow in support of the right to strike. However, also in 1989, the attempt by British Rail to have the NUR ballot declared invalid on grounds which would have made the holding of a legal ballot almost impossible also failed (see p. 96).

Industrial disputes arise out of the conflict of interest between owners, employers and managers on the one side and the employed wage-earners on the other. Each side has some bargaining weapons. Government legislation in the 1980s was directed to strengthen the employers and weaken the employed. Inevitably, because that is their function and their role, whether they like it or not, the courts were drawn into the conflict and, by the nature of the legislation, were required to make political decisions. As Wedderburn has said, the courts see an industrial dispute as essentially one where the enjoyment of private 'property' is being interfered with. It is on this basis that they are so ready to grant interim injunctions, the effect of which is greatly to diminish the workers' bargaining power by wholly suspending the right to strike.

In the 1980s, employers seemed much more intent on testing the extent to which the courts were prepared to go in restraining union activity, particularly in their interpretation of the more recent legislation. The rejection of injunctions by the House of Lords in the Dock Labour Scheme and NUR cases (p. 97) carried echoes of the restraints placed on Lord Denning's enthusiasm, which we have already noticed. On both occasions there was a pulling back from the brink when perhaps the Law Lords sensed that to uphold the employers would have amounted to a denial of the right to strike in most circumstances. Not for the first time in industrial relations, their Lordships required Parliament to take the next steps. So far they have rarely been disappointed. A good example of the restrictive gloss which the courts sometimes attach to statutory words was given by Lord Donaldson MR in *P.O. v. U.C.W.* (p. 96) when, on balloting, he said,

> Where over a long period of continuous action there has been a significant change in the relevant workforce, any call for industrial action following a ballot should be expressly limited to those who were employed by the employer and given an opportunity of voting at the time of the ballot.

This raises the question of what the courts are supposed – in constitutional theory as well as political practice – to be doing in disputes between employers and trade unions. Are they to be arbitrators of last resort? If so, on what basis, taking what factors into account? Once again, Lord Templeman's comments in his interview with Hugo Young give a possible indication.[24] He said, speaking generally of cases coming to the courts (including the House of Lords), that judges were of two kinds: those who ask what is the point of law and those who ask what are the merits of the case. He added however, that even

24. Radio 4, on 13 April 1988.

in the House of Lords 'merits have influence on every case.'

So to ask what is the judicial role in industrial disputes is always to oversimplify, both because there will always be at least two possible interpretations of statute or common law and because individual judges will put different weight on the two considerations: law and merits. What may be true is that in the highly 'political' area of such disputes, merits count for more than law. For in these cases, more than in any others, the consequences of judicial decisions are likely to be far-reaching.

Immigration cases exemplify the kind of social and political choices made by the courts. In *ex parte Swati* (see p. 184), the Court of Appeal took on the role of policy-maker, reducing the caseload on the judiciary. The effect of the decision to limit judicial review was to reduce the number of such leave applications from 697 in 1987 (44 per cent of all applications) to 329 (29 per cent) in 1988. Thereafter the number of immigration applications rose rapidly, though, as a percentage, the figure declined. But in 1994, when the number of such applications rose to 935, its percentage again reached 29 per cent.

Another important choice turned on the interpretation of the requirement that a spouse seeking entry had to show both that the primary purpose of the marriage was not to obtain admission and that the marriage was genuine. But if a would-be immigrant can show the genuineness of the marriage, why should he be obliged to prove also that his primary purpose in entering the marriage is not to obtain admission to the UK? Indeed if the intention to marry is 'genuine', how can the primary purpose be ulterior? So the courts could have argued. But instead we have the opposite in *Bhatia* (pp. 186–7), in part reversed in *Kumar* (p. 187). *Hoque and Singh* (p. 188) supports *Kumar* but still leaves open the ambiguity. It would, however, be unfair to suggest that the courts have positively supported the policy of the government as expressed in rules which are designed to limit the number of Asian and other non-white immigrants. Several of the decisions in the courts show concern at the injustice of this policy, and it was this attitude which, as we have seen, so angered the Treasury Solicitor's Department that the attempt was made to subvert the decision in *Khatab* (p. 50, Note 62) amongst others.

Nevertheless, the general attitude of the courts in England to 'primary purpose' is to look with suspicion on any application for entry and to place the burden of proof firmly on applicants and sponsors. For the Court of Appeal in *Sumeina Masood*[25] it was 'a short step' to conclude that the primary purpose of the marriage was to gain entry, once it had been established that the wife did not intend to live in Pakistan. A different conclusion might have been come to had the hearing been in Scotland where attention was paid to the reality that people may marry out of affection and still genuinely disagree on where they will live permanently.[26]

Again in the deportation cases, we must regret that Lord Bridge concluded in *Patel* (p. 191) that he had to retract his earlier interpretation of parliamentary intention and to entrust the Secretary of State with the largely untrammelled discretion he claimed. Effectively the Law Lords similarly abandoned supervision of the proper exercise of State power in *Budgaycay* (p. 192), *Sivakumaran* (p. 192) and *Oladehinde* (p. 193–4). *Yassine* (p. 193) was politically a more realistic decision.

International law recognizes the status of refugees as victims of political persecution and on this is based the principle of asylum. But governments in western Europe are increasingly reluctant to accept immigrants, especially if they are believed to be seeking entry for 'economic' reasons. So categories arise: persecution must be 'persistent' as in *Sandralingam* (above, p. 195); politicians must not come from 'unsavoury' regimes, as in *Abdullah Conteh* (p. 195); 'terrorism' must be defined as in '*T*' (p. 195); which third countries are 'safe' as destinations as in *ex parte Abdi* (p. 196); the applicability of habeas corpus may need to be limited as in *ex parte Muboyayi* (p. 197); national security once again becomes a cover for obscurity as in *ex parte Chahal* and *Jahromi* (pp. 197, 198); Gerry Adams is excluded one day and admitted soon after (p. 198).

25. See p. 000.
26. *Saftar v. Secretary of State for the Home Department* [1992] lmm.AR 1; see p. 189.

In *ex parte Launder* (p. 200) we are presented with the executive's plea for a corporate decision and the truly Stuart claim that such matters of the prerogation should not be subject to judicial review; and the finding that the Home Secretary should not consult his Cabinet colleagues before exercising his judgment.

M v. Home Office (p. 202) was received with rapturous applause everywhere (except in the Home Office), as if some great new step had been taken in the evolution of the constitution. In reality, had the court not chosen to insist on its right to issue an injunction against officers of the Crown who had failed to comply with an order of the court on a matter clearly within its jurisdiction, the judicial function would have been seriously subverted. As it was the Home Secretary was not held personally responsible or penalized. And the constitutional situation remained unchanged.

Much more significant was the language used by the Court of Appeal in *ex parte JCWI* (p. 203) in striking down the regulations preventing asylum seekers from qualifying for income support or housing benefit unless they applied for asylum immediately on arrival. The Home Secretary was forced to resort to primary legislation and to face Parliament. The similar response by the court in *Akinbolu* (p. 204) was no less important and pushed the interpretation of section 59 of the Housing Act 1985 to its limit, if not beyond. This was a bold decision and a clear example of the new-found robustness of the judiciary when faced with governmental action of which it did not approve.[27]

No one denies the complexity of the problems that surround asylum, extradition and exclusion. The difficulties for the courts arise, in large part, because governments are reluctant to decide on coherent and consistent policies and prefer to keep their discretionary powers uncluttered by principle. But it is also true that the courts have failed to develop a satisfactory jurisprudence which would provide a framework for decision-making. When and in what circumstances and to what extent the courts should intervene in these matters is undefined. In a

27. And see *R. v. Hammersmith and Fulham LBC ex parte A*, *Independent*, 26 February 1997.

period of expanding judicial review, uncertainty is a serious handicap.

We have seen that the legislation on homelessness from 1977 created problems for the courts and reflected the political controversy surrounding the provision of accommodation. Beginning in the mid-1970s but accelerating greatly during the 1980s the shortage of housing at affordable rents, especially in London, became acute. This was largely the result of government policy, which denied to local authorities the necessary financial resources. The passing of the Housing (Homeless Persons) Act 1977 coincided with the emergence of judicial review in its modern form. By the mid-1980s the courts were becoming alarmed at the growth of applications and this led to Lord Brightman's notorious ruling in *Puhlhofer* (1986) quoted above (page 140). Maurice Sunkin has shown[28] that while 'homeless' applications increased from 8 in 1981 to 75 in 1983, they fell in 1984 to 69 and in 1985 to 66. A further sharp fall to 32 in 1986 may have resulted from *Puhlhofer*, but if so the effect was temporary. By 1987 the total had risen to 71, by 1988 to 101 and by 1989 to 177.[29] In 1994 the total was 447, representing 14 per cent of all leave applications. But this must be put in perspective: in 1994, a total of 299,053 households applied for assistance from local housing authorities and just over 127,000 were accepted as being entitled to some help.[30]

Those who were able to establish themselves as having a priority need under the legislation took precedence over other applicants for accommodation. This enabled the courts to make a straight political choice. It strengthened both their reluctance to interpret the statute generously and their resolve to lighten the load of judicial review cases. The decision of the Law Lords in *ex parte Awua* in 1995 (p. 144) following the government's announcement of a future change of policy, and closely reflecting it, was a sharp rejection of judicial precedent and

28. 'What is happening to applications for judicial review?', in 50 *Modern Law Review* 432.

29. Maurice Sunkin, 'The judicial review case-load 1987–89', in [1991] *Public Law* 490.

30. Bridges, Meszaros, Sunkin, *Judicial Review in Perspective* pp. 11, 27–31.

eased the way for the harsher regime for the homeless introduced by the Housing Act 1996.

The Thatcher administrations of the 1980s changed the relationship between central government departments and local authorities. Under the Local Government, Planning and Land Act 1980, ministers acquired powers to withdraw government grants from local authorities who raised more money through local taxation than the government wished. Local authorities began to challenge such restrictions in the courts. And the courts had to decide what their role was in such disputes. Loughlin instances Lord Templeman in the *Nottinghamshire* case (p. 134), taking the view that the courts should not act as referees in such disputes. But, as in other circumstances, the judges are always anxious to retain their traditional power to interpret statutes.[31] On substantive matters, they usually supported the government's view, perhaps being influenced by the knowledge that the statute was meant by the government to represent government policy.

The courts may also have been influenced by their unfamiliarity with the complexities of local government finance. In the later cases, concerned with the swaps market and the limits of local government borrowing powers, judicial decision-making had most of the attributes of a lottery. When local authorities sought to challenge the centralizing policies of the 1980s by resorting to litigation, the judiciary gave the impression of being lost in a maze. The situation was novel and public law had not developed principles applicable to conflicts between public authorities at this level.

Loughlin says that the basic objective of the courts appears to be to ensure and promote elementary standards of fairness, reasonableness, and legality in the conduct of public administration.[32] This is indeed what the courts claim to be doing, but it imports a measure of formalism which, while giving an air of constitutional propriety, conceals a number of policy decisions and political attitudes. At earlier periods, the judges would have run for cover or simply taken an overtly political line (as in *Bromley v. GLC*, above, pp. 126–33). Today, as

31. Martin Loughlin, *Legality and Locality* (1996), Chapters 5, 6.
32. *Op.cit.*, p. 402, and see generally his Chapter 7.

they seek to broaden their horizons and become active partici-
pants in the constitutional premier league, their trumpet gives
forth an uncertain sound.[33] Accustomed to act as referees,
making their own rules and intervening when either of the
principals gives them an opening, they find that to be too busy
is some danger.

Cases where the courts come down quite heavily on the
exercise of ministerial powers include those where ministers
deliberately seem to push the exercise of their powers beyond
their natural limits. In the radio interview with Hugo Young
on 13 April 1988, Lord Templeman spoke of 'bullying' by
ministers and local authorities who 'throw their weight about
too much'. The comment is revealing because it suggests that
the senior judiciary needs to have evidence of positive oppression on individuals not easily able to withstand such treatment.
This seems to fall far short of Lord Atkin's famous claim that
judges should 'stand between the subject and any attempted
encroachments on his liberty by the executive, alert to see that
any coercive action is justified in law'.[34]

Why, for example, should the courts not take a more robust
line in cases like *R. v. ILEA ex parte Ali* (p. 145)?

It was, no doubt, easiest to duck the issue, to fall back on
the proposition that the failure to provide school places for
scores of Asian children in east London, although a statutory
duty cast on the local education authority, is not one to be
enforced at the instance of a parent whose son has been denied
schooling for over twelve months. The Education Act 1944
requires local education authorities to ensure that schools in
their area are sufficient in:

> number, character and equipment to afford to all pupils
> opportunities for education offering such variety of
> instruction as may be desirable in view of their different
> ages, abilities and aptitudes, and of the different periods
> for which they may be expected to remain at school,
> including practical instruction and training appropriate
> to their respective needs.

33. See, for example, M. Loughlin, *op.cit.*, Chapter 6 on the judgments
in *Hazell v. Hammersmith and Fulham LBC* pp. 135–6.
34. *Liversidge v. Anderson* [1942] AC 206; see p. 152.

In another context it is easy to imagine the courts insisting that that duty was mandatory and should be fulfilled. Such a rule would, of course, have been deeply embarrassing to the government, whose refusal to provide adequate funds was the cause of the crisis.

Again, in *R. v. Secretary of State for Social Services ex parte Stitt* (p. 150), the domestic help was necessary to enable an unemployed man with a wife and six children to take an offered place on an employment training scheme. It was refused because of a blanket ministerial direction excluding all payments for this purpose. The Court of Appeal expressed concern that Parliament should have given the minister such wide powers, and Lord Justice Purchas thought it might be 'an unwelcome feature of a dominating executive in a basically two-party democracy'. He suggested that Parliament must have been asleep when it permitted such 'wholly exceptional and, it might be thought by some, objectionable powers' to be given to ministers without any parliamentary fetter or supervision. The Court of Appeal could have used the familiar formula for the exercise of judicial authority: that Parliament 'could not have intended' the power to be exercised in this way. But it chose not to do so and merely to wring its hands.

We have seen (p. 203) how the courts reacted to changes in social security regulations affecting asylum seekers. One suspects that the underlying reason for their attitude was the belief that the minister was using his power of, in effect, deliberate impoverishment of a group of persons to discourage applications for asylum, without any attempt to distinguish the more genuine cases from the less genuine.

Similarly antagonistic were the judicial decisions in the cases on compensation for victims of violence, on the Pergau Dam payment, and on the powers of the rail franchising director.

The first[35] is instructive of the ways in which different judges approached the case. The non-statutory scheme had been in force since 1 August 1964 and had been modified on a number of occasions, most recently in February 1990 and January

35. *R. v. Secretary of State for the Home Department ex parte Fire Brigades Union* [1995] 2 All ER 244; see pp. 122–5.

1992. In 1978, a Royal Commission had recommended that the scheme should continue on the existing basis but should be made statutory. In 1984 an inter-departmental working party recommended a statutory form for the scheme, and it was substantially this that appeared in sections 108 to 117 of the Criminal Justice Act 1988.

Section 171 provides that the Act shall come into force on such day as the Secretary of State may by order made by statutory instrument appoint, and different days may be appointed for different provisions. No order was made for sections 108 to 117 and the non-statutory scheme continued subject to minor amendments made under prerogative powers.

The new non-statutory scheme was published on 9 March 1994 and on 16 March the respondent trade unions applied for judicial review. The first question was whether the minister could decide not to bring into force the statutory scheme.

Two judges in the Queen's Bench Divisional Court refused to make an order against the Secretary of State. In the Court of Appeal, Sir Thomas Bingham MR held that the minister was under a duty to bring the statutory scheme into force, but that he had not been shown to be in breach of this duty. The other two judges held that the minister was under no such duty. The second question was whether the minister acted unlawfully in introducing the new prerogative scheme. Sir Thomas and Morritt LJ decided he had acted unlawfully; Hobhouse LJ held that the minister had acted lawfully.

So all five judges held that the minister was not in breach of a statutory duty to bring the statutory scheme into force. And this was supported by all five Law Lords.[36] This might be thought to be conclusive because if the minister was not under such a duty, surely he could continue to rely on his prerogative powers to make the new scheme? And that indeed was what Lords Keith and Mustill decided. But the majority decided otherwise and held that the minister was under a different duty: to keep under review the question whether sections 108 to 117 should be brought into force; and that it was an abuse or excess

36. It was said that several Law Lords had disqualified themselves from sitting because of their outspoken attacks on the policy of the Home Secretary.

of power for him to exercise the prerogative power in a manner inconsistent with that duty.

As Professor Ganz has written, 'The majority in the House of Lords had to jump through some complex legal hoops to reach the desired result.'[37]

In June 1994, Lord Ackner had successfully moved an amendment to the Criminal Justice and Public Order Bill ordering the minister to implement the statutory scheme within six months, but this was defeated in the Commons. In the event, as we have seen, the government subsequently legislated to achieve its purposes, but made important concessions modifying the tariff scheme to include payment for the cost of care and loss of earnings. The whole exemplifies the way in which the courts and Parliament act and react on each other within the terms of the political constitution, as they have done for at least 400 years. The rules of the game entitle government, backed by a parliamentary majority, to win but not necessarily hands down.

The political debate over the Pergau Dam affair was conducted before the Foreign Affairs and the Public Accounts Committees of the House of Commons as well as on the floor of the House. It was stimulated by the unusual overruling by a minister of the advice of the responsible senior civil servant (as accounting officer for the Overseas Development Administration) who considered the scheme to be 'unequivocally bad' in economic terms.[38] In April 1989, Prime Minister Thatcher had given a firm commitment to the Malaysian government that the project would receive finance from the Aid and Trade Provision (ATP) administered by the ODA and the Department of Trade and Industry. The Secretary of State for Foreign and Commonwealth Affairs was the responsible minister.

In 1988–89 there was a 'brief entanglement' (as the Foreign Secretary in 1994 described it) of Mrs Thatcher's promise with contracts for the export from the UK of defence equipment to Malaysia. The belief was that Mrs Thatcher struck a deal, using ATP money as a sweetener. The Foreign Secretary justified

37. 59 *Modern Law Review* (1996) 95.
38. See F. White, I. Harden, K. Donnelly, 'Audit, accounting officers and accountability', in [1994] *Public Law* 526.

his overruling of ODA on the ground of this commitment as well as the benefit to the UK economy generally of increased trade between the two countries.

In the Pergau Dam litigation[39] the arms deal did not feature. It seems also that the question of the possible illegality of ATP aid was not considered by the various government agencies involved, and that legal advice within or outside the department was not sought. But the adverse view of the ODA was of crucial importance because, without it, there would have been much greater difficulty in persuading the court that the purpose of the Overseas Development and Co-operation Act 1980 was to promote 'sound' economic development. That word did not appear in the Act. It would have been easy for the court to have concluded that all the minister had to show was that the aid was to promote economic development (building a dam) and that the economic merits of this development at this time and in this place were for the minister to decide. But the court took the opposite view and struck down the minister's policy decision. This could be said to be consistent with the 'purposive' approach stemming from the *Padfield* (p. 105) approach, which encourages courts to consider for themselves what is the purpose of particular legislation even though their conclusion may surprise ministers.

Less complicated were the facts and holdings in the passenger rail franchising case of 1995,[40] but it is noteworthy because it is doubtful whether it would have been so decided in the 1980s. Sir Thomas Bingham MR fell over himself in protesting against any possible suggestion that politics had anything to do with the decision of the Court of Appeal. Only 'lawfulness' mattered. But, of course, the Secretary of State was involved and the objectives he prescribed had to be laid before Parliament and published. So were his instructions and guidance.

The Court of Appeal recognized that the franchising director had been 'in constant touch' with the minister's instructions which must be read in a 'practical down-to-earth way' as a com-

39. *R. v. Secretary of State for Foreign Affairs ex parte World Development Movement* [1995] 1 WLR 386 (above, p. 125).

40. *R. v. Director of Passenger Rail Franchising ex parte Save Our Railways*, *The Times*, 18 December 1995; see p. 125.

munication by a minister to a responsible public official. Nevertheless, the document containing those instructions 'means what
it means, not what anyone — Franchising Director, Secretary of
State or member of the public — would like it to mean.'

The applicant's argument was that the specifications to franchisees were not 'based on' British Rail's existing services
and not in conformity with the objectives. Sir Thomas concluded that changes had to be 'marginal, not significant or
substantial', only 'relatively minor'; and the minimum service
level had to correspond 'reasonably closely' with BR's pre-
franchising specification.

The franchising director had been 'cautious in including
loss-making services', because a subsidy would be payable to
the operator. But, said Sir Thomas, no one reading the minister's instruction and guidance could have appreciated that this
approach would be adopted or that the subsidy payment factor
would be given so much weight. So the Court of Appeal
accepted the applicant's argument and did so 'without regard
to the parliamentary materials' put before them, as these were
not admissible when considering the proper interpretation of
the ministerial document.

Applying this finding to the facts, the court held that many
of the reductions in the minimum services to be provided meant
that the franchising director did not correctly understand or
did not comply with the Secretary of State's instruction.

In the court below, the judge had held that judicial review
should be reserved for 'clear cases of unlawfulness', and that
in his opinion the present was not such a case. The Court of
Appeal decided that it was.

What is law and what is politics in this story? No one
supposes that either the judge at first instance (Macpherson
J) or the Court of Appeal decided as they did because they
respectively supported or opposed privatization either generally or of the railways in particular. Macpherson J 'roundly
rejected' the applicants' arguments and, as counsel for the
franchising director argued, held that the limitation on the
director's powers was only that he had to take BR's timetabling
as 'the starting point'. But the difference between this view
and that of the Court of Appeal was not primarily a matter of
documentary interpretation. It was about the deeper political

question of the nature and extent of judicial review and so of the proper relationship between public officers – including ministers – and the judiciary. The prior question is how far the courts will extend their range of review. The Court of Appeal could as easily have ruled that these matters were for the Minister and his subordinate to decide and for Parliament, not the courts, to scrutinize. As counsel for the director argued, the minister could at any time have amended his instruction to the director. But the Court of Appeal decided that the range of judicial review was broad enough to embrace a case of this kind. This was a political decision.

These three cases show the willingness of the courts to intervene and the panoply of reasons at their disposal for doing so. But they show also, and by the same token, how easily they could have decided in the opposite direction. In *Fire Brigades* they could have said that the minister had full parliamentary authority to postpone indefinitely the commencement date of the new scheme and to continue with a modified form of the old scheme. In *Pergau Dam* they could have said that the wording of the statute gave ample authority for the minister to act as he chose. In *Rail Franchising* they could have said that although the proposed changes were extensive the primary purpose was to give to franchisees a wide range of choices and, so long as the minister was content, the court should not intervene.

Means and ends

When on 14 June 1995, it was put to the Lord Chief Justice that 'the very top judges' had in recent years been more 'robust' in standing up to the executive, Lord Taylor said, 'It is not that they have been more robust. We have developed judicial review. It did not exist as such before 1977.'

The reply was significant but evasive, suggesting that the judicial attitude to the executive had not changed, only that the means of review at the disposal of the judiciary had improved. Later, in his evidence to the Select Committee, Lord Taylor emphasized that the courts 'were very careful not to go too far' in overturning ministerial decisions and he cited challenges to Maastricht by Rees-Mogg, to the Anglo-Irish Agreement, and to the use of a statute brought into existence in 1939 for the national emergency.[41] But these were surely examples of deliberate use of the courts for political propaganda. It was not surprising that the applications were dismissed.

However the question is answered, what is undeniable is that the courts have, during this decade, become more severe in their criticism and more strict in their scrutiny of the exercise of executive powers in some areas. Why has this occurred? I have discussed some of the broader aspects in Prologue.

First, government itself became more forceful and on occasion acted in ways which almost invited legal challenge. Perhaps this was attributable to the arrogance which came from long periods in office. A clear example was the failure to heed judicial indications on extradition in *M. v. Home Office* (p. 202).

The second cause of judicial animosity was that the government, pursuing its policy of challenging the powers of professional groups, decided to confront the judiciary. Managerialism was applied to the administration of the courts and we have seen how this was resented by Lords Taylor and Browne-Wilkinson (pp. 48–9), speaking no doubt for most, perhaps all, of their brethren and sisters. More serious was governmental interference with sentencing policy, resulting in a major dispute between Lord Taylor CJ and his successor Lord Bingham CJ on the one side and the Home Secretary on the other. Most important were the Lord Chancellor's proposals to reform the profession (p. 53). The general public was not prepared for the remarkable outburst of anger from many of the most senior judges when they first learnt of the reforms proposed by Lord Mackay early in 1989, nor for the continued opposition by (especially) Lords Donaldson and Ackner when the proposals were debated in Parliament. The profession did not expect to be put to the sword by a Conservative government. Many of the lawyers, those on the bench and those appearing before it, seem to have regarded this interference

41. Third Report of the Home Affairs Committee on Judicial Appointments Procedures (HC52-II of 1995–96) Q283, 290.

with their practices as a breach of the trust which they had thought bound together political leaders and lawyers in unspoken allegiance. Their reaction was the measure of their outrage. Along with this deep feeling went minor irritants for judges: a failure to keep the salary structure in decent relationship with comparable jobs; pique; damage to amour propre. These may seem trivial but their hurt is real. In short, the Mackay proposals were seen as demeaning the profession and not to be borne in dignified silence.

A third major cause of the increased robustness shown by the judges in their dealings with the executive was the political temper in the late 1980s and the early 1990s among the professional classes. The government was disliked and seen as untrustworthy. Aspects of its policies and, even more, of its style offended. I do not mean to portray the senior judiciary (even with obvious exceptions) as middle-aged benchers disturbed by *arriviste*, upstart politicians. But many of the judges did seem to regard ministers as mildly disreputable and not very intelligent.

Judges today mostly reflect moderate Conservative opinion of the middle 'consensus' years of this century. Nor is this surprising. At 1 January 1994, the average age of the 4 Heads of Divisions was 63 years; of the 10 Law Lords, 66½ years; of the 29 Lords Justices of Appeal, 63 years; of the 95 High Court judges, 57½ years.[42] The oldest began their practice at the Bar soon after 1945; only the youngest began after 1960. It is not unreasonable to suppose that a large proportion of the present judges, educated in private schools and the older universities, in practice at the Bar in the 1950s and 1960s, were influenced in their outlook by the settled political climate of those middle years of the century. Their generation was more likely than that which preceded or that which succeeded it to react against the radical and disruptive political changes of the last ten years.

Politically the judges remain conservative, with their homogeneity largely unaffected. But Conservative ministers since the mid-1980s have adopted policies and practices (particularly emanating from the Lord Chancellor's Department, the Home

42. HC 52-II of 1995–96, p. 162.

Office and the Department of Social Security) with which many judges disagree.

There is no doubt that the judges today are far more willing to let their opinions be known on a wide range of political – if not party political – matters. They are also more ready to listen to public opinion, even when it is critical of their performance. That criticism is also more common and directly communicable. The press and television give more publicity to criminal and civil proceedings, and to the judiciary, than at any earlier time.

Replying to a question from Mr David Ashby MP, Lord Taylor (then Lord Chief Justice) said:

> I think some of those old judges that you and I appeared before did not consider they were accountable to anybody and they did not care what anybody said about them. Nowadays, first of all, the press is much more ready to weigh in than it used to be. Perhaps some would say too ready to weigh in without knowing all the facts. But there is certainly a greater consciousness of public interest and concern about how the courts perform. It may be partly as a result of the miscarriages cases too that the courts are much more conscious of being in the public eye and I think people generally – the boundaries between classes I would not say have necessarily gone, but certainly the boundaries have become more smudged and there is a much more homogeneous community now than there was when we began at the Bar. This has rubbed off generally and judges usually realise that the public expects them to be courteous, reasonable, approachable and patient.[43]

This responsiveness by judges contrasts sharply with the former tradition. They could so easily have withdrawn behind barriers of self-regarding rectitude, and it is wholly to their credit that they have not done so.

The senior judiciary have themselves advanced one general justification for their increased robustness. Lord Mustill has said that the courts are required on occasion to step into the

43. Evidence to Home Affairs Select Committee on 14 June 1995 (HC 52-II of 1995–96 Q260).

territory which belongs to the executive not only to verify that the powers exercised by the executive accord with what the substantive law created by Parliament must have intended. Concurrently with this, Parliament has its own special means of ensuring that the executive performs in a way which Parliament finds appropriate. He continued:

> In recent years, however, the employment in practice of these specifically Parliamentary remedies has on occasion been perceived as falling short, and sometimes well short, of what was needed to bring the performance of the executive into line with the law and with the minimum standards of fairness implicit in every Parliamentary delegation of a decision-making function. To avoid a vacuum in which the citizen would be left without protection against a misuse of executive powers the courts have had no option but to occupy the dead ground in a manner, and in areas of public life, which could not have been foreseen 30 years ago. For myself, I am quite satisfied that this unprecedented role has been greatly to the public benefit.[44]

This is an argument conducted largely in metaphors. More common than Lord Mustill's 'vacuum' and 'dead ground' is the description of the parliamentary shortcomings as the 'democratic deficit', and as such it has been applauded by Labour and Liberal Democrat spokesmen. Lord Mustill advances it as justifying judicial intervention. The argument is difficult to accept.

Lord Mustill's words are taken from the *Fire Brigades* case. As we have seen (p. 123), compensation for victims of violence had been considered and reconsidered by Parliament on several occasions since 1964. In November 1992, the then Secretary of State (Kenneth Clarke) gave notice of the government's intention to introduce a new scheme, details of which were given by his successor (Michael Howard) in a White Paper in December 1993. As Lord Mustill said, 'The government's radical change of course has engendered much controversy, both

44. *R. v. Secretary of State for the Home Department ex parte Fire Brigades Union* [1995] 2 All ER 244.

within Parliament and outside.' There were heated debates in the House of Lords.[45]

Whatever the decision in the *Fire Brigades* case may have achieved, it could hardly be said to have filled a vacuum or occupied dead ground vacated by Parliament. While the Law Lords by a majority concluded that the minister could not on this occasion change policy without introducing new legislation (a useful reminder), Parliament fully debated the merits of the change. So also in the Pergau Dam affair, Parliamentarians on the floor of the House and upstairs examined the events in great detail. Parliamentary scrutiny in both instances was thorough and meticulous. All the opposition lacked was a majority in favour of their view of what was 'appropriate'.

More power to the judges?

Most recently the 'democratic deficit' argument has broadened into claims by some judges for a bigger and better place in the political scheme of things. Not content with building on the base provided by Lord Reid and the reformed rules of judicial review, they seek an enlarged constitutional role. This movement is noteworthy because in its less extreme form it is advanced by Lord Woolf, now Master of the Rolls and in the strongest position to give it political reality. Writing in 1995 and noting 'dramatic' changes in the principles of public law he said, 'It is one of the strengths of the common law that it enables the courts to vary the extent of their intervention to reflect current needs, and by this means it helps to maintain the delicate balance of a democratic society.'[46]

This pleasing conceit is popular among writers on the constitution. Historically, it derives from ships of state on even keels. In truth, there is little that is delicate about democracy and even less that can be rectified by judicial touches on the tiller. Over the last few years judges have been moved to deny validity to acts and decisions of ministers and other public

45. 555 HL Deb. col. 1828–1851 (16 June 1994); 558 HL Deb. col. 496–518 (25 October 1994).
46. 'Droit Public – English Style', in [1995] *Public Law* 57.

authorities, not so much on the ground of illegality but from a sense of injustice and unfairness. There is a willingness, especially amongst some of the more recently appointed judges of the High Court, to find against ministers whose decisions are oppressive on those least able to help themselves. This has particularly been seen in judicial reaction to the treatment of destitute asylum seekers. Arguments advanced by local authorities that such people were not 'in need of care and attention' within the meaning of the National Assistance Act 1948, but only in need of money, were not favourably received by the courts.[47]

Judicial quashing of ministerial decisions may have immediate, if shortlived, political consequences by lowering the government in public esteem. It may even force the government temporarily to alter its course. In these ways judicial intervention resembles political comment in the press or on television. It is part of the political context in which government works.

But fine tuning or delicate balancing it is not. The constitution and 'democratic society' remain unchanged. The attitude of governments in the 1990s to judicial decisions that criticised or nullified government decisions confirms this. Where parliamentary or other action to restore the status quo was possible, it was taken. If not, alternative action could generally achieve the same or a similar result.

In like vein, Lord Woolf claimed that the changes in judicial review were made in 1978 'at a time when the public felt a greater need for protection from the abuse of administrative power'. One wonders what is the evidence for this. There had certainly been a growth in judicial activism under Lord Reid in the 1960s and the Law Commission, which from 1966 had been considering questions on the reform of administrative law, produced a final report in 1976. But it is not clear what were the special abuses of administrative power of the 1960s and 1970s.

Lord Woolf then made the case for judicial powers which could override Acts of Parliament. He takes an extreme

47. *R. v. Hammersmith and Fulham LBC ex parte A, Independent*, 26 February 1997; and see *ex parte Kihara* (p. 203).

example: legislation which removed or substantially impaired 'the entire reviewing role of the High Court on judicial review'. It is not clear why Lord Woolf chose to pose this question. One is tempted to ask what he knows that we do not, or what conspiracy is afoot that he wishes to impede by premature disclosure. Legislation wholly to prevent the courts from questioning the legality of government action would grossly disrupt the present relationships between Parliament, government and the judiciary and result in a constitutional crisis of major proportions. No one would be surprised if, in these circumstances, the judges declared such legislation invalid. And many would support them. The propriety of the judges' action would be the least of our worries.

In the same issue of *Public Law* which included Lord Woolf's article there appeared another, by a judge of the High Court, Sir John Laws. He said,

> My thesis is that the citizen's democratic rights go hand in hand with other fundamental rights: the latter, certainly, may in reality be more imaginably at risk, in any given set of political circumstances, than the former. The point is that both are or should be off limits for our elected representatives.[48]

There would be a 'higher-order law' which could not be abrogated by government legislation. The judges would be empowered to strike down offending legislation including Article 9 of the Bill of Rights 1989. Neither the democratic nor the fundamental rights are spelt out; nor is the higher-order law, but emphasis is laid on 'ethical principles about how the state should be run' and on 'the virtuous conduct of the state's affairs'. It is a form of judicial evangelicalism which may not prosper.

Reference to basic or fundamental rights leads to another set of propositions. These are contained in the European Convention on Human Rights, to which treaty the United Kingdom is a signatory but which has not yet been incorporated into UK domestic law. Many members of the senior judiciary, past and present, urge this incorporation. In 1995 Lord Lester intro-

---

48. 'Law and Democracy', in [1995] *Public Law* 72.

duced a Human Rights Bill in the House of Lords. Lords Ackner, Browne-Wilkinson, Scarman, Lloyd, Simon, Slynn, Taylor and Woolf spoke or voted in its favour; so also was Lord Bingham CJ. Lord Lester claims the support of 'most other Law Lords, both serving and retired'. Lord Donaldson (former Master of the Rolls) opposed. The bill died for want of parliamentary time in the Commons, but Lord Lester thought that most MPs would favour incorporation.[49]

This then is another of the political movements to which judges feel free to subscribe even though it is a cause which divides the parties, Labour and the Liberal Democrats being in favour of incorporation and the Conservative party being opposed. Other commentators are divided in their opinions.

Opposition is based primarily on the view that because of the generality of the provisions of the convention, judges would inevitably be drawn into wide-ranging political judgments. For example, the convention provides that everyone has the right to freedom of expression but that this freedom may be subjected 'to such formalities, conditions, restrictions or penalties as are prescribed by law and are necessary in a democratic society'. Whether or not an Act of Parliament prescribing such limitations is valid will depend on whether judges consider they are 'necessary in a democratic society'. The ultimate question is whether so political a matter should be determined by judges or by elected representatives.

Conclusion

In suggesting that the senior judiciary look to a view of the public interest to inform their attitude to the controversial matters of law and order, of political and economic conflict, of sexual and social *mores*, of personal liberty and property rights, of protest, of governmental confidentiality, of race relations, of immigration and the rest, I mean to absolve them of a conscious and deliberate intention to pursue their own interests or the interests of their class. I believe that in these matters and within the considerable area of decision-making open to

49. See [1995] *Public Law* 198.

them they look to what they regard as the interest of the whole society. However, we are left to consider why it is that their view of that public interest is what it is.

It is common to speak of the judiciary as part of the system of checks and balances which contains and constrains the power of the government; or as one of the three principal institutions of the State, each of which acts to limit the powers of the other two. The image has a pleasing and mechanistic appearance, suggesting some objective hidden hand which holds the constitution in perpetual equilibrium. The extent to which the image reflects reality is less obvious.

If we limit our examination to the working of the three institutions – Parliament, the government, and the judiciary – in their relationships with each other, then it is clear that each of these groups influences the way in which the others act. And it is clear, in particular, that the judiciary may oppose the government to the extent of declaring its actions invalid or requiring it to pay compensation or even subjecting one of its members or servants to penalties.

In our society, as in others, political power, the power of government, is exercised by a relatively small number of people, consisting of ministers, senior civil servants, a few heads of industry, banking and commerce and some influential advisers close to government departments drawn from the party machine and universities. Until recently the most senior judges – including the Law Lords, the Lord Chief Justice and the Master of the Rolls – have been part of this oligarchy. For reasons I have discussed, they have today lost that high status. Nevertheless there is no doubt about the importance of judges in our society. Their professional eminence, their influence on the development of the law, the extent of their powers, their habits of mind, the extrajudicial uses to which they are put, the circles they move in and the way they are regarded by members of the oligarchy, confirm that they maintain their position as part of established authority. And I have suggested that part of the reason for their present robustness is to be found in their attempt to regain what status they have lost. As members of established authority they show themselves alert to protect the social order from threats to its stability or to the existing distribution of political and economic power.

I have said that judges look to what they regard as the interests of the whole society. That, in itself, makes political assumptions of some magnitude. It has long been argued that the concept of the whole society suggests a homogeneity of interest among the different classes within the society which is false. And that this concept is used to persuade the governed that not the government but 'the State' is the highest organization and transcends conflicts in society. It is a short step to say that it is the State which makes the laws, thus enabling those in political power to promote their own interests in the name of the whole abstracted society. Inevitably the judiciary reflects the interests of its own class. Lord Wedderburn has written that 'the eras of judicial "creativity", of new doctrines hostile to trade union interests, have been largely, though not entirely, coterminous with the periods of British social history in which the trade unions have been perceived by middle-class opinion as a threat to the established social order'.[50]

A central thesis of this book is that judges in the United Kingdom cannot be politically neutral because they are placed in positions where they are required to make political choices which are sometimes presented to them, and often presented by them, as determinations of where the public interest lies; that their interpretation of what is in the public interest and therefore politically desirable is determined by the kind of people they are and the position they hold in our society; that this position is a part of established authority and so is necessarily conservative, not liberal. From all this flows that view of the public interest which is shown in judicial attitudes such as tenderness towards private property and dislike of trade unions, strong adherence to the maintenance of order, distaste for minority opinions, demonstrations and protests, support of governmental secrecy, concern for the preservation of the moral and social behaviour to which it is accustomed, and the rest.

Professor Mancini of the University of Bologna has singled out 'the susceptibility of English judges to be analysed as a politically cohesive group' – what I have called their homogeneity – as the factor distinguishing them from judges in Italy,

50. See *Industrial Law Journal* (June 1980) at p. 78.

France and Spain. 'What I mean', he says, 'is (a) that English judges seldom make decisions of a nature to challenge a universally received notion of public interest; and (b) that when they happen to do it, their decisions are a result of strictly individual options.' He draws a very sharp contrast: 'the trend towards a more politicized and politically polarized judiciary ... in Italy, France and Spain ... has ... acquired, or is in the process of acquiring, traits so neat and forcible as to rise to the dignity of a major national issue.'[51]

One reason for this continental phenomenon is historical and political: the greater divergence between the right and the left in Italy and France as compared with Britain. But it is made possible by the fact that in those countries judges are appointed in their early or mid-twenties after open competitive examinations. It is therefore possible for men and women with widely different, and (at the time of their examination) unknown political opinions to reach the bench and to remain there, effectively, until retirement. If they display political attitudes of which their superiors disapprove, their promotion may not be speedy. And these superiors continue to be 'politically cohesive'. But to remove the dissidents from office is much more difficult. This split between right and left among the judiciary in those countries is highly significant and wholly without parallel in Britain.

Any analysis which places the judiciary in the United Kingdom in a wholly subservient position to the government misreads history and mistakes the source and nature of the common law. Those who criticize existing institutions in the United Kingdom need always to remember that, in comparison with most other countries, this country enables its citizens to live in comparative freedom. To what extent is this a consequence of our judicial system and of our judges?

Because the powers of governments in Britain are limited by law (even though governments may make new laws and change existing laws), there is always the possibility that the exercise of power by governments may be challenged; and because judges, however much they share the values and aims

51. G. F. Mancini, 'Politics and the Judges – the European Perspective', in 43 *Modern Law Review* (1980) 1.

of governments, are not governmental servants, the challenge may be successful.

There is a sense, however far it falls short of what is claimed for it, in which those who exercise legalized force in our society must have regard to the existence of a judiciary which may be prepared to condemn them in some circumstances and will be supported in so doing. Nevertheless, in the event of an attempt by a government to exercise arbitrary and extensive powers, curtailing individual liberty, it cannot be forecast how the judges would react. The political circumstances would be crucial and the judiciary would be divided, as Lords Parker and Gardiner were divided over official torture in Northern Ireland (see p. 33–6). A left-wing attempt would meet with judicial opposition more immediately than a right-wing attempt. And there is little evidence to suggest that the judiciary would be quick to spring to the defence of individual liberty wherever the threat came from.

Judges are the product of a class and have the characteristics of that class. Typically coming from middle-class professional families, independent schools, Oxford or Cambridge, they spend twenty to twenty-five years in successful practice at the Bar, mostly in London, earning very considerable incomes by the time they reach their forties. This is not the stuff of which reformers are made, still less radicals. There are those who believe that if more grammar or comprehensive schoolboys or schoolgirls, graduating at redbrick or new glass universities, became barristers and then judges, the judiciary would be that much less conservative. This is extremely doubtful, for two reasons. The years in practice and the middle-aged affluence would remove any aberration in political outlook, if this were necessary. Also, if those changes did not take place, there would be no possibility of their being appointed by the Lord Chancellor, on the advice of the senior judiciary, to the bench. Ability by itself is not enough. Unorthodoxy in political opinion is a certain disqualification for appointment.

Her Majesty's judges are unlikely to be under great illusions about the functioning of political power in the United Kingdom today. And I think we come close to their definition of the public interest and of the interests of the State if we identify their views with those who insist that in any society, but especially societies in the second half of the twentieth century, stability above all is necessary for the health of the people and is the supreme law.

It follows that governments are normally to be supported, but not in every case. Governments represent stability and have a very considerable interest in preserving it. The maintenance of authoritarian structures in all public institutions is wholly in the interest of governments. This is true of all governments of all political complexions, democratic and dictatorial. Whenever governments or their agencies are acting to preserve that stability – call it the Queen's peace, or law and order, or the rule of law, or whatever – the judges will lend their support and will not be over-concerned if to do so requires the invasion of individual liberty. But individual property rights have a strong claim on judicial protection as is shown in the *Laker, Padfield* and *Anisminic* cases. And judges are occasionally moved to protest against, and even to strike down, ministerial action which seems to them to be unjust. Ministers are not amused by this and, as we have seen, seek to circumvent the decisions. It is interesting to speculate what would happen if the judges seriously tried to restrain governments from acting against the public interest. Lord Devlin, writing about the *Padfield* decision, wondered 'whether the courts have moved too far from their base' which, he said, was 'the correction of abuse'. He continued, and here he was also speaking of the *Tameside* decision:

> One may also share to some extent the apprehensions of the Civil Service. All legal history shows that, once the judges get a foothold in the domain of fact, they move to expand. Questions of fact become in a mysterious way questions of law. The fence between error and misconception crumbles with the passage of time. The civil servant may fear the day when he dare not reach a conclusion without asking himself whether a judge will think all the deciding factors as relevant as he does. I do not think that the judiciary should be thrust out of the domain of fact.

Lord Devlin wanted above all to see judicial review 'preserved as a weapon against arbitrary government and I am conscious that its efficacy depends upon the good will of Whitehall'. Because of the power of government to exclude judicial review by statutory provision 'judicial interference with the executive cannot for long very greatly exceed what Whitehall will accept'.[52] Or, as the Prime Minister said in 1977 in the House of Commons: 'We should beware of trying to embroil the judiciary in our affairs, with the corresponding caveat that the judiciary should be very careful about embroiling itself in the legislature.'[53] And in *Duport Steels Ltd v. Sirs* Lord Scarman said: 'If people and Parliament come to think that the judicial power is to be confined by nothing other than the judge's sense of what is right ... confidence in the judicial system will be replaced by fear of it becoming uncertain and arbitrary in its application. Society will then be ready for Parliament to cut the power of the judges.'

Sometimes, no doubt, the 'judge's sense of what is right' cannot be applied even by so devoted and self-confident a judge as Lord Denning, as he reluctantly concluded in *Smith v. Inner London Education Authority* (1978) when some parents sought to prevent the authority from closing St Marylebone Grammar School as part of the change to comprehensive schooling. 'Search as I may,' said Lord Denning, 'and it is not for want of trying, I cannot find any abuse or misuse of power by the education authority ... It is sad to have to say so, after so much effort has been expended by so many in so good a cause.'[54]

To some, the judicial view of the public interest appears merely as reactionary conservatism. It is not the politics of the extreme right. Its insensitivity is clearly rooted more in unconscious assumptions than in a wish to oppress. But it is demonstrable that on every major social issue which has come before the courts during the last thirty years – concerning industrial relations, political protest, race relations, governmental secrecy, police powers, moral behaviour – the judges have supported the conventional, established and settled inter-

52. *The Times*, 27 October 1976.

53. 941 HC Deb. col. 909 (15 December 1977) (Mr Callaghan).

54. [1978] 1 All ER 411; see also *North Yorkshire County Council v. Secretary of State for Education and Science*, *The Times*, 20 October 1978.

ests. And they have reacted strongly against challenges to those interests. This conservatism does not necessarily follow the day-to-day political policies currently, associated with the party of that name. But it is a political philosophy none the less.

The two outstanding groups of cases in the second half of the 1980s were those concerned with miscarriages of justice – the Guildford Four, the Maguire Seven, and the Birmingham Six – and those concerned with freedom of speech. Of the first, the best that can be said of the judicial performance is that the courts were shown to be worse than useless as protectors of innocent persons charged with highly unpopular offences. The second – comprising *Spycatcher*, the other curtailments of press freedom, and the protection of government information – demonstrates, as I have said, the deep reluctance of the courts to stand on principle when opposed by special interests.

During the same period the courts failed to develop a coherent doctrine of judicial review. In *Oladehinde* (pp. 193–4), where the Court of Appeal overruled Lord Justice Woolf by the use of semantic trickery, Lord Donaldson MR said, 'It would be a mistake to approach the judicial review jurisdiction as if it consisted of a series of entirely separate boxes into which judges dipped as occasion demanded. It is rather a rich tapestry of many strands which cross, re-cross and blend to produce justice.'

This is rhetorical nonsense. Each of the three possible bases of judicial review – illegality, irrationality, procedural impropriety – is sufficiently imprecise to enable judges to jump with the cat in any direction they choose. Illegality contains all the possible variations of statutory interpretation based on what the courts decide Parliament may or may not have intended. Unreasonableness sometimes seems to be limited to a rule or decision which, in Lord Diplock's words, is 'outrageous in its defiance of logic or accepted moral standards',[55] but may also include one which is merely 'so unreasonable that no reasonable authority could ever have come' to it,[56] or even one which

---

55. *In re the Council of Civil Service Unions* [1984] 3 All ER 935.
56. Lord Greene MR, in *Associated Provincial Picture Houses Ltd v. Wednesbury Corporation* [1948] 1 KB 223.

is partial and unequal, or manifestly unjust.[57] Procedural impropriety includes or excludes a great variety of action or inaction. If this is tapestry it is very loosely woven.

Far more than on the judiciary, our freedoms depend on the willingness of the press, politicians and others to publicize the breach of these freedoms, and on the continuing vulnerability of ministers, civil servants, the police, other public officials and powerful private interests to accusations that these freedoms are being infringed. In other words, we depend far more on the political climate and on the vigilance of those members of society who for a variety of reasons, some political and some humanitarian, make it their business to seek to hold public authorities within their proper limits. That those limits are also prescribed by law and that judges may be asked to maintain them is not without significance. But the judges are not – as in a different dispensation and under a different social order they might be – the strong, natural defenders of liberty.

Judges are concerned to preserve and to protect the existing order. This does not mean that no judges are capable of moving with the times, of adjusting to changed circumstances. But their function in our society is to do so belatedly. Law and order, the established distribution of power both public and private, the conventional and agreed view amongst those who exercise political and economic power, the fears and prejudices of the middle and upper classes, these are the forces which the judges are expected to uphold and do uphold.

In the societies of our world today judges do not stand out as protectors of liberty, of the rights of man, of the unprivileged, nor have they insisted that holders of great economic power, private or public, should use it with moderation. Their view of the public interest, when it has gone beyond the interest of governments, has not been wide enough to embrace the interests of political, ethnic, social or other minorities. Only occasionally has the power of the supreme judiciary been exercised in the positive assertion of fundamental values. In both democratic and totalitarian societies, the judiciary has naturally served the prevailing political and economic forces. Politically, judges are parasitic.

57. Lord Russell CJ, in *Kruse v. Johnson* [1898] 2 QB 91.

That this is so is not a matter for recrimination. It is idle to criticize institutions for performing the task they were created to perform and have performed for centuries. The principal function of the judiciary is to support the institutions of government as established by law. To expect a judge to advocate radical change is absurd. The confusion arises when it is pretended that judges are somehow neutral in the conflicts between those who challenge existing institutions and those who control those institutions. And cynicism replaces confusion whenever it becomes apparent that the latter are using the judges as open allies in those conflicts.

Thus it is usual for judges in political cases to be able to rely on the rules of law for the legitimacy of their decisions. As we have seen, there are innumerable ways – through the development of the common law, the interpretation of statutes, the refusal to use discretionary powers, the claims to residual jurisdiction and the rest – in which the judges can fulfil their political function and do so in the name of the law.

Books referred to in the text

B. Abel-Smith, R. B. Stevens, *Lawyers and the Courts* (1967).

Crispin Aubrey, *Who's Watching You?* (1981)

L. Blom-Cooper, G. Drewry, *Final Appeal* (1972)

L. Bridges, G. Meszaros, M. Sunkin, *Judicial Review in Perspective* (1995)

A. Briggs, J. Saville (eds), *Essays in Labour History* (1960)

T. J. Cartwright, *Royal Commissions and Departmental Committees in Britain* (1975)

S. A. de Smith, *Judicial Review of Administrative Action* (3rd edn, 1973)

Patrick Devlin, *The Judge* (1979)

K. D. Ewing and C. A. Gearty, *Freedom under Thatcher* (1990)

S. R. Gardiner, *History of England 1603–1642* (1883)

B. Hadfield (ed.), *Judicial Review: A Thematic Approach* (1995)

R. F. V. Heuston, *The Lives of the Lord Chancellors 1885–1940* (1964)

Derek Humphry, *The Cricket Conspiracy* (1975)

J. M. Jacob, *The Republican Crown* (1996)

Justice, *Miscarriages of Justice* (1989)

Robert Kee, *Trial and Error* (1989)

Nigel Lawson, *The View from No. 11* (1992)

M. Loughlin, *Legality and Locality* (1996)

C. McCrudden, G. Chambers (eds), *Individual Rights and the Law in Britain* (1994)

Chris Mullin, *Error of Judgment* (1990)

R. Rawlings (ed.), *Law, Society and Economy* (1997)

G. Rhodes, *Committees of Inquiry* (1975)

G. Robertson, *Whose Conspiracy?* (1974)

David Rose, *In the Name of the Law*, (1996).

R. J. Sharpe, *The Law of Habeas Corpus* (1976)

R. B. Stevens, *The Independence of the Judiciary* (1993)

and *Law and Politics: The House of Lords as a Judicial Body 1800–1976* (1979)

Lorraine Thompson, *An Act of Compromise* (1988)

Lord Wedderburn, *The Worker and the Law* (3rd edn, 1986)

S. & B. Webb, *The History of Trade Unionism* (1920)

G. M. Young, *Stanley Baldwin* (1952)

General Index

Aberfan disaster, 30
Ackner, Lord, 41, 53–5, 172, 228, 279, 323, 327, 334
Act of Settlement (1701), 10
Acts of Parliament *see* statute law
ACTSS, 86
Adams, Gerry, 198, 316
Administration of Justice Bill, 43
Advisory, Conciliation and Arbitration Service (ACAS), 82–4
Aid and Trade Provision (ATP), 323–4
air transport *see* civil air transport cases
Aitken, J., 257
Alexander of Weedon, Lord, 241
Amalgamated Society of Railway Servants, 67
Amalgamated Union of Engineering Workers, 76
Amnesty International, 248
APEX, 86–7
Appeal Court *see* Court of Appeal
Argyle, Judge, 12–13
arms-for-Iraq affair *see* Scott Report
Arrowsmith, Pat, 158
Ashby, David, MP, 329
Asquith, Lord, 67
Associated British Ports, 94, 101
Associated Newspapers, 101, 287
Asylum and Immigration Appeals Act (1993), 182, 203
Asylum and Immigration Bill (1996), 203
Asylum and Refugees Act (1993), 195
asylum *see* political asylum cases
Atkin, Lord, 152, 320
Atkinson, Lord, quoted, viii, 86
Attlee, Clement, 1, 9, 16
Attorney-General, 9, 15, 27
 Crossman diaries, 220–1

Scott enquiry, xvii, 239–44
Spycatcher cases, 223–32, 298
 thalidomide case, 216
Aubrey, Crispin, 257

Babies on Benefit, 248
Baldwin, Stanley, 66
ballots *see* under trade unions
banks, leakage of bank rate, 30
Bar Council, 54
barristers
 judges appointed from, xv–xvi, 7, 9, 14–16, 17, 21, 24
 and legal reforms, 53–7
 Recorders appointed from, 7, 9
 Treasury Counsel, 9
BBC, xv, 42, 43, 79, 167, 245–9
Benn, Tony, MP, 198
Benson, Lord, 55
Bill of Rights (1689), 173, 249, 300, 333
Bingham, Lord, xv, 10, 41, 52, 126, 240, 266, 322, 324–5, 327, 334
Birkenhead, Lord Chancellor, 39
Birmingham Six, 209–10, 212, 307, 341
Blackstone, 222
Blom-Cooper, Louis, QC, 38n, 39, 118
BOAC, 70
Bookbinder, David, 245
Bowaters Ltd, 71
Boyd-Carpenter, J. A., 34
Bracewell, Circuit Judge, 46
Braithwaite, Mark, 211
Brandon, Lord, 128–33, 180, 228
breach
 of contract, 71–2, 84–5, 88, 97, 100
 of the peace, 68–70, 94
Bridge, Lord, 41, 54, 61, 101–2, 117, 137, 151, 190–1, 228–9, 248 256, 299

Bridges, Lee, 114–16, 194, 318
Bridgewater, Carl, 118, 213
Bridlington principles, 86
Brightman, Lord, 41, 140–2, 318
British Medical Association, xvi
British Nationality Acts, 175, 182, 303
British Rail, 96, 125–6, 313, 325–6
British Railways Board, 97
British Steel Corporation, 81–2, 95, 98
British Telecommunications Act (1981), 88
Broadcasting Act (1981), 248
Brock, Jenny, 18
Bromley London Borough Council, 126–33
Brown, Lord Justice Simon, 29, 240, 266, 272
Brown, Lord Justice Stephen, 210
Browne-Wilkinson, Lord, 41, 44, 83, 101, 102, 123–4, 146, 225, 287, 327, 334
Bulger, James, 174
Butler-Sloss, Lord Justice, 27, 46

Cabinet Office, Management and Personnel Office, 47
Cameron, Lord, 33
Campaign for Nuclear Disarmament, 161, 266–7
Campbell, Duncan, 246
Campbell, Russell, 137
capital punishment, 13
Cardozo, Chief Justice, (USA), 55
Carson, Lord, 39
Cartwright, Dr T. J., 25
Cassel, Circuit Judge, 13
censorship, 229, 256–9
Central Electricity Generating Board, 271
Chambers, G., 163, 170, 172, 212
Chancery Division, 8, 49
  in courts structure, 23
child abuse, 46
Child Poverty Action Group, 114
children, care of, 147
Children Act, 46
Children Bill, 46
Chronically Sick and Disabled Persons Act (1970), 149

Church of Scientology, 12
Churchill, Sir Winston, 10, 277
Circuit judges, 7–10, 11, 21, 24
  Council of, 45
  in courts structure, 22–4
  participation in public debate, 43, 45
civil
  justice system, 27
  law, xiv, 5, 6, 171, 245, 290–1
  liberties, 29, 35, 297
Civil Aviation Act (1971), 110
Civil Aviation Authority (CAA), 110–11
civil service, xv, 29, 37, 47, 50, 113, 156, 194, 258, 339
Civil Service Appeal Board, 117
Clarendon Schools, 18, 20
Clark, Alan, 37
Clarke, Sir Edward, 15–16
Cleveland inquiry, 46
Coke, Chief Justice, 45, 296
collective bargaining, 82
Commission for Racial Equality (CRE), 178–81
Commissioner for the Rights of Trade Union Members, 94
committees (departmental, etc.), 28
common law, 1–2, 5, 68–9, 100
  natural justice, 105
  nuisance, 68–70
  property rights, 104
Commons
  House of, 13, 16, 17, 20–1, 67
    Foreign Affairs Committee, 257, 323
    freedom of expression, 249–50
    Home Affairs Committee, 2–3, 22
    Maastricht Treaty, 122
    Privileges Committee, 36
    Standards in Public Life Committee, 36
    Zircon affair, 246–7
Communist Party of Great Britain, 161
Community Care (Residential Accommodation) Act (1992), 149
Community Relations Commission, 178

Companies Acts, 67
Compton, Sir Edmund, 33
confidentiality, 220–32
Conservative governments, 27, 72,
 77, 84–90, 110, 134, 310
Conservative Party, 7, 14, 67
 local authorities and councils, 110,
 134
conspiracy, 267–9
 to corrupt public morals, 260–6
 to pervert course of justice, 160
 trade unions and, 63–7, 70
Conspiracy and Protection of Property
 Act (1875), 63, 66, 68, 95
consultative cases, 121
contempt of court, 73–4, 76, 160,
 225, 231
 Harman case, 235
 meaning of, 215–16
 ministerial, 202
 prejudicial statements, 215–19
 protection of sources, 251–6
 in publications and the press,
 205–19
 used against trade unions, 32,
 73–4, 76, 93, 96
Contempt of Court Act (1981), 215,
 217–19, 253–5
Convention on the Status of Refugees
 (1951), 195, 203
Cook, Robin, MP, 29
copyright, 222
County Court
 in courts structure, 23
 judges, 7, 19–20
Court of Aldermen of the City of
 London, 119
Court of Appeal, 7, 295
 appointment to, 8, 17
 confidentiality case, 222
 contempt of court, 214–16
 in courts structure, 23
 disclosure of documents, 232–9,
 243
 discretionary powers cases,
 107–11, 113, 117, 119, 120,
 126–7, 131–7, 140, 143–4,
 145, 147, 149, 150, 324–6
 Harman case, 234–7
 immigration cases, 184, 186–9,
 315

industrial relations cases, 68, 71–3,
 79–84, 84–90, 93–4, 98–102,
 107–9, 287–8, 311–13
judges, 7, 8–9, 13, 18, 24
 and judicial creativity, 286–7
 and judicial review, 43
 and legal reform, 54–7
 Master of the Rolls as president, 17
 miscarriages of justice cases,
 204–13, 307, 309
 moral maze, 267, 271, 273–5, 302
 participation in public debate,
 42–5
 personal rights cases, 156, 157,
 163, 165, 172–4, 190–8,
 202–3, 305, 341
 protection of sources cases, 251–6
 race relations cases, 133, 176,
 180–1
 and sentencing, 46
 Spycatcher case, 226–7, 230, 298
Court of Session, 9
courts
 administration of, 47–8
 attitude to ministers, xvii
 of enquiry, 30–1
 see also
 County Courts; Court of Appeal;
 Crown Court;
 High Court; Magistrates' Courts;
 Supreme Court
 structure, 7, 22–4
Courts and Legal Services Bill
 (1989–90), 41, 54–6, 279
Cox, John, 161
Cozens-Hardy, Lord, quoted, 1
Crime (Sentences) Bill, 52, 61
criminal
 conspiracy, 261
 insider dealings, 254–5
 justice policy paper, 46
 law, 5, 6, 51–2, 115–18, 185, 212,
 291–2
Criminal Appeal Act (1968), 204,
 206
Criminal Appeal Act (1995), 212–3
Criminal Cases Review Commission,
 213, 307
Criminal Damage Act (1981), 269
Criminal Injuries Compensation Bill,
 123–5

Criminal Justice Act (1988), 123–4, 206, 321–2
Criminal Justice Act (1991), 174
Criminal Justice and Public Order Act (1994), 171, 273, 323
Cripps, Sir Stafford, 9
Croom-Johnson, Mr Justice, 30
Cross, Lord, 269
Crossman, R. H. S., 220–1, 231, 233
Crown Agents, 30
Crown Court
  in courts structure, 23
  judges, 7, 156
Crown Prosecution Service, 168, 208
Cullen, Lord, 27
Cunningham, George, MP, 131–2
Customs and Excise, 233
Customs and Excise Management Act (1979), 37

Daily Express, 80–1, 222
Daily Mail, 217–18
Daily Mirror, 222
Daily Telegraph, 43
Dalyell, Tom, MP, 257
Davies, Lord Justice Edmund, 30
Davies-Rees Mr, MP, 138
death (life and) *see* moral maze
death penalty, 45–6
defamation, 245
Defamation Act (1996), 250, 300
Defence of the Realm Act (1914), 153
Defence Regulations, 152
demonstrations and protests, 266–73, 284, 302–3
Denning
  Lord, xiv, 1, 12, 17, 43
    confidentiality case, 222
    CRE cases, 179
    disclosure of documents case, 239
    discretionary powers cases, 107–9, 111
    education authority case, 340
    Harman case, 234–6
    individual freedom cases, 154–5, 157, 196
    industrial relations cases, 78, 79–84, 86, 289, 311–12, 314
    judicial creativity, 278–9, 283–4

judicial reviews and prisoners, 171
miscarriages of justice cases, 210, 307, 309
moral maze, 269–71
police powers, 159
protection of sources, 252
race relations, 178
deportation, 190–204
detention without trial *see* internment
Devlin, Lord, xvii, 3, 26, 70, 204, 206, 208, 281, 283, 286–7, 293–5 301, 339
Dilhorne, Lord, 110, 176
Dimbleby lecture, 43, 278
Dimbleby Printers Ltd, 89
Diplock
  Lord, 29, 34–5, 341
    contempt of court case, 217–18
    discretionary powers cases, 108, 110, 127–33
    Dockers' Club case, 176
    on GCHQ case, 112, 115
    Harman case, 235–6
    industrial relations cases, 80, 87, 91, 311–12
    judicial creativity, 281–3
    moral maze cases, 263
Director of Public Prosecutions, 208–9, 211
disclosure *see* documents
discretionary powers
  control of, 103–51
  early cases, 103–4
  education, 145–8
  fares fair litigation, 126–33
  giving of reasons, 116–19
  growth of interventionism, 104–12
  homelessness, 137–45
  judicial review, 112–16
  local government finance, 134
  local policy, 133–4
  ministerial policy, 119–26
  social security, 149–51
  social services, 148–9
Disraeli, Benjamin, 77
District judges, 7
  participation in public debate, 43, 45
Divisional Court of Queen's Bench, 23–4, 50, 59, 68, 98, 295

control of discretionary powers
  cases, 110, 112, 127, 131–5,
  149
freedom of expression, 244
moral maze, 272
personal rights cases, 156, 168,
  199–201, 203
thalidomide case, 216
docks
  commissions, tribunals etc., 26
  disputes and strikes, 71, 73–6,
  79–80, 94, 298, 310–11
  dockers' club case, 176, 282, 286
  National Dock Labour Scheme, 94,
  97, 313–14
documents
  disclosure of, 232–9, 239–44, 247
  protection of sources, 251–6
  seizure of, 159–61, 168–9
Donaldson, Lord
  cited viii
  confidentiality cases, 223, 225–7
  on the giving of reasons, 117
  industrial relations cases, 86–9,
  97, 314
  and legal reforms, 53–5, 327
  and legislative process, 41
  miscarriages of justice, 308–9
  MR appointment, 17
  personal rights cases, 191, 197,
  341
  as President of NIRC, 59,
  72–9
  and sentencing policy, 51
Drewry, Gavin 38n, 39, 60
drugs (illegal), offences, 160, 164,
  237, 264

Ealing Borough Council, 175
East Ham South Conservative Club,
  176
Economist, 12, 16, 18, 19, 20, 32
Edmund-Davies, Lord, 180, 311–12
education, 145–8, 177–8, 179,
  320–1, 340
  NUT case, 97
  reorganization of secondary
  education (Tameside, London),
  109–12
  school places, 119
Education Act

(1944), 109
(1980), 146
(1981), 147
electricity supply industry, 31
Employment Act
(1980), 84–5, 86
(1982), 88, 93
(1988), 96
Employment Appeal Tribunal, 48,
  101, 181
Employment Bill, 313
Employment Protection Act
(1975), 82
(1978), 33
enquiries *see* Tribunals of Enquiry
environmental decisions, 120
Equal Opportunities Commission, 99
Equal Pay Act (1970), 33
European Commission, 171, 237, 249
European Communities (Amendment)
  Bill, 122
European Community law, 99
European Community Treaty, 273
European Convention on Human
  Rights, xvii, 86, 216, 218, 228,
  232 236–7, 248, 251, 259,
  333–4
European Court of Human Rights,
  171, 174, 197, 216, 231, 256,
  305
European Court of Justice, 199
Eveleigh, Lord Justice, 180
Ewart-Biggs, Baroness, 208
extradition and exclusion, 190–204,
  317

Falklands conflict, 257–8
Family Division, 8, 23, 29, 49
fares fair litigation, 126–33
fiduciary duty, 128–9
Financial Services Act (1986), 254
Finlay, Lord Chancellor, 39
Fire Brigades case, 41, 121, 321, 326,
  330–1
fishing licences, 121
Fitt, Lord, 208
Foot, Paul, 211
Forbes, Justice, 270
Foreign Compensation Commission,
  106
Fraser, Lord, 180, 184, 241

freedom
of expression, 216, 244—51,
299—302
individual, 152—7
Fysh, Michael, 223

Gaming Act (1968), 234
Ganz, G., 123, 240, 323
Gardiner, Lord, 16, 34, 35, 338
GCHQ *see* Government
Communications Headquarters
Gearty, Dr Conor, 170
Gibson, Lord Justice, 100
Glasser, Cyril, xiii
Glidewell, Mr Justice, 17, 131, 156
Goff, Lord, 54
Gordon-Walker, Lord, 40
government
departmental committees, 25—7
and judiciary relationship, 290—343
and legal reforms, 53—7
Government Communications
Headquarters, xv, 17, 112, 156,
297
Greater London Council, 120,
126—33
Grecian, Paul, 242—3
Greene, Lord, 104, 341
Greenham Common case, 253—4,
271—2
Greenpeace, 114
grievance, 267—8
Griffiths, Lord, 54, 230
Guardian, 12, 43, 93, 164, 224,
226—7, 229—30, 253—4, 259,
297
Guildford Four, 206—10, 212, 306,
308—9, 341

habeas corpus, 155, 156, 182—3, 197,
200, 297
Hadfield, B., 114, 147, 163, 172, 307
Hailsham, Lord
function of the LC, 48
industrial relations cases, 76, 78
judicial reviews, 43
legal reform, xiv, 53
moral maze, 268
and public debate, 43—4
reprimands by, 12
resignation, 17

Scott Report, 241
Hain, Peter, 267
Haldane, Lord, 16
Halsbury, Lord, 14, 15, 65, 66, 77,
310
Hamlyn lectures, 43
Harman, Harriet, 234—7
Havers, Lord, 12, 309
health authority cases, 113, 148
Heath, Edward, MP, 17, 78
Henderson, Paul, 37, 243
Herschell, Lord Chancellor, 65
Heseltine, Michael, 240
Heuston, Professor R. F. V., 1, 14,
15, 16, 65, 66
High Court, 7
contempt, 215
in courts structure, 22—4
and legal reform, 54—7
High Court judges, 7, 8—10, 12, 14,
17, 24
appointed to commissions etc., 27,
29, 32
background of, 18—22
and industrial cases, 65, 92, 94
participation in public debate,
42—5
personal rights case, 199
and public service, 46—52
Spycatcher, 226, 298
Highways Act (1959), 158
Hillsborough stadium disaster,
273—4
Hobart, Chief Justice, 278
Hobhouse, Lord Justice, 322
Hoffman, Lord, 144, 149, 250—1
Hollis, Sir Roger, 224
Home Office, 45—6, 118, 164, 329
asylum cases, 202, 317
disclosure of documents cases,
234—5, 238—9
Forensic Science Service, 211—12
Harman case, 234—7
immigration, 193
judges and sentencing policy, 51
livestock exports case, 273
miscarriages of justices cases, 208,
209, 211
homelessness, xiv, 136, 137—45,
318
judicial review, 115—16, 118

homosexuality, 262–3, 265–6
House of Commons *see* Commons, House of
House of Lords *see* Lords, House of
housing, 115–16, 118–19, 136, 137–45, 175, 203–4, 269–70, 317
Housing Act (1985), 203, 317
Housing Act (1996), 319
Housing (Homeless Persons) Act (1977), 137–45, 318
Howard, Michael, 51
Howe, Sir Geoffrey, 37–8
Human Rights Bill, 41, 334
Hume, Cardinal Archbishop Basil, 208
Hurd, Douglas, 208

immigration, xiv, 182–90, 302
   interpretation of rules, 50, 315–16
   judicial review, 115–16
Immigration Act (1971), 154, 182, 193
Immigration Appeal Tribunal (IAT), 50, 182, 186–9, 194
Immigration Rules, 186
impartiality, 290, 292–5
Incitement to Disaffection Bill, 158
Independent Broadcasting Authority, 247–8, 264–5
Independent, 93, 96, 119, 145, 171, 175, 197, 198, 203, 225, 231 245, 254–5, 272, 276, 302
industrial relations, 30–3, 63–102, 293, 310–15
   complaints procedures, 113
   Conservative attack, 84–90
   early cases, 63–7
   inducing breach of contract, 71–2
   the later cases, 98–102
   Law Lords restrain Denning, 79–84, 287
   picketing, 68–70
   right to strike, 70–1
   uses of the labour injunction, 90–8
Industrial Relations Act (1971) 32n, 72–9, 108, 293–4
Industrial Tribunal, 181
injunctions
   against trade unions, 81, 90–8, 98–100, 313

confidentiality cases, 221–2
demonstrations and protests, 270–1, 302
freedom of expression, 246–7
Spycatcher, 226–32
Inland Revenue, 116
Interception of Communications Act (1985), 29, 161–2
International Labour Organization, 85
International Times, 262
International Transport Workers Federation (ITF), 79, 84–5
internment, 152–4, 169
IRA, 170–1, 174, 204, 207, 247–8, 308
Iron and Steel Trades Confederation, 81–2
Irvine, Lord, 52, 57

Jackson, John, 212
Jacob, J. M., 232
Jacob, Sir Ian, 42
James I, 45
Jenkins, Roy, 208
Jenkins of Hillhead, Lord, 241
Joint Council for the Welfare of Immigrants, 202–3
Judge Over Your Shoulder, The, 47
judges, 5
   acceptable behaviour, 11
   appointments of, xiii, xv–xvi, 8–18
   chairing of commissions, tribunals etc., 25–38
   class origins of, 1
   consultative function, 45–6
   creative function in law-making, 6–7
   and discretionary powers, 46–52
   dismissal of, 10–11, 43
   educational background, 18–21, 338
   ethnic minority, 21–2
   impartiality and neutrality of, 35–6, 53–7, 60, 67, 292–5
   legal reforms, 53–7
   legislative process, 38–41
   more power to the, 331–4
   participation in public debate, 42–5, 56–7

judges – *cont.*
  political
    bias and neutrality of, xv, 7–8,
      13–17, 38, 39–41, 51–2,
      56–7, 75, 328
    career as qualification, 14–16,
      17, 20–1
    naïveté of, 78
    role of, 291–343
    and the public interest, 57
    and public service, 46–52
    reprimanded, 11–13
    retirement, xv, 10
    Rules, 112, 237, 303–4
    salaries, xiv–xv
    sentencing policy, xvi–xvii, 51
    social position, 18–22
    survey of, 38–9
    trade unions and intervention by,
      63–72, 75–6
    training, 29
    women, 21–2
Judges Council *see* Supreme Court
judicial
  creativity, 281–9
  misbehaviour, 43–4
  review, xiv–xvii, 42–5, 47, 50, 59,
    98, 333, 341
    contempt, confidentiality and
      censorship cases, 218
    discretionary cases, 112–16,
      116–19, 122, 123, 126,
      137–8, 140–2, 321, 325
    personal rights cases, 161,
      171–3, 180, 182, 192–3, 197,
      200, 202, 315, 317, 341
Judicial Committee of the Privy
  Council, 19
Judicial Studies Board, 29, 46
juries, 6, 34, 258
  contempt of court, 215
  vetting of, 156–7, 257
Justice, 18
Justices of the Peace (JPs), 7, 22–4

Kee, Robert, 207–8, 308–9
Keith, Lord, 101–2, 123–4, 127–33,
  151, 219, 230, 235–6, 245, 311
  322
Kent, Bruce, 161
Kerr, Lord Justice, 131, 179

Kilmuir, Lord, 42
Kilmuir rules, 42–5
King, Tom, 210

Labour governments, 17, 27, 67, 76,
  77, 109, 223, 230, 277
labour law, 63
Labour Party, xvii, 1, 7, 67, 127, 133
  local authorities and councils, 109,
    137
  transport fares, 126–33
Labour Research, 20–1
Laker, Freddy, 110–11, 339
Lambard Archeion, 263
Land Registration Bill, 41
land regulation, 282
Lane, Lord, 44, 49, 53, 190, 208,
  210, 246, 306
Law Commission, xiv, 27, 41, 249,
  332
Law Lords
  appointments, 8–10, 16
  background of, 18, 20
  on commissions, tribunals etc., 27,
    35, 36
  contempt cases, 215, 218, 219
  in courts structure, 22–4
  discretionary powers cases, 120,
    122–4, 127–33, 135–6, 147,
    150–1
  freedom of expression, 250–1,
    300–1
  industrial relations cases, 79–84,
    86–7, 90–1, 94, 99, 101–2, 312
  judges and public service, 46–52
  and legal reforms, 53–7
  and legislative process, 38–41
  moral maze, 260–6, 273
  participation in public debate,
    42–5, 56–7
  personal rights cases, 156, 158,
    164, 168, 170, 172–3, 176, 179,
    183–4, 195, 199–200, 202, 208,
    303–6
  protection of sources cases, 252–6
  Scott Report, 239–44
  social and political issues, 312,
    322
  Spycatcher case, 228, 230, 298
  survey of, 38–9
law and order, 301–9

law reforms *see* legal profession
Law Society, xvi
Laws, Mr Justice, 133
Laws, Sir John, 115, 274, 333
Lawson, Lord, xvi
Lawton, Sir Frederick, 2, 157
lay magistrates, 8, 29
legal
  aid, xiv, 238
  system, independence of, 48,
    292–5
legal profession reforms, 28–9, 50,
    53–7, 327–8
legislative process, 38–41
Leigh, L., 163, 305
Lester, Lord, 41, 242, 245, 281,
    333–4
libel, 249–51
Liberal government, 67
Liberal Party, 7, 67
life and death *see* moral maze
Lilley, Peter, 243
Lindley, Lord Justice, 68
livestock exports, 272–3, 302–3
Livingstone, Stephen, 171, 172,
    305–6
Lloyd, Lord, 41, 101–2, 115, 123–4,
    142, 191, 241, 334
local authorities xv
  and asylum *see*kers, 203–4, 317
  and criminal offences, 171
  freedom of expression, 244
  judicial intervention in
    discretionary powers of, 103–51,
    318–19
Local Authority Social Services Act
    (1970), 149
Local Government, Planning and
    Land Act (1980), 134, 319
Local Government Act (1972), 135
Local Government Commission, 120,
    232
local government finance, 134–7
Local Government Finance Act
    (1988), 136
Logan, Alastair, 212
London
  asylum *see*kers, 203
  Bengali demonstrations, 167
  County Hall, 120
  Court of Aldermen, 119

demolition of listed buildings, 120
dockers, 71, 73–6
Rose theatre, 114
transport, 126–33
Underground, 96, 98
London Residuary Body, 120
London Transport Executive (LTE),
    127–33
Lonrho, 218–19
Lord Chancellor
  appointments made by, 8, 9,
    13–15, 21–2
  appointments of, xiii, 8n, 17
  department of, xiii, 8–9, 22, 43–5,
    47–50, 329
  intervention, xvi–xvii, 12
  judges and public service, 46–52
  and legal reform, 53–7
  participation in public debate,
    42–5
  powers of dismissal, 10–11
Lord Chief Justice, 7, 8, 38, 49
  appointments of, xiii, 10
  confidentiality cases, 221
  and legal reforms, 53–7
  personal rights cases, 157, 158,
    167, 174
Lords
  House of
    Appellate Committee, 8, 23, 219
    contempt cases, 216, 218
    disclosure of documents cases,
      233–4, 238
    discretionary powers cases,
      105–8, 111, 113, 127, 132–3,
      135, 137, 139–40, 147, 151
    and independence of the
      judiciary, 49, 51–2, 295
    industrial relations cases, 65–6,
      69–71, 74–6, 79–84, 84–90,
      94, 101, 287–8, 311–13
    judges, 18
    judicial creativity, 286
    moral maze, 260–3, 267
    Official Secrets, 258–9
    personal rights cases, 152–3,
      167, 175–6, 180, 183, 191–2,
      203, 205
    protection of sources, 255
    sentencing policy debate, 51–2
    Spycatcher, 228, 230, 298

Lords of Appeal in Ordinary *see* Law Lords

Lords Justices of Appeal, 7–10
on commissions, tribunals etc., 27, 29
in courts structure, 22–4

Loughlin, M., 128, 134, 319

Loveland, Ian, 137

Lynskey, Mr Justice, 30

Maastricht Treaty, 115, 121–2, 199, 327

McCluskey, Lord, 44

McCrudden, C., 163, 170, 172, 212

Mackay, Lord Chancellor
and appointments, 10
legal reforms xv–xvi, 50, 53–7, 327–8
and public debate, 44–5
rebukes by, 13
sentencing policy, 52

McKinnon, Judge Neil, 12

Macmillan, Lord, 152

McNeill, Mr Justice, 59, 238

Macpherson of Cluny, Mr Justice, 29, 325

magistrates' courts, 23

Maguire Seven, 207–9, 308–9, 341

Major, Prime Minister John, 37

Mancini, G. F., 336–7

Marshall, G., 122

Massiter, Cathy, 161

Master of the Rolls (MR), 7, 8, 38, 49, 188
appointments of, xiii, 10, 15–16, 17
and court administration, 47
and legal reforms, 53–7
participation in public debate, 42–5
salary, 10

Matrix Churchill, 37, 240–3

Maugham, Lord, 104, 152

May, Sir John, 209, 308

media *see* Press; television

medical profession, xv

Melford-Stevenson, Mr Justice, 12

Mercury Communications, 88

Meredith, Paul, 147

Meszaros, George, 114, 318

metropolitan magistrates, 19

Military Lands Act (1892), 271

Millett, Lord Justice, 99, 224–31

miners'
pay enquiry (1972), 31–2
strike, 92, 94, 313

ministers
enquiries into behaviour of, 30
judicial interference in discretion of, 103–51 *passim*

miscarriages of justice, xv, 204, 298, 306

Miskin, Sir James, 13

Misuse of Drugs Act (1971), 264

Monckton, Sir Walter, 10

Monopolies and Mergers Commission, 218, 254

moral maze
behaviour, 260–6
demonstrations and protests, 266–73
matters of life and death, 273–5

Morris, John, MP, 26–7

Morris of Borth-y-Gest, Lord, 106–7, 263

Morritt, Mr Justice, 231, 322

Mortimer, John, QC, 70

Muggeridge, Malcolm, 217

Mullin, Chris, 2–3, 210

Mummery, Mr Justice, 33

Mustill, Lord, 116–17, 118, 123–5, 196, 265, 322, 329–30

My Country: Right or Wrong, 247

National Assistance Act (1948), 332

National Coal Board, 32, 95

National Council for Civil Liberties, 234–7

National Council for One-Parent Families, 248

National Dock Labour Scheme, 94, 97, 313–14

National Graphical Association (NGA), 89, 95

National Health Service Act (1977), 148

National Industrial Relations Court (NICR), 17, 32–3, 59, 72–9, 108 214, 310

national origins, 5, 175–6

national security, 28, 153–4, 156, 161, 197, 254, 297
Spycatcher cases, 223–32, 298

National Unemployed Workers'
  Movement, 159
National Union of Journalists, 80, 89,
  248
National Union of Mineworkers
  (NUM), 92, 95, 96
National Union of Railwaymen
  (NUR), 96, 97, 313–14
National Union of Seamen, 96–7
National Union of Teachers, 97
nationality, 175–7
neutrality, the myth of, 292–5, 309
New Society, 19
New Statesman, 246
New Unionism, 64
News Groups Newspapers, 215
News International, 95, 168
Nicholls, Sir Donald, V-C, 100,
  123–4, 145
Nicol, Andrew, 257
Nolan, Lord, 29, 51, 131
Nolan Committee, 36
Northern Ireland, 30, 33–6, 198, 299,
  338
  internment, 154
  libel damages to judge, 12
  and PACE cases, 170–2, 305–6
  and prison sentencing, 174
Northern Ireland (Emergency
  Provisions) Act (1973), 35
Nyasaland Commission of Enquiry
  (1959), 26

Obscene Publications Act (1964), 262
obscenity, 260–6
Observer, 93, 218–19, 224, 227,
  229–30
obstruction, 69
O'Connor, Lord Justice, 210
Office of Fair Trading, 254
Official Secrets Acts, 221, 224,
  232–9, 256–9, 266–7, 285
Official Solicitor, 73–4
Oliver, Dawn, 279
Oliver, Lord, 54, 179, 228
Ordnance Technologies Ltd (Ordtec),
  242
Osborne, P., 163
Out of Court, 246
Overseas Development and Co-
  operation Act, 125, 324

P & O, 96
PACE (Police and Criminal Evidence
  Act 1984), 40, 162–71, 211,
  303–4
Parker, Lord, 30, 33, 338
Parliamentary Boundary
  Commissions, 29
Parole Board, 117, 174
Passenger Service Requirements
  (PSRs), 114, 126
Pearce, Lord, 26
The People, 251
Pergau Dam, Malaysia, 125, 321,
  323–5, 326
personal injuries, 123
personal rights, 152–213
  deportation, asylum, extradition,
    exclusion, 190–204
  immigration, 182–90
  individual freedom, 152–7
  miscarriages of justice, 204–13
  police powers, 158–71
  prisoners, 171–5
  race relations, 175–81
picketing, 68–70, 72, 91–2, 95
Pickles, Circuit Judge, 43–4
police
  chief constable case, 105
  and demonstrators/protesters, 68–9,
    158–9, 162, 266–73, 302
  disclosure of documents, 233–4,
    237
  enquiry, 30
  extradition case, 199–200
  interception of communication, 29
  involved in miscarriages of justice,
    204–13, 306–9
  judgement, 265
  jury vetting for trials, 156–7
  methods of obtaining confessions
    and evidence, 158–62, 162–71,
    204–13
  powers, 158–71, 303–5
  suspect's right to silence, 44
Police Act (1964), 237
Police Complaints Authority, 166
Police and Criminal Evidence Act
  1984 (PACE), 40, 162–71, 211,
  303–4
Police (Discipline) Regulations,
  168

political
asylum cases, 151, 190–204, 317,
321
role, 290–343
means and ends, 326–31
more powers to the judges?,
331–4
myth of neutrality, 292–5
public interest and its
application, 295–7
State interests, 297–326
traditional view, 290–1
and social issues, 310–26
Pollock, C. B., 153
Ponting, Clive, 257–8
Popplewell, Mr Justice, 27
port industry *see* dockers *under*
London
Post Office Act (1953), 262
Post Office Engineering Union,
88
Powell, Justice, 225
Prebble & Co., 270
Press
censorship of the, 226, 235
and confidentiality, 220–3
contempt of court (and prejudicial
statements), 93, 96, 215–19
freedom of expression, 244–51,
299–301, 341
Harman case, 234–7
judges and public debate, 42–5
material seized under search
warrants, 167–8
Official Secrets, 256–9
prejudicial statements, 215–19
protection of sources, 251–6
Spycatcher cases, 223–32, 298
union disputes and strikes, 80–1,
89, 91–2, 93, 95–6
Press Association, 80–1
Prevention of Terrorism Act (1989),
198
Prevention of Terrorism (Temporary
Provisions) Act (1976), 156
prime ministers, appointments made
by, 8–10, 15–16, 17, 22
Primodos drug, 221–2
Prison Officers' Association, 100
Prison Rules, 113, 172–3
prisoners, 171–5

judicial reviews brought by, 113,
116–18, 306
property, rights, 103–4, 153–4, 282
Prosser, Lord, 189
prostitution, 260–2
protection of sources, 251–6
protests *see* demonstrations
public debate, participation in, 42–5,
56–7
public interest
arms to Iraq, 239–44
confidentiality cases, 221–2
disclosure of documents cases,
232–9, 239–44
and extradition, 199–200
freedom of expression, 249
immunity certificates (PII), 239–43
industrial case, 94
and intelligence information, 198
and its application, 295–301
and the judiciary, 57, 112, 340–3
law and order, 301–9
miscarriages of justice, 341
protection of minorities, 249
social and political issues,
310–26
Spycatcher cases, 223–32, 298
Public Order Act (1936), 267
Public Service Vehicles (Travel
Concessions) Act (1955), 128
Public Works Loan Board, 135
Purchas, Lord Justice, 142

Quangos, xiv
Queen's Counsel, xv, 8
race relations, 79, 133, 249
CRE cases, 178–81
dockers' club case, 176, 282, 286
personal rights cases, 167, 175–81
racial remarks by judiciary, 12–13
Race Relations Acts, 133, 175–8,
178–9, 281–2, 286–7
Race Relations Board, 175–7, 178
Radcliffe, Lord, 30
Raghip, Engin, 211
Rawlings, R., 115, 122
Recorders, 7–10, 11, 12, 24
in courts structure, 22
training, 29
redundancy pay and compensation, 99
Rees, Merlyn, MP, 208

Rees-Davies, MP, 138
Rees-Mogg, Lord, 115, 121–2, 327
Registrars, 29
Reid, Lord xiv, 16, 69, 95, 233–4,
    261, 263, 281, 283, 285–7,
    331–2
Reiner, R., 163, 305
Reith lectures, 44
Restrictive Practices Court, 32
Review Body on Civil Justice, 49
Review Commission, 213
Rhodesian Opinion Commission, 26
Richardson, Geneva, 172
Romer, Lord, 152
Rose, David, 212, 306–7
Rose, Lord Justice, 125
Rose Theatre Trust, 114
Roskill, Lord, 180, 207, 235–6, 309
Rough Justice, 245–6
Royal Assent, 122
Royal Commissions, 25–6, 28, 55,
    72, 162, 212, 322
Rozenburg, Joshua, 45
Ruddock, Joan, 161
Runciman, Viscount, 212
Rushdie, Salman, 249
Russell, Lord, 110, 342

Salisbury, Lord, 15–16
Salmon, Lord, 39–40, 75, 110, 252,
    312
Salter, Mr Justice, 153
Sampson, Anthony, 1
Save Britain's Heritage, 120
Save our Railways, 14, 114, 125,
    324–6
Scarman
    Lord, 34, 40, 41, 43, 53, 334
    fares fair litigation, 127–33
    Guilford Four, 208
    Harman case, 236
    industrial relations cases, 80, 84,
        288–9, 311
Schiemann, Justice, 147, 193
Schuster, Sir Claud, xiii
Scotland
    commissions, enquiries etc., 26,
        28
    home rule, 11
    judge's dismissal, 11
Scott, Lord Justice xvii, 37–8, 52,

229–30, 239–44, 253, 279,
    300–1
Scott Report, 37–8, 52, 211, 239–44,
    300–1
Scottish Law Commission, 28
Scrutton, Lord Justice, 278
Scum, 264
Sealink, 96
search and seizure, 159
Secret Society, The, 246
Secretary of State, deportations,
    190–3
Security Commission, 29
security *see* national security; Official
    Secrets Acts; security services
Security Service Act (1989), 29
security services, 29, 33, 222–32,
    246–7, 258
sedition, 159
Sedley, Mr Justice, 200
sentencing policy, 44, 51, 173–4
Sex Discrimination Act (1975), 33
Shah, Amarjit Singh, 176
Sharpe, R. J., 155
Shaw, Bernard, 56
Shaw, Lord, 153, 157, 222
Sheen, Mr Justice Barry, 27
Sheriff Courts (Scotland) Act (1971),
    11
shipping industry, 79–80, 84–5,
    96–7, 99–100
shop stewards, union liability for,
    73–5
Silcott, Winston, 211
Simon of Glaisdale, Lord, 10, 41,
    236, 241, 344
Simonds, Viscount, 260–1, 263, 284
Singh, Judge Mohat, 167
Sinn Fein, 248, 299–300
Skytrain, 110
Slade, Lord, 86, 188
Slynn, Lord, 41, 101–2, 196, 241,
    265, 344
Smedley, Mr. Justice, 239
Smith, Professor de, 111
social
    and political issues, 310–26
    services, 148–9, 149–51, 321
Social Fund, 150
Social Security Act (1986), 150
Social Security Commissioner, 151

Social Security (Contributions and Benefits) Act (1992), 203
Society for the Protection of Unborn Children, 217
SOGAT, 95
Solicitor-General, 9, 15
solicitors, 7, 9, 24
  access to clients, 163–4, 169
  disclosure of documents, 236
  and legal reform, 54
  search and seizure of documents, 167–8
Sorn, Lord, 30
Southwark Crown Court, 167
Spycatcher, xv, 60, 93, 223–32, 298, 341
spying, enquiry, 30
squatting, 269
statute law, 5–6
  interpretation of, 47, 63
    discretionary powers cases, 103–8, 112, 120, 123, 133, 135, 136, 147
    personal rights cases, 176–7, 178–9, 201
Staughton, Lord Justice, 194
steelworkers, 81–2
Stevens, Robert, xiii, xiv, 124
Steyn, Lord Justice, 100
stipendiary magistrates, 8, 22–4
Stock Exchange, 51
Street Offences Act (1959), 260
strike, right to, 64, 70–1, 314
strikes, 73–4, 76, 80, 81, 91–2, 94–6, 286, 288, 298, 302, 313
Stuart-Smith, Lord Justice, 29
Sun, 215
Sunday Telegraph, 257
Sunday Times, 19, 60, 215–18, 220, 226, 229–31, 244–5, 298
Sunkin, Maurice, 113–14, 194, 318
Supplementary Benefit Act (1966), 283
Supreme Court, 7, 8, 43
  judges, 18
  Judges Council, 45, 49, 54
  Rules, 112, 237, 303–4
Swift, Mr Justice, 103

T. Bailey Forman Ltd, 89
Taff Vale Railway Company, 66–7, 78

TASS, 93
Taylor, Lord, 2–3, 27, 41, 48, 51, 52, 326, 329, 344
telephone-tapping, 161–2, 164
television, 42–5, 215, 218, 221–2, 224, 235, 247, 249, 252–3, 298
Templeman, Lord, 2, 41, 44, 60, 62, 180, 228, 314, 319, 320
terrorism, 34–5, 170–1, 174, 204, 207, 247–8, 300, 307–8
thalidomide case, 215–18, 298
Thatcher, Margaret, (former) Prime Minister, xiv, 8, 17, 37, 47, 60, 98, 208, 313, 319, 323
Thomas, Sir, 322
Thompson, Lorraine, 138
Thomson, Sheriff Peter, 11
Thomson of Monifieth, Lord, 241
The Times, 12, 59, 60, 340
  demonstrations and protests, 267
  discretionary powers, 114, 117, 119, 125, 129, 133, 136, 149
  education authority, 340
  freedom of expression, 248, 250
  industrial relations, 73–5, 82
  personal rights, 157, 160, 168–9, 171, 174, 184–5, 199, 200, 204
  protection of sources, 254
  Scott Report, 279
Times Education Supplement, 244
Times Group, 95, 244
Tisdall, Sarah, 253
Tottenham Three, 211
trade disputes, 30–3, 66–71, 72, 79–84, 84–90, 287–8
Trade Disputes Act (1906), 66–71, 80
Trade Disputes Act (1965), 71
Trade Union Act (1871), 66
Trade Union Act (1913), 67
Trade Union and Labour Relations Act (1974), 80
Trade Union and Labour Relations (Amendment) Bill, 39
trade unions
  and ACAS, 82–4
  ballots, 93, 94, 96, 97, 98–9, 108–9, 313–14
  banned at GCHQ xv, 17, 112, 156
  'blacking', 73, 79, 81, 84, 88, 99, 311

breach of contract, 71–2
Bridlington principles, 86
collective bargaining, 101–2, 287
and conspiracy, 63–7, 70
contempt of court used against, 32, 73–4, 76, 93, 96
criminal injuries compensation, 123–4
early legal cases, 63–7
funds, 67, 76
industrial relations law, 72–9, 79–84, 84–90, 90–8, 98–102, 287, 310–15
and the judiciary, 29, 39–40, 63–84, 97
liability for members' actions, 93
liability for shop stewards' actions, 73–5
membership, xv, 70, 72, 86, 87–8, 91–2, 100–2, 156
picketing, 68–70, 72, 92, 95
recognition of, 83–4, 87
'secondary action', 84–6, 92
see also injunctions; strikes; trade disputes
unfair dismissal, 87, 89, 99
Trade Unions and Employers' Associations, 72
Trade Unions (No. 2) Bill (1911), 277
Trades Disputes Act (1965), 287
Trades Union Congress, 74, 84, 86
Transport Act (1983), 132
Transport and General Workers' Union, 73, 74, 94
Transport (London) Act (1969), 127–9
Treasury, 51
and court administration, 48–9
Solicitor's Department, 47, 50, 253, 315
Treaty of Rome, 302
trespass, 164, 171, 267–9
Tribunals of Enquiry (Evidence) Act (1921), 30, 31, 34
Trustee Saving Bank, 50–1

Ulster Defence Organization, 248
ultra vires doctrine, 67
Unification Church, 119, 199
Union of Communication Workers, 96
universities, xv, 18–21

Vehicle and General Insurance Company, 30
Vincenzi, C., 194

Wapping, 95–6, 166–8
Ward, Judith, 211
warrants, 159–62, 166–7, 170
Watkins, Lord Justice, 244, 264–5
Webster, Sir Richard, 15
Wedderburn, Lord, 63, 72, 86, 89–90, 91, 97, 98, 311, 313, 336
Wheatley, Lord, 28
White, F., 323
Whitehouse, Mrs Mary, 264–5
Widgery, Lord, 34, 78, 138, 205, 231
Wilberforce, Lord, 298
 courts of enquiry, 31
 discretionary powers cases, 110, 127–33
 industrial relations cases, 31, 74, 81, 312
 personal rights cases, 183–4, 197
 protection of sources case, 252
Wood, Mr Justice, 49
Woolf, Lord, 10, 27, 41, 52, 100, 148, 193, 242, 331–4, 341
Woolwich bombings, 206–7
World Development Movement, 114
Wright, Lord, 152–3
Wright, Peter, 93, 223–32

Young, G. M., 66
Young, Hugo, 2, 19, 60, 314, 320
young offenders, 164–5

Zesko, Stanislaw, 175
Zircon affair, 246–7

Index of Cases

A. Crompton Ltd v. Customs & Excise, 233
A-G v. Associated Newspapers Ltd, 215
— v. Blake, 259
— v. Channel 4 Television Co., 247
— v. English, 218
— v. Guardian Newspapers Ltd and others, 226, 229, 298
— v. Independent Television News Ltd, 215
— v. Jonathan Cape Ltd, 221
— v. Lundin, 252
— v. Mulholland, 251
— v. News Group Newspapers, 215, 217
— v. Newspaper Publishing plc and others, 231
— v. Television Ltd, 218
— v. Times Newspapers, 215, 218, 221
Abdullai Conteh v. Secretary of State for the Home Department, 195, 316
Air Canada v. Secretary of State for Trade (No. 2), 238, 279, 300
Airedale NHS Trust v. Bland, 273–4
Akinbolu v. Hackney LBC, 204, 317
Ali v. Secretary of State for the Home Department, 184
Allason v. Haines, 250
Allen v. Flood, 64
Amalgamated Society of Railway Servants v. Osborne, 67
American Cyanamid Ltd v. Ethicon, 91, 224
Anisminic Ltd v. Foreign Compensation Commission, 106–8, 339
Argyll v. Argyll, 220
Arrowsmith v. Jenkins, 158
Associated British Ports v. Palmer, 100
— v. TGWU, 90, 94, 96
Associated Newspapers Group Ltd v. Wade, 79
Associated Newspapers Ltd v. Wilson, 100, 287
Associated Provincial Picture Houses Ltd v. Wednesbury Corporation, xi, 104, 192, 199, 341

Attorney General for Northern Ireland's Reference, 170

Austin Rover Co. v. AUEW (TASS), 93

Baker v. Cornwall CC, 181

Barclays Bank v. Taylor, 305

Barnard v. Gorman, 153

BBC v. Hearn, 79

Beaverbrook v. Keys, 79

Becker v. Home Office, 171

Bennett v. Commissioner of Police for the Metropolis, 199–200

Bibby Bulk Carriers v. Consulex Ltd, 237

Blackpool and the Fylde College v. Nat Assoc. of Teachers in Further and Higher Education, 100

Bodlington v. Lawton, 100

Bowditch v. Balchin, 153

Re Bowman, 103

Brind *see* Secretary of State for the Home Department

British Rail v. NUR, 96

British Railways Board v. National Union of Railwaymen, 97

British Steel Corporation v. Granada Television Ltd, 222, 224, 252–3, 235, 252, 298

Broadmoor Hospital v. Hyde, 256

Bromley v. GLC *see* R. v. Greater London Council *ex p.* Bromley LBC

Burmah Oil Co. Ltd v. Bank of England, 233, 300

Bushell v. Secretary of State for the Environment, 106

Campbell v. Tameside Metropolitan BC, 238, 339

Carltona v. Commissioners of Works, 103

Carrington v. Therm-A-Stor Ltd, 87

Chahal v. United Kingdom, 197

Chandler v. DPP, 256, 266–7, 285

Charter v. Race Relations Board, 176, 282, 286

Cheall v. Association of Professional, Executive, Clerical and Computer Staff, 86–7

Chief Adjudication Officer v. Foster, 151

Choudhury v. IAT, 188

Church of Scientology of California v. Johnson-Smith, 249

Clarke v. Heathfield, 92

Cocks v. Thanet DC, 137

Commission for Racial Equality v. Dutton, 180

Con-Mech (Engineers) Ltd v. AUEW, 76

Conway v. Rimmer, 233, 235, 300

Council of Civil Service Unions, in re 112, 156, 297, 341

Cozens v. Brutus, 267

CRE v. Amari Plastics Ltd, 179

— v. Prestige Group plc, 179

Credit Suisse v. Waltham Forest LBC, 136

Davendranath Doorga v. Secretary of State for the Home Department, 185

Dawkins v. Department of the Environment, 180

De Falco v. Crawley BC, 138

Derbyshire CC v. Times Newspapers, 245, 300

Devenport v. Salford CC, 138

Dimbleby and Sons Ltd v. National Union of Journalists, 89

Dimskal Shipping Co. v. ITWF, 99

Din v. Wandsworth LBC, 139

Dockers' Labour Club v. Race Relations Board, 176, 286

DPP v. Hutchinson, 271

— v. Jones, 273

— v. Marshall, 165

Duncan v. Cammell Laird, 232

— v. Jones, 158

Duport Steels v. Sirs, 28, 81, 311–12, 340

Ealing LBC v. Race Relations Board, 176

Elias v. Pasmore, 159

Enderby Town Football Club v. Football Association Ltd, 278

Engineers' and Managers' Association v. ACAS, 84

Errington v. Minister of Health, 104

Express Newspapers v. McShane, 80–2, 288, 311–12

Farah v. Commissioner for Metropolitan Police, 169

Farrell v. Secretary of State for Defence, 170

Fender v. St John-Mildmay, 86

Francome v. Mirror Group Newspapers, 222–4

Frank Truman Export v. Commissioner of Police for the Metropolis, 160

Franklin v. Minister of Town and Country Planning, 103

Fraser v. Evans, 220, 225

— v. Mudge, 171

Garfinkel v. Metropolitan Police Commissioner, 160

G.C. Powley v. ACAS, 83

General Aviation Services v. TGWU, 75

Ghani v. Jones, 160

Gillick v. West Norfolk and Wisbech Area Health Authority, 273

Greene v. The Secretary of State for Home Affairs, 152, 155, 297

Grunwick Processing Laboratories Ltd v. ACAS, 83

Hadmor Productions v. Hamilton, 90

Hain v. DPP, 267

Hamilton v. The Guardian, 250–1

Hampson v. Department of Education and Science, 180

Hazell v. Hammersmith and Fulham LBC, 136, 320

Heaton's Transport (St Helens) Ltd v. TGWU, 73, 74, 310

Hehir v. Commissioner of Police for Metropolis, 237

Hill v. Chief Constable of West Yorkshire, 168

Home Office v. Harman, 234–7, 239

Hubbard v. Pitt, 69, 269–70, 284, 302

Hunt v. Broome, 69, 95

Jahromi v. Secretary of State for the Home Department, 198, 316

Jeffrey v. Black, 160

Kamara v. DPP, 268–9, 302

Kavanagh v. Hiscock, 69, 269–70

Khanna v. Ministry of Defence, 181

King v. The Great Britain–China Centre, 181

Knight v. Home Office, 172

Kruse v. Johnson, 342

Lambeth LBC v. Secretary of State for Social Services, 148

Leech v. Deputy Governor of Parkhurst Prison, 113

Lion Laboratories v. Evans, 222, 225

Liversidge v. Anderson, 152–5, 196, 297, 320

Lloyd v. McMahon, 117

London Residuary Body v. Lambeth LBC, 120

London Underground Ltd v. National Union of Rail, Maritime and Transport Workers, 98

London Underground v. NUR, 96

Lonrho plc, re 219

Lord Advocate v. Scotsman Publications, 258

Lyons v. Wilkins, 64, 68

M. v. Home Office, 202, 214, 317, 327

Mackay, re 154

McEldowney v. Forde, 170

McElduff, re 154

McKerr v. Armagh Coroner, 170

Makanjuola v. Metropolitan Police Commissioner, 240, 242

Mandla v. Dowell Lee, 179

Marina Shipping Ltd v. Laughton (1982), 84

Masood v. Immigration Appeal Tribunal, 189, 317

Mercury Communications Ltd v. Director General of
Telecommunications, 113

Mercury Communications v. Scott-Garner, 89

Merkur Island Shipping Corporation v. Laughton, 85

Merthyr Tydfil S.B. Appeal Tribunal *ex p.* Lewis, 283

Middlebrook Mushrooms v. TGWU, 99

Middleweek v. Chief Constable of Merseyside Police, 172

Midland Cold Storage Ltd v. Turner and Others, 59

Mogul Steamship Co. v. McGregor Gow & Co., 66

Mohammed-Holgate v. Duke, 159

Moore *ex p.* 283

Morris v. Beardmore, 160

— v. Crown Office, 215

Moss v. McLachlan, 94

Murray v. Ministry of Defence, 170

Musisi, re 192

Nakkuda Ali v. Jayaratne, 154

National Breweries v. The King, 153

Neilson v. Laugharne, 237, 242

News Group Newspapers and others v. SOGAT 82 and others, 95

North Yorkshire CC v. Secretary of State for Education and Science,
340

Northavon DC *ex p.* Palmer, 137

Norwich Pharmacal v. Customs & Excise, 233

Nottinghamshire CC v. Secretary of State for the Environment, 61,
319

NWL Ltd v. Woods, 79, 84, 311

Ojutiku v. Manpower Services Commission, 180

O'Reilly v. Mackman, 113, 137

Osman v. Ferguson, 169

P & O European Ferries (Portsmouth) Ltd v. NUS, 96

Padfield v. Minister of Agriculture, Fisheries and Food, 47, 105, 109, 112, 199, 324, 339

Pearlman v. Harrow School, 107

Pickwell v. Camden LBC, 129

Piddington v. Bates, 69

Point of Ayr Collieries v. Lloyd George, 103

Post Office v. Union of Communication Workers, 96, 314

Prebble v. Television New Zealand, 249

Prescott v. Birmingham, 128

Puhlhofer v. Hillingdon LBC, 140, 318

Quinn v. Leathem, 65–6

R. v. Absolam, 164

— v. Alladice, 163, 211, 304

— v. Anderson, 262

— v. Army Board of the Defence Council *ex p*. Anderson, 180

— v. Aubrey, Berry and Campbell, 257

— v. Barnet LBC *ex p*. Johnson, 133

— v. Bow St Stipendiary Magistrate *ex p*. DPP, 168

— v. Brent LBC *ex p*. Awua, 144, 318

— v. Brent LBC *ex p*. Macwan, 143

— v. Bristol City Council *ex p*. Browne, 138

— v. Bristol Crown Court *ex p*. Bristol Press and Picture Agency Ltd, 166

— v. British Coal Corporation *ex p*. Vardy, 98, 121

— v. Broadcasting Complaints Commission *ex p*. BBC, 248

— v. Broadcasting Complaints Commissions *ex p*. Channel Four Television Corporation, 249

— v. Brown, 265

— v. Broxbourne BC *ex p*. Willmoth, 139

— v. Cairns, Aitken and Roberts, 257

— v. Cambridge Health Authority *ex p*. B, 149, 274

— v. Camden LBC *ex p*. Gillan, 142

— v. Camden LBC *ex p*. Wait, 143

— v. Canale, 166, 304

— v. Central Criminal Court *ex p*. Adegbesan, 167

— v. Central Criminal Court *ex p.* AJD Holdings, 170

— v. Central Criminal Court *ex p.* Francis and Francis, 167, 305

— v. Central Television, 248

— v. Chief Constable of Devon and Cornwall *ex p.* CEGB, 271

— v. Chief Constable of South Wales *ex p.* Merrick, 169

— v. Chief Constable of Sussex *ex p.* International Trader's Ferry Ltd, 272–3, 303

— v. Chief Constable of the West Midlands Police *ex p.* Wiley, 242

— v. Chief Metropolitan Magistrate *ex p.* Choudhury, 249

— v. Civil Service Appeal Board *ex p.* Cunningham, 117

— v. Civil Service Appeal Board *ex p.* Walsh, 113

— v. Cooper, 205

— v. Corporation of London *ex p.* Matson, 119

— v. Coventry City Council *ex p.* Phoenix Aviation, 272, 302

— v. CRE *ex p.* Hillingdon LBC, 179

— v. Criminal Injuries Compensation Board *ex p.* Lain and P, 123

— v. Crown Court at Inner London Sessions *ex p* Baines and Baines, 167

— v. Crown Court Sheffield *ex p.* Brownlow, 156, 289

— v. Cullen and others, 211

— v. Davison, 164

— v. Delaney, 165

— v. Department of Health *ex p.* Gandhi, 181

— v. Deputy Governor Parkhurst Prison *ex p.* Hague, 172

— v. Derbyshire CC *ex p.* Times Supplement Ltd, 245

— v. Director of Passenger Rail Franchising *ex p.* Save Our Railways, 114, 125, 324–6

— v. Doolan, 165

— v. Dunford, 163

— v. Ealing BC *ex p.* Times Newspapers Ltd, 244

— v. East Berkshire Health Authority *ex p.* Walsh, 113

— v. Ebbw Vale and Merthyr Tydfil SB Appeal Tribunal *ex parte* Lewis, 283

— v. Exeter CC *ex p.* Tranckle, 139

— v. Ford, 157

— v. Foster, 165

— v. Fulling, 165

— v. General Medical Council *ex p.* Virik, 181

— v. Gibson, 263

— v. Gloucestershire CC *ex p.* Barry, 149

— v. Gloucestershire CC *ex p.* Mahfood, 149

— v. Governor of Wormwood Scrubs Prison, 154

— v. Governors of the Bishop Challoner RC School *ex p.* Choudhury, 146

— v. Greater London Council *ex p.* Bromley LBC, xv, 126–33, 319

— v. Greater London Council *ex p.* Kensington and Chelsea LBC, 59

— v. Grecian, 243

— v. Greenwich LBC *ex p.* Cedar Transport, 129

— v. Hackney LBC *ex p.* GC, 147

— v. Halliday, 153—5, 297

— v. Hammersmith and Fulham LBC *ex p.* A, 203, 317, 332

— v. Hammersmith and Fulham LBC *ex p.* Earls Court Ltd, 133

— v. Hammersmith and Fulham LBC *ex p.* Lusi, 139

— v. Hammersmith and Fulham LBC *ex p.* NALGO, 180

— v. Hammersmith and Fulham LBC *ex p.* P., 142

— v. Harvey, 165

— v. Higher Education Funding Council *ex p.* Institute of Dental Surgery, 118

— v. Horseferry Road Magistrates' Court *ex p.* Bennett, 199

— v. Hughes, 164

— v. Hull Prison Board of Visitors *ex p.* St Germain, 172

— v. IAT *ex p.* Hoque and Singh, 188, 315

— v. IAT *ex p.* Cheema, 190–1

— v. IAT *ex p.* Iqbal, 190

— v. IAT *ex p.* Khatab, 189, 315

— v. IAT *ex p.* Owusu-Sekyere, 191

— v. IAT *ex p.* Patel, 191, 316

— v. IAT *ex p.* Secretary of State for the Home Department, 193

— v. Immigration Appeal Tribunal *ex p.* Arun Kumar, 187–8, 315

— v. Immigration Appeal Tribunal *ex p.* Khatab, 50

— v. Immigration Appeal Tribunal *ex p.* Vinod Bhatia, 186–8, 315

— v. Independent Broadcasting Authority *ex p.* Whitehouse, 265

— v. Inland Revenue Commissioners *ex p.* Rossminster Ltd, 160

— v. Inner Education Authority *ex p.* Ali, 145, 320

— v. Inspectorate of Pollution *ex p.* Greenpeace, 114

— v. Islington LBC *ex p.* Rixon, 148

— v. Jones, 69
— v. Keane, 242
— v. Kensington and Chelsea LBC *ex p.* Bayani, 142
— v. Kensington and Chelsea LBC *ex p.* Grillo, 118
— v. Kensington and Chelsea LBC *ex p.* Kihara, 203, 332
— v. Khan (Sultan), 164
— v. Kingsley Brown, 164
— v. Knuller (Publishing etc) Ltd, 263
— v. Lambeth LBC *ex p.* Secretary of State for the Environment, 137
— v. Lambeth LBC *ex p.* Walters, 118
— v. Lewes JJ *ex p.* Home Secretary, 234
— v. LTE *ex p.* GLC, 131—2
— v. M.A.F.F. *ex p.* Hamble (Offshore) Fisheries Ltd, 121
— v. Maguire, 164
— v. Mansfield Justices *ex p.* Sharkey, 95
— v. Mason, 157, 165
— v. Ministry of Defence *ex p.* Smith, 265
— v. Newham LBC *ex p.* McIlroy, 142
— v. Newham LBC *ex p.* R, 147
— v. Newham LBC *ex p.* Tower Hamlets LBC, 143
— v. North Devon DC *ex p.* Lewis, 139
— v. Oldham Justices *ex p.* Crawley, 113
— v. Parchment, 164
— v. Parole Board *ex p.* Wilson, 117
— v. Parris, 163
— v. Paul Deacon, 164
— v. Ponting, 257–9, 285
— v. Preseli DC *ex p.* Fisher, 140
— v. Preston, 161
— v. Quayson, 163
— v. Race Relations Board *ex p.* Selvarajan, 117–18, 178
— v. Radio Authority *ex p.* Bull, 248
— v. Reading Justices *ex p.* South West Meat Ltd, 170
— v. Salt, 157
— v. Samuel, 163, 304–5
— v. Sang, 160
— v. Secretary of State for Education *ex p.* S, 119, 147
— v. Secretary of State for Education and Science *ex p.* Avon County Council, 145

— v. Secretary of State for Education and Science *ex p.* ILEA, 146

— v. Secretary of State for Employment *ex p.* Equal Opportunities Commission, 99

— v. Secretary of State for the Environment *ex p.* Berkshire CC, 121

— v. Secretary of State for the Environment *ex p.* Hackney LBC, 134

— v. Secretary of State for the Environment *ex p.* Hackney LBC and Camden LBC, 134

— v. Secretary of State for the Environment *ex p.* Hammersmith and Fulham LBC, 137

— v. Secretary of State for the Environment *ex p.* Lancashire CC, 121

— v. Secretary of State for the Environment *ex p.* Nottinghamshire CC, 134

— v. Secretary of State for the Environment *ex p.* Tower Hamlets LBC, 204

— v. Secretary of State for Foreign Affairs *ex p.* Rees-Mogg, 115, 122

— v. Secretary of State for Foreign Affairs *ex p.* World Development Movement Ltd, 114, 125, 324–6

— v. Secretary of State for Health *ex p.* United States International Inc., 121

— v. Secretary of State for Home Affairs *ex p.* Anderson, 172

— v. Secretary of State for Home Affairs *ex p.* Hosenball, 154, 196, 198, 257

— v. Secretary of State for the Home Department *ex p.* Abdi, 196, 316

— v. Secretary of State for the Home Department *ex p.* Adams, 198

— v. Secretary of State for the Home Department *ex p.* Al-Fayed, 119, 303

— v. Secretary of State for the Home Department *ex p.* Awa, 184

— v. Secretary of State for the Home Department *ex p.* Brind, 170, 247–8, 265, 299, 305

— v. Secretary of State for the Home Department *ex p.* Budgaycay, 192, 198, 265, 316

— v. Secretary of State for the Home Department *ex p.* Chahal, 197, 316

— v. Secretary of State for the Home Department *ex p.* Cheblak, 196, 198

— v. Secretary of State for the Home Department *ex p.* Doody, 116–18, 172—3

— v. Secretary of State for the Home Department *ex p.* Duggan, 173

— v. Secretary of State for the Home Department *ex p.* Fire Brigades Union, 41, 122, 321–3, 326, 330—1

— v. Secretary of State for the Home Department *ex p.* Gallagher, 198

— v. Secretary of State for the Home Department *ex p.* Herbage, 173

— v. Secretary of State for the Home Department *ex p.* Hickey, 118, 213

— v. Secretary of State for the Home Department *ex p.* Khan, 197, 305

— v. Secretary of State for the Home Department *ex p.* Khawaja and Khera, 184, 190—1, 197

— v. Secretary of State for the Home Department *ex p.* Ku, 186

— v. Secretary of State for the Home Department *ex p.* Launder, 200, 317

— v. Secretary of State for the Home Department *ex p.* Leech, 172

— v. Secretary of State for the Home Department *ex p.* McQuillan, 198

— v. Secretary of State for the Home Department *ex p.* Mehari, 196

v. Secretary of State for the Home Department *ex p.* Moon, 119, 199

— v. Secretary of State for the Home Department *ex p.* Muboyayi, 197, 316

— v. Secretary of State for the Home Department *ex p.* Norney, 174—5

— v. Secretary of State for the Home Department *ex p.* Oladehinde, 194, 316, 341

— v. Secretary of State for the Home Department *ex p.* Onibiyo, 194

— v. Secretary of State for the Home Department *ex p.* Patel, 201

— v. Secretary of State for the Home Department *ex p.*Pierson, 173—4

— v. Secretary of State for the Home Department *ex p.* Ruddock, 161

— v. Secretary of State for the Home Department *ex p.* Schmidt, 200

— v. Secretary of State for the Home Department *ex p.* Sivakumaran, 192, 316

— v. Secretary of State for the Home Department *ex p.* Stitt, 156

— v. Secretary of State for the HOme Department *ex p.* Swati, 184–5, 315

— v. Secretary of State for the Home Department *ex p.* Venables, 174

— v. Secretary of State for the Home Department *ex p.* Walsh, 117

— v. Secretary of State for the Home Department *ex p.* Yassine, 193, 316

— v. Secretary of State for the Home Department *ex p.* Zakrocki, 185

— v. Secretary of State for the Home Office *ex p.* Dew, 113

— v. Secretary of State for Social Security *ex p.* Metropolitan Authorities, 150

— v. Secretary of State for Social Security *ex p.* Britnell, 151

— v. Secretary of State for Social Security *ex p.*JCWI, 151, 203

— v. Secretary of State for Social Services *ex p.* Child Poverty Action Group, 150

— v. Secretary of State for Social Services *ex p.* Cotton, 150

— v. Secretary of State for Social Services *ex p.* CPAG, 114

— v. Secretary of State for Social Services *ex p.* Rose Theatre Trust, 114

— v. Secretary of State for Social Services *ex p.* Stitt, 150, 321

— v. Secretary of State for Trade *ex p.* Anderson Strathclyde, 249

— v. Secretary of State for Transport *ex p.* Greater London Council, 156

— v. Slough Justices *ex p.* Stirling, 169

— v. Social Security Fund Inspector *ex p.* Sherwin, Stitt and Roberts, 150

— v. Solihull Metropolitan Council Housing Benefits Review Board *ex p.* Simpson, 119

— v. Somerset CC *ex p.* Fewings, 134

— v. South Herefordshire DC *ex p.* Miles, 140

— v. Sparks, 164

— v. Surrey Heath BC *ex p.* Li, 139

— v. Swansea CC *ex p.* Thomas, 139

— v. Tameside MBC *ex p.* Governors of Audenshawe High School, 146

— v. Taylor, 219, 305

— v. The Lord Chancellor *ex p.* Witham, 8

— v. Thomson Newspapers, 215

— v. Tower Hamlets LBC *ex p.* Chetnik Developments, 135

— v. Tower Hamlets LBC *ex p.* Monaf, 142

— v. Tower Hamlets LBC *ex p.* Rouf, 139

— v. Vernon, 164

— v. Wandsworth LBC *ex p.* Beckwith, 148

— v. Wandsworth LBC *ex p.* Hawthorne, 139

— v. Wandsworth LBC *ex p.* Nimako-Boateng, 139

— v. Ward, 211

— v. Wealden District Council *ex p.* Wales, 171

— v. Westminster CC *ex p.* Ali, 140

— v. Westminster CC *ex p.* Castelli, 143

— v. Westminster CC *ex p.* Ermakov, 118

— v. Withers, 283

— v. Wolverhampton MBC *ex p.* Dunne, 171

Racal Communications Ltd., re 107—8

Race Relations Board v. Applin, 176

Rantzen v. Mirror Group Newspapers, 251

Raymond v. Honey, 172

Re an application under section 9 of the Police and Criminal Evidence Act (1984), 167

Re an Inquiry under the Company Securities (Insider Dealing) Act, 255

Read (Transport) Ltd v. NUM (South Wales), 95

Richardson v. Mellish, 278

Ridge v. Baldwin, 105, 154

Roberts v. Hopwood, viii, xi

Robinson v. Minister of Town and Country Planning, 103

— v. Torbay BC, 138

Rookes v. Barnard, 70, 282, 286, 310

Rost v. Edwards, 249

Roy v. Kensington and Chelsea and Westminster Family Practitioner Committee, 113

Sandralingam v. Secretary of State for the Home Department, 195, 316

Save Britain's Heritage v. Number 1 Poultry Ltd, 120

Schering Chemicals Ltd v. Falkman Ltd, 221

Scruttons Ltd v. Midland Silicones, 284

Secretary of State for Defence v. Guardian Newspapers Ltd, 156, 253, 297

Secretary of State for Education and Science v. Tameside MBC, 109, 111, 148

Secretary of State for Employment v. ASLEF, 108, 111—12, 148

Secretary of State for the Home Department v. Zalife Huseyin, 191

Shaw v. DPP, 261—4

Shipping Company Uniform v. ITF, 85

Silcott v. Commissioner for Metropolitan Police, 168

Smith v. ILEA, 340

Solihull MB v. NUT, 97

Stafford v. DPP, 205

Star Sea Transport of Monrovia v. Slater 'The Camilla M', 79, 80

Stewart v. Secretary of State for Scotland, 11

Stratford v. Lindley, 71

Swinney v. Chief Constable of Northumbria, 168

T re 275–6

T. v. Immigration Officer, 195–6, 316

Taff Vale Railway Company, 66–7, 78

Taylor v. NUM (Derbyshire), 96

Thomas v. NUM (South Wales Area), 92, 95, 302

— v. Sawkins, 158

Thomson & Co. v. Deakin, 71

Ticehurst v. British Telecommunications, 100

Torquay Hotel v. Cousins, 72

Tynan v. Balmer, 69

Union Traffic v. TGWU, 85

United Kingdom Association of Professional Engineers v. ACAS, 83–4

Universe Tankships of Moravia Inc. v. ITWF, 90

Ward v. Bradford Corporation, 284

Webb v. EMO Air Cargo (UK) ltd, 180

Wednesbury Corporation v. Ministry of Housing and Local Government, 232

Wheeler v. Leicester City Council, 133

Williams v. Home Office, 234, 238–9, 306

X Ltd v. Morgan Grampian (Publishers) Ltd, 256

X v. Bedfordshire CC, 147

Young v. United Kingdom, 86

Zamir v. Secretary of State for the Home Department, 182–4

Whitehall

Peter Hennessy

'The thinking man's *Yes Minister*.'

Lord Hunt, ex-secretary of the Cabinet

'Mr Hennessy has at last produced his magnum opus – more than 800 pages chronicling the history of Whitehall from the Norman Conquest to Norman Strauss. Along the way we also get an analysis of present-day ministries, a reform tract and a succession of the Great and Good . . . It is the best account of the British Civil Service ever produced. More than that, it is also, to use Edward Bridges' favourite word, enormous fun.'

Robert Harris, *Observer*

'The most thorough examination of the civil service and her ways yet published. It is ambitious in intent, sweeping in scope, meticulous in detail and penetrating in analysis. His judgements are fair, and sure to disappoint the ideologies of both left and right. Whitehall looks set to beome the standard work on the ways and byways of a hugely important and underexposed part of national life.'

Jeremy Paxman, *Independent*

'This is an outstanding book by a political historian and journalist who has himself become something of a national institution . . . Present and future ministers, whether seeking to alter the machine or merely to comprehend its puzzling idiom and culture, are certain to regard Hennessy's brilliant investigation as the indispensable guide.'

Ben Pimlott, *Sunday Times*

'*Whitehall* is much the best book on the British civil service ever to appear. Everyone who claims the slightest acquaintance with British government will have to read the book, indeed own it.'

Anthony King, *Economist*

ISBN 0 00 686180 6

Fontana Press

A History of the Soviet Union
1917–1991
Final Edition

Geoffrey Hosking

Winner of the *Los Angeles Times* Book Award for History

Now that the great Soviet empire has finally unravelled, and with the future of the Commonwealth of Independent States looking precarious at best, and violent at worst, as long-subdued territorial conflicts flourish from Moldova to Siberia, never has it been so important to understand the vast continental bureaucracy that for seventy years held so many disparate peoples together. How it did so, and the tactics it employed, form the spine of this acclaimed study of the world's last great land empire.

Geoffrey Hosking traces the evolution of the Soviet political system from its revolutionary origins in 1917 to the collapse instigated by the reforms of Gorbachev's *perestroika*. By providing a vivid picture of what it felt like to be a Soviet citizen during the prodigious upheavals of the twentieth century, *A History of the Soviet Union* reminds us that we cannot afford to ignore the impact of this empire, globally and locally – an impact whose legacy will be with us well into the twenty-first century.

'The outstanding merit of Professor Hosking's book is that the author knows and understands Russians, and brings this understanding to bear on his study of history.'   R. W. DAVIES, *THES*

'This is a first-rate introduction to Russian history since 1917... No-one reading it can fail to be impressed by its sound sense, its mature weighing up of the issues and its considered judgements... It should be in the hands of everyone wishing to be informed about present-day Russia.'   PIERRE WALTER, *TES*

ISBN 0 00 686287-X

FontanaPress
An Imprint of HarperCollins*Publishers*

Fontana History of the Ancient World
Series Editor: Oswyn Murray

Democracy and Classical Greece

Second Edition

J. K. Davies

The art of classical Greece, and its political and philosophical ideas, have had a profound influence on Western civilization. It was in the fifth and fourth centuries BC that this Greek culture – material, political and intellectual – reached its zenith. At the same time, the Greek states were at their most powerful and quarrelsome.

J. K. Davies traces the flowering of this extraordinary society, drawing on a wealth of documentary material: houses and graves, extant sculpture and vases, as well as the writings of historians, orators, biographers, dramatists and philosophers.

Much of the material from these, the best-documented centuries in Greek history, presents a formidable challenge to the interpreter. J. K. Davies builds, chapter by chapter, a coherent narrative of events from often sketchy or inconsistent sources, and shows how sometimes the same evidence can throw up quite different interpretations. He uses the material to create a rich and vivid picture of a changing society whose values and achievements have so influenced our own.

ISBN 0 00 686251 9

Fontana Press

A Darwin Se

Edited by Mark Ridley

Charles Darwin, almost uniquely among great scientists, wrote for the general public. For this *Darwin Selection*, Mark Ridley has chosen the key passages from Darwin's nine most important books, and for each of them he has filled in the context of the selection, annotated the few obscure points, and drawn on the latest Darwin scholarship to explain their history.

From the *Origin of the Species*, we have Darwin's beautifully clear exposition of natural selection and of the case against creationism; fom the *Descent of Man* we have his explanation of human intelligence and morality, and his theory of sex differences; and from *Coral Reefs* we have his theory of the origin of coral atolls – a theory that is still widely accepted today. We see him as an experimentalist, unveiling the loves of the plants; as a travel writer describing 'that little world within itself', the Galapagos Islands; and as a natural philosopher, serenely calculating how the actions of worms over long periods emerge as a geological force and the agency of archaeological preservation. *A Darwin Selection* contains many memorable details too; we can rediscover, for instance, the rudimentary tip of the human ear – the curiosity that finally introduced evolution to the polite conversation of the Victorian sitting-room . . .

ISBN 0 00 686321 3

...he I...ssible

...of Anarchism

Peter Marshall

'To be governed means that at every move, operation or transaction one is noted, registered, entered in a census, taxed, stamped, priced, assessed, patented, licensed, authorized, recommended, admonished, reformed . . . exploited, monopolized, extorted, pressured, mystified, robbed; all in the name of public utility and the general good.'

So said Proudhon in 1851, and from the Ancient Chinese to today's rebel youth many have agreed – among their number Godwin and Kropotkin, Bakunin and Malatesta, Tolstoy and Gandhi, the Ranters and the Situationists, de Sade and Thoreau, Wilde and Chomsky, anarcho-syndicalists and anarcha-feminists. Peter Marshall, in his inclusive, inspirational survey, gives back to the anarchistic, undiluted and undistorted, their secret history.

'Reading about anarchism is stimulating and funny and sad. What more can you ask of a book?' Isabel Colegate, *The Times*

'Massive, scholarly, genuinely internationalist and highly enjoyable . . . this is the book Johnny Rotten ought to have read.'
David Widgery, *Observer*

'Large, labyrinthine, tentative: for me these are all adjectives of praise when applied to works of history, and *Demanding the Impossible* meets all of them. I now have a book – Marshall's solid 700 pages and more – to which I can direct readers when they ask me how soon I intend to bring my *Anarchism* up to date.' George Woodcock, *Independent*

'This is the most comprehensive account of anarchist thought ever written. Marshall's knowledge is formidable and his enthusiasm engaging . . . he organizes a mass of diverse material with great subtlety and skill, presenting a good-tempered critique of each position with straightforward lucidity.' J. B. Pick, *Scotsman*

ISBN 0 00 686245 4